B E Y O N D

C O N T A C T

B E Y O N D

A GUIDE TO SETI AND COMMUNICATING WITH ALIEN CIVILIZATIONS

C O N T A C T

Brian McConnell

O'REILLY®

BEIJING • CAMBRIDGE • FARNHAM • KÖLN • PARIS • SEBASTOPOL • TAIPEI • TOKYO

BEYOND CONTACT: A GUIDE TO SETI AND COMMUNICATING WITH ALIEN CIVILIZATIONS
by Brian McConnell

Copyright © 2001 O'Reilly & Associates, Inc. All rights reserved.
Printed in the United States of America.

Dish photo on cover copyright © Harald Sund/The Image Bank.

Published by O'Reilly & Associates, Inc.
101 Morris Street, Sebastopol, CA 95472.

Editor:	Chuck Toporek
Production Editor:	Sarah Jane Shangraw
Cover Designer:	Ellie Volckhausen
Interior Designers:	Melanie Wang and Alicia Cech

PRINTING HISTORY

March 2001:   First Edition.

Library of Congress Cataloging-in-Publication data is available at:
http://www.oreilly.com/catalog/alien

ISBN: 0-596-00037-5
[C]

CONTENTS

Part I ~ ARE WE ALONE?

1 SETI for Everyone 3
2 Listening to the Stars 11
3 The Drake Equation 21
4 Evolution 35
5 Communicative Civilizations 57

Part II ~ GETTING A DIAL TONE

6 Radio Communication 75
7 Lightwave (Laser) Communication 99
8 Signal Processing and Confirmation 119
9 Bringing SETI Home 147
10 Teleporting Bits 159

Part III ~ COMMUNICATING WITH OTHER WORLDS

11 CETI—Communication with
Extraterrestrial Intelligence 181
12 Binary DNA 197
13 Symbols 213
14 Memory and Programming 239

15 Concepts and igenes   255

16 Sequencing the Binary Genome   275

17 Pictures   293

18 Simulations   313

19 Abstract Symbols and Language   329

20 Semantic Networks   347

21 Content   359

    Epilogue   371

Part IV ~ APPENDIXES

A   Message Replication   375

B   SETI Resources on the Internet   385

C   SETI Program Timeline   387

    Glossary   391

    Selected Bibliography   401

    Acknowledgments   403

    How to Contact Us   405

    Index   407

ARE WE ALONE?

SETI FOR EVERYONE

Since the early 1960s, scientists, engineers, and astronomers have been on the greatest quest for new lands since Christopher Columbus sailed west across the Atlantic. The Search for Extraterrestrial Intelligence, or SETI, began with a simple goal: to search the skies for signs of intelligent life from alien civilizations beyond our own solar system.

The idea behind SETI is straightforward: eavesdrop on wireless communication traffic from civilizations orbiting other stars within our galaxy. Although the technical challenges of detecting a radio or optical signal emanating from a source trillions of miles away are significant, our computing and communication technologies are evolving at such a rapid pace that we can now seriously discuss the possibility of communicating with other civilizations.

SETI has been widely criticized by politicians, and even members of the technical community, as being a waste of time and money—money that could supposedly be better spent on other scientific projects. This, despite the fact that SETI research costs a small fraction compared to other space science programs (such as the Hubble Space Telescope). Yet all the while, public interest in SETI has never waned.

In fact, there's been a great deal of attention for SETI in recent years, particularly with the discovery of planets orbiting nearby stars. At the time of this writing (November 2000), over 50 extrasolar planets have been discovered. These are mainly large, Jupiter-sized planets, which orbit stars not unlike our own. While we're not able to detect Earth-sized planets yet, each new planet we find teaches us more about the universe in which we live, and how planets (and whole solar systems) form over time. It won't be long—perhaps another 10 years—before we're able to detect Earth-sized planets. In the meantime, our hopes of finding a signal from an alien source remain high.

While governmental funding for SETI research has been a political hot potato, the public has taken SETI into its own hands, thanks to a talented team of programmers, scientists, and engineers at the University of California, Berkeley's Space Sciences Laboratory.

Every day, over 2 million people in 226 countries participate in the search for signs of extraterrestrial intelligence. These are not tabloid-reading UFO aficionados sitting in their backyard lawn chairs, binoculars in hand, waiting for first contact. They are ordinary computer users who have downloaded a groundbreaking program from the Space Sciences Laboratory called SETI@home (*http://setiathome.berkeley.edu/*). One of the biggest costs in SETI research is not the gathering of data (which is already being gathered for other purposes by astronomers) but the cost of the computers required to analyze it. The Space Sciences Laboratory created a small program—a screensaver—that people could run on their personal computers at work and at home to process radiotelescope data.

Through the SETI@home project, people with an interest in SETI research have "donated" their computers' processing power to sift through data collected by the Arecibo Radio Observatory in Puerto Rico. Initially planned as a small experiment in a technique called *distributed computing*, the response to SETI@home far exceeded the organizers' wildest dreams. Initially hoping for 5,000 people to download and run the SETI@home screensaver, the project team was taken by surprise as nearly 50,000 people downloaded SETI@home within the first month. In six months, this was up to nearly 1 million downloads, and by its first anniversary, the SETI@home screensaver had made its way to over 2 million computers around the world. As a result, the SETI@home team has, in effect, built the world's fastest (and cheapest) supercomputer.

SETI@home is, in a literal sense, the world's first hands-on space exploration program. SETI@home is a unique project, not just because it is an ingenious way to circumvent the challenge of processing huge amounts of data on a limited budget, but also because it is an outstanding demonstration of the power of distributed computing. With only a few part- and full-time staff, the SETI@home team, led by David Anderson and Dan Werthimer, created a program that turns any personal computer connected to the Internet into a node of a giant, distributed supercomputer.

Tapping into the computing power grid

The concept behind SETI@home is rather novel. Instead of buying a supercomputer that could cost millions of dollars to purchase and support, why not take advantage of the fact that most personal computers are idle more than 90 percent of the time? While each individual computer may not be particularly fast (a typical PC can perform a few million calculations per second), there are hundreds of millions of PCs in use around the world, the majority of which are connected to the Internet at least part of the time. So rather than process all of the raw data in a central location, SETI@home enlists idle desktop computers to process small parcels of the raw data, referred to as *work units*. The SETI@home program can run as a stand-alone application or can be activated by the computer as a screensaver if it is idle for more than a few minutes.

As of November 2000, the project was processing data at a rate of 27.24 teraflop/s,* faster than any supercomputer in use today. In fact, the project has been so successful that the SETI@home team is able to process raw data faster than it is collected. And just as the SETI@home client has evolved over its short life span, the designers are taking advantage of their newfound surplus of computing power by building new versions of the software to perform more sophisticated analysis to look for different types of signals.

The experiment in distributed computing shows how you can combine a large number of relatively slow, networked computers to form a very fast virtual computer. Consider networked computers as constituting a computing power grid. Instead of building your own supercomputer, you can simply harness the distributed nature of the Internet and the processing power of other machines, much like you hook up to the electrical grid to obtain electricity instead of building your own generating plant.

Computers running the SETI@home screensaver interact with servers at UC Berkeley using standard Internet protocols to transfer data back and forth. Upon analyzing a block of data, the SETI@home program connects to the servers to send its tabulated results back for further analysis, and then picks up a new block of raw data that is awaiting analysis.

A living universe?

Since a growing number of scientists believe there is a real possibility that life—perhaps intelligent life—has developed on worlds outside our solar system, SETI@home couldn't have come at a better time. We now know that planets, once thought to exist only in our solar system, are relatively common, and probably circle the majority of stars we see in the night sky. We also know that life, once thought to exist only in comfortable, moderate

---

* A *teraflop* is equivalent to one trillion floating point operations; in this case, 27.24 trillion calculations are being performed by SETI@home each second.

SOLVING PROBLEMS WITH DISTRIBUTED COMPUTING

Many types of computing problems can benefit from the use of distributed computing, including:

- Weather forecasting and climate modeling, which can be efficiently handled through massively parallel computing projects. In a weather simulation, you could subdivide a mathematical model for the environment into a grid of millions of smaller cells. Each cell would represent a small piece of the larger system whose behavior you want to model.

- Cracking encryption systems once thought to be unbreakable. In this application, many computers participate in the electronic equivalent of trying different codes on a combination lock.

- Analyzing data collected by the human genome project. The challenge here is to detect predictable patterns within the raw data collected by the project. This task requires a lot of computation, and like the SETI@home project, lends itself to a distributed approach, where lots of relatively small work units are doled out to a large number of personal computers.

- Creating censor-proof publishing systems. One of the best-known systems, Freenet, developed by Ian Clarke, allows an author to publish a document and remain completely anonymous. The document is automatically copied across Freenet servers worldwide. This makes it virtually impossible to delete or censor a document once it has been published on Freenet.

Distributed computing, however, is still in its technological infancy. In five to ten years, computing and communication devices will be pervasive and most will have continuous connections to the Internet.

climates, can thrive in hostile conditions from the vacuum of space to superheated vents miles beneath the ocean surface.

There is now serious discussion about the past or present existence of microbial life on worlds within our own solar system—specifically on Mars, three of Jupiter's moons (Europa, Ganymede, and Calisto), and Saturn's moon, Titan. Mars and Europa are two prime candidates in the search for past or present life in our solar system.

For the first time in the history of science, statistics now favor the development of life elsewhere in our universe. Considering there are about 400 billion stars in our galaxy, and over 100 billion galaxies in the observable universe, it seems highly unlikely that life has evolved only here and nowhere else.

The idea that intelligent life might exist elsewhere is hardly new. People have pondered this question for thousands of years—probably since the beginning of human existence. However, it is only in recent years that we have developed the technological tools to answer the question of whether life might exist on other planets. We can only guess what we might discover as our technology advances, enabling us to peer deeper into the universe and into time.

Our technology, and with it our ability to detect simple and intelligent life on other worlds, has advanced dramatically in recent years. We have made great strides in astronomy and the advancement of computing technology over the past few decades, and because of these advancements, we have learned more about the surrounding universe than we have in all of recorded history.

New telescopes, such as the Hubble Space Telescope, the twin 10-meter telescopes of the W. M. Keck Observatory in Hawaii, and others, have enabled us to capture stunning and detailed images of distant suns, galaxies, and black holes. These telescopes have captured images of huge stellar nurseries where stars similar to our own sun are formed by the hundreds. They've also captured images of protoplanetary disks around many new stars, suggesting that where there are stars, there may be planets close by.

In the coming years, new optical telescopes and interferometers will enable us to detect Earth-sized planets and, using a technique called spectroscopy, analyze the chemical composition of these planets and their atmospheres. With this capability, we will be able to detect the chemical signature of life on a remote world.

Radio telescopes, such as the Arecibo Radio Observatory and the SETI Institute's planned Allen Telescope Array (ATA; formerly known as the One Hectare Telescope, or 1HT), enable us to analyze the radio signatures of stars and galaxies with the same kind of precision as with optical telescopes. They also enable us to detect artificial signals, similar to our own TV and radio broadcasts (the hallmark of an intelligent sender, should such signals exist).

At the same time that space- and land-based telescopes have advanced, so has computing and networking technology. Fast computers and networks enable us to share and analyze data in ways that were not possible even a few years ago.

What is emerging from these two trends, the rapid improvements in our sensing instruments and computing technology, is a system that can peer further into the universe to look for signs of both simple and intelligent life.

In a literal sense, we have already left the Earth to explore the stars; only we have done so without leaving the safety of our own atmosphere. While we've yet to develop the technology to physically visit distant worlds, we have developed the ability to virtually visit these places. With each improvement in telescope and computing technology, we extend the range over which we can look for signs of life on other worlds long before we have the capability to visit these places in person.

With the growing realization that life may not be unique to Earth, the search for extraterrestrial life—both simple and intelligent life—has become one of the highest priorities in space exploration and one of the most important scientific endeavors of the 21st century. What's most remarkable about SETI is that it is the first expedition in which most of the exploration will be done virtually—either with robots probes, or by telescope.

At this point, nobody really knows what we will find on Mars, Europa, or Earth-like worlds orbiting distant stars. But, for the first time in human history, we've developed the ability to search for life beyond our own solar system. One thing is certain: whenever we have expanded our ability to see and understand our environment, we've been surprised by what we've learned.

Talking to aliens

This book describes how we would communicate with an extraterrestrial civilization, were we to find one. While this may seem like a topic of science fiction, all of the technology and techniques described in this book are in use today in some form. In fact, many of the techniques described later in this book can be reproduced on an ordinary desktop computer. By employing a combination of radio communication and using numbers as symbols, it is possible to send and receive many types of messages, including abstract messages, images, and even computer programs over interstellar distances.

In addition to explaining the nuts and bolts of detecting a radio or laser signal from a distant civilization, this book poses the question of what comes next. If we detect a signal from another planet, what might they say? How might we expect them to say it? Or, if we turn things around, how might we tell our own story to another world?

Suppose you wanted to communicate with someone else. It could be a person who speaks a completely unknown language, another civilization, or perhaps a machine. It doesn't really matter what or where the other party is for the purposes of this exercise. All you know about the other party is:

- You share no common spoken or written language.

- You share no common culture or assumptions about who or what the other is.

- You both possess the ability to transmit coded messages using electro-magnetic radiation (radio, flashes of light, etc.).

- You both possess computing technology.

- There may be a long time delay between transmission and reception.

With this information, how could you build a system for communicating with an unknown party who knows nothing about you, your language, or your mode of communication? How could you send a message that can be interpreted by the other party?

A hopeless problem? Not really.

Biology offers some insight into how to build a system for communication that is so flexible it will allow us to overcome the greatest language barrier imaginable (and provide many real-world benefits for Earth-based software developers and ordinary computer users, even if we never bag an alien).

The purpose of this book is to educate you about the basic technology required to complete the ultimate long distance call, and to pose questions about how we might communicate with another civilization should we detect signals from another world (or discover that we have already been detected).

Most importantly, the book demonstrates that interstellar communication is feasible, and that it will be possible to communicate in depth with other civilizations that choose to communicate with their neighbors. Whether there are other civilizations to compare notes with is another matter.

While this might sound far out, this book is not about speculation. All of the technology and techniques described in this book can be tested and veri-fied. This book doesn't speculate about what we might learn from ET or when we might make contact; nor does it contain lurid stories of interplane-tary sex play. The book merely explores how we can communicate with another civilization using the tools we have at our disposal today.

This book is organized in three major sections. Part I, *Are We Alone?*, intro-duces the basic concepts related to SETI research. This section includes an overview of various SETI projects and introduces the Drake Equation, which estimates the number of possible communicating civilizations within our reach using a simple equation that Dr. Frank Drake sketched on a blackboard over 40 years ago. The Drake Equation tries to determine the number of possible planets within our galaxy (and for that matter, the universe) that could be home to intelligent life. This section also introduces recent revisions to the Drake Equation, and new concepts such as the Rare Earth Hypothesis proposed by Peter Ward and Donald Brownlee, as well as David Brin's equation.

Part II, *Getting a Dial Tone,* discusses the fundamentals of radio and optical (laser) communication over interstellar distances. This part of the book introduces the basic techniques used for detecting weak radio and optical signals and discriminating between bona fide extraterrestrial (ET) signals and background interference. It also describes the limits of current technology.

This book has a secondary audience in addition to people who are interested in SETI research. In describing how to communicate with another civilization, Part III, *Communicating with other Worlds*, describes new techniques that can be employed to develop better computer software. This part of the book shows how we can compose binary (digital) messages for transmittal with a standard radio or lightwave carrier. You'll also learn how we can transmit symbols, equations, computer programs, and, ultimately, abstract language to a receiver who knows nothing more than basic arithmetic. Even if we never use these techniques to communicate with aliens, computer programmers will use them to create very compact programs for distribution over public data networks (i.e., the Internet).

At the end of the book, we've included three appendixes, a bibliography, and glossary. Appendix A, *Message Replication*, looks at two possible scenarios for exchanging messages across extremely long distances through a technique known as *message replication*, where messages originating on one planet get combined with messages from other planets, similar to forwarding an email. Appendix B, *SETI Resources on the Internet*, and Appendix C, *SETI Program Timeline*, provide a list of SETI resources on the Internet and a historical timeline of various SETI projects since 1959.

LISTENING TO THE STARS

The idea of communicating with other civilizations is an ancient one. For eons, people have pondered the idea that the stars might be inhabited, whether by gods or by other civilizations. Ancient civilizations attempted to communicate with the stars by building monuments to the gods thought to live in them. In modern times, many of the people who contributed to the invention of wireless communication also used their inventions to communicate with other worlds. Martian civilizations were the topic of much speculation early in the 20th century.*

The modern SETI era can be traced back to 1959 with the publication of "Searching for Interstellar Communications." This landmark paper, authored by Philip Morrison and Giuseppe Cocconi, describes the idea of using radiotelescopes to detect weak radio signals from other civilizations. It addresses the key technical issues involved in interstellar communication and provides a blueprint upon which most modern SETI programs are based. A related paper, "Interstellar and Interplanetary Communication by Optical Masers," published by doctors Charles Townes and Robert Schwartz in 1961, provided a blueprint for optical (laser) communication across interstellar distances. These papers transformed the search for other civilizations from a fantastical, entrepreneurial activity into a branch of mainstream science.

SETI's beginnings

The first SETI searches were relatively simple and, because of limitations in the computing hardware of the day, could not search many frequencies simultaneously. The ability to listen for a signal on millions, or billions, of

---

* Some of these communication schemes are described in greater detail in Chapter 11, *CETI—Communication with Extraterrestrial Intelligence*.

frequencies at once is critical to detecting a signal. In light of what we now know about detecting a weak signal, it's not surprising that early SETI efforts failed.

Project Ozma

In 1960, Frank Drake, then a young astronomer at the National Radio Astronomy Observatory (NRAO) in Green Bank, West Virginia, conducted the first scientific experiment attempting to detect evidence of intelligent extraterrestrial life outside our own solar system. Drake used the NRAO's radiotelescope to search for a specific type of radio signal emanating from a short list of nearby stars.

Dubbed *Project Ozma*, in reference to L. Frank Baum's *Land of Oz*, the experiment searched for artificial radio signals from the stars Tau Ceti and Epsilon Eridani. Dr. Drake chose to focus on these stars because both are approximately the same age as our own sun, and are about 11 light years* away. From April to July 1960, Project Ozma used the 85-foot NRAO radio telescope to search for possible signals coming from these stars. The receiver used in Project Ozma was nearly one trillion times less selective than today's SETI detection hardware, which can listen to hundreds of millions of frequencies simultaneously.

Drake's experiment looked for a signal centered on the frequency 1.420 GHz (1.42 billion cycles per second). A narrowband radio signal, when converted into sound waves, is audible to the human ear and will sound like a steady tone. Drake analyzed the collected data to look for repeating signals, or blips, that could be translated into binary numbers. Drake was surprised to find a candidate signal soon after he started his search. As it turned out, the signal he detected was the radio emission from a top-secret military project. Not only was Drake the first to put the principles of SETI radio-astronomy to work, but he was also the first person to be faked out by an apparently extraterrestrial signal produced by our own technology.

Although the experiment failed to detect evidence of extraterrestrial life, Project Ozma led to the development of much more sophisticated SETI programs and planted in the public consciousness the idea of communicating with aliens on other worlds.

---

* A *light year* is the distance at which light travels through space in a year—approximately 6 trillion miles.

Big Ear and the "Wow!" signal

The longest running SETI program in the world (22 years, from 1973 to 1995) was hosted by Ohio State University, where a group of volunteer and professional observers used the Big Ear Radio Observatory to search for signs of extraterrestrial intelligence. The Big Ear antenna, which covered an area of three football fields, detected the unusually strong and now famous "Wow!" signal* on August 15, 1977.

The detected signal was over 30 dB (1000 times) stronger than the background noise on the survey frequency, which, like Project Ozma, was also centered on the 1.42 GHz frequency. The signal was estimated to be at least 72 seconds in duration, and matched the characteristics of a radio signal originating from space. Unfortunately, the signal was only detected once, so astronomers were never able to conduct follow-up analysis of the signal's origin.

The telescope has since been taken out of service and is no longer being used.

NASA High Resolution Microwave Survey

The NASA High Resolution Microwave Survey (HRMS) was one of the few publicly funded SETI research programs, and was a precursor to the privately funded Project Phoenix program.

The HRMS program consisted of two searches: an all-sky search designed to look for extremely powerful beacons, and a targeted search designed to pick up weaker signals from nearby sun-like star systems. The targeted search program would have surveyed stars within 100 light years. The all-sky survey was capable of detecting powerful beacon signals over an even greater range (several thousand light years). Some of the large radio telescopes that were to be used included the 305-meter (1000-foot) Arecibo Radio Observatory in Puerto Rico, the 64-meter (210-foot) diameter antenna in Parkes, Australia, and the NRAO's 42-meter (140-foot) diameter antenna at Green Bank. Unfortunately, the U.S. Congress canceled the HRMS program in the early 1990s.

After the HRMS program was killed, the privately funded SETI Institute, and Project Phoenix, sprung up in its place. Fortunately, the SETI Institute was able to capitalize on the money already invested to develop signal processing hardware, and to incorporate this technology into Project Phoenix.

---

* Additional information about the "Wow!" signal can be found online at *http://www. bigear.org/wow20th.htm.*

Project SERENDIP

Project SERENDIP (short for Search for Extraterrestrial Radio Emissions from Nearby Developed Intelligent Populations) is a SETI program that's sponsored by the University of California, Berkeley. SERENDIP's primary goal is to focus on the detection of microwave band radio transmissions.

Project SERENDIP is a parasitic search program, which means that it piggybacks onto other radioastronomy observation projects. Currently, Project SERENDIP is attached to the Arecibo Observatory in Puerto Rico, and conducts other tasks while the telescope is used for other observations. Project SERENDIP provides the data analyzed by participants in the SETI@home project (see Chapter 9, *Bringing SETI Home*, for additional information about the SETI@home project).

SERENDIP IV, the most recent generation of the search program, examines 168 million channels every 1.7 seconds in a 100 MHz band centered at 1.42 GHz. This represents a million-fold improvement in sensitivity compared to Project Ozma.

Project Phoenix

Project Phoenix rose from the ashes of the cancelled NASA HRMS program. This program, still active today, searches a targeted list of nearby star systems to look for both intentional (*beacon*) and unintentional (*leakage*) signals. The program operates from several different radiotelescopes, although not on a full-time basis. As of this writing, the most recent observations were conducted by the Arecibo Radio Observatory in Fall 2000.

Project Phoenix employs detection equipment that is more powerful and more sensitive than its predecessors, with the ability to simultaneously monitor over 20 million narrowband channels. The survey also analyzes a 2 GHz band of frequencies, ranging from 1 to 3 GHz.

Unlike SERENDIP, Project Phoenix is a targeted search program. This program systematically surveys the microwave band for a targeted list of stars, mostly within 100 light years from Earth. SERENDIP studies each star for an extended period of time, surveying most of the microwave spectrum in detail, performing follow-up analysis. This search limits researchers to fewer stars, but permits a more systematic and extended study for each star.

Billion Channel Extraterrestrial Array

Harvard University and the Planetary Society sponsor the Billion Channel Extraterrestrial Array (BETA), as well as its predecessor program, META. Led by Dr. Paul Horowitz of Harvard, the BETA survey is a high-resolution microwave search program similar to the SETI Institute's Project Phoenix. Like Project Phoenix, BETA is designed to monitor a large number of channels simultaneously, enabling researchers to tease out weak signals that may be masked by background noise.

Based in part on technology developed by the SETI Institute for Project Phoenix, BETA is also a targeted search program. This system can listen on several hundred million radio frequencies simultaneously, and can be used to analyze the radio emissions from a star system through most of the microwave band. Additional information about Harvard-sponsored SETI programs can be found online at *http://mc.harvard.edu/seti/*.

SETI League

The SETI League (*http://www.setileague.org/*) is a grassroots organization that encourages private citizens to build their own small-scale SETI receivers using modified versions of commercially available satellite receiving equipment.

Because the participants use less sensitive receivers (a 3-meter dish compared to a 50- to 300-meter dish), the SETI League's strategy is to use a large number of small receivers to look for strong beacon signals. By comparison, the Project Phoenix and SERENDIP programs are capable of detecting relatively weak signals, particularly from nearby stars. However, these programs are limited to searching a small piece of the sky at any given time. The SETI League hopes to have hundreds or thousands of people observing target stars for longer periods of time. While they won't be able to detect a weak signal, such as a TV broadcast, they may be able to detect a strong beacon.

The idea is to use this large network of amateur scientists and hobbyists to increase the amount of night sky being observed at any given time. Just as amateur astronomers are often the first to spot new comets (such as the Shoemaker-Levy 9 comet, which impacted Jupiter), a backyard radioastronomer may be the first to discover the signature of an extraterrestrial beacon.

An excellent example of amateur science, the SETI League has demonstrated how to build a functional radiotelescope for a few thousand dollars or less. In the process of doing this, it has shown how to do radioastronomy on a budget, opening the door for secondary schools and private citizens to build their own backyard radiotelescopes.

European and Australian SETI programs

Australian SETI researchers are conducting a search for extraterrestrial signals in the Southern Hemisphere. This program, sponsored by the University of Western Sydney, is modeled after UC Berkeley's SERENDIP search program. This Southern SERENDIP search program piggybacks on the 64-meter Parke's radiotelescope, enabling SETI researchers to use the telescope to search for ET signals without requiring the telescope to be dedicated exclusively to SETI research, as with the upcoming Allen Telescope Array. Details about Australian SETI programs can be found online at *http://seti.uws.edu.au/*.

Dr. Stelio Montebugnoli of Bologna, Italy, leads a major European SETI effort, Project StarVoice. This program uses SERENDIP IV detection equipment to conduct piggyback observations at the 32-meter VLBI dish antenna located at the Medicina radioastronomy station. European researchers hope to install piggyback SETI hardware at up to 40 radiotelescopes throughout Europe. These telescopes will be networked together to share their data. The system, slated to begin operation in 2002, will include some of the largest radiotelescopes in the world.

The Allen Telescope Array

The Allen Telescope Array (ATA) is a joint project between the University of California, Berkeley and the SETI Institute that will commence operation sometime in the next five years. It was formerly known as 1HT (for *one hectare telescope*) array, until Microsoft alumni Paul Allen and Nathan Myrhvold donated $12 million to help fund the project. This program uses a large array of inexpensive antennae (similar to backyard satellite receiving antennae) to create a virtual antenna with a very large aperture diameter—much larger than we could practically achieve with a single dish.

The array's collecting area will increase the antenna's gain by several orders of magnitude, enabling it to focus on an even more selective patch of sky. The ATA will primarily be used to conduct SETI research, but will also be available for conventional radioastronomy use. The first prototype telescope arrays were unveiled in April 2000, and the telescope array is slated to be fully operational by 2005.

Optical SETI

Instead of looking for radio signals, Optical SETI (or OSETI) programs look for visible or infrared laser pulses coming from planets that could be circling distant stars. One of the interesting things about OSETI is that it can piggyback onto conventional optical astronomy experiments and requires less complicated hardware than traditional microwave SETI equipment. OSETI allows scientists to send larger volumes of information, generate an easily detected signal, and use cheaper hardware on both ends.

OSETI searches can look for either continuous beacons that shine at a very precise color (and hence appear brighter than the background star at a very specific color of light) or for pulsed beacons that concentrate their transmission power into very brief flashes (e.g., billionths of a seconds). We'll discuss the theory behind OSETI in Chapter 7, *Lightwave (Laser) Communication*.

Although microwave (radio) SETI research is now 40 years old, OSETI (optical SETI) is a relatively new field. The idea itself is not new (the concepts behind OSETI were proposed by doctors Charles Townes and Robert Schwartz in their 1961 *Nature* paper "Interstellar and Interplanetary Communication by Optical Masers." Many universities and private research organizations around the world are operating or gearing up to conduct OSETI search programs. The University of California at Berkeley, Harvard University, Princeton University, University of Western Sydney, and the Columbus Optical SETI Observatory are a few of the groups currently looking for optical signals. More programs are slated to go live over the next two years.

NOTE

Appendix C, SETI Program Timeline, contains an expanded list of past, present, and future radio and optical SETI projects. Sky & Telescope magazine's web site, http://www.skypub.com/, also publishes a comprehensive list of microwave and optical SETI programs.

Funding for SETI research

Most people are surprised to learn that SETI receives little or no public funding. Although SETI research is cheap compared to other space science programs, the federal government ceased public funding for SETI research in the 1990s. This was largely due to ignorance on the part of members of Congress who did not understand the indirect benefits of the program. Politicians were eager to convince voters that they were cutting wasteful programs, and subsequently gutted the program, which accounted for one hundredth of one percent of NASA's total annual budget. In the end, Congress saved the average American taxpayer something on the order of 10 cents or less per year. Or, put another way, the cost of one B-2 bomber would have supported a greatly expanded SETI program for over a century.

Since the 1990s, SETI has relied on private funding, mostly from individual contributors, corporations, and non-profit organizations such as the SETI Institute and The Planetary Society. The amount of private funding has increased substantially since the NASA budget cuts but still falls short of what is needed to complete the construction of new facilities. Major projects, such as a lunar telescope array, will certainly not happen unless the program receives public funding.

Despite the high level of popular support for SETI, the government has provided scant support for SETI research. Even during peak public funding, such as the NASA HRMS program, SETI never accounted for more than one-tenth of a percent of NASA's overall budget. Despite its limited resources, the program has received an incredible return for its investment, mainly due to the program's paid staff and volunteers.

SETI is unique among science programs because of its mass appeal.It has tapped this public interest to privately fund its programs and has enlisted volunteers to donate their idle PCs to perform SETI computation work via the SETI@home project. Many leading technology companies—such as Hewlett Packard, Sun Microsystems, and others—have contributed money, technology, and expertise to the effort. SETI relies heavily on computing technology, creating an interesting overlap between the computing industry and SETI, which is bolstered by computer scientists who, as a group, have demonstrated a high level of interest in SETI research.

The benefits of SETI

SETI is a technological frontier in telecommunications. In order to successfully detect a distant civilization, we must push the technological envelope in many areas, from radioastronomy to information theory. In the course of gearing up to communicate with aliens, we will advance our own expertise in telecommunications, computer science, and astronomy, and will advance the state of the art in these and other related fields. Even if we never detect an alien civilization, we will improve our own technology in the process—and we will all benefit as a result.

The astounding economic growth we've seen in recent years is largely due to improvements in information technology, which have led to the creation of a digital nervous system that efficiently coordinates the delivery of goods and information throughout our economy. This was sparked by a subtle shift in the way computers communicate—we shifted from a system based on incompatible, proprietary communication networks to a worldwide standard for exchanging information (the Internet) among machines. This subtle improvement in our ability to communicate has affected nearly every industry.

While at first glance this has nothing to do with interstellar communication, this shift underscores how an improvement in our basic ability to communicate can translate into unanticipated benefits for the general public. Few people would have predicted the long-term dividends from the work done by Vinton Cerf and his colleagues when they invented TCP/IP,* the set of protocols that forms the foundation of today's Internet.

---

* *TCP/IP* stands for Transfer Control Protocol/Internet Protocol.

What real-world benefits will we get from SETI research? Whether we succeed or fail in making contact with an alien civilization, we'll develop new technology that can be applied in many different areas. If we detect an alien signal, we may discover a vast source of knowledge about the universe and about other civilizations. The former is a guaranteed result. The possibility of the latter is more remote. Even if we fail to detect anything, we'll be better off for trying.

Through SETI research, we can learn to send more bits of information with less power. This is a basic goal for wireless data networks because they must use a finite amount of radio spectrum to satisfy ever-growing demand. These techniques are also directly applicable to conventional radioastronomy. The beneficial results of SETI research include:

- The development of advanced radiotelescopes that can be used for conventional astronomy work. These new telescopes, such as the forthcoming ATA, will be the most advanced radiotelescopes in the world.

- The development of new techniques in computing. SETI has already produced one breakthrough in computer science. As already discussed, the SETI@home project is a cutting-edge example of distributed computing. The SETI@home team has in effect created , the world's fastest supercomputer by simply tapping into millions of mostly idle personal computers. This technique will soon be used for weather forecasting, analyzing data collected by the Human Genome Project, and numerous other applications.

- The development of algorithms (computer programs), which in the future may potentially be applied to terrestrial wireless communication by increasing the sensitivity of receivers (e.g., phones). This will allow transmitters to operate at lower power levels, which increases the number of users that can be served within an area (and will also increase the battery life of handheld communication devices).

These are just a few examples of the benefits we'll derive from SETI. There will probably be others we haven't thought of yet. Even if we never receive an alien encyclopedia, we'll learn how to improve wireless communication, write computer programs that are faster and more efficient, and advance the state of the art in related fields.

Then there is the big question: "What happens if we succeed in making contact with another civilization?" Here we can only speculate about what we might learn. If a civilization decides to share its knowledge with others, we could learn an immense amount about them and the other worlds they have explored or communicated with. Although the idea of receiving an encyclopedia may seem fantastical, it is fairly easy to do. (We'll demonstrate how we could transmit our own encyclopedia to other civilizations in Part III, *Communicating with other Worlds*.)

If we do succeed in detecting an information-rich signal, the implications will be nothing short of staggering. We might learn more in a few years than we did in the entirety of our existence. This is a long shot, and may not be likely, but it is a possible outcome that should be taken seriously.

Before we start pointing our telescopes to the heavens in hope of picking up a signal, it will be helpful to know which stars are most likely to harbor life and why. This is the subject of Chapter 3, *The Drake Equation* and Chapter 5, *Communicative Civilizations*, where we explain the Drake Equation, the Rare Earth Hypothesis, and David Brin's equation, all of which attempt to estimate the possibility of intelligent, communicative civilizations in our galaxy.

THE DRAKE EQUATION

The Search for Extraterrestrial Intelligence (SETI) is a serious scientific effort to detect signs of civilizations outside our own solar system. SETI searches listen for specific types of radio transmissions from sun-like stars throughout the galaxy. While this might sound like science fiction, this is simply a branch of astronomy—the only difference is that we're looking for signals that betray an intelligent source.

The modern SETI program is the brainchild of Dr. Frank Drake, an astronomer and now head of the SETI Institute. Dr. Drake developed a formula in 1961 (now known as the *Drake Equation*) that estimates the number of technological civilizations in our galaxy. It's a simple equation, and at the time it was originally written, many of the factors in the equation were unknown. Today, there is a growing consensus that the odds for the development of life in the universe are quite favorable, although whether that means intelligent life really exists is anybody's guess. The Drake Equation was developed as a chalkboard exercise to estimate the number of detectable civilizations in our galaxy.

$$N = R \times f_s \times f_p \times n_e \times f_l \times f_i \times f_c \times L$$

Each item in the Drake Equation is used to factor in the possible existence of intelligent, communicative life elsewhere in the universe. The final product of the equation, N, gives a rough estimate of the number of technological civilizations currently broadcasting detectable radio or optical signals. The nine factors in the Drake Equation are:

R The rate of star formation in our galaxy.

f_s The percentage of stars that is suitable for the development of planetary systems. Main-sequence stars are long-lived and produce a relatively stable amount of energy for several billion years (range of possible values: 0 to 1).

f_p The fraction of those suitable stars that could be orbited by planets (range of possible values: 0 to 1).

n_e The number of possible Earth-like worlds surrounding those sun-like stars that may also have planets (range of possible values: 0 to n, where n is a number greater than 0; range of likely values: $0 < n_e < 10$).

f_l The fraction of those Earth-like worlds where life could develop (range of possible values: 0 to 1).

f_i The fraction of those life-bearing worlds where life, at some point, could evolve to produce an intelligent species (range of possible values: 0 to 1).

f_c The fraction of those worlds where intelligent species may have developed, and also may have technologically advanced civilizations comparable to or exceeding our own (range of possible values: 0 to 1).

L The average lifetime of a communicating technological civilization (range of likely values: < 50 years to millions of years).

Simply multiply all of these factors by one another and you have an estimate for the number of civilizations with which we can potentially communicate.

Some of the factors in the Drake Equation have been researched thoroughly by astronomers and are well known. For example, we have a fairly good estimate for the value of R and we have good evidence that planets are commonplace throughout our galaxy. However, for some of these factors, we only have one example—Earth—to work with. A statistical sample can be interpreted in as many ways as there are interpreters (often with much disagreement and consternation).

The Drake Equation doesn't answer the question of whether intelligent life exists elsewhere in the universe. Instead it demonstrates that in order for intelligent life to be unique to Earth, the cosmological odds have to be stacked against the formation of life.

R—Rate of star formation

The first factor we encounter in the Drake equation is R, which stands for the rate of star formation in our galaxy. New stars are constantly being formed throughout the galaxy. The Hubble Space Telescope (HST) has captured many striking images of new stars forming within collapsing clouds of gas, as shown in Figure 3-1.

Star formation has been occurring throughout the history of the universe. In a literal sense, solar systems like our own are formed from the debris of long-

Evaporating Globules · M16   HST · WFPC2
PRC95-44c · ST ScI OPO · November 2, 1995
J. Hester and P. Scowen (AZ State Univ.), NASA

Figure 3-1: *The Eagle Nebula, a virtual birthplace of stars, as imaged by the Hubble Space Telescope in 1995. New stars are forming in the tendril-like structures at the edge of the gas cloud. (STScI/HST image courtesy of Jeff Hester and Paul Scowen [Arizona State University], and NASA.)*

dead stars. When the galaxy was young, it consisted almost entirely of hydrogen and helium. It was very poor in heavy elements such as carbon, oxygen, iron, and other materials required to form rocky planets and organic material. These heavy elements are formed during the latter stages in a star's life cycle and are cast off into space when a dying star throws off material in a nova or supernova explosion.

These materials are then recycled into new stars that form when the gas clouds collapse once again. The excess material left after the formation of a new star then condenses to form comets, asteroids, and planets. If the metallic content of the new system is high enough, it will likely form rocky planets such as Earth and Mars.

Over the course of billions of years, stars throughout the galaxy gradually generated generous quantities of carbon and other heavy elements—materials that were recycled to form new solar systems such as our own.

Currently, about 10 to 20 new stars are formed each year throughout the Milky Way, but not all of them are similar to our sun.

Likely value for R:

R=10 to 20 stars/year

f_s—Sun-like stars

The next factor we encounter in the Drake equation is f_s. This factor describes the percentage of newly formed stars that are suitable for the formation of planetary systems like our solar system. This factor isn't concerned with the percentage of habitable planets, or even the percentage of newly formed stars that have planets orbiting them. This factor measures the percentage of stars that could potentially host a solar system. This factor will be a number ranging from 0 (0 percent) to 1 (100 percent). By multiplying the factor R by f_s, we can determine the number of new sun-like stars formed in the galaxy each year.

The most important factor that feeds into this is the percentage of *sun-like* stars formed each year. We're most interested in main-sequence stars whose mass is similar to that of our sun. A star's mass is an important factor in its ability to host life because its lifetime is determined by its mass. Stars that are much more massive than our sun burn out much more quickly (within millions of years, as compared to our sun's expected 10 billion year lifespan). While stars that are much less massive than our sun may shine for trillions of years, they do not produce a large habitable zone.

One of the prerequisites for carbon-based life is a stable source of energy, like our sun. Main-sequence stars have life spans measuring billions of years and produce a stable amount of energy throughout most of their life. This stability is important. If the sun's energy output varies significantly, the amount of energy received by planets varies, causing great disruption to their climates (if the sun's energy output were to decrease by just one or two percent, Earth would be thrust into another ice age).

Approximately 10 percent of stars are similar to our sun in terms of mass and lifespan. This implies that one to two new sun-like star systems are formed in our galaxy each year; hence, $f_s = 0.1$.

There are other factors that impact the value of f_s. One of the more important of these to come to light in recent years is the prevalence of heavy elements in a newly formed system. Because these materials are pre-requisites for the formation of rocky planets and organic material, a new star system must not only have a main-sequence star, but it must also have sufficient quantities of heavy elements to support the formation of rocky planets. This will reduce the value of f_s further, although at this stage we do not yet know the minimum required amount of heavy elements. These, and other newly discovered factors, will be discussed in further along with the Rare Earth Hypothesis.

There are about 100,000 sun-like stars within 1,000 light years of our system. We can detect a strong or well-aimed radio signal using current technology out to a range of several hundred to 1,000 light years depending on the strength of the signal and the size of our receiving antenna. Even if we exclude stars outside of the main sequence (i.e., stars that are much lighter or much heavier than our sun), we will still need to investigate 100,000 potential life.

Possible range of values for f_s:

$0 < f_s < 1$

Estimated value of f_s:

$f_s \approx 0.1$

f_p—Planets, planets, everywhere

The late 1990s have witnessed one revelation after another as new telescopes and sensing instruments have given scientists the ability to peer further and further into the universe. Once thought to be extremely rare, extrasolar planets (planets orbiting stars outside our solar system) are now thought to be commonplace.

The planet hunters

Dr. Geoffrey Marcy, a professor at San Francisco State University and a visiting scholar at the University of California, Berkeley, is one of the pioneers in the search for extrasolar planets. Since Didier Queloz and Michael Mayor's 1995 discovery at the Geneva Observatory of an extrasolar planet in orbit around 51 Pegasi, Dr. Marcy and his colleagues have detected planets orbiting approximately four dozen stars.

NOTE
The first planet outside our solar system was discovered by Penn State astronomy professor Alexander Wolszczan in 1991 (confirmed in 1994). Wolszczan's planet orbits the neutron star PSR1257+12. The first planet discovered in orbit around a sun-like star was discovered in orbit around 51 Pegasi by Didier Queloz and Michael Mayor in 1995.[*]

---

[*] Wolszczan, A., Frail, D., "A Planetary System around the Millisecond Pulsar PSR1257+12," *Nature*, Vol. 255, p. 145 (1992).

Because stars are so bright, any planets orbiting stars are obscured by the glare from their sun, making it extremely difficult to directly observe distant planets using today's telescopes. However, a large planet will subtly influence the star it orbits. Its gravitational tug causes the star to wobble as the planet spins around the star. When the planet is orbiting on the near side of the star, the planet pulls the star towards the telescope. Likewise, when the planet is on the far side of the star, it pulls the star away from the observing telescope.

Dr. Marcy and his team used a clever technique called *Doppler shift analysis* (also referred to as *spectroscopy*) to measure the gravitational signature of a large planet. Dr. Marcy and other astronomers detect the wobble by measuring the Doppler shift in the star's light. When a planet pulls the star toward the observing telescope (see Figure 3-2), it's the star's light appears slightly more blue than normal. When a planet star pulls the star away from the observing telescope, it's the star's light appears slightly redder than normal. By detecting this subtle change, Marcy and others were able to detect the presence of large planets orbiting many of the stars they observed. This wobble is invisible to the naked eye, but can be detected with the aid of a spectrometer. Marcy's team was even able to determine the details of the planet's orbit, its approximate size, and the general parameters of its climate.

A spectrometer is, in effect, a prism that splits incoming beams of light into constituent colors (see Figure 3-3). By measuring the intensity of the light at different points along the spectrum (rainbow), astronomers get a detailed picture of the chemical composition of a star and observe how the spectrum shifts over time (the technique used to sense variations in the star's motion).

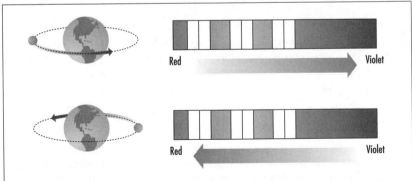

Figure 3-2: *A spectrometer splits an incoming beam of light into its constituent colors (wavelengths) and measures the intensity of the light at many points along the spectrum.*

Astronomers are able to detect minute shifts in the color of a star's light because the light is absorbed at very specific wavelengths by materials in the star's atmosphere. Hydrogen, for example, absorbs light at specific wavelengths, which are different than the set of wavelengths through which oxygen absorbs. These absorption lines appear as dark lines in a star's spectrum and can be used as calibration marks to detect minute shifts in the overall color of the star light (see Figure 3-3).

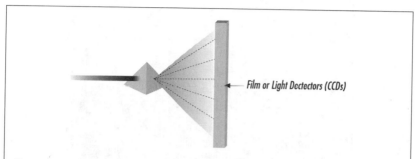

Film or Light Detectors (CCDs)

Figure 3-3: *Astronomers detect extrasolar planets by looking for a wobble in the spectral signatures of stars.*

All of the extrasolar planets detected in this manner are Jupiter-sized planets. (So far, researchers have not succeeded in detected Earth-sized worlds using Doppler shift analysis because the technique is not sensitive enough to detect the small wobble induced by less-massive planets.) Some of these giant worlds orbit in their star's habitable zone. Although a gas giant itself is unlikely to host an environment conducive to complex life, these giant planets are likely to be surrounded by several moons, much like Jupiter and Saturn. Some of these moons may have liquid oceans. As of today, we can see only the giants.

The HST provides important data by capturing images of new stars surrounded by disks of dust and debris (see Figure 3-4). Scientists believe these protoplanetary disks provide raw material for planet formation. They surround the majority of new stars that have been photographed. We know that these disks collapse into planetary systems within a time frame of several million years (which is quick by geological standards). The material in a disk weighs quite a bit, and over long enough periods of time, the force of gravity compels the material to clump together. Over the course of millions of years, the disk of material consolidates into a collection of planets, comets, and asteroids.

When we have the ability to directly photograph planets orbiting other stars we'll get a better picture of what a typical solar system looks like. Our

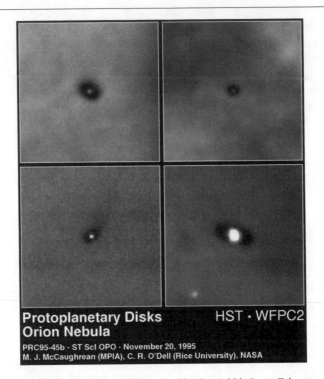

Protoplanetary Disks HST · WFPC2
Orion Nebula
PRC95-45b · ST ScI OPO · November 20, 1995
M. J. McCaughrean (MPIA), C. R. O'Dell (Rice University), NASA

Figure 3-4: *Protoplanetary disks photographed by the Hubble Space Telescope. These false color images reveal extensive disks of debris orbiting newly formed stars. (STScI/ HST image courtesy of Mark McCaughrean [Max-Planck-Institute for Astronomy], C. Robert O'Dell [Rice University], and NASA.)*

system, which has smaller inner planets and large outer planets, may be common, or it may be unusual. We won't really know until we've imaged other systems to compare their features.

Why is this important? Until recently, many scientists assumed that planets were rare and their formation required a unique set of events. As far as we knew, ours was one of a few solar systems orbited by an inhabitable world. If there are no planets to live on, we thought, ET would have no home; therefore, the search for extraterrestrial life (intelligent or otherwise) seemed a waste of time.

The discoveries of other planets confirm the theory that planet formation is commonplace. It now appears that many—perhaps most—stars have orbiting planets. Some planets will be large. Some will be tiny. Some will be baked by their stars. Some will be frozen, desolate worlds like Pluto. But some will fall into what is called the habitable zone (see Figure 3-5). The habitable zone is the area from a star to the orbit at which liquid water cannot be formed. This is a relatively narrow region in which an orbiting planet would receive just enough energy from its sun to melt ice, but not so much that its water boils. If the planet is too far away, it's water freezes. If the planet is too close, the water boils into vapor. Within the habitable zone the temperatures aren't too hot, and they're not too cold—they're just right for harboring life.

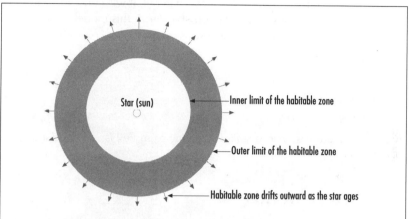

Figure 3-5: *The habitable zone surrounding our sun. Today, the habitable zone includes Earth. This zone drifts further out over time, as the sun heats up as it ages.*

In addition to detecting direct evidence of extrasolar planets, we have also developed a better understanding of why planets are likely to form. The *raison d'être* for planets can be summarized with one word: *gravity*.

We've known for sometime that the force of gravity forms stars. A star forms when a large cloud of gas begins to collapse under its own weight. While it is hard to imagine a cloud of gas having much weight, consider that a gas cloud that spans a region the size of our solar system will be quite massive. As the gas falls in on itself, the central region of the cloud heats up as it is compressed. Eventually, the central region reaches a high enough temperature that hydrogen atoms begin to fuse to form helium. This process powers stars. It also releases prodigious amounts of energy and slows or stops further accretion of material from the gas cloud.

As the gas cloud condenses, it tends to rotate in one direction, much like water circling an open drain. While much of the material in the gas cloud is drawn into the newly formed star, a fraction of the material orbits the star in a halo or disk. Instead of being drawn into the star, material within this halo clumps together to form asteroids, comets, and small planets. Although the clumping tendency is initially weak, larger objects form and begin to exert a significant pull on nearby material, accelerating the rate at which the disk consolidates into a small number of dense objects.

What's important to understand is that the general process is universal. Nearly all newly formed stars will have excess material orbiting them in a disk. Gravity compels this debris to go somewhere—either to clump together, or to fall inward into the star. Some material will be left in orbit around the star. If there is enough excess material, it will consolidate to form planets, or in some cases, a companion star. From this model we conclude that planets orbit many of the sun-like stars in our galaxy.

Possible values for f_p:

$0 < f_p < 1$

Current estimates for f_p:

$0.05 \ (5\%) < f_p < 0.5 \ (50\%)$

This estimate has been steadily increasing as more planets are discovered orbiting other stars.

n_e—Watery worlds

The factor n_e refers to the number of possible planet-bearing solar systems that host Earth-like worlds. The key criteria here is that the planet must have a source of liquid water to sustain life. Such worlds are most likely to exist in the habitable zone (although the moons of large planets, such as Jupiter's moon Europa, may also have liquid water oceans).

While we have detected nearly 30 large (Jupiter-sized or larger) planets orbiting other stars, we have yet to detect planets with liquid water outside of our system. We now know of four worlds in our solar system that are likely to have liquid water. Earth (obviously) and Jupiter's moon Europa, (and possibly its moons Ganymede and Calisto*). In January 2000, the Galileo probe conducted measurements that indicate what could be a saltwater ocean hidden beneath Europa's icy surface.

We have failed to detect Earth-sized worlds outside our solar system due to the inherent limitations of techniques currently used to detect extrasolar planets. The technique used by Mayor, Marcy, and others is not sensitive enough to detect small planets. Nonetheless, nearly all astronomers expect that smaller worlds exist alongside their larger neighbors. Scientists are developing space-based telescopes called interferometers specifically to detect

---

* Johnson, Torrence V. "The Galileo Mission to Jupiter and Its Moons." *Scientific American* 282 (February 2000): 40–49.

Earth-sized planets orbiting nearby stars. These instruments will be online within the next 10 to 20 years and will allow us to take low-resolution pictures of these worlds. In addition to confirming their existence, we will be able to determine the chemical composition of their surfaces and atmospheres.

Interferometers employ interference effects. The interference phenomenon occurs because light has wave-like characteristics, like a sound wave or a ripple traveling across a pond. These interference effects make it possible to create a device that selectively amplifies some light waves, while canceling others out.

An interferometer can selectively cancel out light from a bright point source (i.e., a star). Therefore, when aimed at a distant star, an interferometer will detect only the light reflected by nearby objects, such as planets and cometary debris.

The Terrestrial Planet Finder, a NASA program slated for launch in 2011, will be a space-based telescope that employs both interferometry and spectrometry.* The telescope is designed specifically for the task of detecting and analyzing the chemical composition of Earth-sized planets orbiting stars within 50 light years of our system. This project will compliment conventional space telescopes designed to replace the aging HST.

Figure 3-6 graphically illustrates the power of spectrometry. By comparing the intensity of reflected light at differing infrared wavelengths, we can take a detailed chemical snapshot of a planet. The example above compares Venus, Earth, and Mars. Even at a glance, one can see that Earth has a more complex infrared signature than do Venus and Mars. The primary feature on both Venus and Mars is a sharp dip that betrays the presence of carbon dioxide in the atmosphere. Earth has a CO_2 marker, but also absorbs infrared light at wavelengths associated with water (H_2O) and ozone (O_3, a marker that indicates an oxygen-rich atmosphere). The presence of ozone, together with water, would be strong evidence of biological activity. This is because free oxygen is highly reactive; unless it is constantly replenished, it is quickly flushed out of the atmosphere through chemical reactions (such as rusting iron).

Water, the product of combining hydrogen and oxygen, is one of the most common compounds in the universe. There is an abundance of it throughout our solar system and the majority of star systems we have observed. The only problem is that most of this water is not in a liquid state. However, a large or small planet orbiting within a star's habitable zone may have large amounts of liquid water.

---

* For additional information about interferometers, see Chapter 6, *Radio Communication*.

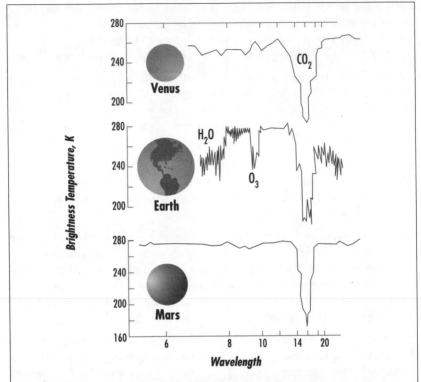

Figure 3-6: *By combining an interferometer with a spectrometer, it is possible to determine the chemical composition of a planet's atmosphere. This example compares the infrared signatures for Venus, Earth, and Mars.*

Just as we have been discovering new planets on an almost weekly basis, we have made breakthrough discoveries about the resilience of life. Until fairly recently, scientists assumed that life could survive only in a relatively tame environment. Life, according to what was then conventional wisdom, is delicate; it survives only in a very specific environment (so specific that life on Earth must be an extremely rare thing—perhaps unique in our galaxy).

In the past 20 years, we have discovered life in nearly every crevice on our planet. We have discovered rich ecosystems around undersea hydrothermal vents (in superheated water that's hot enough to melt lead). We have discovered bacteria that thrive on the cooling rods in nuclear power plants. We have discovered bacteria that can hibernate for thousands—even millions— of years without water (and can even survive the harshest climate of all— outer space). We have discovered bacteria that live in rocks buried miles under the Earth's surface (scientists estimate that these subterranean bacteria, if they lived on the surface, would cover the entire planet in a blanket several feet thick). Contrary to our belief, the life we see on the surface of the Earth is but a tiny fraction of the life on our planet.

The only common thread in all of these environments is liquid water. Anywhere on Earth where there is liquid water (no matter how scarce or infrequent), you will usually find life.

The discovery of an ecosystem beneath the Earth's surface that is larger than that on the surface is also important. It tells us that life could thrive on any world with liquid water. This is why scientists are so interested in Jupiter's moon Europa. Europa probably has a liquid ocean beneath its mantle of ice. Europa's surface is constantly stretched by the tidal forces of Jupiter's immense gravity field (see Figure 3-7). The side of Europa closest to Jupiter is pulled toward Jupiter more strongly than its far side. This causes the entire moon to stretch, causing friction, which translates into heat (much like when you bend a paperclip back and forth until it breaks). This provides the moon with a source of energy to power undersea volcanic activity and maintain a liquid ocean beneath its surface.

If Europa has a watery ocean, it may also have undersea volcanic vents. Many scientists now expect to find some form of life in Europa's oceans. Perhaps we will find only simple bacterial life, or maybe we'll find whole ecosystems. Nobody will know until we go there.

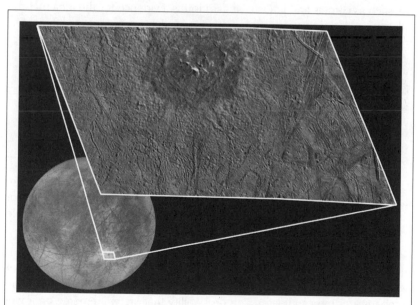

Figure 3-7: *Europa's icy surface, photographed by the Galileo Orbiter (courtesy of NASA/JPL/Caltech).*

Possible values for n_e:

$0 < n_e < n_p$

(Where n_p is the average number of planets in other solar systems.)

Likely values for n_e:

Unknown

(But n_e is likely to be much less than n_p, as only a small percentage of planets in a system will be suitable for the formation of life.)

A universe wired for life?

The most important lessons we've learned in the latter half of the 20th century are that the basic conditions required to support microbial life are commonplace throughout the universe, and life can survive in environments once thought too extreme.

The raw materials from which carbon-based life form are commonplace. Hydrogen, oxygen, carbon, and nitrogen—four of the most important elements for life—exist throughout the observable universe (see Table 3-1). Moreover, many of the chemical precursors for life form naturally. Amino acids, for example, have been detected in locations thought to be devoid of life, such as comets and interstellar gas clouds. Evidence for the idea that the universe is biased to produce the basic ingredients required for life (water, amino acids, hydrocarbons) continues to mount.

Table 3-1: *Relative abundance of hydrogen, helium, and other elements in our galaxy*

ELEMENT	PERCENTAGE
Hydrogen	75
Helium	24
Everything else (carbon, oxygen, nitrogen, etc.)	~1

If the ingredients named in Table 3-1 are common, all life needs to get started is a planet with a liquid ocean and a climate that remains stable for long periods of time. This could be a planet orbiting within a star's habitable zone, or a large moon (like Europa) in orbit around a gas giant.

Whether simple or complex life has developed on these Earth-like worlds is still unknown. There is a real possibility that life has developed on other worlds within our own solar system (as previously mentioned, Jupiter's moon Europa is a prime candidate). The probability that life will emerge on a wet planet, and whether life will evolve into more complex and intelligent forms, is governed by the factors f_l, f_i, and f_c, the subjects of the next chapter.

EVOLUTION

Once we've pinned down a range of estimates for the prevalence of habitable worlds, the next thing we need to do is to estimate the odds for bacterial life emerging on an Earth-like world and then the likelihood that simple life will evolve into intelligent animal life.

The factors at the right-hand side of the Drake Equation (f_l, f_c, and L) are especially controversial. While the idea that bacterial life may be common throughout the universe is gaining mainstream acceptance, the idea that intelligent life has evolved on other worlds is greatly disputed. The reason for the controversy is fairly straightforward. Until we either detect indisputable evidence of intelligent life outside of our solar system, or fail to find evidence of intelligent life after an exhaustive, decades long (or perhaps centuries long) search, the estimates for these factors will be just that: estimates.

f_l—Instant life, just add water

The factor f_l refers to the percentage of Earth-like planets (those having liquid water) on which life develops. This is a trickier factor to estimate because, to date, Earth is the only example of a planet that currently harbors life. We think that bacterial life may have once existed on Mars (Jupiter's moon Europa is another site thought to be hospitable to bacterial life). We have some evidence to support this; the evidence, however, is controversial. We have yet to directly observe life on another planet.

We also haven't looked very hard. We've sent a few relatively simple space probes to other worlds, but we probably won't know what life (if any) developed on neighboring planets until we send people there to look for fossils or other signs of life.

Just as we have learned about extrasolar planets, and life's resiliency, we've also learned that life emerged on Earth much more quickly than many people once imagined. Until recently, conventional wisdom told us that life developed on Earth rather slowly. According to this view, not much happened for hundreds of millions of years until one day, an unlikely accident led to the creation of the first precursor to life: a molecule that could make copies of itself (known as a *replicator*) appeared. Once this happened, the process of evolution took over, and this simple ancestor's offspring became more and more complicated, ultimately leading to bacterial life and eventually to the complex life we see today.

Just as we have been surprised to discover bacteria that thrive on the control rods of nuclear reactors, we've been surprised to discover that simple life emerged soon after Earth became habitable. The first bacterial fossils date to 3.8 billion years ago, when debris still bombarded the Earth. Life took hold on our planet even while it was still a battered world. This observation runs counter to earlier theories about the emergence of life.

This indicates that life can emerge quickly. Since life on Earth formed quickly from raw materials that are commonplace throughout the observable universe (hydrogen, carbon, oxygen, nitrogen and a few other elements), life could get started under similar conditions on other worlds throughout the universe. This is impossible to prove until we visit other life-bearing worlds, but the logic is straightforward.

So, what is a reasonable estimate for the value of f_l? We are still working with a sample size of 1 (Earth), so it is impossible to estimate the value of this number for other solar systems. The consensus among scientists is that the processes that led to the emergence of simple life forms (bacteria) on Earth are possible on other planets that have liquid water oceans and sufficient amounts of heavy elements (carbon, nitrogen, iron, etc.). We're not concerned with the odds for intelligent life here, just simple, single-celled life. The possible values for f_l range between 0 (0 percent) and 1 (100 percent).

We'll have a better idea of the odds once we have explored other worlds within our solar system (Mars, Europa, and Titan, in particular). If we discover evidence of life on other worlds in our own solar system—especially if that life has developed along different lines than ours—we will have strong evidence that f_l is, as many people suspect, closer to 1 (100 percent).

Space exploration

A wide range of space exploration missions have been proposed in order to search for evidence of past and present life on worlds in our solar system and beyond. These missions can be broadly divided into two categories: unmanned space probes and spaced-based telescopes.

We will use unmanned space probes, similar to the Mars Pathfinder probe, to analyze surface materials on other planets and moons in our solar system. In some cases, these probes will return materials to Earth for detailed analysis. These missions will enable us to search for evidence of microbial life throughout the solar system.

We will also launch a series of space-based telescopes to observe distant solar systems and eventually directly photograph Earth-size planets orbiting nearby stars.

UNMANNED PROBES

Over the next 10 to 20 years, we will send unmanned probes to planets and moons throughout our solar system to look for evidence of life. Two worlds at the top of our list are Mars and Europa.

We have been sending unmanned probes to Mars since the 1970s, and have been doing so quite frequently since the 1990s. We've been sending unmanned probes to Mars for a number of reasons, chief among them to survey the planet's geography and climate in detail. Since the discovery of the Allan Hills meteorite, which contained structures that looked to some scientists like bacteria fossils, we have added the search for fossilized evidence of life to the list of reasons to visit Mars in the 21st century.

The most ambitious Mars mission on the books is a sample return mission planned for launch in 2011. In this mission, a robot probe similar to the Mars Pathfinder will collect soil samples from the surface of the planet. These samples will be returned to the Earth for detailed analysis. During previous missions, on-board equipment has analyzed rock and soil samples. However, spacecraft weight limitations restrict the sophistication of such tests. Returning soil samples to Earth will enable us to conduct a wide range of tests to search for evidence of biological activity.

Also scheduled is an unmanned probe that will land on Europa, and if all goes well, a heated probe will melt through the Europa's icy surface to the ocean below. (Heat generated by the radioactive decay of plutonium powers the probe, helping it melt through the ice.) This concept will first be tested at Lake Vostok, a lake in Antarctica that has been buried beneath several kilometers of ice for millions of years. This will be a difficult mission—much more so than the Mars Lander missions—because of the several miles of ice through which machines must drill.

THE VIKING MARS MISSIONS

The first search for life on Mars was conducted over 20 years ago with the Viking missions. The Viking Landers performed a series of tests designed to look for evidence of microbial life.

The Viking Landers performed three main experiments to test for evidence of microbial life in Martian soil, including:

Pyrolytic release experiment

This experiment is designed to detect photosynthesis or carbon dioxide or carbon monoxide processing. Samples are incubated for several days in the presence of a radioactive gas mixture, some samples with simulated sunlight and some without. The samples are then heated to several hundred degrees. The resulting vapors are analyzed to determine whether the carbon dioxide or carbon monoxide gas reacted with the sample.

Labeled release experiment

This experiment is designed to detect metabolic activity through radiorespirometry by detecting waste gases produced by biological activity. Liquid nutrients labeled with radioactive carbon are added to the samples and the atmosphere is continuously monitored to detect any radioactive gases released from these nutrients.

Gas exchange experiment

This experiment measures the production and uptake of carbon dioxide, nitrogen, methane, hydrogen, and oxygen by an incubated soil sample. The sample is sealed and purged with helium gas before a quantity of a nutrient solution (saturated with neon) is added. At certain intervals, samples of the atmosphere are removed and analyzed by a gas chromatograph to measure the production of gases associated with known biological activity.

Although the Viking tests initially suggested the presence of microbial activity, this was later attributed to the highly reactive chemistry of the Martian soil. Mars has no ozone layer to filter ultraviolet (UV) radiation. UV radiation from the sun reacts with the exposed soil, creating peroxides, highly reactive compounds.

SPACE TELESCOPES

Next-generation space telescopes (which will replace the aging Hubble Space Telescope [HST]) will compliment unmanned space probes. These instruments will allow us to peer further into the universe and take photographs at even higher resolutions than we can today. We'll also be flying completely new categories of instruments, such as the Terrestrial Planet

Finder, which directly detect and photograph Earth-sized worlds in nearby solar systems. Other space telescopes, designed to take photographs in the X- and gamma-ray parts of the spectrum, will enable us to learn more about what's happening in more active regions of the universe, such as the center of our galaxy.

NEXT-GENERATION SPACE TELESCOPE

The Next Generation Space Telescope (NGST), slated for launch in 2008, will replace the aging HST. The NGST will be used to take high-resolution infrared spectrographs of other stars, nebulae, and protoplanetary disks (which are thought to be the first stage in planetary development). This will enable astronomers to study the formation of solar systems in great detail. Astronomers will study the physical structure of young solar systems as well as the chemical composition of protoplanetary disks. These surveys will teach us how solar systems and planets typically form and more about their chemical composition. For example, if Earth-sized planetary formation is common in our galaxy, and organic compounds are abundant in these systems, the odds will be stacked in favor of the emergence of life (i.e., we can expect to see higher values for n_e and f_l).

TERRESTRIAL PLANET FINDER

The Terrestrial Planet Finder, described in Chapter 2, *Listening to the Stars*, is a forthcoming space telescope designed specifically to detect and photograph Earth-sized worlds orbiting stars within 100 light years of our own system. When the TPF detects an extrasolar planet, it will use infrared spectroscopy to determine the chemical composition of the planet's atmosphere.

These next generation telescopes will accelerate the search for life directly and indirectly. Because we'll learn more about the processes occurring throughout the universe, we'll learn more about the factors in the Drake Equation. Among other things, we'll learn:

- The percentage of sun-like stars that develop solar systems similar to ours

- The percentage of solar systems that have planets orbiting within their habitable zones

- The percentage of solar systems with potentially inhabitable planets that exhibit evidence of biological activity

- What parts of the galaxy have conditions suitable for the formation of Earth-like planets and the emergence of life (i.e., what are the habitable areas of the Milky Way galaxy)

Fifty years from now, we'll have learned not only how many planets are suitable for life, but we will also have detected (or failed to detect) evidence of carbon-based life on Earth-sized planets. With this information, we will be able to calculate much more reliable estimates for the values for the factors of n_e and f_l.

The Darwin machine

Once life gets started, natural selection and evolution take over. Charles Darwin's theory of natural selection—a disarmingly simple theory—offers tremendous insight into how a simple system can lead to incredible variety and complexity in living things. The principles of natural selection are universal. They can be applied to life on Earth. They can be applied to businesses and social organizations. They can even be applied to computer programs. If life exists on other worlds, its development, like that of life on Earth, will also be driven by Darwin's principle of natural selection. The primary rule in the game of evolution can be simply described as: *the most efficient population wins*.

There are a couple of ways to measure efficiency for a situation in which life is just getting started. One measure is how efficiently an organism makes copies of itself. Efficient reproduction has the greatest impact on how quickly the population can grow. The species whose population grows quickest has the best opportunity to take over the primordial environment, and therefore has the best chance to become the descendant species from which new life forms evolve. Let's define this as a measure of copies made per unit of energy consumed by the organism, since we're interested in knowing how effectively an organism can convert an external source of energy into making copies of itself.

Let's compare two strains of a hypothetical bacteria. Specimen A makes one copy of itself per unit of energy consumed. Specimen B makes 1.01 copies of itself per unit of energy consumed—a difference of just 1 percent. Specimen A reproduces once every six hours (360 minutes). Specimen B accomplishes the same feat once every 356 minutes. Both populations have access to an equal amount of energy that they can convert into offspring. When we start our comparison the populations of both organisms are equal, a 50/50 split. While this seems like a trivial difference, in just 30 days specimen B is able to make 2.5 times as many copies of itself than specimen A. Within the course of a year, specimen B will have made nearly 70,000 times as many copies of itself than specimen A. If the two strains are competing for limited resources, it is pretty obvious which specimen will win and which specimen will be pushed to the sidelines.

The central rule of evolution is that fitness is a relative concept. Whichever organism is most efficient or most adapted to its environment as compared to its competitors will become dominant, given enough time. Once started, evolution favors the development of progressively more efficient organisms.

Efficient doesn't always mean small and simple. For example, photosynthesis (the process of converting sunlight into chemical energy that can be used by an organism) is a very complicated process. The energy cost of building this machinery is quite high, which is why it took a long time to evolve. However, it also gives its owners access to a new source of energy, the sun. Bacteria that can convert sunlight into chemical energy had a huge advantage over those that were dependent on fuels found near hydrothermal vents. The photosynthetic bacteria could expand into habitats that were rich in sunlight, yet poor in the type of chemical fuels their ancestors consumed. Hence, the planet was carpeted in algae, and later plants, while ancestral bacteria were confined to their original habitats.

Sometimes the price of improved efficiency is added complexity. This is an important concept. Evolution is not necessarily rigged to produce increasingly complex life forms, as many people assume. Normally, it is biased in favor of simplicity. Yet it occasionally stumbles across a better, though more complex, way of using external energy to do useful work (e.g., move, reproduce, etc.). Incremental improvements are common, while quantum leaps in efficiency are rare. Although they are rare, major advances such as photosynthesis have such compelling benefits that, once developed, they are likely to become commonplace and not disappear. Because major advances involve more sophistication, they do not happen easily, and because of that, they require a long time (hundreds of millions of years to billions of years on Earth) to develop.

Evolving complexity

Life on Earth started off simply, consisting of no more than single-celled bacteria and algae for over 3 billion years. While bacteria may appear to be simple, they are far more complicated than any human-built machine. For example, the smallest machines ever built by humans measure a few millionths (or *microns*) of an inch and are very simple in design—they are microscopic gears (Figure 4-1) that may someday be used to build microscopic robots, which surgeons will use to explore the inner structure of the human body by navigating through blood vessels, organs, etc.

As fantastic as this idea might sound, bacteria are (in a literal sense) microscopic machines. They manipulate chemicals to construct membranes, filters, and other physical structures with which they store energy, move raw

Figure 4-1: *Submicron gears can be used to build microscopic robots and machines. (Courtesy of the University of Wisconsin, Madison; Wisconsin Center for Applied Microelectronics and Micromechanics.)*

materials, eliminate wastes, and maintain structural integrity. Bacteria are microscopic machines that literally build themselves molecule by molecule. No human-built machine comes close to matching them in their compactness or complexity. So while it may be tempting to look down on these simple, "lower" life forms, remember they routinely do things that are well beyond the current reach of our technology.

For the purposes of this book, life on Earth can be divided into four major periods: pre-cellular life, single-celled life, multicellular life, and intelligent life.

During the proto-cellular (*pre-cellular*) period, life had not yet evolved to the bacterial stage. Little is known about this period, as there are no fossil records to examine. Scientists theorize that the precursors for life were simple *replicators,* molecules capable of making copies of themselves. These molecules were the ancestors of the RNA and DNA molecules found in modern organisms. They would have performed two major jobs: storing genetic information, and serving as templates for assembling proteins by stringing together chains of amino acids (much like RNA is used in modern organisms).

These molecules became progressively more complex, eventually leading to the development of RNA and DNA molecules, and structures similar to single-celled bacteria. The details of this transition from the chemical sub-units of life (e.g., amino acids, polymers, etc.) to fully functional cells are still a mystery. This appears to have taken place over a relatively short period in time, since fossils from simple life forms can be dated back to 3.8 billion years ago.

Single-celled life forms, such as bacteria and algae, have been the dominant form of life on Earth for nearly 4 billion years. If you weighed all of the bacteria and algae on Earth, including subterranean bacteria, their total weight would dwarf the weight of "higher" life forms, including humans. Lowly bacteria are the hands-down winners when it comes to weight. If a large comet or asteroid were to collide with our planet (this happened to our neighbor, Jupiter, in July 1994 with the comet, Shoemaker-Levy 9), it would be fair to assume that all life—humans, animals, plants, etc.—would be wiped out. The worldwide cataclysm caused by a collision with a large comet would leave a few subterranean bacteria to become the ancestors of the next wave of creatures to inhabit Earth.

About 540 million years ago, the first multicellular life forms evolved. Multicellular organisms are essentially organized, and sometimes mobile, bacterial colonies. The cells in our bodies are not that much different than bacterial cells; we just have many different types of specialized cells (i.e., bone cells to support our weight, kidney cells to filter wastes, and so forth).

Such organization and specialization evolved slowly, primarily because this required a big leap in terms of complexity. There are huge competitive advantages for multicellular life; multicellular organisms benefit from a division of labor, where different types of cells perform specific tasks. Bacteria cells, on the other hand, are ombudsman. Each individual cell must perform many different tasks.

The emergence of multicellular organisms indirectly led to the emergence of nervous systems. A nervous system enables an animal to perceive its environment, to move itself, and to capture (and eat) other organisms. As animals evolved, they developed complex nervous systems, which ultimately lead to the emergence of the capacity for language and symbolic communication. The emergence of language enabled humans to communicate learned experiences to their peers and offspring. This was the foundation for the development of culture and ultimately technology. Intelligence, as we define it, is really a composite of numerous skills, many of which are necessary survival skills. Human intelligence is unique because it includes the capacity for language, abstract thought, and symbolic communication. When viewed in the context of evolving life on Earth, human intelligence begins to look more like an incremental improvement over existing forms of intelligence encountered throughout the animal world, and less like a bolt from the blue.

HOX GENES: THE BODY BLUEPRINT

Homeobox (or HOX) genes are common to most animals on Earth. These genes regulate the formation of developing organisms. In effect, they determine the animal's body plan and insure that the correct body parts form in the correct places.

These genes act as a genetic on-off switch that serves to activate and deactivate other genes at critical times during an organism's formation. This is conceptually similar to the idea of a conditional statement in a computer program, and would read something like the following:

"When condition *X* is true, activate the genes that direct the formation of a leg."

The development of HOX genes was critical to the development of animals because HOX genes make it possible for DNA to direct the development of macroscopic (large scale) structures (e.g., legs, arms, brains), not just protein molecules that are confined within an individual cell.

This was an important milestone in the development of life on Earth. The fact that it took several billion years for life to progress from microbial to animal suggests that the development of HOX genes was a major accomplishment that took time and much trial and error to complete.

Intelligence can be described as an organism's ability to comprehend and interact with its environment. This takes many different forms, from being able to recognize patterns (e.g., tell the difference between a plant and a camouflaged predator), to being able to remember the location of a nest. In every case, these skills can be thought of as computational problems that require a computing device to solve.

Typically, mobile organisms have some sort of nervous system, however primitive, to coordinate movement, sense, avoid predators, find food, etc. It is helpful to remember the example by which we proved that a small increase in an organism's rate of reproduction over another's rate translates into a huge long-term evolutionary advantage. Let's look at this same example from the perspective of two animals—A and B—that survive by feeding on another animal, C; remember, the more they eat, the faster they reproduce.

Animal B is just slightly smarter than animal A. As a result, animal B is slightly more successful in surviving and finding food (i.e., by spotting predators, by outsmarting its prey, beating A to the meal, etc.). Access to a larger food supply enables B to produce more offspring (all other factors being equal). Even if this difference is very small, animal B has an evolutionary advantage over a long enough time frame. Evolution plays out over very long time periods (thousands to millions of years). Just a tiny efficiency advantage or disadvantage determines the difference between survival and extinction.

Let's assume that B's slight intellectual advantage translates into a 1 percent advantage in reproductive efficiency since it has better access to a food supply. Hence, with access to the same natural resources, B will produce 1.01 times as many offspring as A in each generation. This is the same scenario as the example we used to illustrate bacterial evolution. The only difference here is that our hypothetical animal produces one generation of offspring every year, instead of one every few hours. In one year, the population of B will have grown 1 percent more than the population of A. In 10 years, population B will have grown 10 percent more than population A. In 100 years, population B will have grown 170 percent more than population A. And in 1,000 years, population B will have grown 2,095,000 percent more than population A. The exact number isn't important here. What is important, though, is that we are looking at something similar to compounding interest. The difference between the rates, when measured over a small time frame, is very small, but when measured over a long timeframe (thousands to millions of years), it overwhelms other factors.

When viewed in this context, increased mental abilities seem to give animals an evolutionary advantage over their competitors. If this weren't true, we would be limp blobs floating mindlessly around in the ocean somewhere. (Even jellyfish have a very simple nervous system that enables them to swim and capture food.) So, just as evolution drives organisms to ever-increasing chemical efficiency, it should also drive some organisms toward increasing mental efficiency.

Despite the great variations between different types of animals, nearly all animals that can move about independently share similar sets of mental skills. Most of these skills are necessary to improve the odds of survival and successful reproduction. Among these skills are:

The ability to sense the surrounding environment
> Although different animals employ senses such as sight, hearing, and smell in different ways, sets of such senses serve the same basic purpose: to form a mental map of the environment relative to the animal.

The ability to recognize patterns
> Pattern recognition is a key survival skill. Primitive animals do a better job recognizing patterns recognition than the most advanced supercomputers. Recognizing a camouflaged predator makes the difference between life and death. Recognizing camouflaged prey may keep an animal from going hungry. Avoiding simple obstacles, something that even dumb animals do effortlessly, presents a major problem for robot designers.

The ability to navigate

Even relatively primitive animals have developed impressive navigational capabilities; insects form crude mental maps of their environment and calculate their position relative to landmarks on that map, such as nests, food sources, predators, and so forth. This requires memory and an ability to visualize themselves relative to landmarks in their environment.

The ability to communicate

The assumption that only humans can communicate is incorrect. Many animals communicate with each other, albeit on a simpler level. Even animals as simple as honeybees relate to one another information about the location of food, approaching predators, etc. Animals do, however, lack grammar and the capacity for symbolic communication. (Dolphins and certain primates, however, have demonstrated the ability to learn human-like communication skills).

Humans have added some interesting layers onto this palette of skills, but in many respects, our mental abilities are built on a foundation similar to that of most animals. We have added grammar, the ability to assemble words into expressions (animals, with the possible exception of primates and dolphins, as noted earlier, can communicate with only the equivalent of individual words). We also have the capacity for abstract thought and proactive imagination (versus the capacity to merely react to our environment). These are unique skills, but in many respects, we are standing on the shoulders of the giants of the animal world.

Human intelligence, in this context, isn't a single, unique skill. It is really the result of a combination of skills, some of which are unique to humans, most of which are not.

So, the questions we need to ask when studying other worlds are:

- How likely is it that single-celled life will evolve into multicellular life?

- How likely is it that multicellular organisms will evolve into small animals that can move about independently (locomotion)?

These two events define pre-requisites for the development of intelligent animals. If life never progresses beyond the microbial level, there will be no animals (multicellular life). And if multicellular life forms remain immobile (like sea anemones), they will not require sophisticated nervous systems to survive. In order for intelligent animals to evolve, we first need multicellular animals that can move about independently. If it turns out that they are fairly common, the odds for intelligent life increase dramatically.

The Rare Earth Hypothesis

The conclusion we've attempted to draw so far is that Earth-like planets should be fairly commonplace, and therefore, so should life, and perhaps intelligent life. The Rare Earth Hypothesis, proposed by Peter Ward and Donald Brownlee of the University of Washington in their book *Rare Earth*, challenges the assumption that Earth-like worlds are common.

The Rare Earth Hypothesis is based on the idea that, while bacteria can adapt to and thrive in harsh and unstable climates, multicellular animals are much more sensitive to climate change, and that planets with stable climates are rare. The hypothesis doesn't challenge the idea that bacterial life may be commonplace throughout the galaxy. What it does is to place constraints on the number of life-bearing worlds where *complex* life can emerge and survive long enough to produce intelligent species.

Bacteria have a huge competitive advantage compared to larger, multicellular life forms. Because bacteria have short life –spans, and reproduce quickly and in large numbers, they can quickly evolve to adapt to changes in their environment. Their high rate of production creates, in effect, a laboratory in which to test billions of variations (mutations) at once. The mutants that are somehow better adapted to the environment will fare better and go on to produce more offspring than their counterparts.

Larger animals reproduce much less quickly than bacteria can and produce a single generation of offspring where bacteria produce thousands of generations of offspring. Because of this, complex plants and animals are much more vulnerable to changes in their environment. This trend can be seen firsthand in the mass extinctions of animal species caused by human disruption to the environment.

According to this hypothesis, the key requirement for bacterial life to develop into complex animal life is a climate that remains stable for very long periods of time (hundreds of millions to billions of years). While planets may be commonplace, such long-term stability may be quite rare. This requirement for long-term stability means that planets must have additional characteristics to simply orbiting within a star's habitable zone.

Galactic habitable zone

Ward and Brownlee introduce the concept of a *galactic habitable zone* in their hypothesis. Just as a planet must be orbiting at a certain distance from its star to sustain liquid water, the authors suggest that certain regions within the galaxy are better suited to the development of complex life than others.

The inner regions of a galaxy are much more active—and much more violent—than the relatively quiet outer regions. Stars in the galactic core are packed in closer quarters. Because of this, a solar system in the galactic core is much more likely to be affected by sterilizing radiation from violent events such as supernovae explosions and the formation of black holes. These events can generate enough radiation to sterilize worlds out to a radius of dozens of light years.

The outer regions of our galaxy contain fewer heavy elements than the inner regions. Heavy elements are a requirement for the formation of rocky Earth-like planets and the formation of carbon-based life. Because of this, scientists think solar systems in the outer spiral arms of the Milky Way are more likely orbited by gas giants like Jupiter than by Earth-like planets.

With this in mind, the authors suggest in the Rare Earth Hypothesis that there is a relatively small region within which complex life will have an opportunity to form in our galaxy. At this time, this part of the hypothesis has not been tested. It is difficult to define the boundaries of the galactic habitable zone because of the complex factors involved. Defining the habitable zone for a star is, by comparison, relatively easy; orbital distances that produce surface-temperature ranges permitting the existence of liquid water determine its boundaries.

Continuously habitable zone

Ward and Brownlee also introduce the concept of a *continuously habitable zone* (CHZ) around a star. This concept is born from the realization that stars do not produce a constant flux of energy throughout their lives. In fact, the sun's energy output has slowly increased since the formation of the solar system. Because of this trend, a planet orbiting just within the boundaries of the habitable zone early in the life of a star may find itself outside of the habitable zone as the star ages. This means that a planet may be habitable for only a small part its solar system's life cycle.

The CHZ is the band of orbital distance that will support liquid water *over* a period of several billion years. It turns out that this band is often very narrow, and doesn't exist at all for stars that are much smaller or larger than our sun. Ward and Brownlee conclude that even though it is likely that one or more planets may orbit within a star's habitable zone, it is unlikely that a planet orbits in its CHZ.

This isn't necessarily bad news for bacteria, since bacterial life appears to take root fairly quickly and that it can survive in extreme environments. However, it doesn't bode well for animal life since multicellular requires a stable, long-term environment to evolve.

Geological processes

Merely orbiting within a metal-rich star's habitable zone isn't enough either. A planet must also be geologically active in order to support life for long periods of time. We have an example of a dead, but potentially habitable planet in our own solar system; Mars orbits just within the outer boundary of the sun's habitable zone. If it had a denser atmosphere, Mars would be warm enough to support liquid water. In fact, space scientists are seriously contemplating the prospect of terraforming Mars by introducing super green-house gases to trap more heat. This is a very long-term prospect, requiring centuries of planning, but it may be feasible.

Mars is a dead planet primarily for two reasons: it is smaller than the Earth and it is not geologically active. Because Mars is less massive than the Earth, its gravity is weaker, which causes its atmosphere to be less dense. Also, atmospheric gases can escape Mars altogether because its gravity is weaker, resulting in a gradual long-term loss of atmosphere into deep space.

If Mars were geologically active, gases released from volcanic activity would offset the loss of atmosphere to space and help stabilize the environment. Thus, Earth serves as another example of how important geological processes are to stabilizing the environment.

Carbon dioxide (CO_2), a greenhouse gas, plays an important role in regulating Earth's temperature. When Earth warms up, CO_2 precipitates from the atmosphere to form limestone deposits. This decrease in the amount of CO_2 in the atmosphere prevents the planet from getting caught in a runaway greenhouse effect like its sister planet, Venus. However, if this precipitation process ran unchecked, enough CO_2 would be removed from the atmosphere to cause global temperatures to drop below freezing. The Earth would freeze over in an Ice Age from which it would never recover.

Fortunately, a geological process called subduction recycles the carbon trapped in limestone deposits back into the atmosphere via volcanic activity. Volcanism provides a long-term source of CO_2 that would otherwise be locked up in rock formations. Limestone formation provides a fast-acting mechanism to remove excess CO_2 from the atmosphere when Earth heats up. (Fast-acting in this example means millions of years, which may not, unfortunately, be fast enough to counter the effects of our own pollution.) Over long time frames, Earth's carbon cycle serves as a thermostat that prevents the planet from tipping into runaway cooling or warming cycles.

Ward and Brownlee conclude that a planet must be geologically active and have a long-term mechanism for regulating the levels of greenhouse gases in order to maintain conditions suitable for animal life.

Giant outer planets

Giant outer planets, such as Jupiter, play an important role in protecting smaller inner planets from asteroid and cometary bombardment. Jupiter, because it is over 100 times more massive than Earth, acts as a sort of vacuum cleaner, drawing in debris, such as comets and asteroids, that would otherwise threaten inner planets.

If we did not have giant outer planets, large objects would impact Earth at a higher rate. These impact events, while they would not necessarily exterminate bacteria, would wipe out a large percentage of animal species. Therefore, complex, higher-order life forms would have to start evolving all over again. Earth would be knocked back to the starting line perpetually, and thinking animals would be much less likely to evolve.

Large moons

Another factor cited by Ward and Brownlee in their Rare Earth Hypothesis is how the presence of a large moon contributes to the possible development of life. Earth has an unusually large moon that was formed as a result of a collision with a very large asteroid (best described as a small planet). This impact threw large amounts of material into orbit around the Earth; that material coalesced to form our moon. Scientists consider this type of collision event to be rare.

The moon has an important stabilizing effect on the Earth's axis of rotation, which in turn has an important stabilizing effect on Earth's climate. The moon prevents the Earth from wobbling as it rotates. If Earth's axis of rotation wobbled extensively, this would cause extreme climate variations; over time, the Arctic regions would become tropical, and vice versa. It is less clear that this is a *de facto* requirement for complex life, since one may argue that life would simply adapt to the climate variations.

If the presence of a large, stabilizing moon turns out to be a requirement for the evolution of complex life, the number of sites at which complex life can emerge will be smaller yet.

The net effect of these factors reduces the value of n_e, the percentage of Earth-like planets, since it makes the qualifying criteria for an Earth-like world stricter. Simply orbiting within a star's habitable zone just isn't good enough.

f$_i$–The emergence of intelligent life

The factor f$_i$ refers to the percentage of life-bearing worlds on which one or more intelligent species evolve. For the purposes of this section, we will define intelligent life to mean the life with the ability to interact with other animals, to communicate with and learn from other animals, and to relate learned experiences to peers and offspring. The capacity for technology is not included in this definition. We'll discuss the capacity for making tools when we discuss the factor f$_c$.

On Earth, several species meet these basic criteria for intelligence. Primates, dolphins, and parrots have demonstrated the capacity for many human-like intellectual tasks, including the ability to:

- Identify objects using verbal or symbolic references (using either symbolic icons or sounds)

- Communicate needs or experiences using utterances or symbols

- Craft and use simple tools to capture prey, build shelters, etc.

- Pass human-taught abilities to their peers and offspring

These animals, while they have many human-like capabilities, did not develop the capacity for symbolic communication on their own, and did not develop the capacity (or at least the inclination) to develop tools for hunting, shelter, and other purposes. The ability to build and use specialized tools was a critical precursor to the development of technology.

Table 4-1: *Intelligent animals*

ANIMAL SPECIES	SIGNS OF INTELLIGENCE
Primates	They can correlate verbal or pictoral symbols with objects (nouns) and actions (verbs) and can label objects.
	They can be trained to communicate using sign language.
	Primates in the wild have been observed using simple tools (e.g., fishing termites out of nests using sticks).
Dolphins	They can understand symbolic communication using sounds and pictures (icons).
	They can communicate with each other using sound.
	Experiments suggest that dolphins are capable of unprompted, abstract communication.
	Experiments also demonstrate that some dolphins understand the concept of delayed gratification and have significant plan-ahead capabilities.
Parrots	Some parrots can label objects using spoken words and understand human words and phrases.
	They can also categorize objects (e.g., when asked to describe the color of an object, the bird replies with the correct answer).

We know that several species on present-day Earth meet many of the litmus tests for intelligence (see Table 4-1). We have no way to determine the intelligence of extinct species from earlier epochs. However, it is probably a safe bet that there were other moderately intelligent species on Earth besides those that exist today.

Dolphins

Dolphins are particularly interesting as they are highly intelligent and have also evolved in an environment quite different from that of our primate ancestors. Humans have recognized dolphins' special intelligence for thousands of years. Because they have evolved in a different environment, and are physically quite different than primates, dolphins offer us insight into what intelligence means.

Many experiments conducted since the 1960s measure dolphin intelligence and investigate the possibility of interspecies communication. Since this is similar to the problem of communicating with an alien intelligence, whose mode of communication may be completely different from ours, this is worth our attention.

Dolphins are obviously intelligent animals, as anyone who has had an opportunity to interact with them knows. Many of their behaviors indicate they not only have good memories, but they are capable of abstract communication and understand the concept of time and delayed gratification.

Dr. Javis Batian conducted one well-known dolphin intelligence experiment. In his experiment, two dolphins, Buzz and Doris, were in captivity in a divided pool. In the beginning, they could see each other. In both parts of the pool, two switches had been installed. The dolphins were supposed to push the right switch if a light came on and stayed on, or push the left switch if the light came on and blinked. They learned to do this fairly quickly.

Then the experiment got more complicated. Doris had to wait for Buzz to push the correct button, and then she had to push the correct button in order to get fish for both of them. The next step was to build a wall between the two parts of the pool that would prevent visual contact between the two dolphins. They could only hear each other, and only Doris could see the light signal.

The constant light came on. Doris waited for her turn. Nothing happened because Buzz couldn't see the light signal. Then Doris made a sound. Buzz reacted by pressing the right button for the constant light. Doris continued with her constant light button and they got the fish.

Now, what does this mean? Doris realized that Buzz couldn't see the signal. She told him by sound that he had to press the button for the constant light. The experiment has been repeated 50 times, and although couldn't see the signal, he was correct most of the time. This experiment suggests that dolphins are capable of communicating abstract ideas, such as left and right.

For another experiment, researchers trained a dolphin to remove trash from its tank. Whenever a person appeared on a platform, the dolphin would retrieve a piece of trash from the tank and bring it to the trainer to receive a reward. One particular dolphin surprised its trainer by producing trash when the tank looked completely clean. The dolphin apparently did his own magic trick, retrieving trash from a completely clean tank. Upon further investigation, trainers discovered that the dolphin had stashed all sorts of trash in a bag in the holding tank, creating a savings account of sorts. What was really impressive was the dolphin had developed a strategy to maximize his reward by tearing off small pieces of the trash in the bag.

This behavior is important for several reasons. First, it suggests that this animal understands the concept of delayed gratification, and reasoned that by stashing trash in a hiding place, he could obtain a reward whenever desired. Second, by tearing large pieces of trash into smaller pieces, this dolphin had apparently reasoned that by dividing the stash into many smaller pieces, he could make his stash last longer. We don't know what this dolphin was thinking, but its behavior seems surprisingly sophisticated.

Dolphins are interesting also because they are intelligent but they have not developed technology. Although they are comparable to humans in terms of certain kinds of intellect, they don't build tools. There is an easy explanation for this. Dolphins do not have hands like ours to make and grasp tools. They may be smart, but they haven't made the transition to building technology.

In attempting to communicate with dolphins and other species, we are expanding our understanding intelligence. We're also learning to deal with the challenge of communicating with animals whose perception of the world, modes of communication, and mental processes are very different from our own.

f_c—Emergence of communicating civilizations

While several species of animals on Earth are moderately intelligent, only one species has developed technology, and that has happened very recently in Earth's history. For the other factors in the Drake Equation, we can draw on data collected from various sources. However, f_c is difficult to estimate because we have a sample size of only 1 (us).

We can't rely on data collected from other worlds to fill in the gaps here. However, we can draw some conclusions based on what we've observed in the animal world. Other animals besides humans, such as chimpanzees, do use tools. Tools are an important precursor to the development of technology. Only very recently have humans developed very sophisticated machines such as computers. Before the industrial revolution, most of our tools were fairly simple.

The first human invention wasn't a Saturn V rocket. The first human inventions were clothing and instruments used for hunting—items necessary for the survival of the species. These were decidedly "low tech" inventions, such as stone axes, wooden spears, and clothing fashioned from the hides of other animals. Only in the past few centuries have we worked our way into building machines, and most recently, thinking machines (computers).

What humans have that other animals do not have is the capacity for language and, because of that, a persistent collective memory (culture). The ability to record and communicate learned experiences to others enabled us to develop a collective memory long before we had developed writing, computers, or CD-ROM drives. Once someone happens upon a useful discovery or invention, this information is passed on to others. So, instead of endlessly reinventing spears, we moved on to new challenges like building permanent dwellings, agriculture, boats, and so on.

The key factor affecting the value of f_c is the extent to which the capacity for building tools and a system of symbolic communication affects the reproductive success of a species that is already fairly intelligent. If this additional ability has little or no impact on an animal's reproductive success, the individuals with these additional abilities will fare more or less the same as their less-witty counterparts, and this trait will not proliferate widely. If this additional ability translates into increased reproductive success, the smarter animals will eventually displace their less-intelligent counterparts.

That a tool-developing, communicating civilization has emerged only once on Earth, and very recently in Earth's history, suggests that the capacities for building tools and using symbolic communication are not critical for an organism's success in most situations. However, once this capacity does develop, its owner will have a significant reproductive advantage over its competitors (as humans have demonstrated with their ability to displace many of the species throughout the planet's entire ecosystem, something no other species has done in such a short period of time). Just as the emergence of multicellular life happened unexpectedly, so too did human-level intelligent life. In both cases, the outcome was not guaranteed by evolution, but once it happened, the resulting species gained a considerable competitive advantage over others and spread rapidly to fill many new environmental niches.

L—Average life span of a communicating civilization

We have been unintentionally broadcasting artificial radio signals into outer space for several decades now. The radio transmissions generated by our radio stations, TV stations, and radar sites look quite different than naturally occurring radio emissions. These signals are telltale signs of a technological civilization, since they cannot be produced without the guiding hand of an engineer. Once a species develops the capacity to communicate using radio, it becomes detectable from distant worlds. Several thousand nearby stars could detect our radio and TV broadcasts from the past several decades. Conversely, we could detect radio transmissions from another world with the technology we have today.

Why is L so important? If the value of L is very small, an intelligent civilization will be detectable (on the air) for only a few years before they destroy themselves (i.e., by waging a nuclear war, ruining their environment, etc.). On the other hand, if an intelligent civilization can sustain itself for a long period of time, it will be detectable for hundreds, thousands, perhaps millions of years. We know from our own experience that we have survived this phase for over 50 years without destroying ourselves. It's a safe bet (and we can only guess at this number) that a civilization that can communicate by radio will be detectable for 50 to 100 years at a minimum.

Human civilization as a whole is several thousand years old. Although entire nations and civilizations have died out, many of their inventions have been carried down through generations. Once we invented the wheel and discovered fire, we didn't lose this knowledge. We could go through another destructive period and still retain a lot of the knowledge we've accumulated to date. Even if the vast majority of humans were killed in a nuclear war, plague, or environmental disaster, chances are that someone, somewhere would remember how to build a radio. Our species would eventually bounce back, and many of the inventions from the nearly extinct civilization would be rediscovered and carried forward. We would have to monumentally screw things up to lose this information permanently.

N—The number of detectable civilizations

So, how many other communicative civilizations exist elsewhere in the galaxy? The answer depends entirely on whom you talk to, and ranges from zero to about one million civilizations. Because we have yet to directly photograph the planets orbiting other stars, we have very little information to use to estimate the right-hand factors in the Drake Equation. We can rely only on educated guesses.

What we do know today that we didn't know as recently as 10 years ago is that planet formation is relatively common, and that life is a lot less delicate than we originally assumed. As of this writing, we have catalogued over 50 planets outside our solar system (about 6 times the number of planets in our own system). In the past 10 years, we've also discovered that life can survive wherever there is liquid water.

We've known for a long time that water and organic chemicals are common throughout the universe. The implication of these two discoveries is that the factors in the left-hand side of the Drake Equation (e.g., f_p, n_e, and f_l) are likely closer to 1 than they are to 0. Because microbial life is the foundation upon which more sophisticated life develops, there are likely to be many worlds in which complex life will have the opportunity to evolve. Whether this will happen on most watery, microbe-laden worlds, or just a few, is still an unanswered question.

Because we only know of one world on which complex life has evolved, we still have a very limited understanding of why it happened and what factors will promote or inhibit the progression from microbe to animal to thinking animals. Until we understand what specific steps occurred in the development of multicellular life on Earth, we won't know whether this is an unlikely event, a virtual certainty, or somewhere in between on other life-bearing worlds.

Based on what we know today, any number of scenarios is possible. It could be that, as the late Gene Shoemaker put it: "There's nobody here except us chickens." Or is it equally plausible that we are only one of many civilizations scattered throughout the galaxy?

COMMUNICATIVE
CIVILIZATIONS

The trickiest factors to estimate in the Drake Equation are f_c and L, which represent the percentage of intelligent species that go on to develop technology, and the average lifespan of communicative civilizations. These are very difficult numbers to estimate because as of yet, we do not have any evidence of intelligent, communicative life beyond Earth. So the only way we can estimate f_c is by approaching the problem indirectly and applying to this question what we've learned about the development of human civilization and technology.

The classic Drake Equation produces a number N, which, when all of the factors are multiplied, estimates the number of communicative civilizations we can possibly detect at any given time. While the Drake Equation is useful as a teaching aid, it oversimplifies the task of estimating how many sites may be on the air and is burdened with multiple assumptions, any one of which can greatly influence the final result produced by this equation. With the help of scientist and author David Brin's work, we'll expand on the classic Drake Equation to take other factors into account, such as a civilization's desire to seek or avoid contact with others, and interstellar migration.

f_c—Communicative, intelligent civilizations

Let's first start off by defining upper and lower limits for f_c, the factor that represents the likelihood that an intelligent species becomes a technological species capable of interstellar communication. The possible range of values for f_c is from 0 (0 percent of life-bearing worlds) and 1 (100 percent of life-bearing worlds). We know that f_c is greater than 0 since, if it were exactly 0, we (humans) would not be here and you would not be reading this book. We also know that f_c is less than 1 because not all intelligent species on Earth have developed technology. Dolphins are very smart, but they have not developed the capacity to make tools, a critical precursor for technology. The same goes for intelligent primates as well as certain species of birds, although some primates have the capacity for using simple tools (such as a blade of grass to extract termites from a nest). While many species have impressive intellectual abilities, only humans have developed sophisticated tools and the ability to communicate and retain symbolic knowledge.

So, from the start, we know that f_c is greater than 0 and less than 1. This is admittedly a very imprecise estimate. f_c could be 0.000001, or 0.9999999, or somewhere in between. This means that our estimate for the number N could be off by many orders of magnitude.

What we know from Earth's evolutionary history is that there is some probability that an intelligent species will go on to develop the capacity to communicate and make tools. After all, this is what happened with humans. It has also happened with intelligent primates on a lesser scale. The lesson we can glean from our own history is that it is possible for a moderately intelligent species to develop the capacity for tool-making. If it is possible here, it should be possible on other worlds that evolution leads to the development of moderately intelligent life.

Part of the problem is we do not have a complete understanding of the conditions that prompted our primate ancestors to evolve into humans. There are many theories about why this happened, but because nobody was around to record events as they unfolded over several million years, it is difficult to test them. Until we understand this process in greater detail, we won't know whether it is likely that a moderately intelligent animal species will make the jump to human-level intelligence. Perhaps this is a fairly straightforward scenario that is likely to play out on other worlds, given enough time. Or perhaps it is an extremely unlikely fluke. At this point, we just don't know.

The probability of technological life

The Drake Equation is a great tool for demonstrating why it is likely that intelligent civilizations have emerged elsewhere in the universe. However, it oversimplifies the issues related to the progression from simple life to technological life and is not intended to be used as a tool for forecasting exactly how many worlds host intelligent life.

To better understand the problem at hand, let's look at a modified version of the Drake Equation:

$$N = R \times f_s \times f_p \times f_e \times f_l \times R_i \times f_c \times L^2$$

As you can see, we have replaced the factor f_i with the factor R_i. In this form, R_i stands for the rate of formation of intelligent species on a life-bearing world, and f_c represents the percentage odds that any one of these intelligent species will develop the capacity for communication and technology. We've also replaced L with L^2 so the units of the equation balance out; if L were not squared, the equation would produce a rate (e.g., civilizations/year), rather than a number.

This equation tells us that intelligent species emerge at a rate of R_i species per year, and that of those species, f_c percent will go on to develop the capacity for symbolic communication and tool-making. The equation also tells us is that if evolution produces moderately intelligent animal species throughout the history of life on a planet, there is a chance that one of these species will eventually make the jump to higher-order intelligence and achieve the capacity for tool-making.

Cultural evolution

At some point in our history, our primate ancestors reached a point in their development at which they could share what they learned through language. At this point, they reached a sort of critical mass. The term *extelligence* is often used to describe this. Extelligence refers to the ability to retain and share information verbally (in spoken or symbolic form), whereas *intelligence* refers to the ability to learn and retain information. Many animals are intelligent, but only humans appear to be extelligent.

Once our ancestors reached the point of extelligence, we passed a landmark similar to the hurdle life crossed with the development of the first bacterial cell. Once they could teach lessons to their peers and offspring verbally, they could accumulate knowledge and pass it onto future generations (instead of learning the same lessons over and over again). Instead of being stuck on a treadmill, they could build on what previous generations learned.

Richard Dawkins coined the term *meme* to describe the evolution of culture and technology. A meme is similar to a gene, in that it is a package of information that, instead of describing to another cell how to build a protein, describes to another being how to do something. For example, the description of how to rub two pieces of wood together to start a fire, or how to make a sharp blade from a piece of flint is a meme.

In Dawkins' model, memes proliferate in the same way genes do. Some memes offer great advantages to those who have them. The meme for making a piece of clothing from an animal's skin is a good example. Compare two populations in a climate with cold winters. One population has learned how to make clothes from animal coats. The other population hasn't. Which one is going to have an easier time surviving a harsh winter?

Unlike genes, memes can hop freely among members of a population and can jump from one population to another. Let's say, for example, your mother creates a new recipe for a cake. It's the best cake you and your friends ever had. You decide to email your recipe to your friends, who in turn pass it along to their friends. Fairly quickly, this "creamy chocolate cake" meme "infects" most of the population.

If memes spread like genes, the only way your mother's cake recipe could prosper would be for your mother to produce more offspring, in the hope that some of them would inherit a gene carrying inherent knowledge of the recipe. This is obviously not practical. The big advantage memetic information has over genetic information is that beneficial memes (good ideas) spread rapidly throughout a population, allowing for great accumulation of knowledge.

Genetic versus memetic information

Once we've reached the critical point of being able to share lessons with peers and offspring, another form of evolution may take place. We can call this memetic evolution. Many of the same basic principles apply to memetic evolution as to genetic evolution. However, there are also important differences, including:

- Genetic information cannot be updated "on the fly" as can memetic information; an organism's genetic blueprint is fixed at the time of its conception.

- While useful genetic information (adaptations) may be passed to offspring only, memetic information may also be passed onto peers.

- In addition to sharing memetic information with all members of a population, in certain situations, it can be shared between species (humans have taught other animals how to use vocabularies of symbols).

- The longer an organism lives before reaching sexual maturity, the more slowly its species can adapt to its environment through genetic changes.

- Memetic information is quickly transmitted through communication.

- A population's capacity for communication governs the rate at which it can transmit memetic information (with the invention of wireless technology and the Internet, our capabilities in this respect are quite advanced).

- While genes are coded in digital, perfectly reproducible form, memes are information in shorthand, easily transmitted and simply communicated. (Memes, then, are highly prone to mutation. The children's game of telephone is a good example of this. When relating a story or instructions verbally, it is likely the speaker will introduce his own interpretation. After being relayed several times, the message may be quite different from the original version.)

It is important to note that memes are not the same as genes, and do not behave in the same way; they are merely a useful metaphor for examining the proliferation of knowledge throughout a population, and for examining the competition between populations with different levels of sophistication.

We'll discuss memes in greater detail in the latter half of this book, as we'll be using a variant of this idea to describe a system for communicating with a distant civilization.

Survival of the fittest memes—culture

Just as individual animals and populations of animals compete for scarce resources in the wild, humans behave in similar ways. The big difference for humans is that for most of recorded history, humans have had relatively few natural predators to worry about (with the exception of infectious diseases). So, instead of competing with other animals to survive, we have frequently found ourselves competing with each other for resources.

This sets up a competitive situation in which different populations compete for limited resources, whether they are arable land, water, game, or rare items (plants, minerals, etc.). It is helpful at this point to examine the factors that play a role in determining the relative strength of one population versus another. They are:

Size of population
> Size is important because a larger population can diversify its labor, share effort (expenses), store more cultural information (collective memory), and engage in major efforts with less risk.

Size of knowledge base
> This is the total store of knowledge collected (that can be recalled) by the population over its history.

Technological sophistication
> This refers to the ability to convert knowledge into tools, weapons, and systems for doing things that allow the population to function more efficiently.

Since these parameters cannot be easily defined numerically, we can't easily build something as precise as a mathematical model, but we can use these as guidelines in predicting how different scenarios will play out over the long haul.

The important trend to be aware of is that, all other things being equal, the ability to store knowledge and build technology will result in a reproductive advantage for a society. For example, when humans developed organized agriculture, they vastly increased their available food supply. These populations grew sharply compared to hunter-gatherer societies since they could support more people with less effort. As a result, agricultural societies displaced the hunter-gatherer societies. Although a few still exist today, hunter-gatherer societies have been all but condemned to extinction in most parts of the world. Even though the agricultural societies may not have made a conscious decision to extinguish hunter-gatherer societies, they grew at a much faster rate and eventually overwhelmed or displaced them.

It is not who wins or loses in a specific scenario, but rather the general mechanics behind what is happening. In order to compete in the long-term, a population must maintain its productivity compared to nearby populations with which it competes for resources. The superior culture will be able to support a larger population, to weather periods of scarcity, and to expand into neighboring territories.

NOTE

This also has some ominous implications should we ever encounter an expansionist alien civilization, since they would likely be much more technologically advanced than we are.

The important point to understand here is that societies don't reach a point where their technology is "good enough." This version of natural selection sets up an endless tit-for-tat game that demands that its participants continue to increase their productivity. Societies that become complacent or poorly managed are typically overrun or sidelined in the long run. Because of this, there is a great incentive for societies to continue to expand their knowledge base and invest in developing new technology.

Not all societies, however, will do this successfully. As we see from human history, there are many examples of societies that have failed. Some have failed quickly, while others prospered for a time and then failed. The Greek and Roman empires were examples of long-lived civilizations that ultimately collapsed. The Soviet Union, on the other hand, thrived for only a short period of time before collapsing under its own weight.

On the other hand, some societies have survived for hundreds or even thousands of years. Meantime, the skeletal (sometimes mummified) remains of those ancestors leave useful information behind that is often passed on to future generations. So, while societies may suffer short-term setbacks or die out altogether, human knowledge and technological capacity as a whole has displayed a steady upward trend toward increasing sophistication because, although civilizations collapse and re-organize themselves, much of the information about them is preserved.

Implications for other civilizations

The trend toward increasing technological sophistication in human societies is driven by a form of Darwinian natural selection. The same dynamic should occur in other populations that have similar capabilities, such as:

- The ability to move freely
- The ability to communicate using symbols (and to remember symbolic information)
- The ability to make tools

This suggests that once a species with these basic capabilities emerges, selection pressure will reward the populations that build the most sophisticated tools because the tools will fairly quickly outweigh genetic factors in a population's ability to compete. For example, a hunter with an arrow (and definitely a rifle) will be more successful than one without, regardless of how strong the unarmed competitor is.

While it is no guarantee, the game of tool-making never ends, so it makes sense that over a long enough period of time, an advanced civilization will eventually emerge from a tool-making population. It took less than 100,000 years for us to advance to the level we're at today. In particular, the advances we've made in the past 500 years have dwarfed everything that came previously.

While we can't estimate f_c based on this logical argument, we can make a reasonable case that once an intelligent, tool-making species emerges, it is likely to advance beyond basic tools to develop increasingly sophisticated technology.

Where is everybody: the Fermi Paradox

Renowned physicist Enrico Fermi posed a simple question that has vexed SETI proponents for decades: "Where is everybody?"

Fermi's logic was based on the idea that interstellar travel, while beyond our current capabilities, is not forbidden by the laws of physics. Although traveling faster than the speed of light is probably not possible, there is no reason that a sufficiently advanced civilization cannot build spacecraft capable of traveling at 1 to 10 percent of the speed of light. At this rate, it would take

800,000 to 8 million years to travel across the galaxy. Although this is a long time from the perspective of an individual person, this is a mere instant in terms of the lifespan of the galaxy as a whole.

Fermi reasoned that if just one species launched an interstellar colonization program where settlers would travel to and colonize nearby stars, then after a few hundred or thousand years, set off yet again for other systems, their descendants would have colonized most of the Milky Way within 50 million years. A long time by human standards, this represents less than 1 percent of the age of the Milky Way. Fermi's logic is persuasive because of the exponential rate of growth that an expansionist civilization will exhibit. Even if most civilizations stay in their home system, it takes only one civilization adopting this strategy to populate much of the galaxy.

SETI proponents have suggested a number of reasons why we have not encountered extraterrestrials (although UFO enthusiasts say the *Fermi Paradox* isn't a paradox because they're already here). Among the explanations that have been put forth are:

Low-rent neighborhood
> According to this explanation, Earth is in a relatively boring part of the galaxy, kind of like the remote parts of Utah. Hence, extraterrestrials are busy migrating to busier, more interesting territory like the galactic core.

The Zoo Hypothesis
> Extraterrestrials are aware of our presence, and are observing us, but are not making their presence known.

The Quarantine Hypothesis
> We have been identified as a dangerous species, and as a result, other civilizations are avoiding contact with us.

The Deadly Probes Hypothesis
> An advanced civilization that wants to thwart potential competitors has sent von Neuman probes (self-replicating robots) out to colonize the stars. These probes are designed to detect and destroy any source of modulated electromagnetic radiation. Disturbingly, this theory provides a consistent explanation for the Fermi Paradox, and is discussed further in a moment.

Nobody's home
> We haven't encountered evidence of extraterrestrials because we are the first species in the galaxy to develop space-faring capabilities. Therefore, if we want to, we can become the civilization that colonizes most of the galaxy.

Of these explanations, three are most likely to be correct. One, we're the first space-faring species to evolve in the Milky Way, in which case there is nobody else for us to contact nearby. Two, Earth is being quarantined or observed as a sort of zoo to allow us to develop prior to contact with other civilizations. Three, if the Deadly Probes Hypothesis is true, we've already signed our own death warrant by broadcasting Barney's infamous (and profoundly irritating) "I love you, you love me" song across the galaxy.

The Zoo Hypothesis

The Zoo Hypothesis,[*] the idea that Earth is being observed by extraterrestrials, is favored by many SETI proponents, and was first proposed by John Ball. This explanation allows for interstellar migration and colonization, and does not force us to assume that every intelligent species decides to stay put in its home system. This explanation is also compatible with the theories of many UFO researchers, who argue that UFOs are signs of a systematic research and observation program (not unlike the type of research we do when tracking wild animals).

> NOTE
>
> *Although the subject of UFOs is controversial to say the least, the idea that extraterrestrial probes are observing Earth should be taken seriously. This is not because of the sightings reported in the tabloid press, but because of the fact that we already know how to build interplanetary probes, as well as stealth aircraft that are effectively invisible to radar tracking systems. One can make a logical argument that a civilization capable of building interstellar probes would also be capable of building stealthy and autonomous robot spacecraft that could systematically observe activity on Earth over long periods of time. This might seem fantastic, but when one considers that we dispatched the Pathfinder probe to the surface of Mars in 1996, and that this is a very crude device compared to what we'll be building 100 years from now, the idea that an ET satellite might be looking down on us from a low Earth orbit doesn't seem so unreasonable.*

One problem that arises with the Zoo Hypothesis is the requirement that all civilizations, or at least all of those that occupy our part of the galaxy, agree to observe the voluntary quarantine of our solar system. If only one other civilization decided that our system should be mined for its natural resources or colonized, we would not be here to debate the matter.

von Neuman probes

When asked to imagine a robot, most people think of a large machine, comparable in size to a person. However, it is possible to build extremely small space-faring robots; these hypothetical robots are referred to as von Neuman probes.

---

[*] Ball, John A., *The Zoo Hypothesis*, Icarus, v. 19, p. 347, 1973.

Initially proposed by the mathematician John von Neuman, von Neuman probes are space-faring robots capable of making copies of themselves. These robots could set course for asteroids orbiting a nearby star and use the metals in the asteroids to produce copies of themselves. These robot off-spring would then travel to other asteroids in other star systems in a self-perpetuating reproductive cycle. Within a fairly short period of time, even if the robots could only attain a maximum speed of 1 percent of the speed of light, they would be able to disperse throughout the galaxy in several million years.

What might such a probe look like? The example below (see Figure 5-1) is based a reasonable projection of what we could build in the near-term using presently available technology. When viewed from the top down, it is about the size of a butterfly or medium-sized bird. When viewed edge-on, the device would be only a few atoms thick, except for a delicate scaffold that makes it rigid.

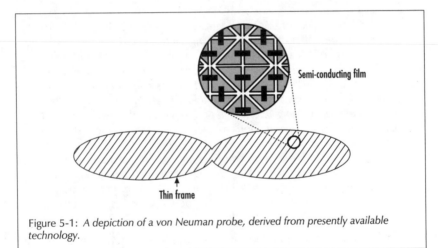

Figure 5-1: *A depiction of a von Neuman probe, derived from presently available technology.*

This hypothetical probe would be capable of processing information, communicating with similar devices, and moving about within the vacuum of space. When viewed at a distance, this machine would be a few centimeters across, and would look a lot like a computer chip manufactured from five major components:

- A very thin layer of semiconducting material (most likely silicon) that forms a wing-like surface

- A lightweight frame that gives the device its shape and rigidity

- A joint that allows the wing-like surfaces to rotate

- When viewed close up, a two-dimensional grid of very small structures that look similar to the circuits etched into microchips

- Electrical or optical pathways that allow information to be passed among these structures

When viewed very close in, for example at the nanometer scale, the smooth surface of the wing is revealed to be a tightly packed grid of microscopic circuits, very similar to what you would see on the surface of a modern microprocessor. Each of these tiny circuits would be a small CPU that could store and process information, and convert incoming light to electricity (to power the device). Tiny electrical pathways connect each of these microcircuits, enabling them to exchange information among themselves.

Although this may appear to be a simple device, it could be a very smart device. Assume that the technology used is comparable to what we will be using ourselves in 20 years. Using even conservative assumptions, a one square centimeter device could have up to 10 billion tiny CPUs, each of them capable of processing information and communicating with each other. This device would control its motion by reorienting its wing-like surfaces to use solar wind or magnetic fields to produce small amounts of propulsive force. Although it wouldn't be able to accelerate from 0 to 100,000 miles per hour in an instant, over long periods of time, it would freely roam an entire solar system. These devices could be produced cheaply since, being made primarily of silicon, there would be no shortage of raw materials needed to build them.

It is certainly within our ability to produce devices like this sometime within the 21st century. Other technologically advanced civilizations should be able to produce devices like this as well.

In his paper "How to Achieve Contact: Five Promising Strategies," Dr. Allen Tough of the University of Toronto has pointed out that the solar system could be swarming with tiny probes. They could be so small that we would be completely unaware of their existence. If one imagines that it will be possible to build very tiny probes in the future (as small as a flea or smaller), it is not hard to consider it possible to blanket a world with such tiny probes without its inhabitants ever knowing.

With this in mind, one scenario that we must seriously consider is the possibility that we are being observed, not by livestock-mutilating UFOs, but by microscopic probes silently communicating with their home world or other probes about their observations.

Deadly Probes Hypothesis

The most disturbing answer to the Fermi Paradox—and the one that requires the fewest arbitrary assumptions—is the Deadly Probes Hypothesis. According to this theory, a civilization somewhere in the galaxy (it only takes one) decides to build and disperse hostile von Neuman probes.

In the Deadly Probes Hypothesis, a civilization builds von Neuman probes whose job is to detect sources of modulated electromagnetic radiation (a clear sign of an intelligent species). Upon detecting a planet emitting this type of radiation, the probe might attach itself (or dispatch sister probes to attach themselves) to a large comet, and over decades or centuries, steer the comet onto a collision course with the planet. The comet would collide with this world, exterminating most of the animal life on the planet in the process. While this may seem far-fetched, the amount of energy required to alter a comet's orbit is not very large if there is a long delay (decades or longer) between the course change and impact with the target planet. While this is beyond our capability, it is feasible for any civilization that is capable of interstellar travel.

It's a disturbing idea, and although it may be an unlikely scenario, it is one that we should not rule out.

Brin's Equation

Scientist and author David Brin expanded on the Drake Equation in his landmark 1982 paper, "The Great Silence: The Controversy Surrounding Extraterrestrial Intelligent Life." In this paper, Brin considers the Fermi Paradox and proposes a new form of the Drake Equation that takes into account two new and important concepts: interstellar migration, and contact avoidance. The simple form of Brin's Equation is shown in Figure 5-2.

$$N' = (1/N^*) \sum_{j=1}^{N} A_j (n_j + 1)$$

Figure 5-2: *Brin's Equation for predicting the number of communicative civilizations.*

The classic Drake Equation ignores the effect of interstellar migration on N, the number of detectable civilizations. Brin's Equation introduces three new factors that can be used to influence the number of detectable civilizations:

n_j This factor represents the number of neighboring star systems colonized—in person or by detectable robot probes—by each parent civilization. This factor is an integer value ranging from 0 to the number of stars in the sampled space.

A_j This factor represents the contact cross-section for each civilization, or the likelihood that a particular civilization will choose to make itself detectable to others. The range of possible values for A_j is from 0 (never detectable) to 1 (always detectable).

$N*$ This factor represents the total number of potentially habitable star systems within the sampled space.

The final result produced by the equation is N', or the number of detectable sites, taking these new factors into account. Notice the number N above the summation symbol in the equation. This is the number N produced by the classic Drake Equation, which is fed into Brin's Equation to produce the revised number N'.

In the simplified form of the equation, the first new factor to consider is n_j, the number of other star systems colonized by each communicative civilization. This factor obviously has a significant effect on the value of N', because interstellar migration, if it is relatively common, greatly increases the number of potentially detectable sites.

Whereas the Drake Equation assumes that intelligent life develops independently on many different worlds, the Brin Equation additionally allows for the possibility that intelligent life will also seed other star systems through interstellar colonization. Even if intelligent civilizations do not expand beyond a radius of a few dozen light years, they may still be able to establish dozens or hundreds of detectable sites, thus increasing the value of N accordingly.

It is also important to note that Brin's Equation does not treat all civilizations as carbon copies of each other. The result N' is produced by repeatedly summing the factor $A_j (n_j + 1)$, where j denotes different civilizations within the sampled space.

The second new factor introduced by Brin's Equation is the contact/avoidance cross section, A_j. This factor estimates the likelihood that a given civilization will seek out or avoid contact with other civilizations. The classic Drake Equation assumes that all technological civilizations will seek to establish contact with their neighbors. Brin's Equation considers that of N sites that develop the capability for interstellar communication, some of these sites will purposefully remain silent and therefore undetectable. For example, if $n_j=0$ and $A_j=1$ for all civilizations within the sampled space, Brin's Equation would reduce to the classic Drake Equation ($N'=N$).

There are many reasons why this contact/avoidance factor will vary. If the likelihood of making contact is very low, civilizations may grow bored and give up their search for neighbors. If there is even a grain of truth to the Deadly Probes Hypothesis, smart civilizations will maintain radio silence to conceal their existence from hostile civilizations. Conversely, if interstellar communication is widespread, and the value of the information to be shared is high, the contact/avoidance cross-section will be much higher. While we can't predict the behavior of any given site, it is important to understand that just because a civilization can communicate with us doesn't necessarily mean they will choose to do so.

When we plug these new factors into Brin's Equation, we can see that the contact/avoidance cross-section is a constraining factor. If it is less than 1 (100 percent) on average, it reduces the number of detectable sites. The colonization factor, on the other hand, increases the number of detectable sites, especially if colonization proceeds in a self-perpetuating cycle of continued migration.

One of the interesting predictions generated by Brin's Equation is that the emergence of technological civilizations may be rare. Yet at the same time, the number of detectable sites can be quite high if interstellar colonization combines with a high contact/avoidance cross-section (e.g., many colonized worlds that actively communicate with neighboring sites).

Likelihood of intelligent, communicative life

The whole point of the exercise in these first chapters isn't to predict how many civilizations are out there, or even to predict that *any* besides our own necessarily exist. The point of the exercise is to demonstrate that in order for human civilization to be unique, the odds have to be stacked fantastically against the formation of intelligent life.

What we've learned about our universe in the past 30 years and what this newfound knowledge implies about the development of life elsewhere in our galaxy raises a lot of doubts about the uniqueness of life on Earth. Nothing in the evidence we've collected to date suggests that it is impossible for life to form elsewhere. We also know that intelligent life on Earth evolved from our less intelligent ancestors.

Knowing this, we really can't say with 100 percent confidence that the existence of intelligent life elsewhere is impossible. If anything, one of the things we've learned in the past century is that if something isn't explicitly forbidden by the laws of physics, it's not only possible, but it's probably happening somewhere.

Black holes are a good example of this. We've known since the turn of the century that the laws of physics predicted objects could be so massive that even light could not escape them. Most scientists greeted this idea with extreme skepticism until 1994, when the Hubble Space Telescope took the first images of a black hole (actually, the rapidly rotating disk of gas surrounding it) in the M87 galaxy.*

If we can't prove that it is impossible for intelligent life to evolve elsewhere, then we should assume the opposite—that it has—and keep a look out for signs of its existence. We may find nothing. Then again, we may discover that communication among technological civilizations is common, and that we are the latest visitors to a party line that has been active for eons.

---

* For more information about this discovery, visit the Space Telescope Science Institute's HubbleSite at *http://hubble.stsci.edu/news_.and._views/pr.cgi?1994+23*.

GETTING A DIAL TONE

RADIO COMMUNICATION

The idea of communicating with aliens by radio is as old as the technology of radio itself. The first SETI experiments were devised not long after the first experiments in wireless communication. Nikola Tesla and Guglielmo Marconi, two of the leading figures in the development of wireless communication, experimented with the idea of interplanetary communication via radio.* Both Tesla and Marconi listened for signals from beyond Earth, and both men claimed to have detected then unexplainable signals. Although the signals they detected were later explained by natural processes such as lightning (which causes odd-sounding signals called whistlers), the idea of communicating with aliens by radio had been discussed early in the 20th century, nearly 50 years before Frank Drake conceived of Project Ozma, the first radioastronomy project designed to detect extraterrestrial radio signals.

The informal attempts to intercept alien radio transmissions in the first half of the 20th century fired the public's imagination. Although they did not detect anything, this work planted the seed for modern SETI programs, which were inspired by a landmark paper "Searching for Interstellar Communications," published by Giuseppe Cocconi and Philip Morrison in the September 1959 issue of *Nature*.† This paper summarized the technical requirements for transmitting and receiving interstellar radio signals, and remains the blueprint from which most of today's SETI projects derive.

Radio communication is really a form of lightwave communication. When we communicate by radio, what we're doing is using a form of electromagnetic radiation (light) that our eyes cannot see.

Why communicate by radio? Radio waves can travel for extremely long distances, and can be generated relatively cheaply. Radio waves, because they

---

* *The Biological Universe: The Twentieth Century Extraterrestrial Life Debate and the Limits of Science*, Steven J Dick, p. 402.
† "Searching for Interstellar Communications," *Nature*, 184 (Sept 1959), 844.

are a form of light, travel at the speed of light, and are the fastest known medium used to convey information from one place to another. While it would be extremely expensive and dangerous to send people to another solar system, radio signals travel at the fastest-known speed allowed, making radio a cheap, low-risk way to initiate contact with neighboring civilizations.

Radio waves can also be used to convey information, allowing the sender to create a signal that stands out against background noise and embed useful information in that signal. Using binary numbers, a simple numbering system we'll discuss later, we can transmit an endless stream of numbers via radio. These numbers, in turn, can be used to build a rich symbolic vocabulary, to describe pictures, and more.

This chapter discusses the basics of radio and laser (optical) communication and describes SETI programs in a way that non-technical readers can understand. We'll build on these concepts in subsequent chapters to explain how SETI researchers deal with interference, as well as how to encode information in a signal.

Long distance communication

Sending a string of digits over interstellar distances is obviously more difficult than sending them across a room. The biggest challenge is overcoming the relationship between the signal's strength and the distance it must travel through space. For every doubling in distance, the effective strength of a signal declines four-fold (Figure 6-1). For example, let's say you measure the strength of a signal at 1 meter (m) and 1000 meters (1 km) from an antenna. The signal at the 1 km distance is not merely 1/1000 the strength of the signal at the 1 m location; it is actually 1/1,000,000 the strength of the signal measured at the 1 m distance (or $1/1000^2$). This is a significant problem because the distances between stars, even relatively nearby stars, are huge. Consider, for example, that it takes a signal from Earth approximately 20 minutes to reach Mars. The same signal would take about four years to reach the nearest star system. To put this in perspective, the signal takes 1/72 of a day to reach Mars and nearly 1500 days to reach the closest star. When the signal reaches Proxima Centauri (a nearby star), it would be nearly 12 billion times weaker than when it reached Mars (and it would already be very weak at that point).

So, why not just build a more powerful receiver amplifier? If the signal isn't strong enough, the receiver could just boost the "volume level" a little bit higher, much like you turn the volume up on a weak AM radio station. This would work fine except that the universe is awash with random, ambient noise. This noise—some of it a by product of natural processes, and some of

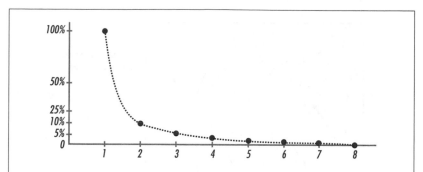

Figure 6-1: *This graph illustrates the inverse square law: as distance doubles, signal strength decreases by a factor of four. At great distances, a signal, even with a very powerful transmitter, will be extremely weak.*

it a relic of the Big Bang—is present throughout the universe. While this noise is very weak, any radio signal crossing interstellar distances will be weaker than this ambient noise level.

If the receiving party attempts to amplify a signal that is masked by noise, they will amplify the noise as well as the signal. Unless they conjure up a way to boost the signal while rejecting background noise, amplifying a noisy signal won't help.

This is why radioastronomers employ very large dish-shaped (or parabolic) antennae in their research. These antennae work by collecting incoming radiation over a large area and refocus it on a much smaller target antenna, or feedhorn, that is coupled to electronic amplifiers, tuners, and related hardware. Although simple in design, this is an elegant workaround to the Catch-22 of amplifying a signal and the background noise that masks it.

Random background noise tends to cancel itself as larger and larger antennae are used because random noise is not coherent. This is difficult to explain without getting into a lot of mathematics. However, a good analogy to use is that of a large body of water.

Consider a lake or ocean dominated by countless small waves, all traveling in different directions (Figure 6-2). Now imagine the same body of water with a strong swell heading toward its shoreline. The long parallel waves in this imaginary ocean are comparable to the radio signals that we're looking for. The chaotic and directionless waves from the first example are comparable to the background noise we'd like to screen out.

An artificial barrier can reflect and refocus the orderly swell waves from the second example (Figure 6-3), because they are traveling in a uniform direction. This is essentially what a parabolic antenna does—it reflects and

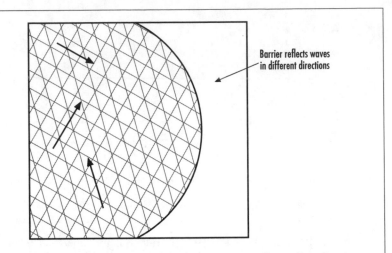

Figure 6-2: *Waves traveling in different directions are scattered in random directions by the barrier.*

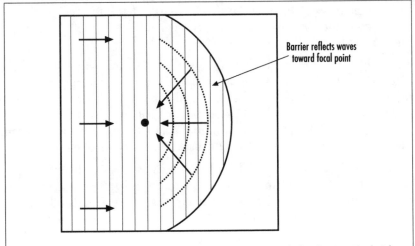

Figure 6-3: *A barrier reflects an incoming wave toward a single focal point. The height of the reflected waves increases toward the focal point.*

refocuses incoming radio "swell waves" to converge on a much smaller target, all without amplifying the chaotic "noise" waves.

This technique permits the construction of extremely sensitive antennae that can amplify weak signals by many orders of magnitude—a trillion fold or more. This is enough to detect very weak radio signals (both natural and artificial signals) from far away sources.

Knowing where to look in space

By photographing the planets orbiting neighboring stars, an advanced civilization will be able to predict which solar systems most likely harbor intelligent life. With this information, an advanced civilization can use the techniques described in Part I to look for chemical markers associated with water and biological activity (intelligent or not).

While this might sound like the stuff of science fiction, we are on the brink of developing this capability ourselves. Our present-day technology is limited to indirect observations. However, within 10 years, we will have space-based telescopes called *interferometers* that will be able to directly observe distant Earth-like planets.

An interferometer is a special type of telescope designed to take pictures of dim objects located close to a much brighter object, such as a star. These telescopes rely on *interference effects*, a result of the wave-like nature of light, to cancel out the light from a bright star without weakening the light reflecting from the dimmer object nearby. Interferometers will allow us to directly observe small planets orbiting distant stars in enough detail to determine their size and chemical composition, and ultimately whether there is biological activity on that planet.

You can collect a surprising amount of information from a picture by using a technique known as *spectroscopy*. A typical color photograph is a composite photo whose primary colors are red, green, and blue. Researchers use spectrometry to break a photo down into hundreds or thousands of individual colors. These images contain an incredible amount of detail about the chemical composition of the objects being photographed. This is because each chemical compound has a distinct spectral blueprint as it absorbs and reflects different wavelengths of light. While this information will be lost in a conventional color or black and white photograph, it is clearly revealed in a *hyperspectral image* (an image that contains dozens or hundreds of primary colors, compared to the three primary colors used in conventional color photographs). Even a blurry image of an Earth-like world will provide an observer with a wealth of information, including:

- The chemical composition of the planet's atmosphere
- The amount of liquid water and water vapor
- The chemical composition of the planet's exposed surface
- Confirmation of the existence of common organic molecules

Although we have yet to use this technique to analyze the makeup of a planet around another star, we have already used this technique extensively to analyze planets and moons within our own solar system; we've used spectroscopy to take chemical snapshots of nearly every major body within our solar system. This technique allows us to conduct detailed chemical surveys of remote worlds without having to go there to take samples directly.

For example, one of the most interesting recent discoveries we've made is the discovery that Saturn's moon, Titan, may have oceans composed of liquid methane (natural gas) instead of the saltwater oceans we have here on Earth. We've also used spectroscopy to learn about the atmospheres of all of the planets in our solar system.

Imagine, for a moment, that an astronomer on a remote world has taken a spectrograph of the Earth. The image is blurry, and does not reveal a great deal of information about the surface of our planet. However, the spectral information tells our hypothetical observer that:

- Earth has a moist, oxygen-rich atmosphere. This is a sign of biological activity because oxygen is highly reactive. Unless it is constantly replenished, it will be removed from the atmosphere as it reacts with other materials, such as iron to form rust. The presence of oxygen is a dead giveaway that something interesting is occurring on Earth.

- Earth has high concentrations of organic compounds on its surface, an indication of plants, oceanic algae, and other materials.

These two pieces of information would instantly tell our observer that Earth could potentially harbor life. This does not necessarily mean that Earth is likely to host intelligent life, but it does suggest the presence of biological activity that could lead to the development of life, microbial or advanced.

An intelligent civilization that wishes to establish radio communication with nearby civilizations will know where possible life sites are located. While this type of analysis will not reveal which life-bearing worlds harbor intelligent life, it will enable a civilization that is hoping to contact others to weed out the stars whose planets are barren.

NOTE

A civilization would need to survey approximately 1 million solar systems to find potential life sites within a 1,000 light-year radius. This is a large effort, but it is not unprecedented in the history of Earth astronomy. We have already catalogued millions of objects in the night sky, so it is reasonable to conclude that other advanced civilizations might have developed this capability as well. Recent advances in computing technology have enabled astronomers to build highly automated systems, such as the system used in the Sloane Digital Sky Survey (http://www.sdss.org/), which are designed to photograph large numbers of stars with minimal human intervention.

Once a civilization has developed a short list of potential life sites, it will know where to spend most of its effort, and where not to waste its time. By narrowing their search, they can focus their efforts, and the energy of their transmitted signals, on a much smaller slice of the night sky. This applies to both radio-based and laser-based strategies.

This has a significant impact on the odds that the civilization will succeed in making contact. Instead of broadcasting a signal uniformly in all directions (where the majority of the energy leaks into empty space), the sender can focus the signal on a well-defined area of the night sky where there is a greater chance of someone being there to receive the signal. This means that the sender can boost the apparent strength of the signal by many orders of magnitude (1000 to 1 million times stronger with a moderately focused signal), or that they can reduce the total power requirement to operate a transmitter without sacrificing detectability.

Knowing where to look in time

A civilization that hopes to make contact with others will not only need to know where to look, but also when to look. This is because we should assume that most civilizations would have a finite life span during which they are detectable by SETI programs. This is where the factor L from the Drake Equation, and from David Brin's modified equation, comes into play. To put this in perspective, Earth has been leaking radio transmissions into space for roughly 100 years (and strong transmissions for less than 50 years). Contrast this against Earth's age, approximately 4 billion years. This means that Earth has been "radio bright" for only 0.0000025 percent of its existence. Hence, if most technological civilizations last for only a few centuries before they self-destruct, even if intelligent life emerges on virtually every habitable planet, the odds of detecting a civilization during this brief window will be very poor. On the other hand, if intelligence has a long-term survival value, technological civilizations may have life spans spanning thousands or millions of years.

The longer a civilization stays on the air, the greater likelihood other civilizations will be able to detect their presence. Unfortunately, there is no easy way to test whether a planet was once home to an intelligent civilization, or to test whether a life-bearing planet is likely to produce an intelligent species. Until we have an opportunity to survey other civilizations, we will have no way of knowing whether long-lived civilizations are the exception or the norm.

The effect of this factor on the search for extraterrestrial beacons is often misunderstood to mean that intelligent life is extremely unlikely. Even if the mean life spans of technological civilizations average several million years, this figure represents less than one tenth of one percent of the age of the Milky Way galaxy. So, even if millions of civilizations have emerged over the course of the Milky Way's life, it is quite possible that we can detect only a few at this particular time. Detecting another civilization is not only a matter of looking in the right place, but looking in the right place at the right time in a particular star's history. The problem lies in the fact that what we perceive as a very long period of time, a thousand years, is barely an instant compared to the age of a typical star system.

Radio basics

The basic messenger in lightwave communication is a particle called a *photon*. The easiest way to visualize a photon is to think of it as a vibrating billiard ball. Photons travel at the speed of light (300 million meters per second). The rate at which the photon vibrates as it travels is known as its *frequency*, which is measured in cycles (vibrations) per second (Hertz); see Figure 6-4. If the photon vibrates back and forth 1 million times per second, it has a frequency of 1,000,000 Hz or 1 MHz (incidentally, this is a frequency used by AM radio stations).

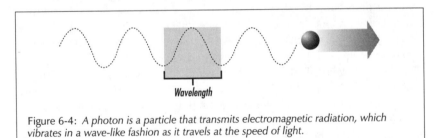

Wavelength

Figure 6-4: *A photon is a particle that transmits electromagnetic radiation, which vibrates in a wave-like fashion as it travels at the speed of light.*

All a radio transmitter does is convert electrical energy into photons. A receiver simply converts the photons into an electrical current. So, in effect, all we're doing is converting electricity into light and then back into electricity. The only peculiar thing about this system is we are using light that is invisible to the human eye, light that passes (with little effect) through solid objects like walls. That's all there is to it. So, the next time you think about how a radio works, think of the radio as a light detector, and the transmitting tower as a flashlight. The tower sends out beams of light that are then detected and converted by the radio.

Building a simple transmitter

Before we build a radio receiver, there are two things we first need to figure out: how to convert electricity into low frequency light (radio) waves, and how to use this transmitter to send binary numbers.

Binary numbers will play in important role in future chapters, where we'll describe how to transmit useful information via a radio or laser signal. We'll focus on binary numbers because they are the simplest possible numbering system, and can be represented in many different ways in a radio or laser signal.

Binary code is a very simple system in which there are two possible numbers, or states. A binary system can be in an ON state (equivalent to the number 1) or an OFF state (equivalent to the number 0). A simple way to build a binary transmitter is to build a receiver that has an ON/OFF (1/0) switch as shown in Figure 6-5. If it is ON, the transmitter is generating a signal. If it is OFF, the transmitter is silent. Using this simple system based on two numbers, we can describe much larger numbers, in the same way that we can string a series of decimal numbers to describe a much larger number.

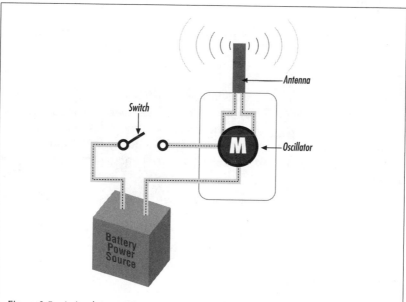

Figure 6-5: A simple transmitter converts a steady electrical current into a single-frequency radio signal.

When we throw the ON switch, an electric current flows through the system, providing the energy required to generate low-frequency light (radio waves). Circuitry in the transmitter converts the steady current from the battery into a continuously varying current called a sine wave, or sinusoid. We do this using a circuit called an *oscillator* (Figure 6-6). This current is fed into an antenna, a long metal rod whose length is related to the frequency of the signal we want to transmit.

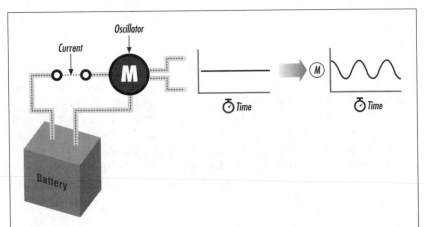

Figure 6-6: *An oscillator converts a constant (direct) current source into a continuously varying (alternating) current. This alternating current can be used to generate a radio signal.*

Without going into a lengthy discussion here about electronics, the sine wave travels up and down the antenna to create a wave, similar to what you see when rapidly whipping a long piece of rope back and forth (see Figure 6-7). Some of this energy is cast off the antenna in the form of low-frequency light waves whose wavelength corresponds to the length of the antenna.

So, what a radio transmitter essentially does is to cause electrical charge (think of it like fluid in a pipe) to slosh back and forth in the antenna. This back and forth motion in the antenna causes the shape of the electrical field around the antenna to change in sync with the movement of the electrical charge. This sets up an electromagnetic wave that travels away from the antenna at the speed of light.

From a practical standpoint, you can think of a radio transmitter as a light bulb. The only difference is that this light bulb generates light that is invisible to human eyes. The light generated by the radio transmitter has two important qualities. One is its intensity or brightness. The other is its frequency, which is analogous to the tone of a sound, or the color of visible light (red light has a lower frequency than green light, which has a lower frequency than blue light).

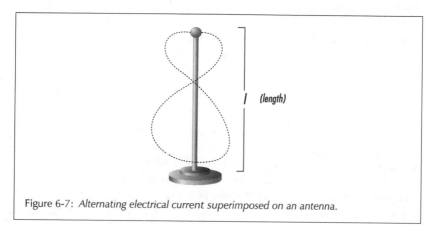

Figure 6-7: *Alternating electrical current superimposed on an antenna.*

Building a simple receiver

On the receiving end of the equation, we need a device that can convert the low-frequency light signal into an electrical current. This electrical current is used to illuminate a small light bulb. If the bulb is lit, or ON, it is assigned a value of 1. If the bulb is OFF (not lit), it will have a value of 0.

This device shown in Figure 6-8 is similar to the transmitter, except the chain of events is reversed. Like the transmitter, this device has an antenna. It also has circuitry that converts electrical currents induced in the antenna into steady state (continuous) electrical currents that flow through the light bulb, which is connected to the output side of the device.

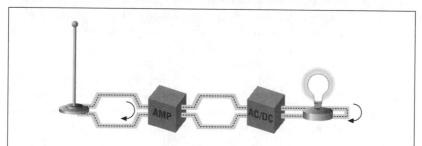

Figure 6-8: *A simplified diagram of a receiver. The antenna feeds a weak current into an amplifier, which feeds an AC to DC converter; the converter feeds electrical current to a light bulb or LED when a signal is detected.*

When radio waves strike the receiver antenna, they induce a small electrical current whose frequency matches that of the incoming radio waves. For example, if we're using a 1 MHz frequency, the electrical current induced in the antenna varies from 1 million times per second. This is far too fast for the human eye to see, so the next thing we need to do is to first amplify this electrical current (it is very weak), and then to convert it into a steady current that corresponds to the radio signal's strength.

The electrical current induced in the receiver's antenna is much weaker than the current in the transmitting antenna. Because of this, it must be amplified before it can be used to do anything useful like power a speaker or lamp.

To amplify the weak electrical signal coming off the antenna, we send it through a device called a transistor. In the old days, we would have used a vacuum tube instead of a miniature solid-state (silicon) transistor. However, the basic principle is the same. The best way to think of a transistor is as a floodgate on a dam. The transistor acts like a valve for the electrical current (Figure 6-9). If the valve is closed, only a small amount of current leaks through; if the valve is open, a lot of the current flows through.

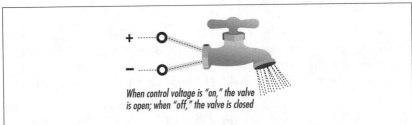

When control voltage is "on," the valve is open; when "off," the valve is closed

Figure 6-9: *This figure depicts a transistor as an electrical valve. In this manner, we can use a small input current to control (modulate) the flow of a much larger current.*

We use the weak input signal to control the "position" of the hypothetical valve (i.e., the transistor). We then use feed a much stronger source of electrical current through the valve. When the weak signal from our antenna is at its peak, the electrical valve is forced wide open, allowing a voluminous current to flow through the device. When the signal from the antenna is at its minimum, barely any current will flow through the device. We can amplify the strength of our signal using this approach by many orders of magnitude, boosting it to useful levels. This explanation oversimplifies this process a good deal, but the objective at this point is to get the basic concept across.

NOTE

This idealized receiver is missing an important component needed to build a real-world radio receiver—a tuner. The purpose of a tuner is to selectively amplify certain signals on certain frequencies, and to reject (ignore) signals whose frequencies are outside the band of frequencies the tuner is designed to pay attention to. By adding a tuner, we can build a pair of receivers, one that is sensitive to signals on one frequency (e.g., 1,000,000 Hz), and another that is sensitive only to signals on another frequency (e.g., 1,000,1000 Hz).

Next, we need to convert the amplified sine wave into a continuous, or direct, current that we can feed into our light bulb. We accomplish this by using a *diode*. As shown in Figure 6-10, a diode is like a one-way street for electricity; it presents little resistance to a current flowing in one direction, and very high resistance in the other. A good visual metaphor to use here is a backflow prevention valve, which remains wide open when water is flowing in the desired direction through a pipe. However, the valve snaps shut if the water starts to flow in the opposite direction.

We can use two diodes in a circuit (Figure 6-11) to create a mirror image of the sine wave. The resulting circuit is called an inverter.

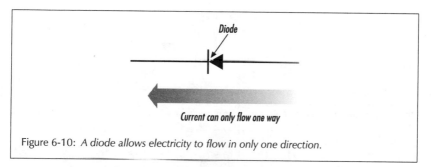

Figure 6-10: *A diode allows electricity to flow in only one direction.*

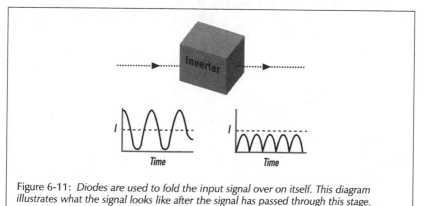

Figure 6-11: *Diodes are used to fold the input signal over on itself. This diagram illustrates what the signal looks like after the signal has passed through this stage.*

What this inverter stage does is change the signal so that it can be averaged over time. The signal that comes out of the amplifier is an alternating current, which means that its value varies, for example, between +1 amp and –1 amp. The important point is that it varies between ± x amps. When this signal is averaged out over time, the average is zero (because the positive values counterbalance the negative values).

What the inverter does is the electrical equivalent of the |x| statement in algebra. The symbol |x| means the absolute value of x, which means "ignore the + or – sign, and convert it to a positive number." Hence the absolute values of +2 and –2 are the same: 2. So, the inverter turns the electrical current from an alternating series of positive and negative values (whose long-term average is zero), into a series of positive numbers (whose average will be a positive number greater than zero).

Notice that in Figure 6-12, the original signal on the left varies between +1 and –1 ampere, while the inverted signal on the right varies between 0 and 1 amps (always positive).

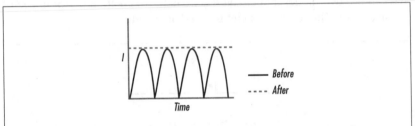

Figure 6-12: *A signal before and after passing through the capacitive (smoothing) stage. The output signal is almost, but not quite, a steady (direct current) signal.*

A capacitor is added to the circuit to smooth, or average, the peaks and valleys of the inverted signal to produce a more (or less) constant electrical current. The capacitor reacts slowly to electrical current, and acts as a sort of reservoir for the electrical charge. If you feed a sine wave into a capacitor, it will charge (or absorb) some of the excess electricity during peaks and discharge during the valleys. As a result, the capacitor smoothes out the waveform.

This stage in the device is doing the electrical equivalent of averaging a series of numbers. The rapidly varying signal from the inverter is converted into a more or less constant current whose value is approximately equal to the long-term average current of the inverted signal.

We now have a steady electrical current that can be fed through an electric lamp or a light-emitting diode (LED). When the received signal is strong, the light is bright. When the signal is not being transmitted, the light bulb is dark.

While this is a fairly simple example, it is enough to illustrate that basic radio communication is not tremendously complicated. This is why we were able to develop radio communication with relatively simple tools and limited knowledge about the laws of physics at the time. It is important to note that this is a dumbed-down example that highlights the basic principles in wireless communication. Real-world systems are much more complex, but they still build on the basic concepts employed in the first, crude wireless sets.

Problems with this simple transmitter

This simple transmitter and receiver form what is called a *two state system*. This means that the system can be in one of two states, ON or OFF, or *sending signal* and *not sending signal*. While this is fine for illustrating how to send a binary signal, this approach has one underlying problem: the failure to receive an ON signal does not always mean that the transmitter intended to send an OFF (or 0) digit. For example, when the transmitter is ON and the receiver is receiving a signal, we know that a transmitter is sending a signal (assuming we're not picking up a signal from another similar transmitter using the same frequency). However, when the receiver is indicating OFF, this could be due to several reasons:

- The transmitter is in the OFF position
- The signal is too weak to be detected
- One of the devices is broken

To deal with this problem, we need to build a four-state system by building two pairs of transmitters and receivers. One transmitter (we'll call it A) is tuned to broadcast on one frequency (e.g., 1 MHz). The second transmitter, B, is tuned to broadcast on a nearby frequency (e.g., 1.001 MHz). Building a receiver that is tuned to receive a specific frequency involves a bit more circuitry. We'll skip the details for now, though, as it's more important to understand the general concept here. When we want to send a 0 digit, transmitter A is placed in the ON position. When we want to send a 1 digit, transmitter B is turned on instead. This system, depicted in Table 6-1, has four states, one of which is unused (or can be used to represent a negative number).

Table 6-1: *Possible states of a four-state transmitter*

CHANNEL A	CHANNEL B	MEANING
OFF	OFF	No data
ON	OFF	0
OFF	ON	1
ON	ON	Unused or –1 (negative 1)

As shown in Figure 6-13, the receiver is connected to two light bulbs instead of the one light bulb in our first example. When we transmit on frequency A, the first bulb lights up, signifying a 0 digit. When we transmit on frequency B, the second bulb lights up, signifying a 1 digit. When we transmit on frequencies A and B simultaneously, we could use this to signify a negative number (e.g., –1).

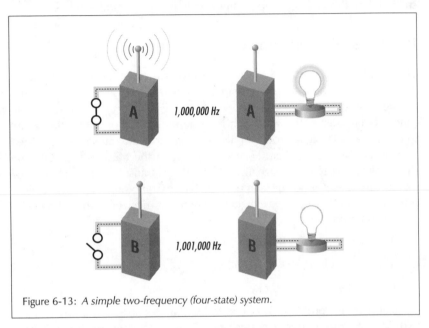

Figure 6-13: *A simple two-frequency (four-state) system.*

If we replace the mechanical switches and light bulbs with connections to "data-in" and "data-out" ports on computers connected to each receiver, the computer connected to the transmitter will send binary digits to the transmitter using a serial port connection (with different voltages signifying 1 and 0, respectively). The computer connected to the receiver receives incoming digits through its data-in port. Conceptually, all we are doing is replacing our mechanical switches and light bulbs with a direct connection to a computer's external data port.

Now we have everything we need to send binary data from one computer to another computer over a simple radio link. This basic principle is the same regardless of the distance between the devices. The only thing that is different when sending a signal over very long distances is that we need to transmit a stronger signal and have more sensitive receiving equipment on the other end.

Building a SETI receiver

Building a receiver that can detect a radio signal from another civilization, though difficult, is an extension of terrestrial wireless communication technology. The primary challenges faced in building these systems are:

- The incoming signals are very weak and easily masked by background noise

- Lack of knowledge about the location and broadcasting schedule of the sender

- Lack of knowledge about the frequencies and signal format used by the sender

The trickiest part, as we'll see later in this section, is not amplifying a weak signal (the solution to this problem is simply to build a larger antenna or an antenna array), but rather overcoming our ignorance about the manner in which an extraterrestrial civilization will transmit their signal. We have no prior knowledge about what frequencies they might use, how they are encoding information in their signal, or whether there is even a signal to detect in the first place. This ignorance is what really complicates the search for alien radio transmissions.

Among the components we need to construct a receiver sensitive enough to detect an interstellar radio signal are:

- A high-gain antenna or an antenna array that can amplify a very weak signal by many orders of magnitude

- Electronic amplification equipment

- Analog to digital converters

- High-speed computers and sophisticated signal processing software, which will be used to analyze the data captured by the receiver

The most important component in a radio-based SETI receiving facility is a high gain antenna or an antenna array because it has a large collecting area. It is helpful to visualize a parabolic mirror, such as those used in solar ovens. Incoming radio waves are reflected by the surface of the antenna, whose shape is designed to focus the reflected radiation on a focal point (see Figure 6-14). Just as a solar oven reflects sunlight onto a small target that can be heated to several hundred degrees, a high-gain antenna reflects radio waves onto a small target, greatly amplifying signal strength in the process (Figure 6-15).

The objective here is to collect incoming radiation over as large an area as possible, and refocus it onto a much smaller target called a feedhorn. The antenna's gain can be roughly calculated by measuring the ratio of the total area of the antenna (or an antenna array) compared to the area upon which the reflected signal is focused.

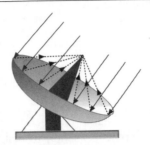

Figure 6-14: *Cross section of a parabolic antenna. The parabolic antenna reflects incoming lightwaves so that they converge on a central, focal point.*

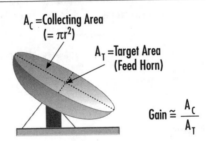

Figure 6-15: *A high-gain antenna works by collecting a signal over a large area and refocusing the signal onto a much smaller target, boosting the intensity of the signal at the focal point.*

For example, if a 10-meter-wide antenna is focused on a target 10 cm wide, the ratio of the antenna's collecting area to the target area is 10,000. This means that, viewed from the focal point of the antenna, the incoming signal's strength is magnified by a factor of 10,000 (40 decibels).

The signal is focused onto an antenna that converts the incoming radio waves into a weak electrical current. This electrical current is very weak and must first pass through an electronic amplifier before it can be processed further.

Depending on its type, an electronic amplifier boosts the strength of the weak electrical signal by 1 million to 1 billion times (60 to 90 decibels, or more). It's interesting to note that the basic technology used here is very similar to satellite television reception equipment. Although the dish is much larger, and the electronic amplifier is chilled in liquid nitrogen (to minimize internal noise generated by the amplifier itself), the basic sequence of events is the same.

The received signal, having been amplified, is then converted from a continually varying analog signal into a digital signal (a series of numbers) through a process called analog to digital conversion. Digitizing the signal allows it to be fed into a computer for detailed analysis.

The signal, having been converted into a stream of numbers, is then analyzed by computer programs (algorithms) designed to look for patterns associated with an artificial radio signal centered on a specific frequency. This is the toughest job in the whole sequence of events because we don't know the details of how an ET radio signal will be formatted. Therefore, we will need to examine billions of individual frequencies on the radio dial. This entails the use of very fast computers capable of performing trillions of calculations per second. This signal processing and follow-up detection stage is discussed in greater detail in Chapter 8, *Signal Processing and Confirmation*.

Building a better transmitter

Next, let's flip this example around, and assume that we want to broadcast a message to other solar systems. We need to design a transmitter specifically for that purpose. To do this, we need a radio transmitter that is powerful, focused, and very accurate.

There are several factors that influence the distance over which a signal can be reliably detected. Among the most significant factors that we need to take into account into building a transmitter are:

Power
> What is the total strength of the signal emitted by transmitter?

Directionality (Antenna gain)
> Is the signal equally strong in all directions, or is it focused on a specific region of the sky?

Noise and interference
> What is the strength of background noise at the selected transmission frequency?

Precision of the transmitter
> What is its ability to transmit on a specific frequency without drifting?

Power

The transmitter power (P) is measured in Watts (W). A *Watt* is a measure of the amount of energy released in a specific period of time—in this case, the number of Joules (a unit of energy) per second (a unit of time). The general trend today is to build low-power transmitters that broadcast at power levels ranging from a few thousandths of a Watt (e.g., digital cellular phones) to about 100,000 Watts (as with the most powerful AM radio stations).

Boosting the transmitter power increases the distance at which a signal can be detected with a particular receiver, but not as much as you might think. As we discussed earlier, signal strength decreases according to the inverse square rule, which means that if you increase the distance to the receiver by a factor of 10, the signal strength decreases by a factor of 100.

If you increase the transmitter's power, the reception range for the signal will increase in proportion to the square root of the increase in power. So, if you quadruple the transmitter power, you'll double the effective reception range for the signal. If you increase the transmitter power 100 times, you'll increase the reception range by 10 times.

What this trend implies is that increasing transmitter power produces diminishing returns since a million-fold increase in transmitter power produces only a thousand-fold increase in detection range (all things remaining equal on the receiving side).

This relationship applies to an omnidirectional antenna, one that sends an equally strong signal in all directions. On the other hand, if we focus an outgoing signal into a tight beam and aim it at selected stars, we can greatly reduce the transmitter power requirements.

Directionality

The next factor to consider is the directionality of the transmitted signal, which is a function of the transmitting antenna gain. Suppose we want to build a transmitter to send a coded message to the 2000 stars closest to our system. An *omnidirectional* transmitter will transmit a signal that is equally strong in all directions, while a *directional* transmitter will enable us to focus a signal, in beam-like fashion, at specific targets in the sky. The tighter the beam, the stronger the signal will be when received at a distance. One problem with using a directional signal is that the receiver must be in the direct path of the beam to receive the strongest signal. If the receiver is outside the focus of the beam, the signal will be much weaker, making it harder to detect.

We can adjust the directionality of the signal by adjusting the design of our antenna. An omnidirectional antenna, like the antenna on a walkie-talkie or cellular phone, is a simple piece of metal. The antenna transmits its energy more or less uniformly so no matter which way you hold your phone; the signal it transmits has almost the same signal strength in all directions.

A directional antenna is shaped differently. Radiotelescopes typically employ a parabolic, or dish-shaped, antenna design, as shown in Figure 6-16. A parabolic antenna reflects radio energy from the transmitter in such a way that it leaves the antenna in a tightly focused beam. One common example of a parabolic design is a flashlight, which uses a parabolic mirror to focus its light into a narrow spotlight.

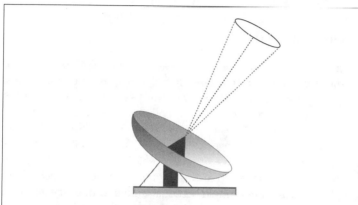

Figure 6-16: *A parabolic antenna has a tightly focused beam, allowing for greater accuracy in transmitting a signal to a specific target in the sky.*

The key factors that determine how tightly focused the radio beam will be are the size of the antenna, and the frequency of the radio waves transmitted by the antenna—and in radioastronomy, bigger is better. The larger we can make the antenna (we can also combine a large array of small antennas to form the equivalent of one big antenna), the more tightly the beam can be focused. Also, we can focus the beam more precisely by using higher radio frequencies (shorter wavelengths).

A measure of an antenna's directionality is its *gain*. A high-gain antenna, such as a large parabolic antenna, will amplify a signal's strength by many orders of magnitude (millions of times). However, there is no free lunch—the more you increase gain, the more you increase directional sensitivity. It is impossible to build a high-gain antenna that looks simultaneously in all directions. This is very similar to looking at an object through a telescopic lens or binoculars. The binoculars allow you to view distant objects in much greater detail; however, the penalty you pay is a limited field of view.

This is why current SETI radioastronomy programs are designed to examine one star at a time. These programs use high-gain antennae to amplify microwave radiation received from individual stars, and analyze the signals for evidence of an orderly pattern. Some search programs hop from one star to another fairly rapidly. For example, the SERENDIP program watches each star for no more than about 12 seconds, while others examine the radiation from an individual star for an extended period of time. This is one of the reasons why it may take years (or decades) to detect a signal from ET. It takes a concerted effort to systematically analyze all of the star systems in our vicinity for signs of intelligent communication.

Noise and interference

Next we must take into account the natural background noise level found in space. The universe is noisy in some frequency bands, and quiet in others, as illustrated in Figure 6-17. Therefore, we want to send our signals in the range of frequencies in which the background noise level is lowest. This happens to be in the microwave frequency band. The noise level in the microwave band, measured in degrees Kelvin ($°K$; a measure of temperature), is barely three degrees above absolute zero ($0°K$, or $-273.15°C$). In fact, the background noise received at this frequency range is an echo from the Big Bang, the explosion that physicists believe gave birth to the universe in which we live.

Background noise is the key technical issue limiting the distance at which a signal can be detected. The further a signal travels from its source, the weaker the signal becomes. Once the signal strength falls below the strength of the cosmic background radiation, it becomes increasingly difficult to detect. Thus the received signal must be amplified to compensate for this degradation of signal strength.

The only way to get around this problem is to increase the gain of the receiving antenna. As a result, we would need to build a larger antenna, or an antenna array, to increase the gain of the signal. Unfortunately, building a larger antenna or array would significantly drive up the cost of the detection system.

The amount of cosmic background noise (background radiation from the Big Bang, noise from naturally occurring processes, etc.) is relatively constant throughout the universe. The only way to overcome this background noise is to increase the gain of the transmitter and/or receiver antenna to boost a signal above the noise level (build bigger antennae).

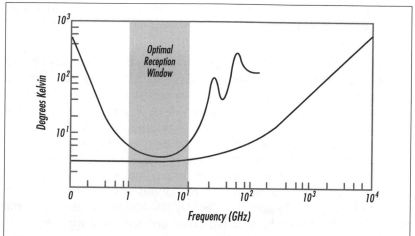

Figure 6-17: *The cosmic background noise level. This graph shows how background noise varies at different frequencies. The universe is quietest in the range between 1 GHz and about 10 GHz. (Courtesy Project Cyclops Manual)*

Long distance toll charges

The primary cost of operating a SETI facility is related to the amount of energy required to power the transmitter. In order to be effective, SETI transmitters and receivers need operate continuously for many years. If we were to look at what it would cost to operate a transmitter array that could target 100 different worlds on a round-the-clock basis, what do you think the annual cost would be for all that electricity?

The total amount of energy required to power the hypothetical transmitter array would be 10 Megawatts (10,000 kW, or 100 kW per targeted star). This energy budget assumes that we use high-gain antennae to focus the outgoing signals on the targeted stars, and that the receiving party will have constructed high gain antennas comparable to the Arecibo radiotelescope or several times larger.

If we assume that wholesale electrical power costs about two cents per kilo-watt/hour (kWh), the cost would be about $200/hour, or roughly $5,000/day. If we translate this into an annual budget, it works out to about $1.8 million/year for power alone. To put this in perspective, the budget for the movie *Titanic* could have covered the electricity bill to run a transmitter array (as described in the second scenario) for approximately 50 to 100 years.

If this cost is converted into a cost per digit, similar to the pricing for a telegram, it would cost, at the very slow data transmission rate of one bit (number) per second, about $0.058 per digit sent.

It's important to note that this estimate is based on the present day costs to operate this type of system, based on our current technology. An advanced civilization will probably have learned how to produce energy cheaply. If you fast forward 100 years or more, we will be able to produce electrical energy in greater quantities and much more cheaply than we do today thanks to technological developments. If we ever see trends in energy technology similar to what we've seen in computing technology, within a few generations, this cost will drop, for all practical purposes, to zero. So, for any advanced civilization (at a stage of technological development 100 years or more ahead of ours), the cost of the energy required to operate a powerful transmitter will not likely be a factor in their decision about whether or not to build and operate such a device.

LIGHTWAVE (LASER) COMMUNICATION

Optical SETI (OSETI) communication can be best compared to the light signals used to send coded messages between ships at sea. The equipment used to generate the coded flashes of light is more sophisticated, and the flashes of light are much more brief (billionths versus fractions of a second). However, the basic concept is not all that different from the communication technique employed by mariners for generations. This chapter discusses the techniques used to generate light signals that can be detected across interstellar distances, as well as the systems used to detect these signals on the receiving end.

Just as we can use radio waves to transmit information, we can do the same thing with visible and infrared light. While the basic principle is the same (we're using photons to convey information), the equipment we use to generate and detect these signals is different than what we use to transmit and detect radio waves.

Interstellar semaphores

OSETI currently looks for two types of laser signals: a pulsed beacon, or a steady, continuous signal. The approach is fairly straightforward. The transmitting civilization aims a tightly focused laser beam at a distant star. Because lasers can be turned on and off within an extremely short period of time (billionths of a second or less), they can be focused into a very tight beam, which can outshine an entire star, if only for an instant. A pulsed beacon would flash, in strobe-light fashion, at the target star. A continuous (always on) beacon works a bit differently. This type of laser is tuned to shine at a very precise wavelength (color).

In both cases, the light from the laser beam focuses on a very small region of the sky, so even at great distances, it's apparent strength is detectable to an observer within the focus of the beam. Either type of signal can be detected over interstellar distances and used to transmit large amounts of information.

The physics of starlight

The light emitted by stars (also known as *starlight*), carries an incredible amount of information. We can learn a great deal about a distant object by studying its spectrum (the color of its light). By shining the star's light through a prism, we can split its light into a rainbow of individual colors. Then, by analyzing the different colors of light emitted by a star, we can learn:

- The chemical composition of the star
- The temperature of the star's surface (which allows us to infer its size and weight)
- The approximate age of the star (which can be inferred from a star's temperature and chemical composition)
- Whether the star is orbited by large planets or a dim companion star (brown dwarf)

We can also detect an intelligent civilization that is attempting to communicate with us via a laser beacon.

Photographing chemistry

Since each chemical element absorbs light at a specific wavelength, we can determine the chemical composition of the star's outer atmosphere by examining the color content of a star's light (see Figure 7-1). In a sense, a star transmits its own chemical "bar code," enabling astronomers to measure the chemical composition of a star.

One of the things we're interested in learning is distant stars' metal content. By analyzing a star's spectrum, we can determine how much carbon, nitrogen, oxygen, iron, and other heavy elements it has. If the star is rich in heavy elements, the star may have a greater chance of developing rocky, Earth-like planets and carbon-based life.

Taking a star's temperature

Since the color and intensity of light closely correlates with temperature, we can measure a star's surface temperature by analyzing the color and intensity of its light. The light emitted by a star follows the rules that govern black-body radiation, which varies according to temperature. As an object's

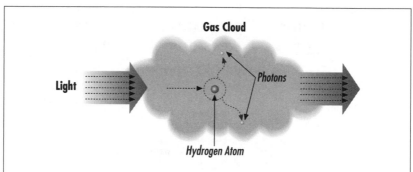

Gas Cloud

Light

Photons

Hydrogen Atom

Figure 7-1: *Atoms in a gas cloud absorb specific colors of light. This light is re-emitted, but usually in a different direction.*

temperature rises, it emits more light overall, and peak intensity occurs at shorter (bluer) wavelengths.

When an object reaches a temperature of several hundred degrees Fahrenheit, it emits nearly all of this energy as infrared (invisible) light. As its temperature increases above this threshold, the object emits some of its energy as red light, which is why molten steel glows red. As the temperature increases to several thousand degrees, its color will shift from red to yellow to white, and eventually to blue. If the object gets hot enough (millions of degrees), it will emit most of its light as ultraviolet or X-ray radiation.

To measure a star's temperature, we must look at its spectrum to find the wavelength (color) where light intensity is highest (brightest), as shown in Figure 7-2.

Weighing a star

Since a star's surface temperature and brightness are closely related to the rate at which the star burns its fuel, and the burn rate is, in turn, directly related to a star's mass, once we know a star's brightness, temperature and chemical composition, we can estimate its mass (similar to its weight). Massive stars burn their nuclear fuel at a much faster rate than do smaller stars. As a result, they emit much more light than their less massive counterparts.

We're primarily interested in stars whose mass is similar to that of our sun. These stars belong to the *main-sequence* category of stars, and have a life span of several billion years. A star's mass is a critical factor in determining its ability to host life, primarily because its life span directly correlates with its mass. Stars that have more than 10 times the mass of our sun will burn much more brightly (which is not necessarily a problem since their habitable zones

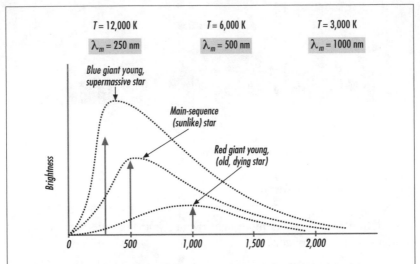

Figure 7-2: *The peak in this graph indicates the color at which a star is emitting most of its energy. This directly correlates with its temperature. This graph depicts several stars with different temperatures.*

will simply be further out). They also have a much shorter life span—a billion years (or less) compared to about 10 billion years for our sun. This shorter life span is a problem because life takes time to evolve from single-celled bacteria to animals. Conversely, stars that are much less massive than our sun, although they have extremely long life spans, have tiny or non-existent habitable zones.

Measuring a star's age

The chemical composition of a star tells us where it is in its life cycle. For example, if a star is rich in hydrogen and has relatively little helium, we know that it is a fairly young star. If a star is poor in hydrogen and has large quantities of helium and heavier elements, this tells us that the star is nearing the end of its life cycle. As a sun-like star ages and depletes its hydrogen fuel, it begins burning helium and heavier elements. When this happens, the star expands and cools to become a red giant. The star becomes redder in color as it cools, a signature that can easily be detected with an ordinary telescope.

Taking the star's size, brightness, and estimated age into account, we can determine whether the star is a likely site for life or not. We're most interested in stable, main-sequence stars that are rich in heavy elements such as carbon and iron, and that are several billion years old. Very young stars aren't good candidates since it takes hundreds of millions of years for planets and life to form; massive stars aren't good candidates since they tend to burn out much more quickly than do main-sequence stars.

Detecting planets

In Chapter 3, *The Drake Equation*, we discussed the technique used by astronomers to indirectly detect planets orbiting other stars. What we're looking for is a wobble in the star as it moves across the sky. Large planets in orbit around a star will exert a large enough gravitational pull to cause the star to wobble back and forth as its planets orbit.

The technique used to detect this wobble is based on the Doppler effect (also known as the *train whistle effect*). An object's motion affects the color of its light. When an object moves toward you, it's light shifts slightly toward the blue (a shorter wavelength) end of the spectrum. When an object retreats from you, it's light shifts toward the red (a longer wavelength) end of the spectrum. A large planet orbiting a star tugs the star, causing it to wobble toward and away from an observer. This wobble can be detected by looking for a cyclical Doppler shift in the star's light.

Detecting ET

It is also possible for an extraterrestrial civilization to use a laser to introduce an obviously artificial signature to a star's spectral fingerprint, one that can be detected by ordinary optical telescopes trillions of miles away.

The basic premise behind OSETI, much like microwave-based SETI programs, is to look for patterns that are obviously different from naturally occurring phenomena. When looking for alien radio signals, we look for signals tuned to a very precise frequency. A signal tuned to a precise frequency is the signature of an engineered device (and is also easier to detect at great distances).

The same principle applies to visible light. Stars emit tremendous amounts of energy as visible light. As an example, our own sun produces 10^{26} Watts (W) of energy, or the equivalent of about 1 septillion 100 W light bulbs (or $10^{24} \times 100$). However, this energy is spread across many colors of the spectrum. The yellow-white light our sun produces is actually a composite of many different colors. So, while a star's total energy output is quite large, it spreads this energy across many colors in a predictable pattern.

Monochromatic (single color) light is the signature of an artificial device. Naturally occurring light emitted by a star will always blur across many colors. The yellow-white light we see from our sun is actually a composite of red, orange, yellow, green, blue and violet light (plus ultraviolet and infrared light, which we cannot see). When we look at the sum of these colors together, the light is white. The laws of blackbody radiation, which we discussed previously as a way to measure temperature, govern this pattern.

By understanding these natural patterns, it is possible to engineer artificial signals that stand out against them; lasers are perfect tools for this. We can use lasers to generate an extremely strong and focused source of light tuned to a very precise wavelength (color). We can also use lasers to transmit extremely brief, but bright, pulses of light. The trick is to generate obviously artificial signals that stand out against the type of light normally emitted by a star.

Knowing how starlight usually behaves, it is possible to build an artificial beacon that, while it is weak compared to a star as a whole, shines brightly at a specific color or for very brief periods of time. The receiving party can then look for evidence of this type of artificial signal by splitting the light into thousands of individual colors, or by measuring the intensity of the light during very short (billionths of a second) timeframes.

Continuous beacons

Even a powerful laser will be very weak compared to its planet's sun. However, a laser transmits its energy into a very precisely focused beam, while a star emits its light equally in all directions (Figure 7-3). One type of laser signal we're looking for is a continuous beacon. This type of beacon can aim at a targeted star continually, giving the signal a greater chance for detection.

For every doubling in distance from the star, its light will grow four times weaker. In looking at the figure, you can see how the intensity of the starlight drops off rapidly as distance increases (e.g., increasing distance by 5× decreases light intensity by 25×).

When viewed from a distance, the laser and starlight merge into a single point of light. Therefore, as shown in Figure 7-4, a distant observer sees the starlight and laser light combined, and would probably have a difficult time determining which light is from which source. However, when viewed close in, the laser light and starlight originate from two different points in the sky.

The apparent brightness of light produced by a star decreases by a factor of 100 for every 10-fold increase in distance. We can simplify this to say that signal strength varies in proportion to distance squared. A laser beam does not distribute its energy uniformly in all directions. It concentrates its energy into a beam shaped like a very narrow cone (Figure 7-5).

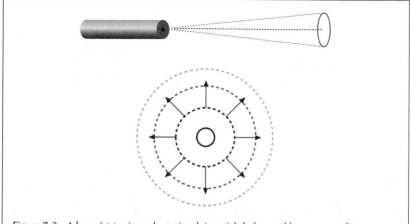

Figure 7-3: A laser (at top) can be trained, in a tightly focused beam, on a distant target, whereas a star (bottom) shines equally brightly in all directions.

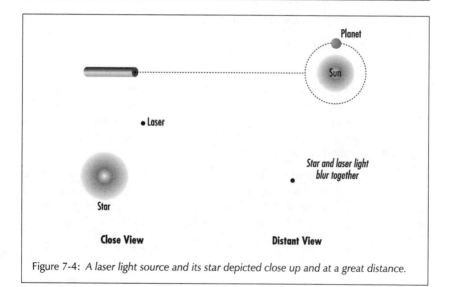

Figure 7-4: A laser light source and its star depicted close up and at a great distance.

The formula used to estimate the intensity (*I*) of the signal at a distance (*d*) can be expressed as follows:

$$I = P / (\pi \times r^2)$$

or:

$$I = P / (\pi \times (d \times \text{tangent}(\phi))^2)$$

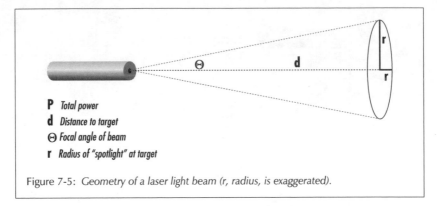

P   Total power
d   Distance to target
Θ   Focal angle of beam
r   Radius of "spotlight" at target

Figure 7-5: *Geometry of a laser light beam (r, radius, is exaggerated).*

The elements in this equation are defined as follows:

I Intensity

P Total laser power output

d Distance from the laser to the target

Θ Focal angle of the laser beam

r Radius of the laser beam's "spotlight" when it reaches its target

This formula tells us that we can boost the apparent strength of the signal by tightly focusing the beam. The angle, Θ, describes how tightly focused the beam is. The smaller we make the angle, the more the intensity of light is boosted at a given distance, compared to an omnidirectional source of light (e.g., a star or incandescent light bulb).

As an example, let's compare two identical beams. Each beam transmits at the same power level, however, beam A has an angle of 1°, and beam B has a much narrower angle of 0.01°. When observed from an equal distance, beam B will appear to be roughly 10,000 times brighter than beam A.

The trick to maximizing the efficiency of a laser beacon is to adjust the angle Θ so that the most intense part of the beam passes within about 100 to 200 million miles of the targeted star. This target radius may extend out as far as one billion miles, depending on the type of solar system. This means that most of the transmitted energy focuses on the region in which habitable planets are likely to exist.

As we transmit to more and more distant stars, we would reduce the angle of the beam to match the desired target radius. There are limits to how tightly we can focus a laser beam. Vibration, atmospheric instability, and the long-term motion of distant stars all impose limits on the accuracy with which the beacon can target distant stars. Vibrations in the device will cause the beam to smear across a larger patch of sky. Atmospheric instability, although not an issue for space-based transmitters, degrades the performance of ground-based lasers by causing the beam to bend and disperse slightly as it passes through the atmosphere (this same effect causes stars to twinkle). In addition, uncertainty about the future position of distant stars also places a limit on the transmitter's efficiency, as the solar system may drift away from the beam by the time the laser light arrives.

Detecting continuous laser beacons

The key to detecting a continuous beacon is to analyze the spectrum of a star's light in great detail. The trick is to analyze the star's light not just at a few wavelengths, but at thousands or even millions of wavelengths. A laser emits nearly all of its energy in a single, precisely tuned wavelength, whereas the star shining behind it blurs its energy across many different wavelengths (Figure 7-6). By measuring the intensity of light at very specific wavelengths, we improve the chances of detecting a laser against the background glare of the star. This is the same strategy used to detect radio signals, except here we're applying it to visible light.

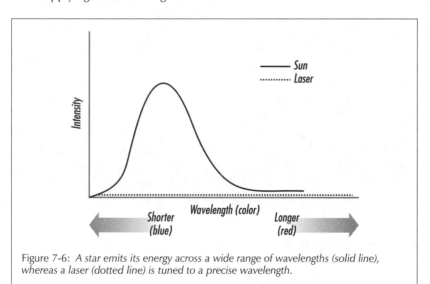

Figure 7-6: A star emits its energy across a wide range of wavelengths (solid line), whereas a laser (dotted line) is tuned to a precise wavelength.

If we look at a wide range of colors, the laser beam's net contribution to the measured light will be hidden in the background glare of its star. This is best illustrated by example. The first step is to graph the intensity of the incoming light from a star as a function of its color (Figure 7-7).

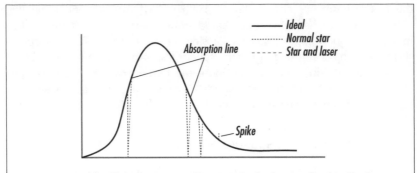

Figure 7-7: *Graph of light intensity as a function of color for a perfect blackbody source, for normal starlight, and for starlight with an embedded laser beacon.*

Figure 7-7 depicts three curves. The solid line is the curve we expect to see from a perfect source of blackbody radiation. Notice how the intensity of the light peaks at a specific color and then tapers off. The solid dashed line is the graph we expect to see from a normal star. Notice how it's similar to the perfect curve. The main difference we notice is the sharp drops in intensity at specific wavelengths. These sharp drops represent the absorption lines caused when light is absorbed by chemicals in the star's outer atmosphere. The dotted line represents the curve we would see if a strong laser beam were embedded in the incoming starlight. It is identical to the other two curves, except for a slight increase in intensity at a specific wavelength. This *spike* above the ideal intensity curve is a red flag indicating something unusual about the star (especially if the spike has an unusual color not typically emitted by known elements).

Continuous beacons will not be easy to spot; however, they can be detected if we know what to look for. Even a very strong, and very well aimed laser will be weak compared to its background starlight. The signature we're looking for will be subtle—and definitely invisible to the human eye—but it may be visible to telescopes equipped to analyze a star's spectrum in detail.

Pulsed beacons

Since we don't really know which signaling method is the *de facto* choice of extraterrestrials (if there are any), we shouldn't assume that any particular method of laser light communication is the sole method that will be used. This is why we're looking for signals in many parts of the electromagnetic spectrum. As mentioned earlier, another type of signal we'll look for is a *pulsed laser beacon*.

Pulsed laser beacons are based on a different strategy. They use strobe-like flashes of light to outshine an entire star for an instant. This is fairly easy to do because lasers can be turned on and off very quickly, and can emit flashes of light measured in billionths or even trillionths of a second. By concentrating their power into such a short period of time, they can generate extremely bright flashes of light without requiring extraordinary amounts of power.

The basic setup for sending and receiving pulsed laser signals is similar to the strategy used for continuous beacons. The main difference is on the receiving (detection) end of the line. The transmitting laser will be off for a majority of the time, emitting its light in brief, but very bright flashes of light. As with a continuous laser beam, the light from a pulsed beacon will also be tuned to a precise wavelength.

On the receiving end, an optical telescope feeds the light it collects into a *photon detector* or *photomultiplier (PMT)*. A photon detector is a sensitive instrument that counts each incoming photon (or light particle) that enters the telescope. This device allows the observer to count each incoming photon one by one, and to do so within very short time intervals (billionths of a second)

On a simplistic level, you can visualize the photon detector as a device that, when a light is shined on it, lights up an indicator. This detector then feeds data to a display. If the detector were seeing a pulsed light signal, the receiver would see something similar to the graph in Figure 7-8.

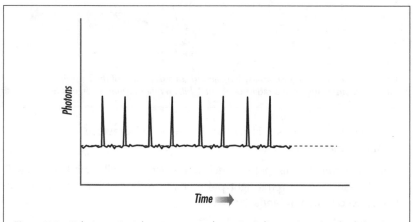

Figure 7-8: *Light intensity (photons captured per second) over time. A pulsed signal will produce a graph like this with regularly spaced spikes coinciding with each light pulse.*

While normal incandescent light might take a tenth of a second to go to full brightness, lasers can flash brightly for billionths of a second, allowing the sender to concentrate the laser's power into a very short period of time. During this brief period of time, the laser will shine thousands, or even millions of times, more brightly than a star. The laser is turned off most of the time, and when averaged out, does not consume an extraordinary amount of power.

Pulsed OSETI transmitter

The key component in an OSETI transmitter is a laser beam that can be cycled on and off very rapidly. This laser beam is aimed at the center of another solar system (at its primary star), and is focused such that the majority of its energy falls into a region within 200 million to 1 billion miles of the target star (Figure 7-9).

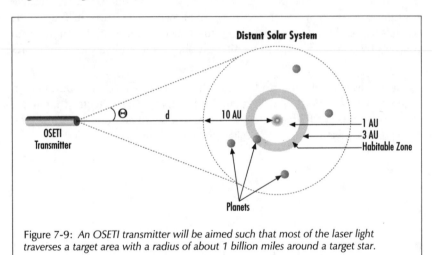

Figure 7-9: An OSETI transmitter will be aimed such that most of the laser light traverses a target area with a radius of about 1 billion miles around a target star.

This configuration makes it likely that the signal will traverse any potentially habitable planets in the system.

When we combine this pulsing technique with a well-aimed and tightly focused beam, we can emit light pulses that briefly outshine a nearby star when viewed from a distant solar system.

Pulsed beacon detection system

Detecting this light pulse is surprisingly simple, actually quite a bit simpler than detecting a microwave radio transmission. A simplified OSETI detector will consist of the following basic components:

- An optical telescope

- Two or more physically separated photon detectors

- A spectrometer, which is used to split light into different wavelengths, further increasing detector sensitivity

- Computers and signal processing software (unlike radio-based SETI programs, OSETI searches do not require high-speed supercomputers)

The first item, the optical telescope, is easily understood. We use an optical telescope to focus on a specific region of the sky so that we can limit the light we receive to that from a single target star. The telescope feeds the light it collects to two or more photon detectors.

PHOTON DETECTORS

A photon detector generates an electrical impulse every time it is struck by a light particle (photon). The nice thing about photon detectors is that they respond instantaneously when they capture a photon. Instead of counting the number of photons received per second, we count the number of photons received during much smaller slices of time (i.e., per microsecond, per nanosecond, etc.).

Photon detectors take advantage of the *photoelectric effect*. Albert Einstein discovered the photoelectric effect, and for his work in this area, received the Nobel Prize (though many people mistakenly assume the prize was awarded for his theory of relativity). Einstein discovered that when light strikes a surface, it knocks negatively charged electrons free from the atoms to which they are bound, causing an electrical current to flow. This same basic principle is employed in solar cells, digital cameras, and other light-sensing devices.

You can think of a photon detector as a pile of sand that has been stacked so high it is on the verge of collapsing. All it takes is one minor disturbance (adding or subtracting a single grain of sand) to trigger an avalanche. In the case of a photon detector, the arrival of a single photon triggers a cascade of events that ultimately triggers the release of a large number of electrons (Figure 7-10). This event is measured as a brief spike in electrical current. So, while the incoming photon has nearly zero energy all by itself, its impact can be magnified to make it an easily detected (and counted) event. This doesn't mean that you can get something for nothing; the device requires an outside power source to amplify the effect of the initial photon's impact to a level that can be detected by an electronic counter.

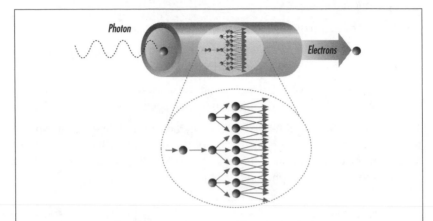

Figure 7-10: *Simplified depiction of a photomultiplier. A single photon triggers a cascade (a chain reaction). This triggers the release of a large number of electrons, which can be measured as a brief electrical current.*

What happens if we look at the output from the photon detector at an interval of once every 10 billionths of a second? If there is no pulsed beacon, the only light we will see is the background light from the star. The photons will arrive at random intervals, with no obviously repeating spikes.

If we add a pulsed beacon to the mix with a transmission time of one pulse once every 3 nanosecond (ns), the receiving telescope will capture photons emitted by the background star at a steady rate (Figure 7-11). During the brief *on* time, the photon detector will detect photons at many times the usual rate. If we average this over an entire second, the photons contributed by the laser will be insignificant compared to the total number of photons emitted by the star.

Output from the photon detectors is fed into a computer that analyzes this data using sophisticated software to look for short duration spikes in the number of photons received compared to the background noise level. A spike might be caused by a laser from an extraterrestrial civilization, but is more likely caused by stray photons entering the detector. One major source of noise is photons generated by the radioactive decay of material in the detection equipment itself.

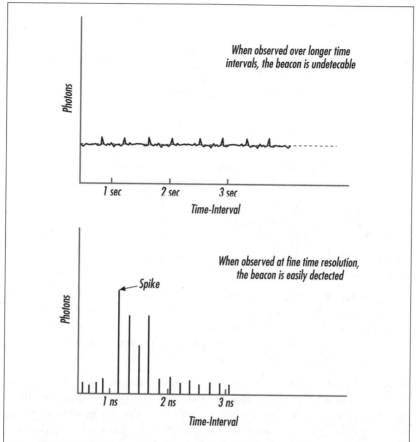

Figure 7-11: *Photons captured per second (top) and photons captured per nanosecond (bottom). The flashing beacon is overwhelmed by background radiation from the star when observed over a long time frame, but is easily seen when observed over a short (i.e., nanosecond) time frame.*

The detector's sensitivity can be further enhanced by splitting the incoming light through a prism, as shown in Figure 7-12. In a simplified form, the detector would split light into four buckets for red, yellow, green, and blue/violet light so the device has a total of eight photon detectors (two for each color of light). This allows us to identify incoming photons by their color, enabling us to improve our chances of detecting a beacon.

Figure 7-12 shows a simplified diagram of an OSETI detection system that breaks incoming light into different color bands. The incoming light passes through a prism and splits into different colors. An array of photon detectors behind the prism counts individual photons as they arrive. This type of arrangement allows the detector to differentiate according to color.

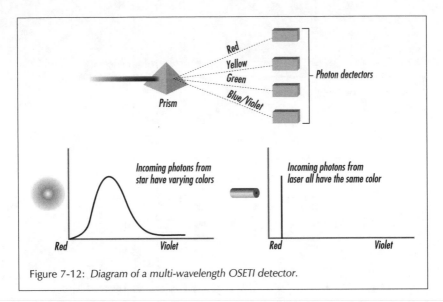

Figure 7-12: *Diagram of a multi-wavelength OSETI detector.*

Incoming light from the target star is a composite of many different colors. For example, some of the star's photons are green while others are red. Since the detector is set up to isolate different colors of light, it will count green photons in one bucket, and red photons in a different bucket. Hence, the intensity of the starlight, at a specific color, is reduced.

Incoming light from a pulsed laser, on the other hand, will concentrate all of its energy at a single precisely tuned wavelength. A single photon detector in the array will count all of the photons from the laser. So, instead of seeing incoming light spread across many wavelengths, the detector sees incoming photons that are precisely tuned to a specific color (e.g., deep red).

This technique can be used to build OSETI detectors that are many times more sensitive compared to the basic setup described earlier. For example, if the detector splits light into 100 different detectors, the apparent intensity of the background light from the star decreases by a factor of 10 to 100 within each color band, while the apparent intensity of the beacon remains the same.

Future OSETI technology

One of the biggest advances in OSETI technology will come in the next 10 to 20 years when we launch the Terrestrial Planet Finder space telescope, which uses interferometers instead of traditional mirrors for imaging. The interferometers, which will primarily search for Earth-sized planets, could also be used to detect laser beacons.

Space-based interferometers will enable astronomers to distinguish between light that is coming from a star and light that is coming from a site in close proximity to the star (e.g., light reflected from a planet, or light emitted by a laser beacon). These telescopes reduce the glare from a star by a factor of 100,000 or more, further improving our chances of seeing the signature from an extraterrestrial laser beam. Astronomers will be able to use the same basic techniques presently used to search for pulsed and continuous beams. The advantage, however, is that they will be able to reduce the background glare from the stars they observe, making it easier to see the nearby beacon.

Technical challenges and limits of OSETI

While transmitter power is important, is not the primary limiting factor in the detection range of an optical or infrared signal. Other factors conspire to impose limits on the detection range for a laser beacon. Among them are:

Pulse duration
> By concentrating the laser's power into the shortest time interval possible, we maximize its apparent intensity during its *on* cycle. By using shorter pulses, we can increase the detection range for a pulsed signal, but only up to a certain point.

Aiming accuracy
> While the stars in the night sky appear to be stationary, they are in constant motion. The effect of this motion is negligible over a short period of time. However, if we aim a laser beam at a star that is 1,000 light years away, it will be in a different location by the time the light beam arrives (see Figure 7-13). (When we look at a star that's 1,000 light years away, we see is the position of that star 1,000 years ago because its light took 1,000 years to reach us.)

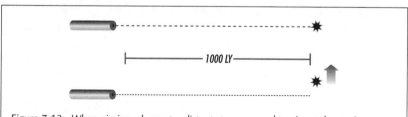

Figure 7-13: *When aiming a laser at a distant star, we need to aim at the star's predicted position when the light beam arrives, not at its current position as seen in our sky.*

Vibration and atmospheric interference will also limit aiming accuracy. As we lower the value of the lasers' angle (Θ), we become more and more susceptible to aiming errors caused by mechanical vibration and atmospheric interference. Even minute vibrations will be enough to cause the laser beam's aiming point to drift off center. Likewise, atmospheric instability (similar to the effect seen when looking at a stretch of asphalt on a hot day) also causes aiming errors. While less of a problem for nearby stars, this becomes a major problem when aiming at more distant sites. Moving the laser to a space-based platform can minimize these issues.

Extinction

Extinction refers to the attenuation (weakening) of the beam due to absorption by interstellar medium. While interstellar space appears to be empty, it is not a perfect vacuum. Interstellar space contains trace amounts of hydrogen, helium, oxygen, and other basic elements. When light transmits over short distances, the chance that an individual photon will collide with a molecule in transit is extremely remote. However, when the light beam traverses a distance of hundreds to thousands of light years, a significant percentage of the photons will be absorbed in transit, making the signal weaker and weaker as it travels.

At long wavelengths (i.e., infrared light), a signal can travel long distances with little attenuation. At shorter, visible wavelengths, attenuation limits communication range to a few dozen light years. We get the best results by using red or infrared light. One of the reasons that microwave (radio) signals are favored for very long-range communication is that microwave band signals are not as susceptible to extinction as infrared and visible light signals.

Dispersion

Dispersion is a particularly important phenomenon that affects pulsed laser beams. As illustrated in Figure 7-14, as a light pulse travels over a long distance, it spreads out over time.

Dispersion imposes a limit on the time resolution we can use to detect a signal. Think of this as being like the frame-rate for a movie projector. If dispersion introduces a 10 ns error into the arrival times for incoming photons, then the smallest time slice we can use to count incoming photons is about 10 billionths of a second. This effect is largely a function of the distance between stars. The farther away the other star is, the greater the effects of dispersion. Dispersion cancels out the benefits of using shorter-duration light pulses once the distance of the target becomes great enough.

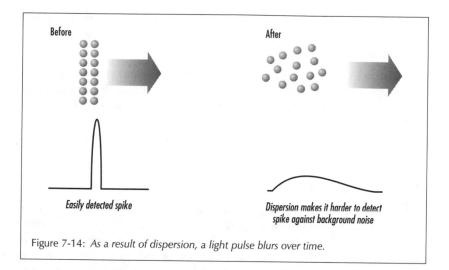

Figure 7-14: *As a result of dispersion, a light pulse blurs over time.*

Optical versus microwave SETI

Sir Arthur C. Clarke made an excellent observation once when he commented on the debate over the relative merits of optical and microwave SETI programs. He compared the debate to arguing over whether the inhabitants of a remote island should use smoke signals or beat on their drums to make contact with the inhabitants of nearby islands. Clarke's point was that our modern technology might be quite crude compared to that of an advanced civilization.

The one thing that we do know is that it is possible to communicate over very long distances using electromagnetic radiation. But will an extraterrestrial civilization use microwave radiation, visible light, or infrared light to establish contact with nearby civilizations? We really don't know. What we do know is that either method—optical or microwave—can be used to transmit coded information across interstellar space.

The main advantage of using microwave signals is economy. Microwave signals can be generated cheaply, and can travel longer distances with less degradation than optical signals. The downside of microwave signaling is the size and complexity of the detection systems. While a pulsed laser beacon can be detected by a modified optical telescope, detecting a microwave signal requires high-speed computers and sophisticated signal processing hardware and software.

Which method is best? This most likely depends on two factors: the senders' ability to cheaply generate energy, and whether or not the location of the receiving site(s) is known.

If the senders have developed advanced energy production technology (e.g., nuclear fusion power plants), the cost of the electricity needed to operate a powerful transmitter will be negligible. In this case, the senders will likely use signal formats that are easiest to detect (e.g., optical beacons). On the other hand, if the senders' energy production technology has reached a plateau similar to ours, they will have a strong incentive to minimize the transmitter's power budget. Microwave signaling is cheaper in this situation, although the signal will be harder for the receiving party to detect.

Next, if the location of the receiving party is known, the senders will want to focus most of the transmitted signal on that part of the sky. In this situation, the senders can use either optical or microwave technology, since both types of signals can be focused into a narrow beam. On the other hand, if the senders do not know where the other sites are, they will want to use a loosely focused beam or an omnidirectional beacon. Lasers are a poor choice in this situation, and so the senders will probably be biased in favor of microwave signaling.

So, what method will another civilization use to contact us? It could be either of these, or perhaps something we haven't even thought of yet. People on both sides of the optical-versus-microwave debate have made convincing arguments that their approach is best. The most likely answer is that both technologies have their advantages and disadvantages, depending on how they are applied. Since we don't know anything about the location or technological sophistication of other civilizations, we should look for both types of signals.

SIGNAL PROCESSING
AND CONFIRMATION

Merely detecting a microwave radio signal or a pulse of light is just one of several steps in a chain of events that would lead to the confirmation of contact with another civilization. As we've touched on in previous chapters, the universe is awash in noise, from the residual background radiation of the Big Bang to electromagnetic pollution resulting from our own activities.

Unfortunately, it is no simple matter to eliminate this pollution. Some noise sources, such as cosmic background radiation, are universal. You simply cannot avoid them, no matter in what direction you point your antenna. Artificial noises are equally difficult to avoid because we employ wireless communication so extensively here on Earth.

No matter where you travel on our planet, you are exposed to radio or lightwave radiation from ground-based and/or airborne transmitters. Even Antarctica is not unpolluted. Satellite telephone systems, such as the troubled Iridium telephone system, enable you to make cellular phone calls from this remote continent to anywhere in the world. While this may be reassuring if you are stranded on an ice floe with only penguins to keep you company, it is a nuisance if you are scouting for a pristine location uncontaminated by our own radio and light pollution.

Radio signals are especially vulnerable to our own interference, which is one of the reasons SETI radioastronomy is so challenging. Detecting a signal is the easy part. Separating *bona fide* extraterrestrial signals from our own noise is the difficult part.

Confirming a signal

SETI equipment and software detect all unusual signals, which get passed on to confirmation and follow-up detection systemsthat weed out interference and false observations. These systems provide human observers with a short list of candidate signals that merit closer attention. The general sequence of events in signal detection and confirmation are as follows:

Signal acquisition

This first stage detects all unusual radio or optical signals. This stage is designed to be very sensitive, and will detect any signal that matches the basic detection criteria (i.e., tuned to a specific wavelength, significantly stronger than the background noise level). As a result, this stage generates a large number of false alarms, most of them caused by our own Earth- and space-based transmitters.

Signal analysis

This stage is responsible for determining which of these "hits" are potential ET signals. This stage is usually highly automated, and is designed to weed out the vast majority of candidates. It examines each candidate signal for signs that it is originating from man-made or natural sources. The candidate signals that cannot be attributed to interference or natural sources of radiation are then passed on to human observers for detailed analysis.

Follow-up detection

The third stage examines especially interesting candidate signals to verify that they are actually originating from a distant source, and not somewhere nearby. This stage typically involves two or more telescopes examining the same target from different locations on Earth. If the signal originates from a satellite or space probe, it will appear to be in a different location, and moving differently with respect to the background star field when viewed from multiple sites. This is an open-ended stage. Astronomers at multiple sites will attempt to disqualify the signal. Only after exhaustive observation and analysis will they declare a candidate signal to be extraterrestrial in origin.

Decoding

The final stage of confirming an alien signal will only be applied if and when a signal has been verified as being extraterrestrial in nature. In this stage, researchers will analyze the signal in an attempt to decipher its contents. This stage may proceed quickly if the signal is designed to be easily decoded, or it may take an indefinite number of years if we inadvertently eavesdrop on a signal that was not intended for us.

The SETI@home project at UC Berkeley has also detected several interesting candidate signals. To date, all of them have been attributed to man-made interference or explained away as statistical anomalies. The second phase of the SETI@home project will examine the best candidate signals detected during the project's first run, in which the program randomly surveyed most of the night sky visible from the Arecibo Radio Observatory.

IS IT REAL, OR JUST AN ANOMALY?

Other unverified signals have been detected throughout SETI's history. Many of these signals have been subsequently identified as man-made in origin. The protocol for detecting an ET signal requires multiple independent observations to rule out any possibility of a non-ET signal being misinterpreted as the real thing.

However, many observed events have not been disconfirmed. Like the "Wow!" signal, they were detected once, but did not recur during follow-up observation. For example, an intermittent signal might be detectable from Earth for only brief periods of time (a matter of seconds). Unless follow-up detection systems can rapidly analyze a candidate signal, it is possible that these signals may pass the first test, but then disappear before they can be double-checked.

For that reason, failure to detect a signal during the follow-up detection stage does not categorically rule out the source since it could be an intermittent source. Unless a signal can be repeatedly observed from multiple locations, it can't be identified.

To date, scientists have detected some interesting signals, but have never gotten past stage three. In every case so far, save one, the signals we have detected have been subsequently attributed to man-made radio interference. The one notable exception, the "Wow!" signal picked up by the Big Ear Radio Observatory in 1977, was thought to pass many of the tests for an ET signal. However, the signal was only picked up once, and lasted for little more than a minute. Astronomers were never able to detect the signal in subsequent observations of the same star system. Without additional observations to confirm the source of the signal, all we can say is that we detected an interesting signal of unknown origin, probably ours, possibly not.

In our 40+ years of searching, we have yet to detect conclusive evidence of an extraterrestrial radio or lightwave transmission. While this may sound discouraging to some, others take this with a grain of salt, as there are many technological (and financial) hurdles we still need to cross. We may succeed in detecting a signal relatively soon, or it might take decades or centuries to detect a signal. The estimates for the odds of SETI's success vary widely, depending entirely on whom you talk to.

Verifying radio signals

The biggest challenge facing radio-based SETI searches is not the task of detecting a weak radio signal from a distant star but rather the challenge of distinguishing between a *bona fide* ET signal and our own radio transmissions.

In the century since we invented radio communication, we have progressed to the point where we are transmitting signals in nearly every piece of the radio spectrum. An extraterrestrial civilization that is broadcasting an intentional signal in a conscious attempt to establish communication will most likely employ the frequencies that are least affected by background noise. The universe is quietest in the band of frequencies from about 1 GHz to 10 GHz. Unfortunately, many of the frequencies we use for other purposes are also in this frequency range.

Communication satellites typically use the GHz band to carry their transmissions. Digital cellular telephones use the frequencies from around 1.8 to 1.9 GHz to carry phone calls. Home-based cordless phones and wireless data networks use frequencies ranging from 0.9 to 2.4 GHz to transmit their data. Although these devices transmit weak signals, they are very strong compared to an extraterrestrial signal that has traveled 100 trillion miles. So, the big challenge in radio SETI isn't detecting a signal, but rather differentiating between the real thing and a stray call from a cordless phone, leakage from a microwave oven, and other sources of radiation.

Fortunately, the signals generated by human activity have distinguishing characteristics. By comparing candidate signals against a checklist of properties, it is possible to develop a largely automated scheme for discarding signals caused by our own radio frequency interference.

Computing is a critical component of radio-based SETI programs. The ability to detect a weak signal is directly related to the computational capabilities of the detection system. We can use computers to test many different assumptions about a signal, and to reject noise.

Radio-based signal detection

Since SETI radioastronomy is based on the detection of radio signals, many people assume that it is simply a matter of listening for a tone on a radio receiver. In fact, detecting a signal—even with a very efficient amplifier—is difficult because the signal can be masked by noise and may be modulated (i.e., the signal strength or frequency may vary over time) in a way that we're not expecting. Once we detect a signal, the pattern will be obvious to us;

however, until we detect it, the signal will likely appear to be part of the radio background noise, making it much more difficult to detect.

Radio-based SETI searches analyze signals in a multistage process. Incoming data from a radiotelescope is converted from a continuously varying electrical signal and is digitized into a series of numbers. This data is then fed into a spectrum analyzer to break up the incoming signal into millions of channels, much like an equalizer in a home stereo system, except the number of channels is much greater. Computer programs then analyze the output from the spectrum analyzer, and look for spikes centered about a specific frequency.

The spikes are ranked based on how well they match the characteristics of terrestrial radio interference. During this stage, scientists look at the signal to see if it stays tuned to a precise frequency or drifts across frequencies, and to see whether its power level remains constant or varies over time. These factors help determine whether the signal is originating from a distant source in the sky, or if it is originating from a more mundane source, like a nearby microwave oven being used to heat a bag of popcorn for a bored and hungry researcher.

This process is fairly straightforward, but it requires sophisticated software and computing hardware capable of performing billions or trillions of calculations per second. The SETI@home project aids in this by enlisting the help of millions of idle desktop computers around the world to analyze data acquired by Project SERENDIP. Additional information about the SETI@home project can be found in Chapter 9, *Bringing SETI Home*.

Signal processing

The process of analyzing a signal can be divided into four general steps: digitization, frequency domain (Fourier) conversion, spectrum analysis, and finally, follow-up analysis and interference rejection. The first three steps are automated, with the work being done by sophisticated computer algorithms. The fourth step may be automated, but usually requires human intervention to further analyze the signal.

Digitization

The first step in analyzing a signal involves converting an analog signal from a receiver into a series of digits. This is called *analog-to-digital conversion*, or A/D for short. A/D conversion works by taking a snapshot of the incoming signal at very rapid intervals. The A/D converter measures the voltage of the incoming electrical signal from the receiver, and converts this voltage level to a corresponding number—the higher the voltage level, the higher the number.

To digitize a signal, the range of frequencies to be analyzed is isolated from the others. Since we do not currently have the equipment to monitor billions of channels simultaneously, we must focus on a narrower swath of the spectrum to analyze. This stage is called *down conversion*. Down conversion makes it easier to convert an incoming signal from analog to digital format. The receiver isolates a block of frequencies (for example, 1.1 to 1.12 GHz), and then converts these down to much lower frequencies (Figure 8-1). This is also done because A/D converters are more effective at processing signals in lower frequencies.

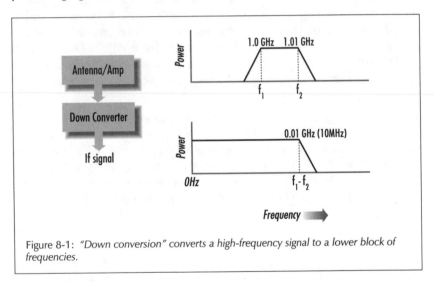

Figure 8-1: *"Down conversion" converts a high-frequency signal to a lower block of frequencies.*

The down-converted signal is then fed into an A/D converter (Figure 8-2). This device continuously converts varying analog signals into a series of numbers which we can then analyze using a computer.

NOTE

If you are having trouble visualizing this analogy, think of this example in terms of sound. You've probably seen an animated movie for which the sound of an actor's voice is manipulated to make its pitch higher or lower. With down conversion, the pitch of the signal is lowered so that it falls within the "hearing range" of the A/D converter.

So let's assume we want to analyze a 100 MHz piece of bandwidth. We'll take a snapshot of the incoming signal at a minimum rate of 200 million times per second. We'll actually sample the signal at a higher rate to

Figure 8-2: *Analog to Digital (A/D) conversion converts a continuous (analog) signal into a series of numeric values. The more frequently the signal is sampled ("photographed"), the greater the accuracy of the digital reproduction of the original signal.*

improve the accuracy, with which we can analyze higher frequency signals within this band. This is called *oversampling*.

The result of each "snapshot" will be a 16- to 32-bit number (digit) that describes the voltage level of the original analog signal. The more bits we use per sample, the more sensitive our analysis.

If we use a 32-bit sample, and sample at the minimum rate, the digitization process will produce a stream of digits at the rate of 6.4 billion bits per second (bps), or 6.4 Gbps. This is a lot of data to analyze, so we will need a very fast computer to do all of this work.

If we wanted to digitize 10 GHz of the spectrum—roughly the amount of bandwidth needed to cover the quietest part of the microwave band—we would generate about 1 Terabit (trillion bits) of raw data per second. This is comparable to the speed of our fastest fiber optic networking technology. We're currently falling well short of having the capability to process this much data in real-time, which is why current microwave SETI searches focus on a smaller piece of the spectrum.

Frequency domain (Fourier) conversion

Once we've converted an analog signal into a series of numbers, we need to convert this signal from the time domain to the *frequency domain*. The frequency domain breaks broad signals down into a large number of component frequencies. This allows us to look for monochromatic ("pure tone") carriers within our signal.

To do this, we perform a *Fourier transformation*, which involves a mathematical formula (algorithm) that allows us to see how power in a signal is distributed across different frequencies (tones). For example, if you apply a Fourier transform to the signal from your home stereo, you would be able to see the acoustic composition of a sound (i.e., strength of high sounds versus low sounds, etc.).

The major difference between the SETI receiver and your home stereo's equalizer is the SETI spectrum analyzer breaks the signal down into millions or hundreds of millions of channels, whereas your home equalizer will have, at most, 10 to 20 channels corresponding to low and high tones.

This is where computing power comes into play. The Fourier transform is a fairly computationally intensive task. The amount of computation required is proportional to the rate at which data flows into the system, and to the number of channels into which we want to parse our signal.

For this process to be effective in SETI research, we want to listen on as many individual channels as we can because this has a direct bearing on our detection capability. If we can listen on 3 billion channels simultaneously, we have a good chance of detecting a narrowband carrier in the microwave frequencies that are most useful for SETI applications. If we can listen on only 100 million channels, we must either tune to parts of the spectrum individually, or use wider channels (which means the signal is more likely to be masked by noise).

The following equation gives you an idea of how much computing power is needed to listen to the microwave spectrum from 1 to 10 GHz. We want to do this with a frequency resolution of 0.1 to 1.0 Hz. This means that we need to break our signal into anywhere between 9 and 90 billion individual channels. The amount of processing power required varies according to the formula:

$$OPS \cong 5 \times BW \times \log_2(n)$$

In this equation, BW stands for bandwidth (in Hz) and n stands for the number of points or channels in which to divide the signal. OPS stands for the number of calculations required per second. If we graph this equation, we see that the dominant factor is the amount of bandwidth we want to monitor. The amount of processing power required is directly proportional to the amount of spectrum we want to monitor. This equation can be roughly simplified to:

$$OPS \cong 100 \times BW$$

In order to monitor 10 GHz of bandwidth, we need a computer capable of performing 1 trillion operations per second. This is well beyond the capability of a desktop computer, but can be attained by a supercomputer, or a large cluster of slower computers. The SETI@home project solved this problem by distributing the computational workload to a very large number of desktop computers.

The equation predicts the amount of processing power needed to detect an ideal symmetric (always on) signal that stays perfectly tuned to a specific frequency. In reality, a signal drifts across a range of frequencies and varies in its apparent power as shown in the waterfall signal plot in Figure 8-3. Notice how the peak frequency varies over time. This pattern tells us that the transmitter is not precisely tuned to a frequency, or that the transmitter is in motion relative to the receiver.

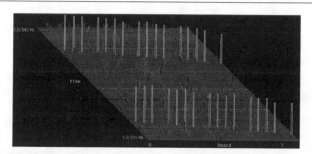

Figure 8-3: A waterfall plot of a drifting signal. This graph depicts signal strength over time across a range of frequencies.

In order to detect a drifting signal, the program that analyzes the raw data would need to repeat the whole process many times, once for each drift rate to be tested. For example, we may test a block of data to look for a signal that is drifting at +1 Hz/second, +1.5 Hz/second and +2 Hz/second. By testing many different frequencies, we improve the odds of spotting a signal that does not stay precisely tuned to a specific frequency. The downside is that we need to budget even more computing power to look for less than ideal signals. This increases the computing requirement by a factor of 1000 or more, depending on the number of different permutations tested.

Searching for an ideal, non-drifting signal in the 1 to 10 GHz band requires a bare minimum of approximately 1 teraflop of computing horsepower to listen to just one star system. To do a rudimentary search for signals that drift across a range of frequencies requires upward of 100 to 1000 teraflops. To put this in perspective, the SETI@home project, whose collective computing power is equivalent to the fastest supercomputer in the world, tops out at an average speed of 10 to 20 teraflops. At this speed, SETI@home covers a small slice of spectrum (about 0.0025 GHz or 2.5 MHz). To use the same system to cover a 10 GHz swath of spectrum would require 4,000 times as much computing power, or 40,000 teraflops. This will be possible in the future as computers become faster and more pervasive. For now, this speed is beyond the reach of our current technology (unless we're willing to throw a lot of money at the problem).

The SETI@home system breaks its 2.5 MHz band of frequencies into 33.5 million distinct channels. Because the system also looks for signals whose frequencies drift over time, it requires much more computation compared to a system that assumes that the signal does not drift significantly with time. The SETI@home project's director, Dan Werthimer, points out that the SETI@home system does the equivalent of monitoring 436 billion channels when the "dechirping" algorithms (which compensate for drifting signals) are taken into account.

In theory, the SETI@home project can muster an almost unlimited amount of computing power. The total computing capacity of the project is determined by:

- The number of volunteers running the client program

- The average speed of the volunteers' computers

- The amount of bandwidth available to exchange data with the volunteers' computers

The primary factors limiting the capacity of the system today are the number of volunteers and the average speed of their PCs. Since computing performance will continue to increase, we can expect SETI@home's capacity to increase as well, even if the number of participants plateaus.

If we want to monitor multiple systems simultaneously, we must also multiply this number by the number of star systems we want to monitor. So, while the basic principle behind interstellar radio communication is fairly straightforward, the computing resources required to conduct a truly comprehensive search are beyond our current capabilities. In 20 years time, the offspring of today's SETI programs will be able to listen to the entire microwave band and watch several star systems simultaneously. As our ability to listen to more and more frequencies and star systems grows, the odds of successfully detecting a signal grow in lockstep with the speed and efficiency of the detection systems.

Until recently, radio-based SETI searches employed custom-built hardware to break an incoming signal into a very large number of channels. These custom-built spectrum analyzers were designed for this specific task. The latest generation spectrum analyzers monitor over 150 million channels simultaneously. By comparison, the first SETI detection systems could only monitor about 100 channels at once, so the hardware has improved a million fold since the early days of the program.

Because we are constrained by the maximum speed of today's computers, we can monitor a relatively small slice of the spectrum at any given time. In order to monitor a much wider range of frequencies, SETI researchers expect that we will require a million- to billion-fold improvement in computing speed. While this may sound extreme, computer speeds have already increased a million-fold in the past 20 years, and are expected to continue to increase exponentially in the future. If the trends from the past persist, we can expect computers to meet or exceed this threshold within the next 20 to 30 years. Then we will be able to build SETI detection systems that can listen on tens of billions of channels in real-time. So, while today's detection systems are quite sophisticated compared to Frank Drake's first SETI experiment, they are crude compared to the systems that will be placed into operation 20 years from now.

As shown in Table 8-1, current radio-based SETI programs monitor from less than 1 percent to about 20 percent of the radio spectrum that can potentially be used for interstellar communication.

Table 8-1: *Comparison of current radio-based SETI searches*

SETI PROGRAM	BANDWIDTH MONITORED	CHANNELS MONITORED	PERCENT OF USABLE MICROWAVE SPECTRUM[a]
SETI@home	~2.5 MHz (0.0025 GHz)	33,600,000	0.025%
SERENDIP IV	100 MHz (0.1 GHz)	168,000,000	1%
BETA	320 MHz (0.32 GHz)	640,000,000	3%
Project Phoenix	2000 MHz (2 GHz)	2,000,000,000	20%

[a] Out of 10 GHz of relatively quiet microwave spectrum (up to ~10 GHz).

Even with the advances in computing hardware and software over the past 20 years, we're still listening to only a relatively small piece of the radio spectrum. Moreover, many SETI programs operate on a part-time basis and do not have 24/7 access to radiotelescope facilities. Future SETI programs will boast much more advanced signal processing hardware and software, and will most likely run around the clock. These programs will be able to detect weaker signals and will be able to monitor billions of individual channels in real-time.

Spectrum analysis

The next stage of signal analysis involves the use of computer programs to process the information produced by the spectrum analyzer. This stage is designed to look for specific patterns indicative of an artificial source.

The primary pattern we're looking for is a signal whose power is concentrated in a very narrow band of frequencies. Only a device engineered by an intelligent source can generate this type of signal. We know this because naturally occurring radio sources spread their power across a wider band of frequencies and typically fail this test. The narrowest naturally occurring radio signals spread their power across a band of frequencies about 1000 Hz wide, about 1,000 to 10,000 times wider than a precisely tuned carrier signal.

This is the first test a candidate signal needs to pass. We can't rule out the possibility that an alien signal, similar to our own radio or TV signals, may be spread across a wider band of frequencies. However, this will considerably weaken the signal, making it much harder to detect at interstellar distances. If we detect a broadband signal using the presently available systems, it is much more likely to be due to our own interference.

At this stage, scientists typically look for spikes, where a signal's power is concentrated into a well-defined narrow band of frequencies. Spikes are relatively common, and have many easily explained causes, such as terrestrial interference. The analysis software will tag spikes that exceed pre-programmed thresholds for follow-up analysis. The type and extent of follow-up analysis varies depending on the type of detection equipment used. In general terms, the follow-up stage will look to rule out local sources as the cause of the signal. This stage in the detection process is fairly dumb. Its job is to comb through all of the spectral data to look for signals that concentrate their power into a narrow band of frequencies. These signals may be tuned to a single precise frequency, or they may spread across a wider band of frequencies (up to about 1000 Hz). The signal may also drift across frequencies (e.g., the signals may increase or decrease steadily in pitch). The primary job in this stage is to separate potential signals from random background noise, and to hand a catalogued list of hits to the follow-up analysis stage, during which false alarms are weeded out.

Follow-up analysis and detection

The spectrum analysis stage hands its results off to a program whose job is to determine whether candidate signals (spikes) come from a local or distant source. The basic goal in this stage is to weed out signals generated by transmitters in Earth's general vicinity as well as signals from our own deep space probes. Since we have not yet sent man-made radio transmitters to other star systems, we can use a process of elimination to determine whether a radio signal is extraterrestrial or not. If we can confirm that a signal originates from a transmitter in another solar system, and cannot attribute the signal to natural causes, we can be confident that it is being generated by a radio transmitter, and hence is evidence of an intelligent civilization.

NO FREE LUNCH: FASTER COMPUTERS MEAN BIGGER EARS

We can reduce the amount of computational time by dividing incoming signals into fewer channels. For example, let's look at how we could divvy up a 1 million MHz band. We could divide this into 1 million 1 Hz channels, or we could divide it into 10,000 100 Hz channels. By using 100 Hz channels, we could reduce the amount of computational horsepower needed to analyze the data by a factor of 100. But there's a catch to this.

If we listen on a wider band of frequencies, the signal will need to be much stronger for us to detect it. This is because the type of signal we're looking for will concentrate most of its power on a specific frequency, and we'll be listening to many frequencies at the same time. The problem is that our receiver will also pick up the background noise on the other frequencies. The result is that the cumulative power of the background noise will be stronger than it would if we were listening on a narrower channel (see Figure 8-4). Because of this, the signal needs to be several times stronger, or we need to have a more sensitive receiver (i.e., a bigger dish).

In order to maximize our odds of detecting a signal, we need to listen on as many very narrow channels as possible. Since we need to listen to 10 to 100 billion channels simultaneously, we should ideally monitor channels with a width of 0.1 to 1.0 Hz. With present-day technology, we can only listen to about 25 to 500 million channels at once, so we still have some ways to go before we'll have a receiving system that can monitor the entire microwave band in real-time.

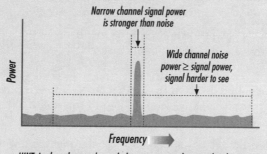

Narrow channel signal power
is stronger than noise

Wide channel noise
power ≥ signal power,
signal harder to see

Power

Frequency ➡

HINT: Look at the area beneath the curve to visualize signal and noise power

Figure 8-4: By listening on a narrow channel, we greatly improve the odds of detecting a signal because the signal rises well above background noise. The shaded area under the curve represents the total power of the background noise; we can reduce the power of the background noise by looking at a narrower band of frequencies.

So, what we're really interested in learning about a candidate signal is its point of origin. At this point, we don't care if the signal is conveying information; we only want to know where it is coming from.

Stage three will pick up all types of candidate signals, including our own. Based on SETI searches conducted to date, we can conclude that we will detect a very large number of false signals before we detect an authentic signal. The SETI@home project, for example, has catalogued over 1 billion spikes (signals powerful enough to stand out against background noise) in its first year of operation. SETI@home has yet to detect a single authentic signal. Even if SETI@home detected one alien signal per year (and that's an optimistic assumption), it would have to sort through 1 billion potential hits for every authentic signal. This is obviously an approximation, but it gives you a sense of the scale of the problem. There is no way you could expect human researchers to manually examine each potential signal. This would give new meaning to the term *busy work*. The trick at this stage is to write a set of analysis programs that look for clues to indicate whether a signal is coming from a nearby transmitter or from a distant source.

Since the vast majority of detected carriers will be the result of local interference, scientists use a process of elimination to rule out signals that can be explained by local interference by looking at several characteristics:

Doppler drift rate
> Does the signal stay fixed on a single frequency, or does it wander about a bit? If so, how does the signal's frequency drift?

Signal power
> Does the signal transmit at a constant power, or does it wax and wane? If so, how does the signal power vary over time?

Frequency distribution
> Is the signal's power focused on a narrow band of frequencies, or is it spread across a wide band of frequencies?

Locality
> Can the signal be detected by another antenna that is physically distant from the primary site? This test is used to rule out interference from a source close to the primary receiving site.

These characteristics tell us a lot about a signal's origin and whether it is our own activities or not.

DOPPLER DRIFT RATE

By examining the signal's Doppler drift rate, we can immediately determine whether the signal is coming from a ground-based transmitter, or from an orbiting satellite. This is because the signal, no matter how perfectly tuned its transmitter, wanders off its target frequency in a specific way because of varying motion between the transmitting and the receiving site. When a transmitter and receiver approach each other, the signal's frequency shifts to a slightly higher frequency. If they are traveling in opposite directions, the signal's frequency shifts to a slightly lower frequency. And, because the transmitter and receiver are both attached to orbiting and rotating bodies (i.e., a planet that orbits its sun), this relative motion changes over time.

Doppler shift, also known as the *train whistle effect*, occurs when the transmitter and receiver move toward or away from each other. Just as a train's whistle is shifted higher in pitch when it moves toward an observer, so too is the frequency of a radio signal when the transmitter moves toward the receiver. Since the speed of light is universal, we can use the shift in a radio signal's frequency over time to determine how the transmitter and receiver move with respect to each other. This tells us a great deal about the signal we're receiving, and can be used to weed out any false alarms. To get a better idea of what we're talking about, let's look at a couple possible scenarios:

No Doppler drift or random shift
> If the detected signal's frequency does not vary with time, we can be fairly certain that this signal is coming from another transmitter firmly attached to *terra firma*. This is because the absence of a Doppler shift tells us that the transmitter and receiver are not in motion with respect to each other (Figure 8-5).

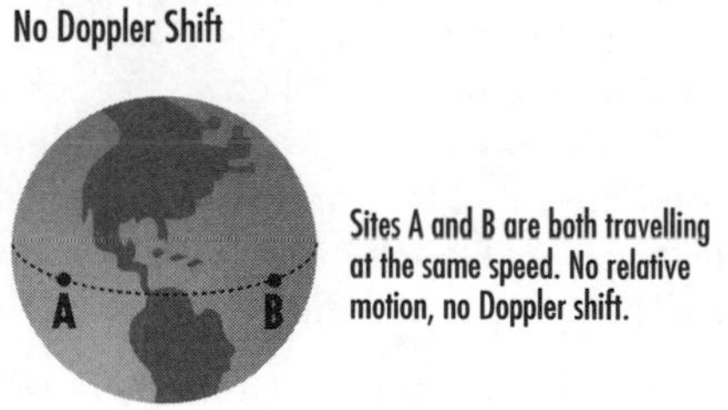

No Doppler Shift

Sites A and B are both travelling at the same speed. No relative motion, no Doppler shift.

Figure 8-5: *If an incoming signal displays no frequency drift (stays precisely on a specific frequency), it suggests that the signal comes from a ground-based transmitter on Earth.*

Doppler drift rate suggesting velocity in excess of ± 3 miles per second
> If the signal's Doppler drift rate indicates a change in velocity of several miles per second, this tells us that the signal is probably coming from a satellite in low-Earth orbit (Figure 8-6). (There is a small chance that the source may be a satellite orbiting another planet, but the most likely

explanation is that the signal is coming from one of our own satellites.) In this situation, the transmitter passes in and out of the antennae's field of view (beams) quite quickly, so Doppler drift is not the only clue that the signal is man-made.

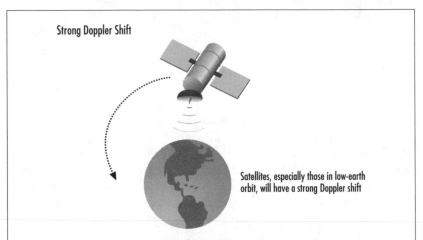

Strong Doppler Shift

Satellites, especially those in low-earth orbit, will have a strong Doppler shift

Figure 8-6: *If an incoming 1 GHz signal displays a Doppler shift greater than ± 20 KHz, this tells us that the source is an orbiting satellite.*

Some of the factors we look for include: a slight Doppler drift that varies in accordance with the Earth's daily rotation (a 24-hour period) and its revolution about the sun (a 365-day period), *plus* an unknown component that is the result of the distant planet's daily rotation and revolution about its star (Figure 8-7). We know the period of rotation and revolution of the Earth, so we can correct a detected signal's frequency drift for these attributes. If, after correcting the signal for local Doppler drift, there is still a varying Doppler drift in the signal whose period does not match that of the Earth's, the signal will warrant further scrutiny.

If there is no Doppler drift in the signal, or if there is a Doppler drift that suggests that the signal source's velocity varies by plus or minus several miles per .second, the probability that the signal was generated by a man-made device is fairly high.

GAUSSIANS AND OFF-AXIS VIEWING

Next we'll want to examine how a candidate signal's power level varies over time or when the signal source is viewed slightly off target. This tells us whether the signal originates from a stationary point source in the sky or a local source.

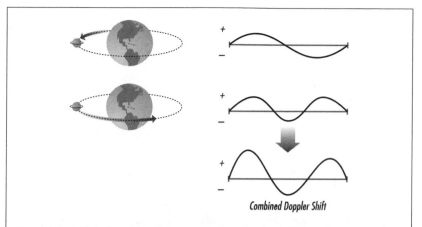

Figure 8-7: A likely Doppler drift rate profile for an ET signal. This profile accounts for the rotation and orbital motion of the Earth as well as the planet on which the transmitter is located.

Drift surveys, where the telescope slews across the sky to examine a large number of stars, are looking for signals that fit a Gaussian power curve. As the signal source passes through the telescope's field of view, the signal's power increases from zero, peaks, and then decreases, as shown in Figure 8-8.

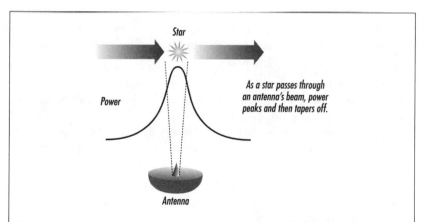

Figure 8-8: As a signal source passes through the telescope's focal point, the apparent power of the source increases, peaks, and then decreases, typically within a few seconds.

If a signal originates from another solar system, we will expect the power level for the signal to vary as shown in Figure 8-9.

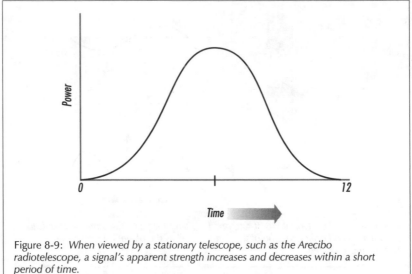

Figure 8-9: *When viewed by a stationary telescope, such as the Arecibo radiotelescope, a signal's apparent strength increases and decreases within a short period of time.*

In the case of the Arecibo radiotelescope, which is used by the SERENDIP and SETI@home projects, a target star passes through the antenna's field of view in about 12 seconds. So, these programs look for a signal whose power level rises and falls to and from peak value in 12 seconds.

So, we will test a candidate signal to see how well its power profile fits this curve. If the event lasts longer than 12 seconds, we can rule it out. On the other hand, if the power curve fits this profile, we can reasonably suspect that the signal is of extraterrestrial origin.

The SERENDIP project uses the Arecibo radiotelescope to conduct a full sky survey. The SERENDIP instrument cannot be arbitrarily aimed and fixed on a single point in the sky. Instead, the telescope views objects as they drift across the sky. While this is not ideal for surveying a specific target for long periods of time, this drift allows researchers to search and analyze large sections of the sky.

Other programs, such as the SETI Institute's Project Phoenix, are targeted search programs. In these surveys, observers train telescopes on specific stars for an extended period of time, allowing them to analyze a much wider swath of radio spectrum.

In these search programs, researchers weed out interference using a technique called off-axis viewing. Whenever a telescope identifies a strong candidate signal, the telescope is programmed to automatically slew slightly off-target while the signal strength is measured. If the signal originates from a distant source, its strength decreases as the telescope drifts off target. If the signal originates from a local source that is not associated with the target star, the signal strength will not change in the same predictable way. This providess astronomers with the means to develop an automated verification step that eliminates a large percentage of false alarms.

When researchers detect a signal that passes these tests, they repeat the observation from different telescopes or at different times. If they detect the same signal at the same frequencies when observed at different times, or from different telescopes, this is strong evidence that the signal is not coming from a local source. Very few man-made signals exhibit this behavior; the exception being deep-space probes such as the Pioneer spacecraft (SETI researchers were once fooled by the signal from a Pioneer spacecraft since it passed all of the tests described above). This example applies to all sky or drift surveys (where the telescope is not fixed on a specific target, but rather drifts across the sky to look at a large number of stars).

In a targeted search, we use a variation on this strategy to determine whether a signal is originating from a distant source. When a telescope detects an interesting signal, it automatically pans slightly away from the target star. The analysis software then notes how the strength of the signal varied when the telescope was on and off target. If the signal originates from a distant source, it should become weaker when the telescope moves away from the target. If the signal does not weaken as expected, the signal is most likely caused by local interference.

FOLLOW-UP OBSERVATIONS

Whenever researchers detect a promising candidate signal, and after they've weeded out obvious false alarms, the next step is to compare observations from two or more antennae watching the same area of the sky. If the signal is local in origin, either only one antenna detects it or it appears differently on the remote antenna (i.e., different strength, different Doppler drift profile, etc.).

Researchers look for differences in the observations from the two sites. If the signal can only be detected by one site, the signal is probably not a *bona fide* ET signal. However, if the signal can be detected at multiple sites, we would then compare the Doppler drift and power characteristics (power versus time, power versus frequency, etc.) of the two signals. This step provides another opportunity to weed out false targets (such as a signal originating from a satellite in an orbit that causes it to appear to be stationary with respect to the background star field when viewed from one location). A signal isn't handed off to a human observer for further scrutiny until it passes all of these tests.

SCORING CRITERIA

Since there is no single criteria that automatically pegs a signal as extraterrestrial, the criteria described in the previous sections need to be considered as a whole. Table 8-2 summarizes the criteria used to score a candidate signal. Notice how a signal can be discarded at several points in this process.

Table 8-2: *Ranking criteria for candidate ET signals*

CRITERIA NUMBER	CRITERIA	YES (PASS)	NO (FAIL)
1	Is this a narrowband signal (power concentrated in narrow band of frequencies)?	Possible ET signal or RFI, go to #2.	Unlikely ET signal, most likely RFI or natural source.
2	Does the signal display a Gaussian power curve (fixed antenna) or decrease in power when an antenna is aimed slightly off target (targeted search)?	Possible ET signal or RFI, go to #3.	Signal most likely due to RFI.
3	Does the signal stay tuned to a precise frequency and not drift over time?	Signal is most likely interference from a ground-based transmitter.	Possible ET signal or RFI, go to #4.
4	Does the signal's Doppler drift suggest the source is traveling at a speed of ± several miles per second?	Signal is most likely RFI from a satellite in low Earth orbit (this signal should have also failed test #2).	Possible ET signal or RFI, go to #5.
5	If viewed over long period of time, does the signal's peak power change?	Not conclusive, but it improves the case for an ET signal because an interstellar radio signal will wax and wane due to absorption by interstellar medium.	If the signal's peak power stays precisely the same, this suggests it is RFI.
6	Can other, similarly equipped, distant telescopes detect the signal?	This rules out interference from a local source.	This suggests the signal is the result of local interference or a malfunction in the detection system.
7	Can the signal be observed over a long period of time at the same apparent point in the sky?	Strong case for an ET signal if it passes these other tests.	Inconclusive: an ET signal may be brief, and only detectable for a short period of time.

Just because a candidate signal passes all of these tests doesn't automatically peg it as an ET signal. At this point, astronomers would observe the source in greater detail and attempt to rule out all possible man-made and natural causes before concluding that it was sent by another civilization. The source of the signal would be placed under the largest microscope (or telescope) possible and scrutinized in every way possible before researchers would finally admit the signal was real. And even then, there would still be some doubt about its existence.

Confirming lightwave signals

Lightwave (laser) signals are, in many respects, easier to confirm than radio signals because laser light is highly directional and projected in a very tight beam. We can take advantage of this characteristic to build receivers that are extremely sensitive to light coming from a specific direction and ignore light streaming in from other directions.

As we discussed in Chapter 7, *Lightwave (Laser) Communication*, we're currently searching for two types of laser signals: continuous (always on), and pulsed (strobe light) beacons. Unlike the radio signals we are searching for, laser signals would almost certainly come from a powerful beacon designed specifically for the purpose of communication. SETI radio searches are designed to look for both intentional beacons and leakage radiation (such as a radar signal used to track comets or asteroids). Because lasers are directional, it is extremely unlikely that another civilization would "leak" laser signals in random directions. If we detect a laser signal, it is much more likely that they have aimed that beam directly at us, knowing that Earth is a life-bearing planet and a possible site for intelligent life.

The good news with laser signals is that they are much less prone to man-made interference. The main source of interference in laser signals is the background glare from the stars they are orbiting. We discussed the techniques that can be used to overcome this background glare in Chapter 7.

Continuous laser beacons

As we discussed in the previous chapter, continuous laser beacons show up as spikes in a star's spectrograph (graph of the intensity of its light as a function of color). How easy this is to detect is primarily a function of the following:

- The strength of the laser.
- The precision of the laser. We will be looking to see if the laser is precisely tuned to a single wavelength, or whether it spreads its energy across a range of wavelengths (colors).

- The resolution of the receiver's spectrum analyzer. We will check to see how many colors the detector splits the incoming starlight into (the greater the resolution of the spectrometer, the greater our chances of seeing the spike we're looking for).

The main problem facing this type of search is background starlight. Because the laser attempts to outshine the star on a continuous basis, it must be very powerful and tuned to a precise wavelength. On the receiving end, we need a high-resolution spectrometer to split the incoming light into a large number of individual colors in order to have a decent chance of distinguishing the laser light from the background starlight.

While a pulsed laser beacon will not be easily mistaken for a natural source of radiation, it will be difficult to distinguish a continuous laser beacon from its background starlight. If the laser beam is extremely strong, and produces a pronounced spike in intensity in the star's spectrum, this will be a clear signal that something unusual is going on. However, if the laser causes a spike that is only slightly above the star's baseline light level, it will be harder to see and not be immediately clear whether the spike is from an artificial or naturally occurring source.

While many OSETI researchers think that pulsed laser beacons are more likely (because they are more energy efficient and easier to detect), we can look for continuous laser beacons in the course of doing conventional astronomy work. It is common practice to map a star's spectrum to learn about its chemical composition, whether it has planets, etc. As we improve the resolution of the spectrometers used to do this work, we will improve our ability to detect a continuous laser beacon embedded in a distant star's light. We're collecting this spectral data anyway, and by doing so, we are enabling SETI researchers to look for these signals after the fact.

Pulsed laser beacons

The basic signature we are looking for in a pulsed laser signal is a brief spike in the number of photons received within a very short period of time (millionths or billionths of a second). Because lasers can concentrate their energy into extremely brief pulses, we can build lasers that briefly outshine an entire star, even though the laser's average power consumption is modest. Lasers can do this because they are off 99.99 percent of the time, and concentrate all of their power into a tiny window of time.

As we discussed earlier, we use sensitive light detectors called *photomultipliers* to count the photons streaming in from a star one by one. The photons from the star will arrive at random intervals, and will be evenly spread out over time. The artificial signal will generate a large burst of photons that will arrive within a very short time period, at a rate much higher than that of the background photons.

The main sources of interference we will encounter in an optical detection system are caused by the radioactive decay of the materials used to build the detector itself, and by Cerenkov radiation, which comes from cosmic rays.

One of the primary sources of interference in an optical detection system is light produced by radioactive decay. This happens because the detection device itself contains trace amounts of radioactive elements. These elements decay, producing photons as a byproduct. This is a problem because the photodetectors can detect individual photons, so while the flash produced by the decay of a single Uranium atom is usually invisible to the naked eye, it is easily detected by the photodetector, as depicted in Figure 8-10.

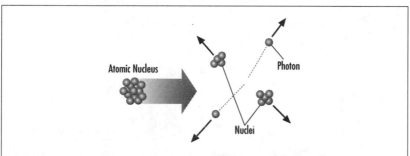

Figure 8-10: *During radioactive decay, an atom's nucleus splits into two smaller nuclei, producing a flash of light (photons).*

The fix for this problem is to use two or more independent photon detectors physically separated from each other. It is extremely unlikely that two radioactive decay events will occur at exactly the same time in both systems. Thus, if a flash is detected in only one detector, we conclude that is probably caused by radioactive decay. If the flash is detected in both detectors, we can be confident that the detected light originated from outside the detection device. Figure 8-11 illustrates what happens when a radioactive decay event triggers the detector, while Figure 8-12 illustrates what happens when an external light source triggers the detection system.

The simultaneous detection of a nanosecond flash of light in both detectors is a strong sign that the light originates from a source outside of the detection apparatus. However, this by itself does not peg the source as an ET signal.

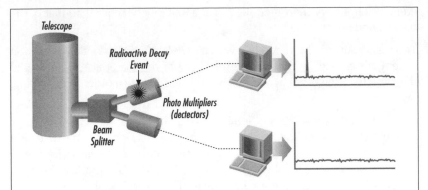

Figure 8-11: *The radioactive decay of material in one detector causes a false reading in one detector, but not the other. This event can be automatically discarded. Notice how one detector registers a spike while the other does not.*

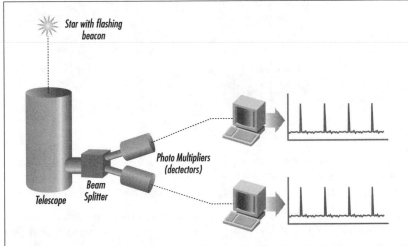

Figure 8-12: *When a flash of light enters from outside the telescope, both detectors detect it simultaneously.*

Because a pulsed laser beam is very likely a beacon signal, we would expect it to be detectable over an extended period of time, and possibly to be transmitting information in the form of coded digits.

The next thing we'll look for is a periodic pattern. A beacon signal will most likely repeat at precisely predictable intervals. We would expect to see flashes of light that repeat at precisely spaced intervals (e.g., the laser is on for exactly 5 ns, off for exactly 600 million ns, then on again for 5 ns). The precise timing of the flashes will rule out natural sources of radiation as the cause, and will increase our confidence that this is an extraterrestrial signal.

When we find a repeating, precisely timed source of light like this, the next step will be to observe the source from other telescopes outfitted to detect this type of signal. By observing the source from multiple telescopes, we can rule out false alarms due to local interference and equipment malfunctions.

If we succeed in detecting such a precisely timed source of light from multiple telescopes, the only possible explanation remaining is that the signal is an extraterrestrial beacon, or the signal is the result of an unknown natural process that can produce accurately timed and very brief flashes of light. Analyzing the signal to determine whether or not it is carrying encoded information can quickly help disprove the latter explanation.

A laser signal, because it must be aimed directly at our solar system to be detected, would most likely be an intentional attempt at communication. The sender would need to aim the laser directly at us, and would probably not do this unless they thought there was a purpose in doing so. Although this is less likely to occur, the job of detecting this type of signal is much easier since the sender is making a deliberate attempt to establish communication. This is the opposite situation compared to a microwave band transmission where we could detect either an intentional or leakage signal. If we detect a laser-based signal, it is more likely that the signal will contain useful information (whether we can comprehend its contents is another matter entirely).

Signal detection

The big question, of course, is: what happens if we confirm the detection of a signal from another civilization? The scientific community has published a detailed set of procedures that should be followed if we were to establish communication with another world. Contrary to popular belief, this information will not be sequestered from the public. In fact, the follow-up detection process, required to positively verify any signal, guarantees that it will be impossible to keep the news secret for any length of time.

These procedures are outlined in the "Declaration of Principles Concerning the Activities Following the Detection of Extraterrestrial Intelligence." The full-text of this document is available online from the SETI Institute at *http://www.seti.org/science/principles.html*.

What this document says, in effect, is that no signal can be confirmed without the involvement of hundreds of scientists around the world, all of whom will most likely have an Internet connection. Even if someone wanted to keep the information secret, it would be impossible. Apart from making it virtually impossible to censor the detection, this process is also designed to provide the scientific community with an ongoing opportunity to debate the origin of the signal—partly to further reduce the odds of a false alarm, and partly to foster a healthy public debate about the cause and source of the signal.

Needle in a haystack

The failure to detect a verifiable extraterrestrial signal is more a sign of the immaturity of our search than it is evidence of our uniqueness in the universe. The reason for this is that the amount of work required to search the entire sky for ET signals dwarfs the work that has been done to date.

To understand the scope of the search, SETI researchers create what is known as a *search space*. Think of this as a geometrical object, like a box, that represents the total volume of territory that must be surveyed. This box does not represent the physical dimensions of space, as we perceive it, but rather the total number of frequencies and positions in the night sky that must be analyzed.

Researchers use a formula similar to the one below to estimate the total number of combinations of frequencies and positions in the sky that must be tried in order to conduct a thorough search:

$$N = n_f \times n_p$$

In this formula, the factor n_f represents the total number of frequency bins, or channels, that need to be analyzed. For microwave SETI searches, this number ranges between 1×10^{10} to 1×10^{11} (10 to 100 billion discrete channels). For optical SETI searches for pulsed beacons, this number ranges between 1 to 100 discrete frequency bins. For optical SETI searches for continuous beacons, like microwave SETI, the number is large because the incoming light must be split into a large number of narrow color (frequency) bins.

The factor n_p represents the total number of positions in the sky that must be searched. This is not always the same as the number of stars to be examined. This number is a function of the sensitivity of the receiving antenna or telescope, which determines the instrument's field of view. The more sensitive the instrument, the narrower its field of view, and therefore, the greater number of possible aiming positions. For example, a telescope that looks at 1 millionth of the sky must be cycled through approximately 1 million different aiming positions to survey the entire sky ($n_p = 1$ million).

So, let's plug in some numbers to estimate the amount of work that needs to be done to conduct a thorough search for an extraterrestrial radio signal.

This search requires that we examine roughly 100 billion discrete frequencies (channels), and that we look at 10 million different positions in the sky.

Using these numbers, we get the following result:

$$N = 1 \times 10^{11} \times 1 \times 10^7 = 10^{18}$$

This result, $N=10^{18}$, means that we have to try 10^{18}, or 1 quintillion, different combinations to survey the entire range of possible sources and frequencies for an ET signal. If the transmitter transmits in our direction only part of the time, the search becomes further complicated due to the addition of a temporal dimension to the search space. For example, if another civilization transmits in our direction only 1 percent of the time (perhaps they cycle their transmitter among a list of target stars), this increases the search space by an additional factor of 100.

Anyway you look at it, this is a large number. This example also understates the scope of the search because it does not take into account other factors that affect the odds of detection, including:

- Receiver duty cycle (percentage of time our antennae look at each target star)
- Civilization lifespan (the L factor from the Drake Equation)
- The odds that a real signal will be misinterpreted as our own radio frequency interference

This situation will change dramatically in about five years, when the Allen Telescope Array, the first radiotelescope designed for full-time SETI use, goes online. The telescope array, which is being built at the Hat Creek Radio Observatory, will be much more sensitive than today's radiotelescope, and will be able to conduct microwave SETI searches on a continuous basis. This will improve the odds of detecting a signal many fold.

BRINGING SETI HOME

On May 17, 1999, a talented group of radioastronomers and computer scientists at the University of California, Berkeley released a revolutionary computer program that would quickly become the world's most successful experiment in distributed computing. The project, called *SETI@home*, instantly attracted tens of thousands of SETI enthusiasts, and re-ignited worldwide public interest in the search for extraterrestrial intelligence.

A typical desktop computer is capable of performing a few million calculations per second. While this is fast by human standards, it is nothing compared to the amount of computing power needed to detect and process interstellar radio signals. For that, you need a supercomputer. But how do you get a supercomputer when you don't have the budget for one? The answer is easy: just commandeer the idle time on other computers to do the work for you through a process known as *distributed computing*.

The basic concept for the SETI@home project was to build a screensaver that could run on any computer (Windows, Macintosh, Unix/Linux, etc.), which could run in the background while the user was doing something else. The screensaver would harness the computer's unused processing power and put it to good use crunching on data collected by the Arecibo Radio Observatory and Project SERENDIP. By splitting the giant flow incoming data from the Arecibo telescope into many bite-sized chunks of data, the SETI@home team was able to turn an overwhelming task into work that could be doled out to many relatively slow computers.

SETI@home solves an important problem in microwave SETI search programs. It makes computing power cheap. Searching for an artificial signal in the microwave band requires the listener to sift through billions of frequencies to look for a fleeting signal that would betray the existence of a civilization orbiting a distant star. In order to have any hope of hearing a faint signal, SETI researchers are forced to build computers capable of performing trillions of calculations per second—a speed that outpaces even the fastest computers in existence today.

Prior to the invention of the SETI@home program, SETI researchers were forced to custom-build their own spectrum analyzers, expensive pieces of computing hardware designed to split incoming signals into millions—and sometimes hundreds of millions—of narrow channels. Such hardware is not cheap. In order to build these devices within a limited budget, researchers were forced to make compromises that limited the sensitivity of the detection systems.

While an individual PC is far too slow to process all of the data collected by UC Berkeley's Project SERENDIP, a network of thousands or millions of personal computers is a different story. That's exactly what the SETI@home team, did by distributing a free program over the Internet. In a little more than a year, over 2 million people worldwide downloaded the SETI@home program, creating the world's fastest supercomputer. So now that we know how signals are analyzed by SETI detection systems, let's take a look at how the SETI@home program works.

How SETI@home works

The SETI@home program can run either as a standalone application in the background while you're doing other work, or it can be set to screensaver mode, in which case it's only activated when your system is idle for a predetermined amount of time.

The SETI@home program does not actually detect signals in real-time. Instead, it is focused on processing archived, raw data collected by the Arecibo Radio Observatory receivers to look for patterns that would betray the existence of extraterrestrial signal. SETI@home works in conjunction with Project SERENDIP,* which is a passive observation program that currently uses the Arecibo Radio Observatory to look for extraterrestrial radio signals. This means that the SERENDIP system looks at whatever other astronomers are looking at. While the SERENDIP team cannot handpick the stars they want to survey, they have the advantage of being able to monitor

---

* SERENDIP stands for "Search for Extraterrestrial Radio Emissions from Nearby Developed Intelligent Populations." Additional information about Project SERENDIP can be found online at *http://seti.ssl.berkeley.edu/serendip/serendip.html*.

the skies on an almost continual basis (a real feat, since dedicated telescope time is a rare commodity). This is a multistage process, consisting of the following steps:

- Raw data from the telescope is first collected and archived. This signal is digitized (converted to numbers) and stored on disk or tape for analysis. This data is also annotated to include a timestamp, sky coordinates, and information about the status of the receiving equipment during the time of the observation.

- The raw data is divided into chunks, or timeslots, which represent approximately 107 seconds each. The signal is also broken down into many different channels (similar to the way a stereo equalizer works). This creates blocks of data small enough for a desktop computer to analyze in a reasonable amount of time. A typical data unit can be processed in 10 to 20 hours, depending on the speed of the computer's microprocessor and amount of memory.

- When SETI@home launches for the first time, or when it finished processing a data unit, the client application connects to a group of servers at UC Berkeley to request a data unit. The SETI@home server assigns a block of data to the user, and sends the data to the PC. The amount of raw data sent in a work unit is actually pretty small (about 340,000 bytes). The computer does not need to have a high-speed Internet connection to participate; a 340-Kbyte data unit takes about 2.5 minutes to download over a 28.8-Kbps connection.

- Signals are broken down into thousands of individual channels. This process is explained in more detail in Chapter 6, *Radio Communication* and Chapter 8, *Signal Processing and Confirmation*. For now, think of this like a stereo equalizer, except it breaks the signal into thousands of channels ("tones") instead of just a few channels.

- The program then examines the resulting signal (now split into hundreds or thousands of channels) to look for signals that spike above a certain power threshold. If it finds a spike, the spike is tested again and bookmarked for additional testing.

- Spikes are examined to determine whether they fit into what is known as a *Gaussian curve*. (In the context of a radiotelescope, "Gaussian curve" refers to how the power of an incoming signal varies over time.) The Arecibo telescope receives signals as the Earth rotates on its axis, giving the signal coming from a distant source a unique signature. As the Earth rotates and a signal comes into "view," the signal's power level will increase from zero, peak, and then decrease to zero in a span of approximately 12 seconds. This is the amount of time it takes a target star to drift across the telescope's narrow field of view. If a signal fails this test, it's most likely coming from a local (i.e., human) source, rather than from an alien source. If the signal passes the Gaussian curve test, it will be subject to further scrutiny and analysis to determine the validity of the signal.

The desktop computer processes the data unit while the system is idle, or as a process running in the background, depending on how the user has set the preferences. Upon completing its work, the SETI@home client uploads the processed results to a bank of servers at UC Berkeley and requests a new block of raw data. The SETI@home client spends most of its time crunching numbers and displaying its results on screen. Typically, it will spend several hours processing each data unit (the amount of time required depends on the speed of the machine and how much time its owner spends performing other tasks).

If a signal passes the Gaussian test, the software notes the event and includes it in the results it sends back to the SETI@home team. All spikes and Gauss-ians are catalogued for further analysis during future telescope passes and for targeted search programs. If a similar signature is found during multiple tele-scope passes over a period of time, this will be strong indicator that there is something out there that merits detailed analysis by other observers.

The SETI@home client analyzes data in many different ways. It does this because, while we know generally what type of signal to expect (we're look-ing for radio waves that are tuned to a very precise frequency), we don't know the details of how a signal might change over time, or how it might be used to convey information. So, the SETI@home client processes the same block of data using many different assumptions to look for different types of radio carriers.

A key component in this system is a centralized task manager. This com-puter, or cluster of computers, serves as a dispatcher by assigning data units to individual computers, much like a taxi dispatcher hands off fares to differ-ent drivers. The server's primary function is to make sure that the desktop PCs aren't unnecessarily duplicating each other's work (i.e., several comput-ers processing the same block of raw data). The server's secondary task is to make sure that the data sent out for processing is completed within a speci-fied time frame. For example, if a computer doesn't return its results within a certain number of days, it reassigns the data unit to another user. As an extra measure of quality assurance, two different users process each data unit. Once the finished results are received and analyzed, the data unit is placed back in the loop to be sent to another user. Only after a data unit has been processed twice is it considered "retired."

Reading SETI@home's results

The SETI@home client presents information to the user in an easy-to-read format. Although it does not tell the user about every candidate signal it has analyzed, it allows the user to see, at a glance, how its work is proceeding. Figure 9-1 shows the key features of the SETI@home display.

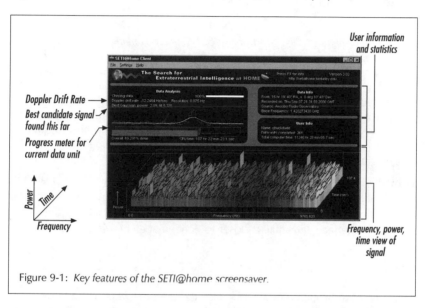

Figure 9-1: *Key features of the SETI@home screensaver.*

The program displays five major pieces of information, separated into three specific sections:

Data analysis

> The upper-left section of the SETI@home program displays information about the type of analysis currently being performed.

> The program also displays the best candidate signal found so far (including its power and Gaussian fit scores).

> The bottom half of the display shows a frequency/power/time graph of the data as it is processed by the program. The program continually updates this display as it makes multiple passes through each block of raw data. The 3D axis shown in Figure 9-1 explains how the information is organized in the graph.

Data information

> Here you'll see information specific to the data unit currently being processed by the SETI@home screensaver. This section indicates the date,

time, and location of the observation, as well as the sky coordinates that were monitored during the Arecibo radiotelescope's 107-second pass.

User information

This section contains information about the user, including username, summary statistics about the number of data units processed, and the total CPU time used by the program.

NOTE

This information is displayed only if SETI@home is being used on a system with a graphical interface, such as Windows or Mac OS, or if the user specifically requests to do so on a Unix or Linux system running a version of the X Window System. Unix and Linux users also have the opportunity to run SETI@home as a shell process on their systems, which is typically faster because the computer doesn't use computational power to draw the graphics in an X Window. To learn how to run SETI@home effectively, see the README file that's included with the program.

With this information, the user can see, at a glance, which star system is being analyzed, the most interesting signals detected so far, and a summary of how the analysis is proceeding. Now that we know about SETI@home's basic user interface, let's take a closer look at what all of this means.

Spikes

In its first pass through a new block of data, the SETI@home client first performs a Fast Fourier Transform (FFT). This process splits the signal into many very narrow channels. This is analogous to a home stereo equalizer, except the number of channels is much, much larger.

When the program is looking at random noise, the signal power level, within each narrow channel, will be more or less equal. If this were played out as audio, you would hear the steady hiss of white noise. When the system picks up an artificial signal, the signal power will be markedly higher within one or more of the narrow channels (frequency bins) produced by the FFT process. This would sound like a steady tone against a background of hissing noise.

This is the type of signature the program looks for on its first pass through the raw data. This pattern is called a spike. A power spike can have many causes, the most likely of which is human-generated radio frequency interference. The antenna might have picked up a satellite transmitter, an earthbound walkie-talkie conversation, or any number of different sources of microwave radiation. In fact, the SETI@home program has cataloged several hundred million such signals since its launch, none of which have yet proved to be extraterrestrial in origin.

Merely detecting a spike is not enough. The fleeting signal must next be examined to measure how it varies in its frequency and power over time. This tells the observer much more about the origin of the signal.

(Im)perfect pitch

Any *bona fide* ET signal will probably drift across several frequencies (tones) during the time it is visible at a rate linked to the Earth's rotation. If the signal originates from a terrestrial source, it will most likely remain fixed on a single frequency or drift randomly due to inaccuracies in the transmitter. If the signal originates from a very distant source, its frequency drifts in accordance with the earth's rotation and orbit around the sun. How a signal's frequency varies over time can then be used to determine, in part, whether it is coming from a local or very distant source.

The SETI@home software builds a three-dimensional plot depicting the incoming signal. This plot divides the horizontal dimension into many frequency bins across the width of the screen. Each bin represents the frequency band, or tone, of the signal. The vertical dimension represents signal strength; the higher the bar, the stronger the signal. The depth dimension represents time. The signal graph scrolls backward, deeper into the display, as the signal is analyzed in discrete time intervals.

If a signal drifts across frequencies, the SETI@home client will not immediately recognize it as extraterrestrial. This is because the power profile of the signal, when watching only one frequency, will not fit a Gaussian curve. The signal will appear to rise and fall in less than 12 seconds, and will not be recognized as a candidate signal.

The SETI@home client compensates for this by using a technique called *dechirping*. The client skews each successive frame of results by a small amount (i.e., 1 Hz) per time interval. For example, if the software tests for a signal that is drifting by 1 Hz per second, a skew rate of 1 Hz per second is applied to that signal by shifting each new row of data one channel to the right. Therefore, when the program looks at a signal drifting at a similar rate, it will closely match the power characteristics expected of a signal emanating from a very distant source.

Another problem is that we won't know the rate at which an incoming signal drifts across frequencies. Because of this, the program needs to test many different skew rates (e.g., look for signals that are drifting to higher frequencies at varying rates and signals that drift to lower frequencies at different rates). This forces the program to repeatedly analyze the frequency/time/power plot to look for signals that are skewed at an unknown rate. This significantly increases the amount of computation required to look for the signal.

The Earth's daily rotation will introduce a Doppler shift of about 2,700 Hz to a signal, as observed from Earth's equator, whose primary frequency is 1.5 GHz. Throughout the course of a 24-hour cycle, this hypothetical signal would drift from about 1,499,997,220 Hz to 1,500,002,780 Hz. The Doppler shift occurs because the speed of light is fixed. As such, the signal will appear to be on a higher frequency when the transmitter travels toward the receiver, and a lower frequency when it travels away from the receiver. A similar, but smaller drift is introduced by the Earth's orbit around the sun. However, since it takes the Earth 365 days to complete one circuit around the sun, this effect is much less pronounced over short periods of time than the effect of the Earth's daily rotation.

Imperfections in transmitting equipment also cause frequency drift. We can make microwave transmitters capable of holding a frequency to within a few parts per billion of accuracy. While we can make very good transmitters, we cannot make receivers that hold a pure tone with absolute perfection. Because of this, imperfections in the transmitter may cause frequency drift. However, we can probably assume that a civilization sophisticated enough to broadcast across interstellar distances will know how to eliminate most of these flaws in their radio equipment, just as we are on the path toward doing ourselves.

Gaussian (power versus time) fit test

A candidate signal must also pass a *Gaussian fit test*. This test is designed to weed out signal spikes that result from terrestrial interference of some sort.

As a signal drifts across the telescope's beam, it displays a curve like the one shown in Figure 9-2, with its power rising from an ambient noise level to a peak signal in about six seconds, and then decreasing back to ambient noise in another six seconds. The signal will not blink on and off. Instead, it will gradually peak and wane.

The SETI@home software tests spikes to see how well they match this Gaussian power curve by comparing peak power levels to power levels measured at 1 to 10 seconds before and after the peak. The software then compares measured values against the ideal values expected for an ideal signal. The program compares the measured and ideal values, and looks for differences (error measurements) in the signal over the 12-second time interval. If a signal is a perfect Gaussian, there is no error. If not, the sum of the errors is a non-zero value. The lower the number, the better the score. Figure 9-3 illustrates this process in simplified form.

The Gaussian fit test is important because it discriminates between spikes made by our own radio frequency interference (RFI), and a *bona fide* signal

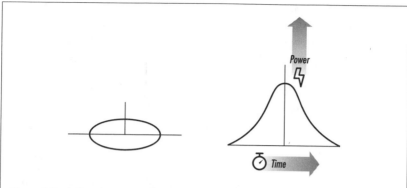

Figure 9-2: *A Gaussian curve, illustrating how an alien signal might look as it passes through the Arecibo radiotelescope field of view.*

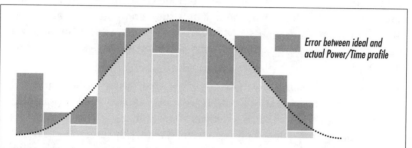

Figure 9-3: *An example candidate signal overlaid onto an ideal Gaussian curve. The shaded area represents the discrepancy between the real and ideal signals. The smaller the shaded area, the better the fit.*

that originated from a very distant source. As discussed in Chapter 6, a distant source passes through the antenna's field of vision within about 12 seconds. If the signal comes from a ground-based source, it will most likely be visible for longer than 12 seconds. If the signal is coming from an orbiting satellite, it will pass through the antenna's field of view in less than 12 seconds. Hence, the duration of a power spike, and the shape of the curve (power versus time), tells us a lot about the source of the unknown signal.

Cataloging and post-processing

The SETI@home software is primarily designed to automate the busy work that requires a lot of computing time and repetitive analysis. Its primary function is to weed out the millions of anomalous signals caused by terrestrial interference and background noise, and to provide human astronomers with a much shorter list of candidate signals that merit closer inspection. The program catalogs all spikes and, upon completion of each data unit, sends the following information back to UC Berkeley in a summary log file:

- Exact date/time of the event, in Greenwich Mean Time (GMT)

- Sky coordinates observed (derived from time stamp)

- Frequency/power/time plot for the signal (to permit further analysis of data)

- Gaussian fit test score

When the program detects a signal with a particularly good power profile and Gaussian score, the SETI@home team performs a detailed and intensive series of calculations on the candidate signal. This type of analysis is done on only a relatively small number of events (compared to the total number of events observed), and can be done on a conventional high-speed workstation, rather than with the aid of a supercomputer. Signals that pass this follow-up test are then sent to human observers who examine the signal's location and power profile to see if it matches any known terrestrial sources.

If a candidate signal passes these tests, the team then requests that a targeted search system, such as the SETI Institute's Project Phoenix or Harvard University's BETA system, take a detailed look at that star system to see if the signal recurs. A truly interesting signal would attract the attention of observatories worldwide. If the same signal could be detected by multiple, independent facilities, it would be strong evidence that radio contact has been made with another civilization. Any unusual signal would be examined in great detail before public announcements were made.

Results so far

Searching for extraterrestrial intelligence is an exhaustive process that requires a lot of computing power. Here are some interesting statistics about SETI@home:

- SETI@home was launched on May 17, 1999 in the hope of getting 5,000 users to register and run the program. As of its one-year anniversary, SETI@home had over 2 million registered users.

- SETI@home makes up one-third of UC Berkeley's computing power.

- SETI@home servers transfer 22 Mbytes of data per second.

- Ten people connect to the SETI@home servers every second.

- The SETI@home web site receives:
  - 1 million hits per day
  - 100,000 unique visitors per day
- The SETI@home servers transmit 15 work units per second.
- Two different users process each work unit twice, to ensure the accuracy of the processing. Once a work unit is marked complete, it's deleted from the server.

To date, SETI@home users have processed nearly 250 million data units. While the SETI@home team has detected many interesting candidates, none of the signals have passed the scrutiny of the candidate signal screening process discussed in Chapter 8. However, the SETI@home team plans to conduct a follow-up survey to take a detailed look at the most promising candidates collected during the project's first pass.

TELEPORTING BITS

If another civilization has gone through the trouble of constructing a power-ful radio or laser beacon, chances are they are doing so in a conscious attempt to establish communication, and not merely to just say "Hi there!" So next, we must consider the different techniques that can be used to embed information in a radio or light wave signal.

To embed information in a radio or lightwave carrier, we use a technique called *modulation* to subtly alter one or more characteristics of the underly-ing signal to represent coded information. We might do this by slightly changing the frequency of a radio signal, or by manipulating the timing between laser light flashes. We'll discuss the specific techniques used to embed information in different types of signals shortly.

Numbers, in turn, can be used to represent virtually any type of informa-tion. Nearly every type of media we encounter today (from newspapers to television broadcasts), at some point in its creation or delivery, is converted into a series of binary numbers. Newspapers, for example, are authored on computers. Television broadcasts transmit in high-definition digital formats for which the images must be reduced to series of binary numbers. The fact that information is now managed in a digital format is not accidental. Digital information can be stored, broadcast, and reproduced without introducing errors.

In this chapter, we'll discuss some of the ways in which scientists can embed digital information in a radio or lightwave signal. This will provide us with some guidance in knowing what to expect should we encounter an informa-tion-bearing signal from another solar system.

Binary code

The simplest scheme for transmitting information is *binary code*. Binary code is derived from the binary numbering system, which has only two digits: 1 and 0. Higher order numbering systems, such as the decimal system (with its numbers 0 through 9) and others, can all be reduced to binary code.

Binary numbers read just like decimal numbers. The only difference between the two is that each digit in a number can have only two possible values, versus the ten possible values in a decimal system. One may represent larger numbers by combining many digits into a long string. As we can see in Figure 10-1, the number 38 is represented in binary form as 100110, or $(1 \times 32) + (0 \times 16) + (0 \times 8) + (1 \times 4) + (1 \times 2) + (0 \times 1)$.

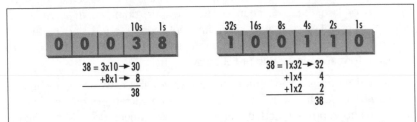

Figure 10-1: *Binary code can represent any number. The example above depicts the number 38 represented in decimal and binary form.*

Numbers can represent all types of information. For example, the 64-digit binary number on the right of Figure 10-2 can represent the black and white image on the left . This image, called a *bitmap*, is laid out on an 8 × 8-pixel grid, consisting of a total of 64 picture elements; each block represents one element, or *pixel*. Each pixel is represented by a binary digit (0 for white, and 1 for black).

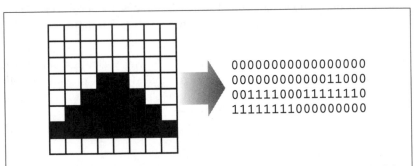

Figure 10-2: *The 64-digit number on the right represents the bitmap image on the left in binary form.*

Sounds and other wave-like signals can be represented digitally as a stream of digits (Figure 10-3). For example, a typical compact disc recording represents sound in a stream of 16-digit binary numbers (44,000 numbers, or samples, per second). The sound wave played by a CD player is sampled at 44,000 times per second, with a 16-digit number used to represent each sample (for a total of 704,000 digits per second).

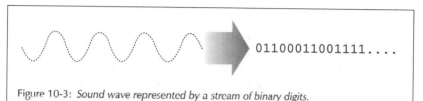

01100011001111. . . .

Figure 10-3: *Sound wave represented by a stream of binary digits.*

Binary numbers can also represent symbols and letters of the alphabet, with digital encoding performed by computers (Figure 10-4). In North America, the ASCII code represents letters, numbers, and other symbols with numeric codes (e.g., $A = 65$, $B = 66$, $C = 67$, and so on). Other encoding systems, such as Unicode, represent the letters in from many different alphabets in a numeric format.

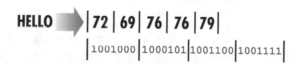

Figure 10-4: *The letters for the word "HELLO" are converted to ASCII code, which can then be converted to binary code for digital representation.*

Numbers are far from boring. They can be used as proxies for symbols, computer instructions, images, and all types of information. This, as we'll discuss shortly, is the key to creating a message that can be easily deciphered on the receiving end. Numbers are also useful because, while we may have a completely different way of communicating, we can assume that any technological civilization will understand mathematics.

Binary computing

Aside from being the simplest numbering scheme, binary code is the foundation upon which we've built computers. Binary code can represent both numbers and logical instructions for computer processing. This crossover capability makes binary code especially interesting as a format for communication.

Digital computers are built upon binary arithmetic and Boolean logic. While a computer may handle complex tasks like editing a document, it does all of its thinking in terms of Boolean statements, such as the following:

If A Is Greater Than B, Then Run Procedure 1, Otherwise (Else) Run Procedure 2.

Computers use hardware to store, manipulate, and compare binary numbers. In order to build general purpose computing devices that can run an infinite variety of programs, we combine this hardware with a system for storing and retrieving instructions from persistent memory (random access memory, or RAM). While the overall behavior of a computer may be quite complex, computers are built from a collection of simple logic circuits. One such device is an *AND gate* (Figure 10-5).

Figure 10-5: *Schematic of an AND gate. This AND gate accepts two inputs (a and b), and produces one output signal (a digit).*

An AND gate compares two or more binary digits, or strings of binary numbers (inputs), and then produces an output number, as shown in Table 10-1. This output number is also a binary number with two possible values.

Table 10-1: *Possible states for an AND gate*

INPUT BIT A	INPUT BIT B	OUTPUT BIT
0 (False)	0 (False)	0 (False)
0 (False)	1 (True)	0 (False)
1 (True)	0 (False)	0 (False)
1 (True)	1 (True)	1 (True)

AND gates and other logic circuits are built using transistors. A transistor, as shown in Figure 10-6, has three wires. Transistors act very much like a faucet. Two of the leads, *a* and *b*, represent piping water that passes through the valve; the third lead, *c*, functions like a valve. By modifying the electrical voltage applied to the third lead, we can adjust the amount of electrical current flowing through the transistor.

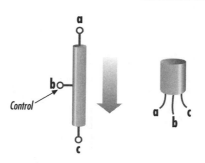

Figure 10-6: *A transistor functions a lot like an electrical valve. By adjusting the voltage applied to the third lead (c) on the transistor, we can modify the amount of electrical current allowed to flow through the device. The symbol on the left represents a transistor in some simplified circuitry schematics.*

A simple AND gate can be built using two transistors (Figure 10-7). The input signals (bits), a and b, control the flow of current through the device. The signals from the input wires a and b control the flow of current through the device. If both a and b are on (a=1, b=1), current flows unimpeded through the device to the output wire (output = 1). If either a or b are off (0), current does not flow through the device, and the output signal is off.

The circuit depicted in the diagram above can be used as an AND gate. Notice now the leads a and b connect to the transistors. A battery connects to a loop of wire that is connected to the transistors in such a way that, if both a and b are ON, the current from the battery flows freely through both transistors, and creates a positive voltage at the output terminal. If either a or b are OFF, one or both of the transistors resists the flow of electrical current, and consequently there is no measurable voltage at the output terminal.

This is just one example of a logic circuit built using transistors. We can build similar circuits to perform basic arithmetic (e.g., add, subtract, multiply, and divide numbers), to store and retrieve digits in persistent memory, and to compare digits and strings of digits (e.g., compare two numbers to determine which is largest). While these are relatively simple functions, when combined, they are the foundation upon which sophisticated computer programs and microprocessors (CPUs) are built.

Binary biology

DNA is an excellent example of a digital storage system. DNA encodes instructions for building proteins using triplet (sets of three) chemical base pairs. DNA base pairs are chemical symbols that represent the amino acids

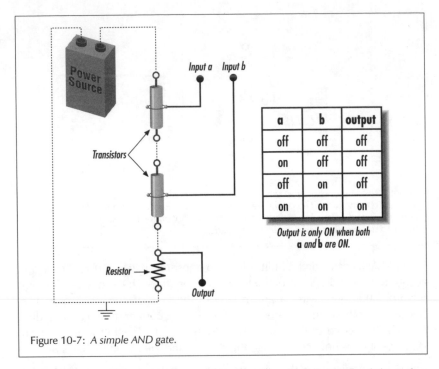

a	b	output
off	off	off
on	off	off
off	on	off
on	on	on

Output is only ON when both a and b are ON.

Figure 10-7: *A simple AND gate.*

from which complex proteins are built. You can literally think of the information encoded in DNA the same way you would think of a file stored on a disk drive, except that this file describes how to build a living organism instead of a spreadsheet program.

This is why numbers are so interesting as a means of transmitting information. While a string of numbers may not appear to be very interesting, we can use numbers to describe an infinite variety of ideas, something we'll discuss at length in Part III, *Communicating with Other Worlds*.

Binary code is especially relevant to interstellar communication because it is easily represented in radio and lightwave signals, and is easily detected and decoded. Each digit in a binary number has two possible states. To transmit binary digits via radio or light wave signals, the transmitter modifies their signals to flip-flop between two possible formats. When the signal is in one state (e.g., the laser's color is red), it represents one digit (e.g., 0). When the signal is another markedly different state (e.g., green), it represents the other possible digit (e.g., 1).

This general approach can be used to transmit a long series of arbitrary binary numbers using a radio or light wave communication link. At this point, we're not concerned with how the digits are organized, or what they mean, just how we can embed them in the underlying signal.

Biology offers great insight into how we can organize information within a coded message that is easy to parse and decipher on the receiving end. This is something we'll cover in detail in the latter half of the book.

Radio signals

We can transmit binary numbers in many ways using a radio signal, each of which has its advantages and disadvantages. The four basic techniques for transmitting information by radio are:

Amplitude modulation (AM)
> This technique modifies the strength of the signal to convey information (e.g., high transmitter power level represents 1, while a lower power level represents 0). This approach has several problems and is not acceptable for interstellar communication, mainly because AM signals are especially prone to interference.

Frequency shift modulation (FSK)
> In frequency shift keying, the sender varies the frequency, or tone, of the signal to convey information. For example, the sender transmits on one frequency to send a "1" digit, and on another frequency to send a "0" digit.

Phase shift modulation (PSK)
> A phase shift keyed signal is always on, and always transmits on the same frequency. This is called a symmetric carrier, and is easier to detect. Altering the phase of the signal helps to convey information, something we'll explain in a moment.

Polarization
> Polarization keying works by altering the polarization of the photons emitted by the radio transmitter. This type of signal is always on and tuned to a precise frequency, so it is easier to detect. We'll discuss polarity modulation in greater detail shortly.

The basic idea is the same in all of these cases. We modify the radio signal slightly during the course of the transmission. By making subtle changes to the signal, it is possible to encode digital information in the form of binary digits, without making the signal itself much harder to detect.

Of these four techniques, the two best schemes to use are phase shift and polarization modulation, which can be used exclusively or together. These two techniques maximize the ease with which the receiver can detect the signal.

BEST BETS: DETECTION AND DECODING

The two methods most favored by SETI researchers are phase shift and polarity shift because these signals can be observed with a receiver that is not specifically designed to be sensitive to phase or polarization changes. A receiver that is not designed to see the information in the signal will merely see a continuous, pure tone. This makes the signal easy to detect during an initial survey to detect sources of microwave radiation.

Once the receiver succeeds in detecting a signal, the signal will be scrutinized to see if it is using these forms of modulation to transmit information, and to see if weaker signals on nearby frequencies are being used to transmit larger quantities of information.

Phase and polarization modulation maximize the initial detectability of the signal while also making it easy to detect the encoded digits overlaid onto the radio carrier.

Amplitude modulation

The simplest scheme for transmitting digits by radio is amplitude modulation (AM). This is the scheme we depicted in our simplest transmitter example in Chapter 6, *Radio Communication*.

With AM, the transmitter's power level conveys information. For example, transmitting at high power might mean 1, while transmitting at a lower power level might mean 0 (Figure 10-8). This approach is acceptable over short distances in an interference-free environment. However, it is not acceptable for long-range communication (and has been largely discarded in our own communication networks).

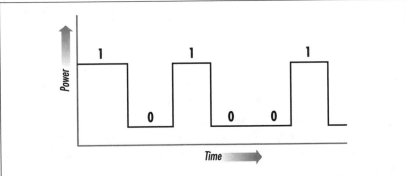

Figure 10-8: *An amplitude modulated (AM) signal indicates digits using differences in signal strength during transmission. In this example, a high power level means 1, while a low power level means 0.*

The main downside to AM is the effect of background noise on the signal. AM signals are more susceptible to the effects of background noise when the transmitter is sending at a lower power level because we have no control over or way to eliminate background noise. In a pristine, noise-free environment, however, the recipient would clearly see the difference between the strong and weak signal (Figure 10-9).

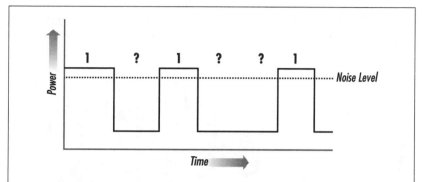

Figure 10-9: *An amplitude modulated signal, when it's competing with background noise, is harder to decode. When the transmitter operates at lower power, the receiver may be uncertain whether the transmitted digit is 0 or 1.*

When a signal competes with background noise, it is harder to detect when the transmitter operates at low power. This leads to a situation in which the background noise confuses the receiver, causing it to mistake a 0 for a 1 digit, or vice versa. This also makes the signal harder to detect because it is easier to see a continuously broadcast carrier than an AM carrier that flashes on and off. This type of pattern requires more effort (and more computation) to detect. It is also not a very efficient way to transmit information (inherently low data transfer speed).

Frequency shift keying

Frequency shift keying was widely employed until recently, and is still used by many older computer modems. The basic premise in FSK is to use the carrier frequency to signify a number. A high frequency might signify a 1 digit, while a lower frequency might signify a 0 digit.

This approach is better than AM because both signals can be sent at an arbitrarily high power level. The intensity of the signal has no bearing on the information being sent, so the receiver can ignore the strength of the signal and focus on its frequency (or tone).

This is conceptually similar to using musical notes to transmit data. A high note would mean "1," while a low note would mean "0." These musical notes could then be combined in any order to send an arbitrarily long series of binary numbers. Just replace sound waves with radio waves, and it's the same principle.

To decode a frequency shift keyed signal, we look at how the primary frequency of the signal varies over time. In Figure 10-10, the signal hops between two frequencies, A and B (A=0 while B=1). This example decodes to the series of numbers 01101101.

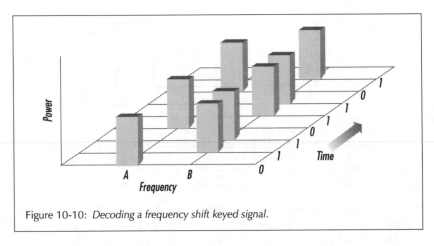

Figure 10-10: *Decoding a frequency shift keyed signal.*

This technique also has problems. The main problem is the transmitter alternates between frequencies. A receiver will see the signal as two "flashing" radio signals, each on different frequencies that wink on and off. This makes the signal harder to detect because the signal appears weaker compared to the background noise. As a result, this type of signal may flunk out in the early stages of the detection process because it is more easily confused with background noise.

NOTE

Phase shift modulation is harder to explain. If you have not studied physics or electrical engineering, you may have a difficult time with this concept. If it's not immediately clear to you, don't worry about it. The concept of phase, and changing a signal's phase, has stumped many students.

Phase shift keying

A radio receiver translates a radio signal into a continuously varying electrical signal. This electrical signal, if we can isolate the radio carrier from all other signals, looks like the sine wave shown in Figure 10-11.

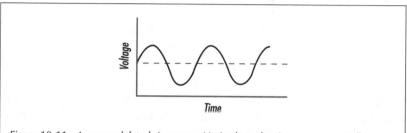

Figure 10-11: *An unmodulated sine wave. Notice how the sine wave repeatedly wavers between high and low values.*

The basic trick employed in phase shift keying is to reverse the phase of the sine wave. The easiest way to visualize this is to flip the sine wave over. When you do this, troughs replace the peaksand peaks replace troughs. The signal's frequency and strength doesn't change, but the sender can alternate between normal and reverse phase to embed information in the signal (Figure 10-12).

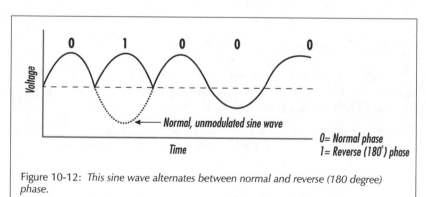

Figure 10-12: *This sine wave alternates between normal and reverse (180 degree) phase.*

Notice how there are three peaks in succession where there should normally be a peak followed by a trough followed by a peak. We can use these two different states to signify digits, for example, a normal phase equals 0, and a reverse phase equals 1. This method of encoding information is superior because it allows the sender to embed information in a signal without making the signal harder to detect. When someone first detects a phase modulated signal, they are unaware there is any information in the signal. They merely know that the strong carrier is always on and tuned to a precise frequency. If you could hear this signal, it would sound like a continuous, unwavering pure tone. Once the recipient scrutinizes the signal in further detail, he would see that the signal's phase flip-flopped over time—a strong sign that the carrier contains encoded information.

This type of continuous tone is ideal from a detection perspective because the receiver can use a long *integration time* to detect the tone. The concept of integration time is difficult to explain without going into more detailed math. Conceptually, it is similar to listening attentively for a specific, distant sound against environmental noise.

The basic principle the receiver employsis to listen to a band of frequencies for a long period of time (usually several seconds, which is a long time in the world of electronics and radio). The random background noise tends to cancel itself out, while an artificial signal reinforces itself. So, the longer the integration time the receiver uses when listening to a frequency, the more a pure tone signal gets boosted above the background noise level. This concept is akin to the idea of using a long exposure time to take a picture. By allowing more light (radio waves) to strike the film (radio receiver), you're able to tease out more detail in dim lighting conditions.

Polarization modulation

One of the unique features of light waves, including radio waves, is the manner in which its photons vibrate. As illustrated in Figure 10-13, all photons vibrate back and forth in a specific direction as they travel.

Photons in this example vibrate in either a left-right or up-down direction. The state of their polarization can convey information (e.g., left-right vibrating photon means 0, up-down vibrating photon means 1). The direction in which the photons vibrate determine the polarization of the signal. The direction of polarization can then be used to convey information (Figure 10-14).

This direction of vibration can also be used to represent information. For example, vertically polarized photons could represent a 1 digit, while horizontally polarized photons could represent a 0 digit. Decoding a polarized light or radio signal only requires the receiver to construct a pair of receivers, one that is sensitive to photons polarized in one plane (direction), and another that is sensitive to photons polarized in a perpendicular plane. The observer monitors the strength of the signal detected by each receiver; if the incoming signal is polarized, it will register more strongly on one receiver than the other. Figure 10-15 depicts a simplified dual receiver system.

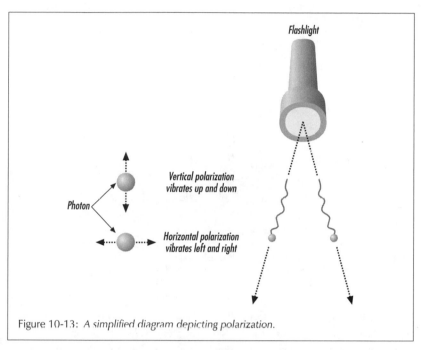

Figure 10-13: *A simplified diagram depicting polarization.*

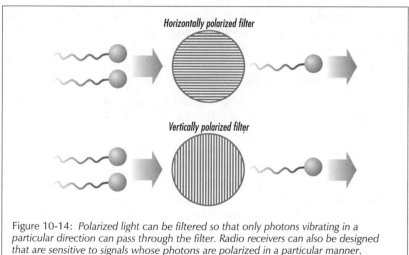

Figure 10-14: *Polarized light can be filtered so that only photons vibrating in a particular direction can pass through the filter. Radio receivers can also be designed that are sensitive to signals whose photons are polarized in a particular manner.*

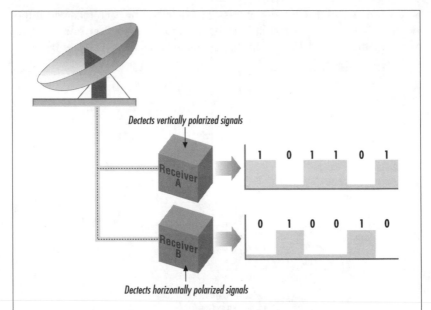

Figure 10-15: *Simplified illustration of dual polarization receiver. Receiver A is sensitive to vertically polarized signals, while receiver B is sensitive to horizontally polarized signals.*

One receiver is sensitive to vertically polarized light while the other is sensitive to horizontally polarized light. This receiver, when listening to a signal using polarization to embed information, will see a signal that is stronger in one receiver than the other. When receiver A detects a stronger signal than receiver B, the signal could be interpreted as a 1 digit. Likewise, when receiver B detects a stronger signal than receiver A, the signal could be interpreted as a 0 digit. When the receivers listen to an unpolarized signal, both receivers would detect an equally strong signal (Figure 10-16).

While this is how it works in theory, the description above is not entirely correct. An interstellar radio signal will most likely use a type of polarization called *circular polarization*. This means that the direction in which the photons vibrate rotates over time, much like the hands on a clock. In this scheme, the direction of rotation denotes a digit. So, clockwise rotation might mean 1, while counterclockwise rotation of the photons means 0. Both types of polarization (horizontal/vertical, clockwise/counterclockwise) can be used to encode information. While it is easier to visualize horizontal/vertical polarization, circular polarization is more likely to be found in interstellar signals because a circularly polarized signal will be less susceptible to interference from interstellar gas clouds.

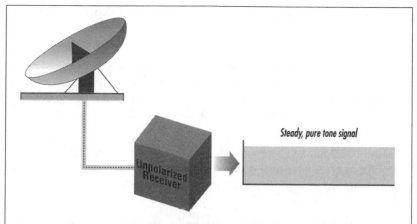

Figure 10-16: *When a receiver that is not sensitive to polarization observes a polarized signal, it sees a continuous (always on) signal that is tuned to a precise frequency (pure tone).*

Light signals

There are several ways to encode information onto pulse and continuous sources of laser light. Although both radio and visible light signals are composed of photons, the technology used to detect laser light is quite different from the systems used to detect radio signals. The key difference between optical and radio receivers is that optical systems have the ability to detect and count individual photons as they arrive. This characteristic allows information to be embedded in laser beams in several different ways (compared to radio signals), without making the signal itself much harder to detect. The following techniques can be used to embed encoded information in a laser beam:

Wavelength (color) modulation

The laser (or pair of lasers) emit light at two or more specific wavelengths. Each unique wavelength can represent a number (e.g., 650 nm = 0, 700 nm = 1). By analyzing the color of the light, the recipient can see that information is encoded in the signal. This is similar to frequency modulation for a radio signal.

Polarization

It is easy to manipulate the polarity of laser light by using polarized filters (commonly encountered in polarized, glare-reducing sunglasses). These filters allow light that is polarized in one direction to pass through, while blocking light that is polarized in an opposite plane.

Likewise, it is easy to measure the polarity of a light signal on the receiving end.

Pulse timing

In the case of a pulsed laser beacon, information can be encoded in the timing of the beacon's flashes. This is similar to Morse code. A long delay between flashes might mean 0, while a short delay between flashes would mean 1. This technique can be applied to pulsed beacons only.

All of these techniques can be employed together in a pulsed laser beacon. This allows information in the signal to be encoded in several layers, and allows the transmitter to send many bits of information with each flash of light.

When an observer first detects a signal, he will see only a flashing laser beacon. He will also notice that the timing between flashes varies between two specific values (for example, 6/10ths of a second and 4/10ths of a second). This pattern in the timing of the signal would suggest the possibility of information encoded in the timing of the signal, with the timing of the flashes providing one channel of information. As shown in Figure 10-17, a short delay between pulses denotes a 1 digit, while a longer delay between pulses denotes a 0 digit in this example. The duration of the pulse itself can also be used to encode an additional bit of information.

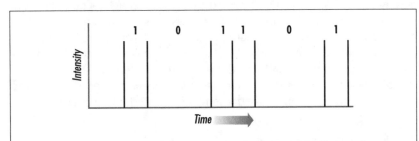

Figure 10-17: *Pulse timing modulation is used to transmit one bit of information per flash.*

When the receiver examines each flash of light in detail, it will be able to see that the flash is composed of several distinct colors of light. For example, let's say the laser emits light at up to 16 discrete wavelengths. When analyzed in detail, the spectrum of the flash of light reveals that each distinct wavelength represents one bit of information. So in this case, the spectrum encodes 16 bits of information in each flash of light.

The human eye can discern between about 16 million distinct colors (or about 24 bits of binary data). Since our eyes are not nearly as sensitive to color as high-resolution spectrometers, it is possible to encode even more bits of information into the spectral fingerprint of a flash of light (Figure 10-18). The transmitter can be designed to emit light at several distinct wavelengths, each of which represents a digit in a series of binary numbers. Hence, a 16-color transmitter can encode 16 bits of information in the spectrum of the light pulse.

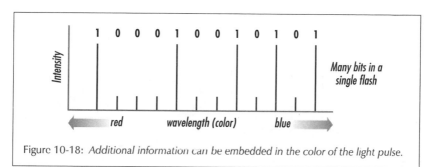

Figure 10-18: *Additional information can be embedded in the color of the light pulse.*

Figure 10-19 illustrates how colors can transmit digital information. The Color Modem program depicted in this figure converts 8 bits of information into light consisting of 8 primary colors (ranging from red to violet). When all 8 bits are set to one, the resulting color is white. If, for example, the two leftmost bits are set to one, the resulting color is a red hue. A more sophisticated system could encode dozens, hundreds, even thousands of bits of information in the color of its light.

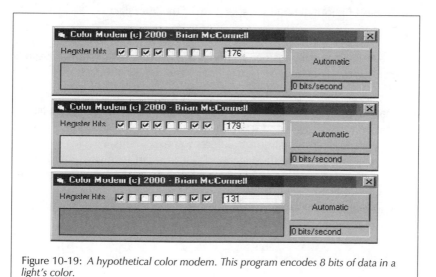

Figure 10-19: *A hypothetical color modem. This program encodes 8 bits of data in a light's color.*

Next, the receiver examines how the polarity of light changes over a very short period of time while the laser is on. For example, if the laser is on for 8 billionths of a second, and the polarity of the light can be updated once per nanosecond, the laser can encode 8 bits of information using polarity (Figure 10-20).

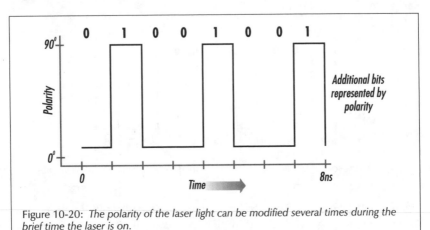

Figure 10-20: *The polarity of the laser light can be modified several times during the brief time the laser is on.*

In this example, the pulsed laser beacon transmits three different signals of varied lengths in the short time that the laser is on:

- 1 bit of information in the timing of the flash
- 16 bits of information in the spectrum of the laser light
- 8 bits of information by rapidly changing the polarity of the laser

If this laser emits 10 flashes per second, this system could transmit 250 bits of information per second, or 21.6 million bits of information per day.

Lasers that employ this kind of multi-layered approach can pack a lot of information into a light signal that is still easy to detect. This approach allows information to be transmitted using several independent encoding channels and can transmit information at different speeds. This enables a distant receiver to easily acquire the signal and quickly start receiving information, though at a very slow pace (1 bit per light pulse). As the receiver examines the signal in greater detail, it can detect additional information encoded in the lights' color and polarity. This will be harder to read, and will most likely require more sophisticated detection hardware on the receiving end.

Detectability versus speed

When deciding which method of communication it's going to employ, the transmitting civilization will need to consider the trade-offs between detectability (the ease with which the remote party can initially acquire the signal), and the ability to transmit large quantities of information across that link.

Detection and data transfer speed are *not* the same thing. A signal can be very easy to detect and quite capable of transmitting very large amounts of information that is difficult to see within the signal. Conversely, a signal can be easy to acquire but incapable of transmitting more than a few bits of information per second.

The challenge for the sender is to engineer a signal that is easy to acquire *and* capable of delivering large amounts of information. One way to do this is to design the signal so that it transmits data using several modulation schemes simultaneously (for example, by using phase modulation and polarity modulation simultaneously). You can think of each modulation scheme as a channel, much like a television channel. The sender would send data at a high speed on one channel, and would send the same data at a much slower speed on another channel. This enables the recipient to capture the information on the slow channel fairly easily, even if they are unable to see the information embedded in the faster channel.

The key factor limiting the speed at which a radio or laser signal can transmit data is the amount of energy used to encode each bit of information. There are two ways to maximize this number. One is to increase the power output of the transmitter. Another is to reduce the speed at which data is transmitted. This forces the sender to deal with an awkward trade-off between maximizing the data transmission speed and keeping power requirements at a reasonable level. Figure 10-21 illustrates this trade-off. With a relatively small antenna, the recipients might only be able to capture data encoded at 100 bits per second or less. However, with a much larger antenna, they could capture data encoded at much higher speeds.

Think of what happens when you take a picture in low light conditions with no flash. If everything in the scene stays still, you can use a long exposure time to capture light, enabling you to take a very detailed picture. However, if there is a lot of motion in the scene, you're forced into a trade-off between adequate exposure and motion detail. If you use a short exposure time to capture the scene with poor lighting, the resulting image will be clear but lack detail. Conversely, if you use a longer exposure time to compensate for low lighting, motion trails will follow the moving objects in the scene.

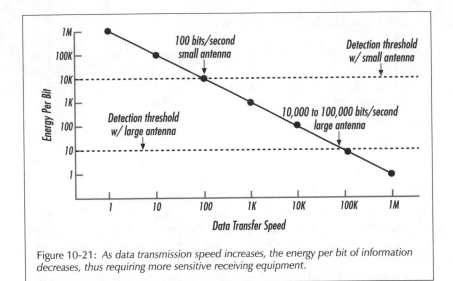

Figure 10-21: *As data transmission speed increases, the energy per bit of information decreases, thus requiring more sensitive receiving equipment.*

We find ourselves in a similar dilemma with transmitting an interstellar message. If we send data too quickly, the bits will appear to blur together on the receiving end. The recipient will still see the underlying signal, but will not be able to separate the bits of data from each other. The recipient can compensate for this by building a larger or more sensitive telescope, but this obviously requires additional work on their part.

Knowing this, we can forecast what to expect in an interstellar beacon signal, and can determine what we would need to do if we wanted to send our own message. The solution is to construct a signal that transmits data using several different encoding schemes at data transfer rates ranging from slow to fast.

The next thing we'll want to do is figure out how to organize an apparently endless stream of binary numbers so that we can use them as symbols, to convey useful information or instructions to a distant party that has no prior knowledge about the sender. The rest of the book focuses on how to structure this coded information so that it is possible to infer meaning from nothing more than binary numbers.

COMMUNICATING WITH OTHER WORLDS

CETI—COMMUNICATION WITH EXTRATERRESTRIAL INTELLIGENCE

Modern SETI programs are based on the realization that it is possible to transmit coded information across interstellar distances using wireless communication. We know with certainty that we have the capability to detect the radio broadcasts of civilizations like our own. As our detection systems improve, the distance at which we can detect another civilization will continue to increase.

The possibility that we detect another civilization, or that another civilization detects our own radio, television, and radar broadcasts, though small, is real. Perhaps the most interesting question to ponder is what kind of communication is possible between civilizations.

Up to this point, we've been discussing the mechanics of moving raw bits of information across interstellar distances. The remainder of the book looks at the kind of information we might expect to receive or—if we reverse the roles—what kind of message we can transmit to neighboring civilizations. While many people assume that any meaningful communication among civilizations is impossible, we can demonstrate that, in fact, it is possible to communicate a wide range of ideas, using only binary numbers as a foundation for composing a message.

This chapter is an overview of historical attempts to send coded messages to other civilizations. Then, in Chapters 12 through 21, we'll discuss one hypothetical system for communication from start to finish. This system, which borrows ideas from both genetics and computer science, enables a sender to convey many different types of information, from symbols to high-resolution images to a general-purpose abstract language.

CETI history

CETI, short for *Communication with Extraterrestrial Intelligence*, is related to SETI, except the roles are reversed. In SETI programs, scientists are passively searching for signals emanating from other civilizations—listening for someone else's signal. However, with CETI, we are the ones who are trying to initiate contact.

The first attempts to communicate with extraterrestrial civilizations via radio can be traced to the invention of radio itself. Many of the people involved in the creation of wireless communication built experiments to listen for or sent coded radio signals to Mars, which was, at that time, thought to be a likely site for life.

In the early 20th century, the notion of an advanced civilization on Earth's sister planet caught the public's imagination. This fascination was vividly demonstrated by the panic caused by Orson Welles and the Mercury Theater's legendary 1938 radiobroadcast of *The War of the Worlds*. This idea not only captured the public's imagination, but also that of many of the day's most prominent scientists, leading some astronomers to interpret canal-like features on Mars as signs of an extensive irrigation system constructed by a race of intelligent beings.

We not only attempted to intercept radio signals from Mars; we also sent our own coded messages in an attempt to initiate communication. Compared to other stars in our galaxy, Mars is much closer to Earth. A radio transmission can traverse the distance between Earth and Mars in about 20 minutes, compared to the years or decades that it might take for a signal to travel the distance between stars. If an advanced civilization had existed on Mars—and if they had the desire to communicate—it would have been relatively easy to establish two-way communication via radio.

Since the invention of wireless communication and space transportation, we've attempted to make contact with other civilizations in several ways: by building monuments, sending coded signals designed specifically for alien civilizations and, unintentionally, leaking electromagnetic radiation into space.

Monuments

The idea of building monuments to be seen by other civilizations is an ancient notion. One could argue that the monuments built by ancient civilizations were, in a sense, attempts to communicate with superior beings.

Since the beginnings of the space exploration program, we have been building our own version of these monuments in the form of spacecraft, some of which will travel across interstellar distances. Both the Pioneer and Voyager spacecraft took this a step further by carrying plaques that are designed to be easily decoded by another space-faring civilization. These plaques were attached to the spacecraft in the event that another civilization might intercept the probes thousands or millions of years from now.

The plaques attached to the Pioneer 10 and 11 probes contained an image with six useful pieces of information about our solar system and the human race, including:

- The figures of a man and woman standing next to each other, with height indicators.

- A diagram representing a well-known change of states in a neutral hydrogen atom. This transition results in a characteristic radio wave with a 21 cm wavelength. This diagram also equates this condition with the binary number 1.

- Horizontal and vertical ticks used to encode the number 8 in binary form. When combined with the above, this is intended to show that the woman depicted in the image is 8 times 21 cm, or 168 cm (about 5'5") tall.

- A radial pattern describing our location in the galaxy by mapping the distance from our sun to neighboring pulsars.

- Solid bars in the radial pattern indicate distance, and the lone horizontal bar is used to denote the distance of our sun to the galactic center at the time of Pioneer's launch (in both space and time).

- A drawing that describes the layout of our solar system, with ticks beneath each planet denoting its relative distance to the sun in binary code. Pioneer's trajectory is also shown as starting from the third planet, Earth.

Together, these indicators explain, in a nutshell, who built the spacecraft, what they look like, where they live, and when they launched the craft. The Pioneer plaques should be intelligible for millions of years, far longer than any structures we build here on Earth. The Voyager probes took this concept a step further by including an audio and visual record, in the form of a gold-plated phonograph disk that stores both sounds and several color images. The technique used to record sounds on the disk is basically the same technique used to record sounds on an LP record album.* Sound is

---

* A detailed explanation of the techniques used to encode information on the Voyager record can be found at *http://cedmagic.om/featured/voyager/voyager-record.html*.

recorded in analog form in the form of grooves whose track corresponds to the waveform of the sound to be reproduced.

The disk is also used to store 20-color images. The images were stored on the disk by tracing successive scan lines of a two-dimensional image, in much the same way that a television's cathode ray tube draws an image as a stack of horizontal lines. The color images are actually recorded as a set of three individual images (one each for the three primary colors we see; red, green, and blue). The first image in the series depicts an image of the Sun's color spectrum. This serves as a calibration image that guides the recipient in decoding the color information in the image. We'll discuss several techniques for transmitting images in encoded form in Chapter 17, *Pictures*.

It is unlikely these plaques will be intercepted by another civilization, as it will take tens of thousands of years to traverse the distance to the nearest star systems.

We're not only building our own monuments, but we are also looking for signs of monuments built by other civilizations in our own backyard. The renowned science fiction author, Arthur C. Clarke, vividly described this scenario in the classic *2001: A Space Odyssey*. Clarke's hypothesis was that one of the ways in which an advanced civilization may initiate contact is to build an obviously artificial structure somewhere near our planet, such as on our moon or in the asteroid belt.

The reason for doing this is to build a type of "tripwire" that will only be crossed when a developing civilization acquires the capability to leave its home planet. This capability requires the civilization to understand science, develop advanced technology, and presumably, to be intelligent enough to anticipate the possibility of extraterrestrial life (and therefore be better prepared to deal with this event).

While this may sound like a far-fetched idea, we know that the laws of physics do permit interstellar travel (although it is difficult, and involves very long transit times). If other civilizations have developed space-faring capabilities, we can't rule out the possibility that one way they may choose to make contact with others is to build structures that will only be discovered by a civilization when it reaches a fairly advanced state of development.

In the past 30 years, we have developed technology to conduct detailed radar and photographic surveys of other planets and moons within our solar system. Over the course of this century, we will reach a point at which we will be able to map even relatively small artificial structures on other worlds. While it's unlikely this will happen, we can't rule out the possibility that some day we may stumble across something like Clarke's monolith.

Leakage radiation

Our civilization has been "on the air" since the early part of the 20th century. Although our initial radio and TV broadcasts were sporadic and relatively weak, the total power of our radio broadcasts has been steadily increasing with each passing year. This leakage radiation, though it may be meaningless to anyone who intercepts it, will nonetheless betray our presence to any advanced civilization with equal or better radio reception capability within a range of about 60 light years.

It's important to understand that the initial detection of a civilization does not require the party on the receiving end of the line to understand the contents of the signal. By merely detecting a radio carrier, a civilization will be able to gather two pieces of information right away:

• Whether an intelligent civilization exists outside its solar system

• From which solar system the signal emanates

So, even if the broadcast is transient, and completely unintelligible, it will still betray the presence and location of its sender. Let's imagine what this might look like to an advanced civilization that is looking at Earth through a high-resolution radiotelescope (as shown in Figure 11-1).

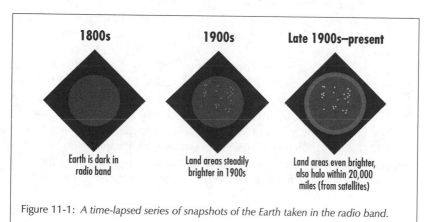

1800s	1900s	Late 1900s–present
Earth is dark in radio band	Land areas steadily brighter in 1900s	Land areas even brighter, also halo within 20,000 miles (from satellites)

Figure 11-1: *A time-lapsed series of snapshots of the Earth taken in the radio band.*

Figure 11-1 illustrates how Earth's appearance, as seen in radio wavelengths, would have changed over the past 100 or so years. The image on the left shows Earth as it would have been in the 1800s, before we started generating powerful radio signals. In this image, both the Earth and the space around it would have appeared dark in the radio band.

The middle picture in Figure 11-1 depicts Earth as it appeared in the middle of the 20th century, just prior to the development of man-made satellites. In this image, the Earth's landmasses would be lit up in areas where there were human settlements, while the rest of the Earth would be dark. This image would look a lot like the photos taken of Earth from orbit at night, where city lights are clearly visible from space.

The image on the right of Figure 11-1 depicts the Earth as it appears today and into the 21st century. In this image, the inhabited areas on Earth are brightly lit because of all of the radio, TV, radar, and telecommunications broadcasts emanating from populated areas. In addition, the observer would also notice a faint halo extending out to about 20,000 miles away from the Earth. This halo would betray the signals emitted by man-made satellites, although these signals would be much weaker and harder to see compared to ground-based transmitters, which are more powerful but not very well focused.

This imaging technique, although it is beyond our current capabilities, will be within our reach eventually. We should assume that civilizations thousands or millions of years more advanced than ours will be able to see Earth in this fashion.

The implication of this is that with each passing year, we announce our existence to a larger number of star systems. Already, our first strong radio broadcasts can be detected out to a distance of about 70 light years. It's important to note that our broadcasts radiate outward in such a way that for every doubling in detection range, the number of star systems reached increases by a factor of eight. This is because of something known as *spherical geometry*. With spherical geometry, if you double the radius of a sphere, you increase its volume by 2^3, or 8. Since stars are distributed relatively evenly out to a distance of about 1000 light years from Earth, we can say that each time we double the amount of time we've been on the air, the number of stars that can potentially hear us increases by a factor of 8. Table 11-1 illustrates how the volume of space, which is filled with our unintentional broadcasts, increases depending on how long we remain on the air. Even if we never make a conscious attempt to transmit a message to another civilization, we are already providing ample clues about our existence.

Table 11-1: *Relationship of duration of broadcast, detection range, and volume of space filled by broadcast*

YEARS "ON THE AIR"	MAX DETECTION RANGE	VOLUME OF SPACE
10	10 LY[a]	4188 LY^3
20	20 LY	33509 LY^3
50	50 LY	523587 LY^3
100	100 LY	4188000 LY^3

Table 11-1: *Relationship of duration of broadcast, detection range, and volume of space filled by broadcast (continued)*

YEARS "ON THE AIR"	MAX DETECTION RANGE	VOLUME OF SPACE
200	200 LY	33509000 LY³
500	500 LY	523587000 LY³
1000	1000 LY	4188000000 LY³

a   LY stands for light year; LY³ stands for cubic light years.

Coded signals

In addition to our unintentional broadcasts, or leakage radiation, we have made several attempts at communicating with other civilizations via radio broadcasts. Early in the last century, we tried to establish communication with Mars, both by attempting to eavesdrop on their radio traffic (none was found), and by transmitting our own coded messages.

In that era, radio was still in its infancy. The people experimenting with Martian communication were not radioastronomers; they were largely the same people who invented radio. These attempts at communication, although crude by today's standards, forced people to realize that, in principle, the only difference between sending a signal from New York to Washington, and from New York to Mars is the distance. The underlying laws of physics were expected to be the same everywhere, so in principle, radio communication between planets should work (and it does; we've demonstrated this in present-day communication with remote space probes).

These early attempts at communication, although they did not produce evidence of a Martian civilization, were not fruitless. One proposal, which got fairly serious attention, was published in 1920 in *Scientific American*. The system proposed to send a series of images using a signaling format similar to Morse code (a combination of short and long signals, typically represented by dots and dashes).

Many of the usual signals that were originally thought to be coded messages from Mars turned out to be the byproduct of naturally occurring processes, such as thunderstorms, noise from the Earth's ionosphere (whose presence enables long-range communication via short-wave radio), and others.

In 1959, Giuseppe Cocconi and Philip Morrison published their landmark paper "Searching for Interstellar Communications" in *Nature*, at about the same time that Frank Drake was gearing up to run his Project Ozma experiment. These two events marked a turning point in SETI history. From that point on, SETI was no longer the provenance of entrepreneurs and inventors. Instead, it became an extension of the emerging field of radio-astronomy. In 1961, R. N. Schwartz and C. H. Townes published their paper, "Interstellar and Interplanetary Communication by Optical Masers" in *Nature*. As mentioned in previous chapters, this paper became the blueprint for Optical SETI programs.

The idea that interstellar radio communication was possible quickly gained widespread acceptance. The debate over SETI has never been about whether it is technically feasible to broadcast a radio signal across inter-stellar distances. We know it is possible because we can detect naturally occurring sources of radio waves from over 10 billion light years away in the form of the cosmic background radiation that was predicted by the Big Bang Theory. The debate has always been about whether there is another intelligent civilization to talk with, not whether radio waves can travel dozens or thousands of light years to reach us.

This realization prompted scientists in many different fields to give serious thought to the subject of how we can communicate with an alien race that would have no common language or frame of reference compared to ours. People quickly realized that, while we might not speak remotely similar languages, or even communicate in the same way, any technological civilization is likely to understand mathematics, because mathematics are the foundation upon which much scientific understanding is built.

Therefore, if one wished to communicate with an alien civilization, the best way to do so would be to create a simple mathematical language. This understanding led to the development of two main types of systems for communicating with alien civilizations, both of them based on numbers as symbols. One approach is to transmit pictures, or *bitmaps*, in coded form, and to use these pictures as a means of communicating abstract concepts. The other approach is to transmit numeric sentences, or *equations*, using a mathematical language that is designed to be easily understood by a technological civilization.

Pictographic communication systems

The basic idea behind pictographic communication is rooted in the cliché: "A picture is worth a thousand words." This is especially true when the recipient of a message doesn't even know what the words are to begin with. Pictographic communication systems attempt to relay information through the use of two-dimensional bitmaps, or black and white images. These messages are typically brief, and attempt to describe basic concepts and symbols in a schematic form. The odds of successfully communicating an idea are often much higher if the sender paints a picture of the idea instead of describing it with words, which the recipient may or may not completely understand.

The systems used to send images via interstellar radio broadcasts are based on the idea that you can send a long string of binary digits that can then be converted in a two-dimensional grid to form a black and white image (as shown in the example in Figure 11-2).

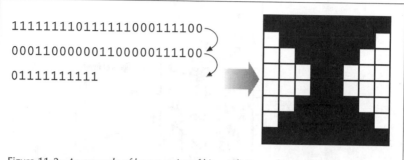

Figure 11-2: *An example of how a series of binary digits can be displayed as a two-dimensional image.*

The hourglass shape depicted in Figure 11-2 is represented by a series of 64 binary digits, which read as follows:

1111111101111110001110000011000000110000011110001111110111111111

When looking only at the series of digits, it is hard to see how these numbers can be mapped into a two-dimensional image, but the process is relatively straightforward. Any civilization smart enough to build radiotelescopes would be smart enough to figure this out. This is the basis of pictographic communication, and most of the systems that employ this technique use variations of the same basic theme.

ARECIBO PICTOGRAPH

In 1975, scientists sent a powerful transmission carrying a pictographic message (Figure 11-3) designed to be easily decoded by an alien civilization from the Arecibo Radio Observatory.

The Arecibo Message was designed to pack a lot of information into a relatively small (1679-bit) message. The message depicts, among other things:

- The Arecibo radiotelescope (shown at the bottom of the image)

- A simplified map of our solar system, with earth highlighted (this is shown directly above the upside-down Arecibo Radio Observatory graphic, near the bottom of the image)

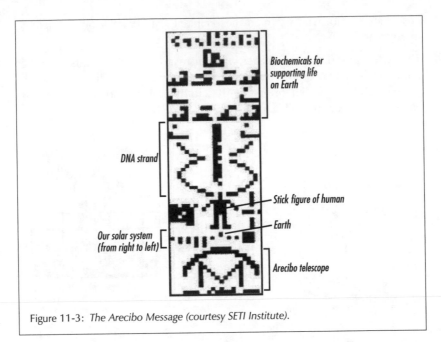

Figure 11-3: *The Arecibo Message (courtesy SETI Institute).*

- A stick figure of a human (although it is unlikely the recipient would recognize a human without having seen one already)

- A depiction of the DNA molecule, and some of the biochemicals found in early Earth life

The scientists aimed the signal at the M13 globular cluster near the edge of the galaxy where there are about 300,000 stars. The signal will reach its target in about 21,000 years.

DUTIL-DUMAS PICTOGRAPHIC SYSTEM

The most recent pictographic message was sent in 1999. The message employs a sophisticated system developed by Yvan Dutil and Stephane Dumas and shown here in Figure 11-4. This message differed from previous messages in that it can be used to build a basic symbolic vocabulary and convey a surprising amount of information in a short message. Although it draws on the basic concepts employed in the Arecibo Message, its authors take the concept further to develop a general-purpose math and science vocabulary.

This figure depicts a "page" from their message. This page introduces the concept of numbers and basic arithmetic and is organized into five major sections. The symbols in the upper left corner of the page denote the page

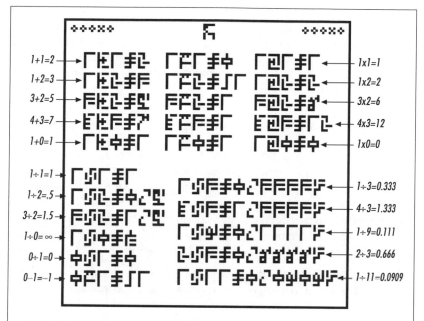

Figure 11-4: *An excerpt from the Dutil-Dumas pictographic message (marked up to show the meaning of the expressions contained in the image).*

number in binary form. X denotes a 1, while O denotes a 0. Hence, the page number reads 00010, or decimal 2.

The approach Dutil and Dumas took was to use a series of two-dimensional images to teach the recipient to recognize a vocabulary of numbers and symbols that can then be combined to form higher order expressions. These images can be likened to flashcards designed to depict key mathematical and scientific ideas in an easily recognizable symbolic format.

Below the top row of the page, there are three columns or blocks of symbols that occupy the upper-half of the page. The upper-left column contains several examples of addition. The upper-center column contains several examples of subtraction. The upper-right column describes several examples of multiplication. The lower half of the page contains several examples of division, as well as floating-point numbers.

Notice how it is easy to learn what the different symbols stand for. This system is particularly interesting because of its ability to describe a progressively more and more complex lexicon of basic symbols.

A 23-page message compiled using Dutil and Dumas' technique, along with links to related sites, can be found on the web at http://www. matessa.org/~mike/dutil-dumas.html. *This message was broadcast in 1999 to several target star systems from the Evpatoria radiotelescope in the Ukraine.*

Non-pictorial communication systems

Along with these pictographic systems for communication, numerous symbolic systems have also been proposed. These systems rely heavily on mathematics as a common language, not on images, to convey ideas (something we have to take into consideration since we cannot necessarily assume that an alien species sees things the same way we do). A species that perceives its world through sound, much like bats do here on Earth, may not recognize a bitmap image, but it may be able to recognize basic mathematical concepts.

Not surprisingly, mathematicians developed these systems. Carl L. DeVito and Hans Frudenthal developed two especially noteworthy systems.

LINCOS

Dutch mathematician Hans Freudenthal created a language called *Lincos* (short for *Lingua Cosmica*), which was designed specifically for the purpose of interstellar discourse. The language is expressed purely in mathematical form, and uses symbols that are created by combining short and long radio pulses (dots and dashes), much like Morse code. Each distinct word has a unique series of short and long pulses. These words can then be combined to form equations (e.g., $1+1=2$) and to group words into categories (e.g., symbol *xyz* belongs to category *abc*).

These equations and categories can then be used in combination with still more expressions, enabling the sender to build a rich vocabulary of mathematical and scientific concepts.

Lincos is described in detail in Freudenthal's 1960 book *"LINCOS: Design of a Language for Cosmic Intercourse."*

DEVITO'S NUMERIC LANGUAGE

Mathematician Carl L. DeVito described a similar system for interstellar communication that relied on numbers—not pictures—to build a vocabulary of symbols. His system was also capable of describing numerically coded symbols and explicitly describing their context within an expression.

DeVito's system is very straightforward and also uses a form of signaling similar to Morse code. In his system, the sender transmits numbers and symbols by transmitting a series of radio or light pulses. This is similar to the semaphore lamps used by the Navy to send messages in Morse code between ships at sea. DeVito added an interesting twist to his system by using the duration of each pulse to describe the context of the symbol.

Trains of short pulses (dots) were used to describe numbers, while trains of long pulses (dashes) were used to describe symbols or commands. Hence, the duration of the pulse tells the recipient whether it is describing a command or data. Following this basic principle, let's use DeVito's system to describe a simple equation, such as "2+2=4." This statement would be expressed as:

```
_ _ * * _ _ * * * _ _ _ _
```

or:

```
dash dash dot dot dash dash dot dot dot dash dash dash dash
```

or:

```
(dash dash) (dot dot) (dash dash) (dot dot dot) (dash dash dash
dash)
```

We can see in this example (depicted graphically in Figure 11-5) how we can describe a simple mathematical language by combining the dots (short pulses) and dashes (long pulses) to describe equations. This system could be used to describe higher order mathematical symbols such as sine and cosine, as well as fundamental concepts such as addition and subtraction.

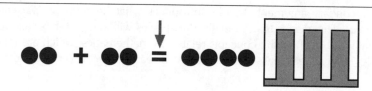

Figure 11-5: *Excerpt of message "2 + 2 = 4" described using DeVito's system (the symbol "=" is represented by three short pulses).*

This system can be used to build up a lexicon of symbols for a wide variety of mathematical concepts, and ultimately to build a symbolic language derived from these fundamental concepts.

Will it be possible to converse with aliens?

The idea that we could communicate in depth with an alien civilization strikes many people as preposterous. At first glance, the technical issues create an insurmountable barrier to real communication. The distances involved make it very difficult to detect radio or optical signals from other star systems. Even if we do succeed in detecting a signal, it is likely that another civilization will have evolved differently than humans, and therefore is likely to see the universe from a vastly different perspective than ours. That's the conventional wisdom.

Marvin Minsky, one of the pioneers in artificial intelligence research, offers an interesting perspective on the challenge of communicating with alien civilizations in the article *"Communication with Alien Intelligence."*

Minsky points out that any intelligent, communicative species will be forced to develop symbol systems to represent objects, actions, and causes in their environment. His *economic argument* reasons that because the surrounding environment can be described in abbreviated form through the use of symbols and categories of symbols, this is a much more economical way to communicate. For example, it's much easier to say the word "apple" than it is to draw a detailed picture of an apple. Using a symbol for an apple is much more efficient in terms of the amount of memory required to remember the concept, the amount of information required to describe the concept in communication, and the amount of time required to transmit the concept in conversation. Because of this, Minsky suggests that symbolic communication systems and intelligence will likely go hand in hand.

In a secondary argument, Minsky introduces what he terms a *sparseness argument*. This means that an intelligent species will encounter certain very special ideas, such as the concepts related to mathematics, which are much simpler than other ideas—and interact with each other in very predictable ways.

One example is addition. Addition is a universal concept. The equation $2+2=4$ will always be true, regardless of the perspective of the reader. These special concepts, because they are rare and universal, will form the basis for a common language from which other concepts can be derived (as Hans Fruedenthal did with Lincos).

Far from encountering a hopeless communication gap, if Minsky, Freudenthal, and others are right, we may discover that it is possible to communicate in much greater depth than many people have imagined.

Bridging the ultimate language gap

At first glance, the idea of communicating with an alien race, with which we have no common language (and perhaps completely different modes of communication), seems like an impossible task. However, in approaching this problem, it's important to clarify our definition of intelligence. The SETI Institute's Jill Tarter has a very simple, objective test for defining intelligence. If a civilization can build a radio or optical telescope capable of sending or receiving interstellar signals, they're intelligent. If they can't do this, while they might be very smart (as dolphins are), we won't be able to detect them.

With this litmus test in mind, we can construct a mathematical language based on concepts that both parties must understand in order to be able to pass Dr. Tarter's test. In order to be able to build radiotelescopes, a civilization must have the following knowledge.

- They must understand the basic laws of physics, especially those related to electromagnetic radiation (light).

- They must understand three-dimensional geometry. They need to know this in order to build the high gain-antennae required for radioastronomy.

- They must understand mathematics on a level comparable to ours. Without math, it is hard to make sense of science, especially physics.

With these things in mind, we can start to define a numeric language that is versatile and easy to learn. Throughout the remainder of this book, we'll expand on the ideas explored in previous SETI programs. By combining ideas from biology, math, and computer science we'll describe a complete system for communication that is both easy to learn, and that is also capable of communicating a wide range of ideas and many different kinds of information.

BINARY DNA

While it's interesting to be able to send a block of binary numbers across interstellar distances, this whole exercise is pointless unless we can use those bits to convey something meaningful. This is probably the biggest challenge SETI researchers face, because it forces them to think about how we share knowledge ourselves. Whether we are communicating verbally, in written form, or sending a file across the Internet, our communication can ultimately be reduced to a small set of basic elements—binary numbers, letters in the alphabet, or the basic utterances of our speech. By themselves, these basic elements have no meaning. Yet, when combined, they can be used to form words and phrases that represent everything we see and experience.

The challenge is to work out a system that enables someone to see structure (and, with the help of that structure, to derive meaning) within an otherwise endlessly repeating series of numbers. One way to visualize this is to imagine that someone who speaks a completely unknown language is sending you a coded radio message. This message consists of nothing more than short and long beeps, similar to Morse code, except the key to decoding the message is unknown. Since the sender speaks a language nobody else has encountered, you can't consult a dictionary as a guide. The only clues about how to read the message are embedded in the message itself.

So far, we've discussed the technology required to transmit a radio or light-wave carrier that can be detected at interstellar distances, as well as the techniques used to detect extraterrestrial signals and filter out various types of noise and local interference. This chapter focuses on the techniques that can be used to transmit useful information (images, text, multimedia, etc.) over a carrier signal. Throughout this chapter and the remainder of the book, we explore the various ways to organize numbers so that they convey meaning, and also contain hints about how to read the message itself.

Assumptions about alien communication

While we can only guess about what an intelligent alien species might look like, or how they might talk to each other, we can make some predictions about what types of signals and messages they will be capable of understanding. Among other things, we can assume that an alien civilization that is capable of communicating with us can understand electronics, digital computing, math, and Boolean arithmetic. We make these predictions based on the minimum level of technological capability required to detect an interstellar signal. An understanding of electronics is a prerequisite for building the sensitive amplifiers and signal processing circuitry needed to detect a weak radio signal. An understanding of math and geometry is also a perquisite for building a properly shaped antenna for a radiotelescope.

We make these predictions because we understand the technological requirements for interstellar communication using electromagnetic radiation. These requirements define a minimum level of understanding of physics and telecommunications on both ends of the broadcast. Any civilization that is capable of communicating in this manner will, by definition, have reached a minimum level of technological sophistication.

This lowest common denominator, the understanding of electromagnetic radiation and digital computing, serves as a foundation upon which we can build a system for communication, even though we may know absolutely nothing else about the party on the other end of the line.

Aliens and electronics

One thing we do know is that communicative aliens will understand electronics. The process of transmitting or detecting radio or optical signals requires the use of electronic devices such as transistors and diodes, each of which perform specific functions within an electronic system. As we learned in Chapter 10, *Teleporting Bits*, transistors act like electronic valves, allowing a very small electric current to control the flow of a much larger electric current. This is the basic premise behind an amplifier.

There are several important devices required to build SETI transmission and detection systems, among them: basic electronic components (resistors, capacitors, transistors, and diodes), and digital computing devices (AND gates, memory registers, etc.).

NON-LINEAR DEVICES (ELECTRONIC VALVES)

A non-linear device, or electronic valve, is a device that can adjust its resistance to carry an electrical current. A diode, for example, allows a current to flow easily in one direction through the device, but not the other; it is a one-way street for electrical current. A transistor (a basic component used to build amplifiers, logic circuits, and memory) behaves like an electrical valve. Current flows into the device through one connector and out through another. A third connector is used to control the amount of current that flows through the device by applying a small electrical signal to the device. This is conceptually similar to adjusting the valve on a water faucet, where a small mechanical force controls the flow of water through the faucet.

These devices make it possible to build a wide range of devices, including:

Amplifiers
> A weak signal is used as the control signal to modulate the flow of a much larger current through a device.

Logic circuits
> Transistors can be combined to form devices that process binary data (e.g., to add two binary numbers or compare two numbers, etc.).

Memory
> Transistors can also be combined to form a special class of logic circuit that remembers the last binary number presented to it. This is the basis of random access memory (RAM).

PHOTOELECTRIC DEVICES

Photoelectric devices convert light into electrical signals, or convert electrical energy into light. These devices are especially important in Optical SETI (OSETI), and are important for astronomy and scientific research as a whole. These devices can be divided into two broad categories: *light capturing devices* and *light emitting devices,* which may be defined as follows:

Light capturing devices
> These devices convert incoming light into an electrical current. They are based on the photoelectric effect, the phenomenon that Albert Einstein described, and for which he won the Nobel Prize in Physics in 1921. Among the devices we've developed in this category are solar cells and charged coupled devices (sensitive light detectors that are used in a wide variety of applications in astronomy).

Light emitting devices
> These devices convert electrical energy into light. One example is a light emitting diode (LED), which efficiently converts electrical energy into

light. Unlike an incandescent light, which emits many colors of light, an LED emits light that is tuned to a narrow range of colors. Solid-state lasers, which were derived from the work done on LEDs, operate in a similar manner, except they emit a narrowly focused beam of coherent light.

It's not important for an alien inventor to build a carbon copy of our silicon transistor, or to invent each of these things in the same sequence. However, it is necessary that it build devices that are functionally equivalent to many of these components in order to build the equipment required to detect an interstellar signal. This is important because the civilization, while it may not have invented these devices in the same order, must have discovered most of them in order to build the hardware required to communicate wirelessly.

Aliens and digital computing

Electronic valves and computing are closely related, so the next thing we must assume is that aliens understand digital computers. A digital computer, with its ability to process information presented in the form of minute electrical signals, is built from a large array of simple circuits that are built using interconnected non-linear devices. One such example is the flip-flop memory register shown in Figure 12-1.

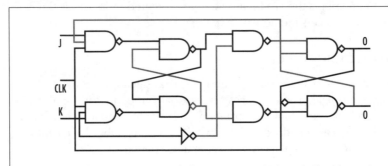

Figure 12-1: *This circuit, composed of NAND gates, which are built with transistors, stores a single bit of information.*

NOTE

A NAND gate is the equivalent of an AND circuit, followed by a NOT circuit. This means that a NAND gate will produce a 1 when either of its inputs A or B are 0.

Once a civilization has invented an electronic valve, whether it is a vacuum tube or solid-state transistor, it will only be a matter of time before it also discovers that these devices can connect together to build digital memory and information processing circuitry. While it's impossible to predict the sequence of invention, it's reasonable to conclude that a civilization capable of communicating by radio or laser has also discovered transistor-like devices, and is therefore likely to have discovered digital computing.

Any civilization that makes a serious attempt to communicate must understand the importance of computing in communication, especially computing related to the detection of radio signals. Because of this, we can expect that a civilization capable of building an interstellar beacon has probably discovered digital computing in some form.

Aliens who understand math

An understanding of mathematics and geometry, as we know them, is another implicit requirement for interstellar communication. The best shape to use for a radiotelescope is a parabolic dish. If you cut a cross-section through the antenna of such an antenna, the shape of the cross section would be a parabola (Figure 12-2). The reason for this has to do with geometry. A parabola is defined by the formula $y=ax^2+bx+c$. This equation should be familiar to most people who've taken algebra or geometry. The curve this formula describes is also an ideal shape for a mirror, thus an antenna with this shape reflects incoming radiation in such a way that it converges on a single focal point, much like a solar oven (Figure 12-3).

The development of electronics and math are closely related because electricity is invisible. It's impossible to see the current flowing through a wire, or to see what's happening inside of a transistor, as shown in Figure 12-4 and Figure 12-5. To reliably design electronic devices, the inventors must be able to model their behavior using mathematical equations.

The following equations describe the behavior of the simplified transistor depicted in Figure 12-5:

$$Iab = Vab / R$$

$$R = Vcb * 1000$$

The first equation tells us that the current flowing through the device (Iab) is equal to the voltage applied to the device (Vab) divided by its resistance to electrical current (R). This value, R, is in turn determined by the voltage applied to the third connector (Vcb). The resistance of the device is equal to the control voltage multiplied by 1000. By increasing the control voltage applied to the device, we increase its resistance to electrical current, and decrease the amount of current flowing through the device.

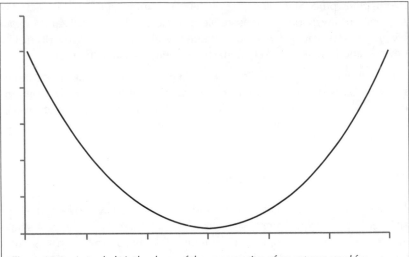

Figure 12-2: *A parabola is the shape of the cross-section of an antenna used for radioastronomy.*

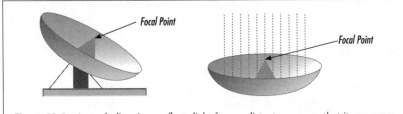

Figure 12-3: *A parabolic mirror reflects light from a distant source so that it converges on a central focal point.*

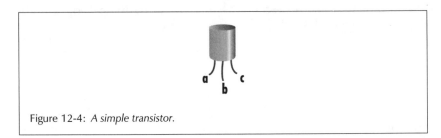

Figure 12-4: *A simple transistor.*

This example greatly oversimplifies the behavior of a transistor; however, the basic idea is the same. By modifying the control voltage (Vcb), it is possible to control the flow of a much larger current through the device. The equations used to describe a real transistor are more complex and take a large number of factors into account, such as the temperature of the device, the effect of current leaking from the control input through the device, and

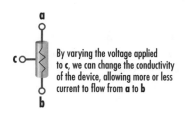

By varying the voltage applied to c, we can change the conductivity of the device, allowing more or less current to flow from a to b

Figure 12-5: *A simple transistor shown as part of an electrical circuit.*

many others. The important point in all of this is that to build transistor-like devices, it is very helpful to know how to use mathematics to first model their behavior.

Therefore, any civilization that is capable of interstellar communication must have discovered electronics. It is also likely that it understands math and geometry. While it's possible that a civilization could have discovered electricity without understanding math, it's hard to imagine it constructively using electricity without being able to model devices mathematically.

Aliens and binary code

We can conclude from these predictions that a communicating alien civilization will most likely understand electronics, digital computing, and mathematics. Therefore, it's a reasonable assumption that it will understand, or at least be capable of understanding, binary arithmetic. If it learns to build digital memory and logic circuits, it will learn binary code (since it is closely related to the behavior of these devices).

Even though we may have very little in common with an alien civilization, it is likely that both parties will be able to understand and manipulate digitally coded information. This is a fancy way of saying that using binary code, we will be able to communicate with computer programs written in binary code.

The point isn't to speculate that aliens would instantly recognize a binary encoded message, but merely to point out that in order to detect a signal at all, they would need to have developed most of these skills. Even if they had stalled out at our level of technological development, a minimum requirement to detect an interstellar signal, they would already know most of what is required to detect and begin deciphering this type of interstellar message.

Lingua numerica

The real challenge in all of this is figuring out how to embed meaning in a string of binary numbers. This forces us to think about what communication and symbols really mean, without getting caught in the trap of assuming that aliens will automatically understand ideas or concepts that are obvious to us (like the concept of emotional states).

Instead of speculating about what message aliens might choose to send to us, we will look at how to construct a message that can convey large amounts of useful information while at the same time can be easily decoded. This is just one of many possible approaches we could use to do this. The goal of this section is not to provide an encyclopedic overview of every SETI communication system that has been proposed. Instead, we focus here on describing one system from start to finish and how it can be applied to the task of sending a detailed message to an alien civilization.

The system that this book describes is the outgrowth of the author's work on a system for developing and distributing software via public data networks, such as the Internet. The general approach borrows ideas from genetics and artificial intelligence research (especially semantic networks). By combining these ideas, it is possible to create a system that is useful not only as a way to demonstrate how an alien message might be organized, but also as a framework for a new system for developing and distributing computer software.

The basic objective of the technique is to devise a system for transmitting machine instructions (computer programs) and for building a symbolic vocabulary based on numbers. We do this because we can describe computer programs using a basic vocabulary of less than 100 mathematical and logical symbols, all of which can be easily described to a recipient who understands electronics and digital computing. Although their underlying instructions may be simple, computer programs can exhibit complex behavior. We can use computer programs to perform an infinite variety of tasks, from displaying a compressed image to illustrating a complex situation, such as a simulated fly-by of the Earth. These computer programs, embedded throughout the message, will be the built-in clues that guide the reader in deciphering the message itself and in learning the meaning of symbols that represent abstract ideas.

The important point here is that it is possible to use computer programs to describe complex ideas in an abbreviated format. Take the idea of gravity, for example. Gravity is an abstract concept that cannot be seen directly, and as such, is hard to describe to someone who does not already know what you're talking about. Imagine trying to explain the word *gravity* to an alien using still images or symbols alone. It's kind of like playing a game of *Pictionary*™ over the telephone. If you can describe the idea with a computer program, you can recreate the behavior of objects under the influence of gravity in a simulation.

Imagine, for a moment, that you write a short computer program that simulates the interaction of several objects according to the laws of gravity. Such a program can be quite brief, consisting primarily of the equations used to describe the gravitational force between two objects based on their mass, velocity, and distance from each other.

The simulation would automatically run through an endless series of randomly generated examples. Some examples would depict two large objects orbiting each other at a distance, while another would depict a large number of smaller objects interacting with each other. This program could run for as long as the viewer allowed it. The program itself would only be a few hundred or a few thousand bytes long, yet it could depict an infinite variety of situations, all of which are consistent with the laws of gravity. The recipient viewing this program is going to notice a common theme in all of the simulated scenarios: they're all consistent with the laws of gravity. They will then be able to infer that the program is related to the concept of gravity. So, with one small statement, we can describe a comprehensive description of gravity, and later use this to define symbols related to this idea. We can apply this approach to a wide range of ideas, and use it to build a vocabulary of practical and abstract concepts that can be used to build a simplified language.

By using this approach, which we'll describe in detail in the upcoming chapters, we can create a message format that is very easy to decode and that can also convey an infinite diversity of messages, from computer programs to high-resolution color images. We're not limited to sending scientific equations or digital stick figures; we can build a general-purpose symbolic language that allows us to say pretty much anything we'd like to.

Just as we can use this general technique to tell our story to anyone who cares to listen, we can use this as a guide to anticipate how other civilizations might initiate contact with their neighbors.

Genes, memes, and igenes

The blueprint stored in DNA, an organism's genome, is, in effect, the program that describes how an organism builds itself and functions throughout its life. This information is subdivided into many discrete packages of instructions (genes). Each gene is typically associated with a particular function or trait (such as the instructions for producing the hemoglobin molecule used by red blood cells). An organism's DNA program is not read in its entirety from start to finish, but is broken down into many smaller units, each of which can be accessed as needed.

An *igene*, like a gene, is a set of computer instructions that can be incorporated into other, more complex programs. Just as the gene for hemoglobin doesn't describe how to build an entire blood cell, an igene that describes how to calculate the sine of a number is a component that deals with a small part of a larger task. This modular approach for packaging instructions allows us to create symbols that are shorthand for an otherwise complicated set of instructions, and to combine these symbols to describe complex processes in shorthand form. The key difference between an igene and a gene is the igene contains computation instructions whereas a gene describes how to build a protein that is used by an organism.

igenes can be used to build a symbolic vocabulary that allows us to perform a wide variety of math and computational tricks. The igenes can be combined to create complex systems, even though their building blocks are quite simple. We can use igenes to describe computer programs, and reusable segments of computer programs. We can then use these programs to do all sorts of things, like perform calculations, simulate systems, display images, or anything we normally do with conventional programs; the possibilities are limitless.

In Chapter 15, *Concepts and igenes*, we'll describe how to build programs composed of igenes to describe memes, or abstract symbols. Memes, as we discus in Chapter 19, *Abstract Symbols and Language*, are shorthand for abstract ideas. We'll do this by writing computer programs that display pictures of objects, simulate the situations or processes we'd like to describe, and so forth. This memetic vocabulary will form the foundation for an abstract language that we can use to describe a wide variety of concepts. All of this can be done starting with an apparently meaningless sequence of ones and zeros.

Hiding structure in numbers

When an alien civilization first encounters our hypothetical radio message (or we detect a similar message ourselves), all they will see is an apparently endless stream of binary numbers. At first, the message will appear to be hopelessly jumbled and devoid of meaning. If it is not formatted so that it contains clues about its structure, the party on the receiving end may never figure out how it is organized, and will never be able to get beyond receiving the signal.

The first step on the path to comprehension is to figure out how the series of numbers is organized into the equivalent of words, groups of words, groups of groups of words, and so on. A good metaphor to use is the general format of the information encoded in DNA. Learning the format of DNA is not the same thing as learning the meaning of the instructions encoded in DNA. The first step is to figure out how the information encoded in a genome is broken down into smaller subunits of information. Knowing how genetic information is organized doesn't mean that we understand what every gene does, but merely that we know how to parse this data into the equivalent of words and sentences.

DNA does this by using special sequences of base pairs, the genetic equivalent of letters, to denote the end of a sequence of instructions. We will do something similar with our series of binary numbers by using special sequences of binary digits to play the role of parentheses. We'll use these parentheses to bracket other numbers and to create groups of numbers, and groups of groups of numbers, as in the following example:

    ((((1001)(1010)) ((1000)(1010)) ((1001)(0101)) ((1000)(1100))
    ((1001)(0101)))

Which can be read in decimal form as:

    ((((9)(10)) ((8)(10)) ((9)(5)) ((8)(12)) ((9)(5)))

This example, thanks to the parentheses, is easy to break down into words and groups of words, and groups of groups of words. While this doesn't tell us anything about what this statement means, it does tell us where to start in breaking the message down for analysis. Now compare the above example with the following statement:

    1001101010001010100101011000110010010101

This is merely the first example without the parentheses. Imagine that you had received a message like this, except that instead of a few digits, you were looking at millions or billions of digits. Where does one word end and the next begin? How could you tell whether words are combined to form groups or groups of groups? Without a clue about how the message is organized into subunits, it would be very difficult to interpret. This type of structure tells the receiver how to parse the message, or break it down into its basic units.

Binary biology

So, how can we describe the idea of a parenthesis to an alien? Biology can teach us a lot about how to pack an immense amount of information into a small package. The entire human genome, in effect the program required to build a human being, consists of about 3 billion DNA base pairs, or roughly 6 billion bits of information. This is roughly equivalent to the amount of information stored on a single CD-ROM. What this demonstrates is that nature can condense everything it takes to build a human into this space, whereas Microsoft can barely manage to squeeze its suite of Office software into the same real estate. We can learn a great deal from nature's economy of words.

The DNA molecule encodes the information needed to build most life forms on Earth. The DNA molecule uses different combinations of base pairs to represent different amino acids, which are used to assemble more complex molecules, called proteins. Special combinations of base pairs represent the *start* of a series of instructions to build a protein. The DNA molecule encodes information using four different molecules: adenine, thymine, cytosine, and guanine (Figure 12-6).

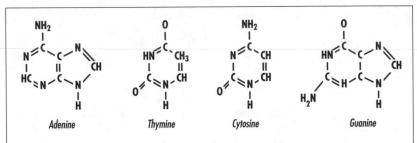

Figure 12-6: *Adenine, thymine, cytosine, and guanine: the basic units used to form genetic words in DNA.*

These four molecules, when found in groups of three (or *triplets*), form basic genetic words. These words can represent an amino acid (a building block for proteins), or they can represent a special "stop" word to mark the end of a sequence (or a word at the end of a sentence).

It's helpful to think of DNA encoding as we would an alphabet, just like the English alphabet. Forget, for a moment, about the fact that we're dealing with chemicals here. Think of each base pair as a letter: *A* for adenine, *T* for thymine, *C* for cytosine, and *G* for guanine.

By itself, a single letter means nothing. In order for them to mean something, these letters must be combined to form words. The information in DNA is organized in triplets, or sets of three base pairs. These triplets are analogous to words in English. For example, the sequence *GAC* is the word that represents *aspartic acid*. The format of DNA is more rigid than English. Every word in DNA is built from three base pairs (letters), no more, no less. These triplets are also referred to as *codons*. Since DNA uses three letters (molecules) to represent each word, and the letters have four possible values, DNA can encode a total of 64 different states in each three-character (letter) word. This means that DNA could, in theory, encode a maximum of 64 different words.

In practice, DNA encodes a total of 22 amino acids (see Table 12-1). This is because several different combinations can code for a single amino acid. (This appears to be an error-correction mechanism, so a random error in transcribing one letter in a DNA word will not necessarily produce the wrong amino acid.)

Table 12-1: *DNA codons and their meanings*

AMINO ACID	ABBREVIATION	DNA CODONS
Alanine	Ala	GCA, GCC, GCG, GCT
Cysteine	Cys	TGC, TGT
Aspartic Acid	Asp	GAC, GAT
Glutamic Acid	Glu	GAA, GAG
Phenylalanine	Phe	TTC, TTT
Glycine	Gly	GGA, GGC, GGG, GGT
Histidine	His	CAC, CAT
Isoleucine	Ile	ATA, ATC, ATT
Lysine	Lys	AAA, AAG
Leucine	Leu	TTA, TTG, CTA, CTC, CTG, CTT
Methionine	Met	ATG
Asparagine	Asn	AAC, AAT
Proline	Pro	CCA, CCC, CCG, CCT
Glutamine	Gln	CAA, CAG
Arginine	Arg	CGA, CGC, CGG, CGT
Serine	Ser	TCA, TCC, TCG, TCT, AGC, AGT
Threonine	Thr	ACA, ACC, ACG, ACT
Valine	Val	GTA, GTC, GTG, GTT
Tryptophan	Trp	TGG
Tyrosine	Tyr	TAC, TAT
Stop	.	TAA, TAG, TGA

These words can, in turn, be combined to form groups of words. The German language offers a good analogy. Many German words are formed by combining several words to create a single compound word. In the same way, several DNA words can be strung together to describe a protein that is formed using several amino acids. For example, combining the words arm, band, and uhr forms the word Armbanduhr. This example translates in English to *wristwatch*, or literally, "arm + band + clock."

A typical DNA instruction can be read in a format such as the following:

```
STOP : Alanine + Aspartic Acid + Glycine + Alanine : STOP
```

This instruction can be read as: "Build a protein by combining alanine, aspartic acid, glycine, and alanine." It would be coded in DNA as:

```
TAA GCC GAT GGA GCC TAA
```

The Stop instruction is important because an organism would otherwise produce infinitely long, tangled blobs of amino acids, instead of useful proteins that perform a specific function such as transporting oxygen in blood (i.e., hemoglobin).

We're going to do something similar with our endless stream of binary digits by creating two special series of "start" and "stop" instructions. One series, 111000111000111000, will always indicate the start of a word. Another series, 101000101000101000, will always indicate the end of a word. So, whenever we see the sequence of digits 111000111000111000, we see an *open parenthesis*, "(", and whenever we see the sequence of digits 101000101000101000, it can be interpreted as a *close parenthesis*, ")".

NOTE

The number 111000111000111000 doesn't have an inherent meaning. This number was chosen at random to use as an example throughout the book. In a real system, the sender could use any string of digits as a delimiter to separate symbols and groups of symbols.

Parentheses can also be described by assigning special states to the transmitted signal itself. If, for example, the message is embedded in a pulsed laser beacon, the sender could use special colors to describe "(" and ")" symbols (e.g., red=0, orange=1, yellow="open parenthesis," green="close parenthesis").

At first, the recipient of the message will see nothing more than a series of binary numbers with no apparent beginning or end. However, upon closer inspection, there will be certain sequences of digits that recur throughout the message. One of the first things our recipient will do is to start analyzing the series of digits to look for order or repeating patterns in the message. The open parenthesis and close parenthesis sequences will appear repeatedly throughout the message. The recipient will most likely look for repeating patterns in the message by analyzing the frequency with which different combinations of digits appear. This type of analysis, although it is requires a lot of computation, is fairly easy to do.

The trend that this frequency analysis will reveal is that these two series of digits occur repeatedly throughout the message. They also occur in a predictable order. An open parenthesis symbol will be followed by some data, and then by a close parenthesis symbol. The open and close parentheses symbols will also be encountered in equal numbers throughout the message as a whole.

This, by itself, does not reveal the meaning of the open parenthesis and close parenthesis sequences, but their use throughout the message is a strong indication that these sequences are important to deciphering the message.

The recipient will also know that, if the message contains useful information, it will most likely be organized into smaller units and subunits of information. So, the first thing the recipient will want to do is figure out how to parse the message, or to break it down into those smaller blocks of data.

Once the recipient discovers that the "(" and ")" sequences appear throughout the message, and sees that they almost always occur in pairs, it should be fairly easy to figure out that they are being used to bracket information—to define the start and end of a word or group of words. They will most likely try many different approaches before finding the right solution. When the recipient figures out that the "(" symbol equals 111000111000111000 and the ")" symbol equals 101000101000101000, the basic structure of the message will be revealed. For example:

```
11100011100011100011100011100011100010011010001010001010001110001
11000111000110011001010001010001010001110001110001110000001101000
10100010100011100011100011100001010110100010100010100011100011100
01110001100110010100010100010100010100010100101000101000
```

Although we can see a repeating pattern in this sequence of digits, it is difficult to see how this message is organized. What we'll do now is to replace the sequence 111000111000111000 with a "(" symbol to denote the start of a word. We'll replace the sequence 101000101000101000 with the symbol ")" to denote the end of a word. When we perform the translation, the series of digits above is reduced to:

```
((1001)(11001100)(0001)(010101)(11001100))
```

Now the structure to this message is revealed. We can see relatively short words bracketed by "(" and ")" symbols, and can also see groups of words bracketed by "(" and ")" symbols to create *expressions*.

While this doesn't tell the recipient anything about what the words mean, it does reveals the basic structure of the message. Once the recipient can parse the message into individual words and groups of words, they can then set about the task of determining what these numeric words mean.

The basic trick we're using here is to introduce an obvious, repeating pattern into an otherwise unintelligible message. In effect, what we're doing is repeating the following message over and over:

```
{useful information starts here}101010111001101101010101
11111010101010100000011001101001101{useful information ends
here}{useful information starts here}1011111100000111{useful
information ends here}
```

This approach allows the recipient to discern the basic structure of the message using only simple statistical analysis tools. This approach may also be easy to decipher because it mimics the way information is coded in biological systems, and therefore may look familiar to our distant recipient (assuming biological information is encoded in something similar to DNA on other planets, which it may not be).

Once these special symbols are known, a simple computer program could be employed to perform a search and replace operation, much like a word processor does. At this point, the goal is not to translate the message itself, but to figure out how it is organized into symbols, groups of symbols, groups of groups of symbols, and so on. Next, we'll look at how we can use this system to create a vocabulary of symbols that we can use to build a progressively more and more sophisticated message.

SYMBOLS

In the previous chapter, we learned how to add structure to a seemingly endless and incomprehensible string of binary digits. This important step enables the recipient to discern basic structures in the message, but says nothing about the meaning of the message itself. We're still a long way from our goal of sending information-laden messages to a party on the far end of our galaxy. The next critical step is to build a basic vocabulary of symbols that can be used to describe simple instructions, such as arithmetic operators. What we're talking about doing here is defining some of the basic elements of a simple programming language.

This programming language will enable us to perform the basic tasks required to build more complicated programs. In this chapter, we'll discuss how to:

- Describe algebraic expressions (such as $A+B=C$)

- Make decisions based on input conditions (e.g., "if condition A is true, then perform task X, otherwise perform task Y")

- Build a lexicon of symbols using previously defined symbols to create a progressively sophisticated palette of commands

- Label symbols according to their context, or usage, within an expression

- Group symbols into categories

This next step requires us to be part linguist and part teacher. In the previous chapter, we discussed how to recognize the basic structure of the message, or how to recognize the equivalent of words and sentences. In this chapter, we'll describe a basic vocabulary of symbols and a system for combining these symbols to create expressions that can then be combined to create machine-readable instructions (programs), and ultimately, a general-purpose language.

Interstellar flash cards

Using the simple system we developed in the previous chapter, we can now teach the receiving party a basic set of symbols. This is accomplished by sending sets of positive (good) and negative (bad) examples. This technique will be used throughout the remaining chapters.

The first thing we need to do is define a basic set of arithmetic symbols (or operators) that are used to build formulas. For example, we all know that = means "equals," and that > means "greater than." Most of us learned these concepts using a skill called *pattern recognition*.

Pattern recognition is a key component of learning and intelligence. This refers to the ability to discern patterns within a noisy background. A good example of this is the ability to spot an animal that is camouflaged by vegetation.

Intelligent animals expand upon this ability to visually identify potential threats. Some animals can understand labels, where a sound or visual symbol is used to refer to an object. Some of the most intelligent animals can group objects into categories (e.g., identifying objects by their general shape or color). This ability isn't limited to humans; some species of primates, dolphins, and parrots have the ability to understand the concept of categories.

Pattern recognition is a basic animal survival skill. The ability to spot a camouflaged predator in the bushes can literally mean the difference between life and death. The ability to recognize hiding prey makes the difference between finding a meal and going hungry. In these scenarios, the pattern the animal recognizes is the shape of another animal that is partially obscured by terrain or vegetation. Since the ability to quickly recognize a predator (and flee if necessary) is so important, it is easy to understand why natural selection will favor this trait. What highly intelligent animals, namely humans, have done, among other things, is expand upon this capability to recognize patterns in the mind's imagined universe, as well as in the real world.

The technique we use to define symbols takes advantage of an intelligent reader's ability to recognize patterns. The general process can be compared to teaching something using flashcards.

While a few of us are smart enough to learn new skills purely through explanation, most of us learn new skills through a combination of repetition and trial and error—once something becomes rote, we can pretty much operate on autopilot for most tasks. Our teachers presented us with many positive and negative examples of the concepts they were trying to explain. Once presented with enough examples, we learned to recognize that X>Y means that the number X was larger than the number Y, or that (1+2) is the same as 1+2=3. We're going to do the same thing in our coded message. The only difference is that instead of using flashcards, we'll use sets of equations to get our point across.

The equals symbol

One of the first mathematical concepts we will want to teach the receiver is the concept of equivalence. While this is an obvious idea to us (we've already learned it), it is difficult to teach using words alone, especially if you don't have a shared language to start with. As a challenge to yourself, try to define the concept without getting into a loop (this is similar to describing the color red to someone who has never seen the color red). However difficult equivalence is to explain verbally, it is easy to explain by example to someone who understands math.

The first thing we need to do is create a numeric symbol for what we refer to as an equal sign (=). Let's say, for example, that the number 10 (binary 1010) is an equals sign (=). The specific sequence of bits does not matter for our example; all we are going to do is say that the sequence 1010 is the same thing as our (=) symbol. This sequence of bits will not be used to say anything else except (=). At the same time, we want to create a symbol that means, "not equal to" (≠). We do this by assigning the number 11 (binary 1011) to mean not equal (≠).

The party receiving our message for the first time will have no idea that the sequence 1010 means = or that the sequence 1011 means ≠. These will just be one of many millions of bits of information. To the naïve listener, these sequences will have no special meaning.

To teach the other party how to interpret these symbols, we simply transmit examples. Using the technique we learned in Chapter 12, *Binary DNA*, the message we send might look something like this:

```
((1111)(1010)(1111)) : 1111 = 1111
((1111)(1011)(1100)) : 1111 ≠ 1100
((1111)(1011)(1101)) : 1111 ≠ 1101
((1111)(1011)(0000)) : 1111 ≠ 0000
((1101)(1010)(1101)) : 1101 = 1101
((1100)(1011)(1111)) : 1100 ≠ 1111
...
```

NOTE

The parentheses sequences have been replaced by (and) characters for brevity and readability.

Also, software developers will probably notice that these introductory examples do not differentiate between commands (operators) and numbers (data). I have glossed over this issue for now, and will address it later, in order to keep this particular example simple. We'll come back to this in a moment.

In the sequence above, we're doing nothing more than sending a series of examples to define the = and ≠ symbols. When analyzing this series of messages, the receiver will notice that 1010 is *always* placed between two identical numbers, and that 1011 is *always* placed between two unequal numbers. This is akin to a teacher showing a student a series of positive (good) and negative (bad) examples of a concept.

With a few examples, we are able to define the concepts of *equal* and *not equal*. We can now proceed to describe additional arithmetic symbols, which will be used to build the foundation for a general purpose programming language.

Interstellar algebra

The next hurdle we need to cross is to define a set of symbols used for basic arithmetic and Boolean logic. These symbols will give us the foundation upon which we can build simple computer programs.

Now that we defined equal and not equal, we can teach new concepts using sets of positive and negative examples. Starting with addition, we can create a set of symbols used in basic arithmetic, as shown in Table 13-1.

Table 13-1: *Basic arithmetic symbols and their binary translations*

SYMBOL	DESCRIPTION	DECIMAL NUMBER	BINARY EQUIVALENT
+	Add	12	1100
−	Subtract	13	1101
×	Multiply	14	1110
÷	Divide	15	1111

To describe these symbols, we merely transmit a set of short examples. These messages might read as follows:

```
((0001)(1100)(0001)(1010)(0010)) : 1 + 1 = 2
((0010)(1010)(0001)(1100)(0001)) : 2 = 1 + 1
((0001)(1011)(0001)(1100)(0010)) : 1 ≠ 1 + 2
...
```

```
((0001)(1110)(0001)(1010)(0001)) : 1 x 1 = 1
((0010)(1110)(0010)(1010)(0100)) : 2 x 2 = 4
((0001)(1110)(0010)(1010)(0010)) : 1 x 2 = 2
...
((1111)(1101)(0001)(1010)(1110)) : 15 - 1 = 14
```

Using this technique, we can define symbols for basic arithmetic operations. We can do this without resorting to drawings, and without assuming any special knowledge on the part of the receiver (except that they can add). Most of these basic concepts can be explained by sending a relatively small set of examples.

Using numbers as symbols

The important point to grasp here is that we are using numbers as symbols for ideas, or concepts. This is another important point that we will come back to throughout the book.

In the examples, we have used the number 1100 as a numeric equivalent of the plus sign (+). This number itself has no inherent meaning; we could have used 0101010101 or any other sequence of digits to mean +. The point is, we have defined a unique sequence of digits and are consistent in the way we apply it (i.e., we don't use 1100111100 to mean + in one place, and 11010101 to mean + in another).

Although this may seem like an odd system, we have been doing this with computers for decades. The central processing unit (CPU) in a computer executes programs in a form called *machine code*. Machine code is a series of numeric instructions that the CPU recognizes as commands. Although computer programs are often written in an English-like format, they are converted into numeric instructions prior to execution.

To understand this, let's look at an Intel microprocessor. Table 13-2 lists some of the commands recognized by an early Intel CPU, the 80186 microprocessor (a predecessor to the Pentium™ chips widely used in desktop computers).

Table 13-2: *A partial list of Intel 80186 CPU Instruction Set*

COMMAND	DESCRIPTION
AAA	ASCII Adjust for Addition
AAD	ASCII Adjust for Division
AAM	ASCII Adjust for Multiply
AAS	ASCII Adjust for Subtraction
ADC	ADDition with Carry

Table 13-2: *A partial list of Intel 80186 CPU Instruction Set (continued)*

COMMAND	DESCRIPTION
ADD	ADDition
AND	Logical AND
BOUND	Detect Value Out of Range
CALL	Call Procedure (Subroutine)
CBW	Convert Byte to Word
CLC	Clear Carry Flag
...	

Each of the commands in the instruction set is identified by a unique 8-bit number (an integer ranging from 0 to 255). We've used mnemonic identifiers for readability. However, the CPU responds exclusively to numeric symbols.

So, for example, when we send the *ADD* command to the CPU, it sums the two numbers in its registers (temporary memory locations). When we apply the *IDIV* command, the CPU will perform an integer division. The *JUMP* commands are used to branch off to different parts of a program (sequence of instructions), depending on the outcome of comparisons. For example, "If R1 is greater than R2, JUMP to location X in program."

With a few dozen basic computational symbols, we have everything we need to build simple computer programs. The point of this example isn't to say that this is the only way to organize things, but to offer an example of how we can treat numbers as mathematical and computational symbols.

Using this technique to define symbols, we can quickly build a basic mathematical and logical vocabulary that describes the core symbols used in computer programs. Table 13-3 contains an example of what the basic symbolic vocabulary might look like.

Table 13-3: *Lexicon of basic arithmetic symbols*

SYMBOL ID	SYMBOL	DESCRIPTION
7	Next symbol is a register	The word following this symbol identifies a memory register (storage location)
8	Next symbol is a command	The word following this symbol is a command (operator)
9	Next symbol is a number	The word following this symbol is a number
10	=	Equal(s)
11	≠	Not equal

Table 13-3: *Lexicon of basic arithmetic symbols (continued)*

SYMBOL ID	SYMBOL	DESCRIPTION
12	+	Addition
13	–	Subtraction
14	×	Multiplication
15	÷	Division
16	AND	Logical AND
17	OR	Logical OR
18	XOR	Exclusive OR
19	NOT	Not (binary inverse)

Using this example vocabulary of symbols, we can then build expressions that can be combined to create simple computer programs:

((((9)(1)) ((8)(12)) ((9)(1)) ((8)(10)) ((9)(2)))

This example statement, when translated into English would read:

1 + 1 = 2

This is a simple example, but we can use this technique to build progressively more and more complex igenes that can ultimately be combined to create programs that do some really interesting and useful things.

Context

Another lesson we need to teach ET is how to tell the difference between a command (an *operator*) and data (a *number*). This is a potential stumbling block, because we're sending our entire message as a series of binary numbers. In some cases, we will use a number as a placeholder for a symbol or command (e.g., the number 10 means =), and in others, we may use the same number (10) as data. This dilemma is easily illustrated in the following example.

The number 10 will be the equivalent of an equal sign (=), and the number 12 will be the equivalent of a plus sign (+). Using the format we've described so far, here's how we would say "10+2=12":

((1010)(1100)(0010)(1010)(1100))

or:

((10)(12)(2)(10)(12))

The problem here is that the recipient cannot easily decide when the number 10 is to be interpreted as a command, and when it is intended as a number to be manipulated by a command. So, the recipient could just as easily read this message as:

= + 2 = +

This clearly leaves a lot of room for error. So, before we teach the recipient a large library of arithmetic symbols, our first order of business is to teach them to recognize the context of the numeric words in the message. This is analogous to teaching someone to recognize whether a word is being used as a noun or as a verb in a sentence.

Symbols or words, by themselves, often convey no meaning unless they are combined with others. The context in which a symbol is used is often just as important as the root meaning of the symbol itself.

The notion of *context* is something we're all familiar with. Although, once we've mastered grammar, we are not often consciously aware of its importance in communication. In most human languages, words may be used in several different contexts. Among the most important uses are nouns, verbs, and modifiers. Often, the same root word can be used in any of these contexts. This context tells the listener whether a word is being used to refer to an object, to an action or event, or to describe another word in an expression.

Context allows the author to describe how a symbol is used within a larger collection of symbols. This may seem like a trivial invention, but it allows us to combine symbols to express an infinite variety of ideas and situations.

Context is just as important to the comprehension of a coded numeric message as it is in the spoken or written form. The purpose of this section is to describe the importance of context as it relates to how a symbol enables the author to interleave many different types of information into a single message to create expressions that combine symbols, variables, and numeric data.

When a number is just a number

The hypothetical message we're building is composed entirely from a string of binary numbers. This string of numbers, as we discussed in Chapter 12, can be parsed into individual words, groups of words, groups of groups, and so on. This parsing operation does not allow the listener to automatically translate the message, but merely to break it down into a series of numeric words that can be arranged to form the equivalent of sentences and paragraphs.

So far, we've limited the discussion of context in this chapter to discerning the difference between a symbol for an arithmetic command, and a number or data that is processed by a command. Even with this limited, either-or grammar, we can build equations and sets of instructions that resemble computer programs. By extending this further, we can build a grammatical framework that allows us to combine numbers, symbols, variables, images, and grammar elements to create general-purpose languages.

Just as we developed a basic vocabulary of numeric symbols to represent concepts such as addition, subtraction, and so on, we can develop a similar vocabulary of numeric symbols to denote the context in which other symbols are used within an expression. One way to do this is to combine pairs of numeric words, as in the following example:

    (((1001)(1100)) ((1000)(1100)) ((1001)(1100)) ((1000)(1010))
    ((1001)(11000)))

Which can be read as follows in decimal form:

    (((9)(12)) ((8)(12)) ((9)(12)) ((8)(10)) ((9)(24)))

Which can be read as follows in shorthand form:

12_{number} $12_{command}$ 12_{number} $10_{command}$ 24_{number}

Which can be translated to:

    ([12](12)[12](10)[24])

Or:

    ([12](+)[12](=)[24])

In this system (which is not the only way to denote context), we build an expression by combining two numeric words to form a compound symbol. These symbols are then grouped to form a complete expression. Each pair of numeric words follows a predictable format. The first numeric word denotes the context of the word that follows it.

The number 8 (binary 1000) means that the number next to it should be interpreted as a symbol or command. The number 9 (binary 1001) means that the number following it should be interpreted as a number that is operated on by another symbol or command (e.g., the "2" in the statement "1+2=3").

This general formula for denoting context is simple to decode, and can be extended to describe other contexts. Consider the following example:

    ((1024)(9819)) ((1025)(7162)) ((1024)(6555))

The symbols in this example might be decoded as follows in Table 13-4.

Table 13-4: *Meaning of symbols used in example*

DECIMAL ID	USE	MEANING
1024	Context	Noun
1025	Context	Verb

Table 13-4: *Meaning of symbols used in example (continued)*

DECIMAL ID	USE	MEANING
6555	Symbol	Cat
7612	Symbol	Chase
9819	Symbol	Dog

In this example, the numeric word 1024, when paired with another word, means the symbol should be interpreted as a noun. The numeric word 1025 means the symbol should be interpreted as a verb. Hence the example above can be read as "noun^{dog} verb$^{chase(s)}$ noun^{cat}."

This is a simplified example, but it illustrates how this general approach can be extended to create an abstract language for communicating with other civilizations, something we will discuss in detail in Chapter 19, *Abstract Symbols and Language*.

Semantic building blocks

We can incorporate many types of symbols and data in a message. What is unique about the message we are building is that it can contain both machine instructions (computer programs) and symbols for representing abstract ideas. This gives the sender a great deal of flexibility for explaining ideas, and in combining symbols to form complex expressions.

Symbols and commands

The first type of word we described in Chapter 12 was a symbol, or command. Numeric words were used as placeholders for symbols or machine-readable commands to build a basic vocabulary of arithmetic and logic symbols that, in turn, form the foundation for a simple computer programming language. This programming language can then be used to create progressively more sophisticated programs, capable of performing a wide range of tasks (such as simulating the behavior of a complex physical system).

Data

Commands are useless unless they have data to act upon and process. To do this, we need to be able to differentiate between a command and a number. Since the entire message is composed of numbers, there needs to be a system for denoting when a number is being used as a placeholder for a symbol (i.e., the number "12" means "+" in one context), and when it represents raw data (i.e., "12" simply means the number "12" in another).

Local and global variables

Local and global variables, which will be discussed in detail in Chapter 14, *Memory and Programming*, are used as storage containers for information. Variables enable programs to store, recall and process information on the fly.

With variables, we can create general-purpose programs that are composed of generic instructions like the following:

```
V3 = V1 + V2
V6 = V4 + V5
V7 = V3 x V6
```

The first expression in this example says, "Add the contents of variable 1 and variable 2, and store the results in variable 3. The program does not make any implicit assumptions about which numbers are stored in variables 1 and 2; it merely processes whatever data is presented to it at the time the program is run.

This convention allows the sender to create general-purpose programs that can be run in an infinite variety of configurations.

Images

Images, which we'll discuss in Chapter 17, *Pictures*, are a powerful tool for illustrating a wide variety of ideas. It is fairly easy to represent images in coded form by using bitmaps. Bitmaps are two-dimensional arrays of binary numbers which, when displayed in a grid, depict an image.

However, these images, like everything else in the message, are reduced to a string of binary digits. Without a way to tag these numbers to say, "These digits represent an image," it will be difficult for the reader to determine how the numbers should be interpreted.

So, just as we created context labels for symbols, raw data, and variables, we'll assign another context label to indicate that the series of digits that follows it will describe an image. This will enable the sender to interleave numbers, symbols, variables, and images (such as the example in Figure 13-1) into a single, easily parsed message.

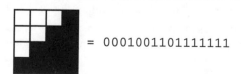

Figure 13-1: *An example of a two-dimensional bitmap represented in numeric and graphical form.*

Abstract language: Nouns, verbs, and modifiers

The goal of this part of the book is to demonstrate how these tools can ultimately be used to create a general-purpose abstract language. To do this, we also need to define several additional contexts in which numeric symbols can be used; this will be described in Chapters 18 through 21. At the most basic level, we need to define three contexts in which numeric words can be used to create an abstract language—nouns, verbs, and a modifier that describes the relationship between the two:

Nouns (object symbols)
> One context in which we'll use symbols is as placeholders for objects, or the equivalent of nouns (e.g., "The *spacecraft* orbits the nearest moon"). In this context, the word *spacecraft* is used as a symbol for an object or idea.

Verbs (difference of action symbols)
> Another context in which we'll use symbols is to depict an action, change of state, or event (e.g., "The spacecraft *orbits* the nearest moon"). In this context, the word *orbits* is used to describe how an object changes or interacts with another object.

Modifiers (descriptors)
> The final context we'll use to describe, or provide further information about an object (noun) or action (verb) within an expression is a modifier (e.g., "The spacecraft orbits the *nearest* moon").

While it may seem outlandish to assume that an alien civilization will use language in the same way we do, the concepts behind nouns, verbs, and modifiers are universally applicable. A noun is simply a placeholder for an object in an expression. A verb is a placeholder for an action or process (change of state over time). A modifier simply provides more information about nouns or verbs in an expression.

Shorthand notation

For future reference, we will use shorthand notation to describe the context of the words in an expression, much like we replaced the number 000111000111000111 with the open parenthesis "(" symbol. We did this to make the examples easier to read, and will apply a similar form of shorthand notation to denote the context and arrangement of words.

Word structure and grouping

In Chapter 11, *CETI—Communication with Extraterrestrial Intelligence*, we discussed a simple scheme where two unique series of digits would be used as open and close parentheses. These symbols allow the sender to easily delimit the boundaries between words, and to group words into nested assemblies of words, and groups of words. This simple invention allows the author to create elaborately structured expressions, and is also easy to decode on the receiving end.

In this system, the series of digits 111000111000111000 means "(", and the series 101000101000101000 means ")". Recall that the numbers themselves are not special. We could have used any arbitrary series of digits, or special carrier signal states, to do this. What is especially useful about the parenthesis symbols is they can be combined to create elaborate nested structures. From now on, we'll always use the shorthand symbols in place of the actual binary numbers to denote open and close parentheses in example programs.

Context labels

We'll also use shorthand notation to describe the context in which words are used in an expression. Table 13-5 summarizes the verbose and shorthand expressions used to denote context in future example programs.

Table 13-5: *Shorthand notation used to denote context*

CONTEXT	VERBOSE FORM	SHORTHAND FORM
Local variable/memory register	((6)(x))	|x|
Global variable/memory register	((7)(x))	{x}
Symbol/command	((8)(x))	(x)
Data/number	((9)(x))	[x]

The shorthand form used to denote context is a simple substitution. So, ((9)(2)) becomes ⌊2⌋, while ((7)(2)) becomes {2}. The purpose of this is to make the examples tighter and easier to read. Let's look at some example expressions (see Table 13-6) that use basic arithmetic.

Table 13-6: *Plain text, verbose, and shorthand forms of expression*

PLAIN TEXT	VERBOSE FORM	SHORTHAND FORM
1+1=2	(((9)(1))((8)(12))((9)(1))((8)(10))((9)(2)))	([1](12)[1](10)[2])
1×1=1	(((9)(1))((8)(14))((9)(1))((8)(10))((9)(1)))	([1](14)[1](10)[1])

Table 13-6: *Plain text, verbose, and shorthand forms of expression (continued)*

PLAIN TEXT	VERBOSE FORM	SHORTHAND FORM
2+2=4	(((9)(2))((8)(12))((9)(2))((8)(10))((9)(4)))	([2](12)[2](10)[4])
2×2=4	(((9)(2))((8)(14))((9)(2))((8)(10))((9)(4)))	([2](14)[2](10)[4])
3+3=6	(((9)(3))((8)(12))((9)(3))((8)(10))((9)(6)))	([3](12)[3](10)[6])
3×3=9	(((9)(3))((8)(14))((9)(3))((8)(10))((9)(9)))	([3](14)[3](10)[9])

Notice how the shorthand form allows us to display expressions in a more compact format. Keep in mind that all of these expressions, whether we read them in shorthand or longhand form, are ultimately converted to strings of binary numbers. So, we're primarily doing this to make the expressions easy for humans to read.

Mapping ideas in two dimensions

By assigning numbers to ideas, we're creating a type of coordinate system that allows us to create a form of map. One way to visualize this is to imagine a map of California. The map has two dimensions: a horizontal (East-West) axis, and a vertical (North-South) axis. Any point on the map can be identified using a pair of East-West, North-South coordinates.

We can apply this same idea to the practice of mapping ideas and their usage (or context). Like the map of California, this idea map has two dimensions. The coordinates on the horizontal axis identify a specific idea according to its numeric address (e.g., 12 for +, 13 for −, etc.) The coordinates on the vertical axis identify the context in which the idea is used, as shown in Figure 13-2.

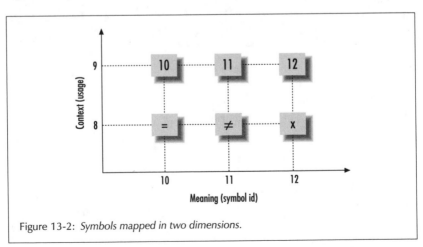

Figure 13-2: *Symbols mapped in two dimensions.*

Figure 13-2 depicts how three symbols (10, 11, and 12) appear in a two-dimensional coordinate system. In this mapping system, the ideas are expressed using *xy* coordinates, where *x* identifies the symbol to be used, and *y* describes the context in which it is used. We can use this information to build a translation table, as shown in Table 13-7.

Table 13-7: *Translation table with two-dimensional (x,y) addresses for symbols*

SYMBOL ADDRESS	MEANING	SYMBOL ADDRESS	MEANING
(10,8)	=	(10,9)	10
(11,8)	≠	(11,9)	11
(12,8)	+	(12,9)	12

Notice how the same idea (e.g., 10) can take on different meanings, depending on the context in which it is used. This system for mapping ideas will be especially important later, when we discuss how to create a general purpose language that combines symbols for objects (nouns), actions (verbs), and modifiers (adjectives and adverbs).

Later in the book, we will also discuss how a third dimension can be added to this mapping system, to allow for concepts from multiple senders to be combined into a single lexicon (the third dimension, or *z* axis, would identify the source or author of the symbol).

Boolean logic

Using what we've learned, we can now send simple equations to our distant neighbors. However, they have most likely figured out that 2+2 does *indeed* equal 4, and the novelty of these messages will quickly wear off if we don't give send them something that's more interesting.

By combining basic arithmetic with Boolean logic, we can create a simple programming language that can be used to build progressively more and more sophisticated programs. Boolean logic allows us to compare numbers and to make decisions based on these comparisons. All of computer programming can really be boiled down to the following:

If condition *X* is met, then do *this*, otherwise do something *else*.

While this is a very simple concept, it allows us to create programs that perform complicated tasks, such as forecasting the weather from a mathematical model or creating an artificial environment for a video game.

The challenge here is to explain the concepts of Boolean logic and program control without resorting to flowcharts, Cliffs Notes™, or other shortcuts.

Remember, we are not playing Pictionary. Our only means of communicating with the folks on the far end of the galaxy is via a stream of digits. There is also going to be a minimum 10-year time delay in the conversation. So if the folks on the other end of the line don't "get it," they will have to wait a long time for a hint.

There are many ways to do this; what follows is just one way of defining the symbolic vocabulary needed to create a simple programming language.

Boolean arithmetic

Boolean arithmetic is a special form of math that applies to binary numbers. While the ordinary rules for addition, subtraction, and other basic math apply to binary numbers, there are also special operations we can perform on binary numbers. A partial list of the symbols we need to define are shown in Table 13-8.

Table 13-8: *Short list of symbols related to boolean arithmetic*

COMMAND	DECIMAL	BINARY	MEANING
FALSE	0	0	Means that a test condition is not met
TRUE	1	1	Means that a test condition is met and is true
AND	2	10	Performs AND operation on two or more binary numbers
OR	3	11	Performs OR operation on two or more binary numbers
XOR	4	100	Performs Exclusive OR (XOR) operation on two or more binary numbers
NOT	5	101	Returns the inverse of a binary number

This is a partial list of the symbols we'd need to describe, but their explanation should give you the basic idea of how they can be used.

TRUE OR FALSE?

The two most basic concepts in Boolean logic are *true* and *false*. This is a fundamental concept in computing. If a certain condition is met, it is true. If a condition is not met, it is false. So, the first thing we need to do is define two numeric symbols, or sequences of binary digits, to mean true and false, respectively. True and false are basic concepts in binary arithmetic, so we'll use the numbers 0 and 1 as symbols (0 means false, 1 means true).*

---

* For the sake of brevity, we will define the symbols as *T* for "true" and *F* for "false" rather than spelling them out each time.

To demonstrate this idea, we'll send a series of positive and negative examples to highlight true and false conditions as follows:

```
((([1](+)[2](=)[3])) (=)(1))
((([1](+)[2](=)[4])) (=)(0))
((([1](-)[0](=)[1])) (=)(1))
((([1](-)[1](=)[1])) (=)(0))
```

Now, let's look at two of these statements up close:

```
((([1](+)[2](=)[3])) (=)(1))
```

which means:

```
([1] (+) [2] (=) [3]) (=) (1)
```

and:

```
((([1](+)[2](=)[4]) (=)(0))
```

which means:

```
(1 + 2 = 4) = (0)
```

In both instances, we've built a *nested expression*. The first statement uses the statement (1+2=3) as a term in another equation (1+2=3)=1 to show that 1+2=3 equates with another symbol. This basic principle is used to send several statements that show the relationship between a number and a particular symbol.

To define a symbol for *T*, we'll send equations that are obviously correct (e.g., 1+2=3). The first statement in the two examples above is used to define a symbol for a true statement. Likewise, when we want to define an *F* symbol, we send equations that are obviously incorrect (e.g., 1+2=4).

Given enough examples, the receiver will notice a pattern in the series of examples. They will see that the correct equations are equated with one symbol, while obviously invalid equations, such as "1+2=5," are equated with another symbol. We don't need a huge number of examples to do this. A few dozen examples should be enough to get the ideas of *true* and *false* across. Then, we'll proceed to define symbols for other Boolean operations such as *AND*, *OR*, and *NOT*.

AND

The AND operation compares two binary numbers as follows. Let's first look at two single digit (bit) numbers, A and B. The AND result will produce a result C (Table 13-9). If either A or B is equal to 0, AND will give a result of 0. If both A and B are equal to 1, AND will give a result of 1.

Table 13-9: *A List of the possible states for AND operation (two bits in, one bit out)*

A	B	RESULT (C)
0	0	0
0	1	0
1	0	0
1	1	1

An AND operation can be applied to single digits, but it can also be applied to large numbers. The following example shows how the AND operator works on larger numbers. If there are two 1s in a column, the corresponding digit in the result is 1. If either of the two upper digits in a column is 0, the resulting digit is a 0:

```
    00111001
AND 00011001
    00011001

    11111000
AND 00011000
    00011000

    01010101
AND 10101010
    00000000

    11111111
AND 11111111
    11111111
```

We can define the AND symbol by transmitting a series of positive and negative examples as follows:

```
([101111001](10)[000111000](=)[000111000])
([1100](10)[0100](=)[0100])
([1100](10)[0011](=)[0000])
([1100](10)[1100](=)[1100])
```

The idea is to send a sufficient number of examples so the recipient can deduce the use of the unknown symbol (0010) in the example set. Given enough examples, the recipient will be able to see that the symbol 10 (decimal 2) means AND.

OR

The OR operator works slightly differently than the AND operator. The behavior of this operation can be described as:

```
If A or B = 1 Then C = 1
```

This operation is described in Table 13-10. An OR operation is typically used to test whether one or more input digits are equal to 1 (true).

Table 13-10: *Table of possible states for an OR operation (two input bits, one output bit)*

A	B	RESULT (C)
0	0	0
0	1	1
1	0	1
1	1	1

When we apply this operator to larger numbers, we'll get results like those below:

```
    00011100
OR  00110010
    00111100

    01010101
OR  10101010
    11111111

    00011000
OR  00000000
    00011000
```

To define our OR symbol, we do the same thing we did when we defined the AND symbol; we send a series of positive and negative examples:

```
([101111001](11)[000111000](=)[101111001])
([1100](11)[0100](=)[1100])
([1100](11)[0011](=)[1111])
([1100](11)[1100](=)[1100])
```

NOT

The NOT operator is a simple operation that's used to generate the inverse of a binary number. As illustrated in the following example, if digit A = 1, we simply flip the value of A to 0 (and vice versa):

```
NOT 011000 = 100111
NOT 111100 = 000011
NOT 010101 = 101010
NOT 000000 = 111111
NOT 111111 = 000000
```

We can express this example in the form of:

```
((101)[111001])(=)[000110])
((101)[111111])(=)[000000])
((101)[000111])(=)[111000])
((101)[010101])(=)[101010])
((101)[000000])(=)[111111])
```

Comparative statements

Once we have defined symbols to perform basic arithmetic functions (true, false, etc.), the next thing that we need to do is define symbols that describe comparative relationships between numbers. The greater than symbol (>) is used to say number X is larger than number Y. These statements are an important part of computing since computer programs rely on comparisons (IF-THEN statements).

We can use the same technique we used to teach basic arithmetic symbols to describe most of the Boolean arithmetic symbols. These symbols are defined in Table 13-11. These symbols are used to compare other symbols or numbers, and can also be used to describe how one symbol relates to another symbol.

Table 13-11: *Symbols used to compare other symbols or numbers*

SYMBOL	DESCRIPTION	DECIMAL CODE	BINARY EQUIVALENT
>	Greater than	16	10000
≥	Greater than or equal to	17	10001
<	Less than	18	10010
≤	Less than or equal to	19	10011
⊂	Member of a set/category	20	10100
⊄	Is not a member of a set/category	21	10101

The >, , <, and ≤ symbols are good examples of operators that can be used to compare numbers against each other. These symbols are a crucial component in machine language programs because they are the basic building blocks for computer programs (e.g., if X is greater than Y, execute procedure Z).

The ⊂ and ⊄ symbols can be used to describe how symbols relate to each other. For example, symbol X is a member or is not a member of category Z. These symbols, and others like them, will be used to group symbols into categories and to build a map of the relationships among symbols.

DEFINING COMPARISON OPERATORS

To define comparison symbols such as >, , <, and ≤, we'll send a series of examples to illustrate positive and negative examples of each concept. For example:

```
((TRUE)[1101](>)[1100])
((TRUE)[1101](>)[0111])
((TRUE)[1101](>)[0110])
((TRUE)[1101](>)[0101])
((FALSE)[1101](>)[0100])

..
((TRUE)[1101](≥)[1101])
((TRUE)[1101](≥)[1100])
((FALSE)[1101](≥)[1110])

..
((TRUE)[1101](<)[1110])
((TRUE)[1101](<)[1111])
((FALSE)[1101](<)[1101])

..
((TRUE)[1101](≤)[1101])
((TRUE)[1101](≤)[1110])
((TRUE)[1101](≤)[1111])
((FALSE)[1101](≤)[1100])
```

NOTE

The symbols >, ≥, <, and ≤ are represented in their shorthand form for readability. In an actual message, the labels TRUE, FALSE, >, ≥, <, and ≤ would be replaced by numeric symbols.

This series of examples has been designed to reveal patterns we want to display to the recipient of our interstellar message. Once deciphered, the recipient can easily deduce the meaning (or usage) of each new symbol.

DEFINING RELATIONAL SYMBOLS

The ⊂ and ⊄ symbols can be used to describe how one symbol relates to another symbol (i.e., whether the symbol is or is not a member of a category). This type of symbol will be very important when we start building a lexicon of symbols for objects, categories and, ultimately, abstract ideas.

The ⊂ symbol is intended to mean, "X is a member of category Y." In contrast, the ⊄ symbol is intended to mean, "X is not a member of category Y."

This is an interesting example because we haven't described the concept of a category or set. We can use categories to group symbols into families, and ultimately, to build a translation table that describes each symbol in terms of other symbols (a semantic network). First, we need to get the idea of a category across to our audience.

We can define the concept of a category by defining several symbols that are associated with certain types of numbers, and then incorporate these symbols into sentences that define the $\subset$ and $\not\subset$ symbols.

For this example, we will create three symbols to represent three types of numbers: even numbers (i.e., 2, 4, 6, ...), odd numbers (i.e., 1, 3, 5, 7, ...), and prime numbers (i.e., 1, 2, 3, 5, 7, 11, 13, 17, ...). Table 13-12 describes the symbols used to represent these ideas.

Table 13-12: *List of categories used to describe different types of numbers*

DESCRIPTION	DIGIT	BINARY EQUIVALENT
Even Number	2, 4, 6, 8, etc.	10110
Odd Number	1, 3, 5, 7, etc.	10111
Prime Number	1, 2, 3, 5, 7, 11, 13, 17, etc.	11000

These symbols can be defined by sending a set of examples as we've done before, such as the following:

```
([0010](1010)(10110)(1010)(11000))      2=even=prime
([0100](1010)(10110)(1011)(11000))      4=even≠prime
([0110](1010)(10110))                   6=even
([1000](1010)(10110))                   8=even
([0001](1010)(10111)(=)(11000))         1=odd=prime
([0011](1010)(10111)(=)(11000))         3=odd=prime
([0101](1010)(10111)(=)(11000))         5=odd=prime
([0111](1010)(10111)(1010)(11000))      7=odd=prime
([1001](1010)(10111)(1011)(11000))      9=odd≠prime
([1001](1011)(11000))                   9≠prime
```

The recipient will quickly see that we're associating the symbols 10110, 10111, and 11000 with different classes of numbers (odd, even, and prime, respectively).

The next thing we will do is send a series of examples to introduce the $\subset$ and $\not\subset$ symbols. We will use some basic rules from arithmetic in these examples. For example, we know—and we assume the recipient will know—the following:

- All prime numbers, except 2, are odd numbers.
- No even numbers, except 2, are prime numbers.
- Not all odd numbers are prime numbers.
- The sum of an odd number and an even number is an odd number.
- The sum of two even numbers is an even number.
- The sum of two odd numbers is an even number.

We can express these rules symbolically with the following:

```
((1) (((10110)(10000)[10])(10101)(11000)))
```

which can be read as:

```
((TRUE)((EVEN NUMBER)(>)(2))(⊄)(PRIME NUMBER))
```

Additional rules can be expressed in shorthand as follows:

```
((FALSE)((EVEN NUMBER)(>)(2))(⊂)(PRIME NUMBER))
((TRUE)((EVEN NUMBER)(+)(ODD NUMBER)(=)(ODD NUMBER))
((TRUE)((ODD NUMBER)(+)(ODD NUMBER)(=)(EVEN NUMBER))
((TRUE)((EVEN NUMBER)(+)(EVEN NUMBER)(=)(EVEN NUMBER))
```

NOTE

Remember that in an actual message, the labels TRUE, FALSE, etc., would be replaced with numeric symbols.

We also repeat some of our earlier examples, substituting the = symbol with the ⊂ symbol. These will read as follows:

`([0010](10100)(10110))`	2 is member of even
`([0100](10100)(10110))`	4 is member of even
`([0110](10100)(10110))`	6 is member of even
`([1000](10100)(10110))`	8 is member of even
`([0001](10100)(10111))`	1 is member of odd
`([0001](10100)(11000))`	1 is member of prime
`([0011](10100)(10110))`	3 is member of odd
`([0011](10100)(11000))`	3 is member of prime
`([0101](10100)(10110))`	5 is member of odd
`([0101](10100)(11000))`	5 is member of prime
`([0111](10100)(10110))`	7 is member of odd
`([0111](10100)(11000))`	7 is member of prime
`([1001](10100)(10110))`	9 is member of odd
`([1001](10101)(11000))`	9 is not member of prime

Although the difference between = and ⊂ is subtle, the recipient will be able to see that, in the second example, we are using expressions, such as, "Even numbers greater than 2 are not members of prime numbers," to create groups or categories. Therefore, a statement like ((1001)(⊂)(10110)) will be read as "5 is a member of ODD NUMBER," and not as "1001 = 10110."

We've now advanced to a point where we can describe simple equations and Boolean arithmetic. We can also group symbols into simple classes or categories, a capability that will enable us to create a higher-level language. We now have most of what it takes to create a simple programming language. Once we can describe self-running computer programs, we can describe almost anything to our distant neighbors.

We can use the same general approach to teach the recipient to recognize a wide variety of arithmetic and logic symbols, for example, the concept of fractional or floating-point numbers. The purpose of this chapter is not to define an entire encyclopedia of basic arithmetic symbols, but to illustrate the general process that can be used to do this.

The examples we've used so far should be obvious to anyone who understands algebra. These symbols can be defined using a relatively small set of examples. Some ideas are much more esoteric, and as such, do not lend themselves to a simple "A+B=C" definition. Just as some concepts were very difficult for you to learn in school, while others were a relative no-brainer, the same will be true of the symbols in this numeric vocabulary.

One of the benefits of this general approach is that we can adjust the number of training examples as needed, based on the difficulty of the concept being described. This allows us to adjust the number of examples we use to describe any given symbol. Some concepts, such as addition, will be immediately obvious to the recipient, and therefore will require few examples to describe. Other concepts, such as randomness, do not lend themselves to a neat algebraic definition. These types of symbols will require a large set of positive (good) and negative (false) examples.

When we send large example sets, we're giving the recipient a greater opportunity to recognize a pattern among the examples. This allows us to define more difficult concepts that cannot be defined precisely in terms of other concepts. This allows us to optimize our message for maximum readability by adjusting the number of training examples used to define a symbol based on how obvious, or esoteric, it is.

Fractions and floating points

So far, we've discussed how to denote whole numbers (i.e., 0, 1, 2, 3, 4, etc.), but what do you do if you need a number that is greater than 0 and less than 1? We typically describe numbers that have fractional components (e.g., 3.14159, an approximate for the value of pi) by adding a symbol that allows us to describe a *floating point* (the binary equivalent of a decimal point). Floating-point binary numbers work the same way decimal numbers do. The example shown in Figure 13-3 illustrates how a floating point number works.

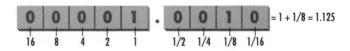

Figure 13-3: *A floating-point number shown in binary form.*

This number 00001.0010 equates to 1 1/8 when expressed in decimal form, or 1.125 in integer form. The numbers to the left of the floating point can be combined to form integer values (i.e., 0, 1, 2, 3, etc.). Numbers to the right of the floating point can be combined to form fractions (e.g., 1/2, 1/4, 1/8, 1/16, etc.).

The first thing we need to do is to create a floating-point symbol (i.e., a period, "."), which we can insert between two numbers to create a floating-point number. Let's define the number 4 (binary 100) to mean "." for this example. Table 13-13 below contains some examples of floating-point numbers.

Table 13-13: *Examples depicting floating-point numbers.*

SHORTHAND NOTATION	PLAIN TEXT EQUIVALENT
([0010](.)[001])	2.125
([0001](.)[11])	1.75
([1111](.)[1111])	7.9375

Teaching the concept of the floating point is done in the same way that we taught other basic arithmetic symbols. The easiest way to do this is to send equations that produce the same results. One equation uses division to produce a fraction. The other defines a number using the floating-point symbol.

As we did before, we will send several examples in our message to help the recipient define the floating point symbol. One such example is:

([0001](÷)[0100](=)([0000](.)[0100]))

or:

1 ÷ 4 = 0.25

Thus, our earlier example of 00001.0010 would read as:

[00001](.)[0010]

If we describe a series of equations where we divide the number 1 by another number whose value is 2 or greater, the concept of a floating point is pretty easy to explain. The recipient would know that the result of this operation will be less than 1, and will quickly figure out that a period (.) symbol is being used to describe a floating point. Table 13-14 shows some examples that were written in the format used elsewhere in the hypothetical message.

Table 13-14: *Examples of floating-point numbers expressed in several formats*

EXPRESSION	BINARY FORM	DECIMAL FORM
(([1](1111)[10]) (1010) ([0](100)[1]))	1 / 10 = 0.1	1 / 2 = 0.5
(([1](1111)[100]) (1010) ([0](100)[01]))	1 / 100 = 0.01	1 / 4 = 0.25
(([1](1111)[1000]) (1010) ([0](.)[001]))	1 / 1000 = 0.001	1 / 8 = 0.125
(([1](1111)[10000]) (1010) ([0](.)[0001]))	1 / 10000 = 0. 0001	1 / 16 = 0. 0625

All we are doing is teaching the recipient to the meaning of the (.) symbol by using division, which we've already taught. The recipient will already know that the left-hand side of each equation involves division that produces a fractional number. The right hand side of the equation contains the new and unknown (.) symbol. With a few examples, the recipient should be able to deduce that the (.) symbol is being used as a floating point.

Before we go about building a general-purpose language, the next thing we need to do is to define some additional concepts that are required to describe truly useful computer programs: memory and branching. *Memory* refers to the ability to store and recall information on demand. Just as the ability to remember is essential to our daily lives, it is an essential part of computing. *Branching* refers to the ability to make decisions within a program (for example, to perform one list of tasks when a test condition exists, and another list of tasks when it does not). We will cover both of these concepts in the next chapter.

MEMORY AND PROGRAMMING

By now, we could tell a distant civilization a great deal about what we know about physics and chemistry, by sending a simple list of equations. Equations from Albert Einstein's theory of relativity ($E=mc^2$) would tell them that we understand the equivalence of matter and energy, with all of the destructive capability it entails. Another concept to share would be Werner Heisenberg's uncertainty principle, which would tell the recipient that we understand quantum mechanics.

We already have most of what it takes to create a simple programming language. By adding a few more concepts, we can use our message to describe self-running computer programs. Computer programs are important because they can be used to transmit information in abbreviated form. Programs allow the sender to do much more than simply remove a few extra bits from the message. They can be used to depict complex situations, model physical systems, and to display compressed images, just to name a few things. They also allow the recipient to interact with the program while it is running.

They also allow the sender to squeeze more information into a signal that can only carry a finite number of bits. We accomplish this with two programming concepts we've yet to discuss: *memory* and *branching statements*, without which it is impossible to write a useful program.

Memory is a critical component in computing because it allows programs to store and recall information on the fly. Without memory, we wouldn't be able to write even the most basic of programs. Branching statements allow a program to make decisions based on various test conditions. Although this is a relatively simple extension to what we've already described, branching statements allow the sender to write very sophisticated programs from a small vocabulary of basic symbols.

Memory

The next logical building block we need to make the program useful is *memory*. Memory gives the program the ability to store (remember) and retrieve (recall) information for future use. Memory is a critical feature in computing; without it, we can't write a useful program.

In Chapter 11, *CETI—Communication with Extraterrestrial Intelligence*, we worked out a simple scheme for parsing a stream of binary digits into words and groups of words. We also learned how to use binary numbers to reference symbols or commands that do something, and numbers that can be used to represent raw data that gets processed by these commands. We added a simple scheme to describe the context of each word in an expression (e.g., used as command, raw data, etc.). For example, we can use the symbols 8 (1000), 9 (1001), and 12 (1100) to describe whether a numeric word in an expression should be interpreted as a command or as data:

```
((1000)(1100))          Symbol 12 (the + sign, for addition)
((1001)(1100))          The number 12
```

Notice how these examples are structured; the words are grouped in pairs. The first word in each pair is used to indicate the context of the word that follows it. On the first line, the symbol 8 (1000) is used to tell us that the number following it should be interpreted as a command (1100, which can be interpreted as a + sign). On the second line, symbol 9 (1001) tells us that the number following it is raw data, in which case 1100 would be interpreted as the number 12.

So far, the words in the message have been used in one of two possible contexts, either as data or as a command. The next concept we need to introduce in the message is the concept of memory. Fortunately, the concept of memory should be familiar to a civilization that is capable of receiving a radio message from across the galaxy. This is because in order to detect the signal in the first place, they need to be able to store and manipulate digitally recorded data.

The next step is to define a couple more symbols that we'll use to describe additional contexts of the numeric words in an expression. One symbol, 6 (0110), will be used to describe a *local variable*, or *private memory location*. Another symbol, 7 (0111), will be used to describe a *global variable*, or *public memory location*. We'll talk about the difference between private and public memory locations in Chapter 15, *Concepts and igenes*, but first, let's look at a simple example:

```
(((0111)(0001)) ((1000)(1010)) ((1001)(1111)))
```

Which would read as:

```
M1 = 15
```

This statement means that the number 15 should be stored in public memory location, or variable, 1 (M1). The example depicts a common operation performed throughout computer programs, which is to store a number in memory where it can be used for other purposes.

Memory is a trickier concept to explain to our extraterrestrial audience because it is difficult to visualize. The challenge here is to design a message that explains the concept of memory by example. We can do this by sending several statements that produce identical results:

```
(
(((0111)(0001)) ((1000)(1010)) ((1001)(0010)))
(((0111)(0010)) ((1000)(1010)) ((1001)(0011)))
(((0111)(0011)) ((1000)(1010)) (((0111)(0001)) ((1000)(1100)) ...
((0111)(0010))) ((1000)(1010)) ((1001)(1001)))
)
```

Which can be displayed in shorthand as:

```
(
({1}(=)[2])
({2}(=)[3])
({3}(=){1}+{2}(=)[5])
)
```

and further interpreted as:

```
M1=2
M2=3
M3=M1+M2=5
```

NOTE

The symbols { and } refer to memory registers in shorthand form. {1} means memory register 1, {2} means memory register 2, and so on.

The program above provides a simple example of how we can explain the concept of memory. This example program stores the numbers 2 and 3 in memory locations 1 (M1) and 2 (M2), respectively. Then it adds the contents of M1 and M2, and stores the result in memory location 3 (M3). The final statement in this program, M3=M1+M2=5, provides the recipient with the key for deciphering the way information is stored in memory. This statement tells the recipient that the sum of M1 and M2 and the value for M3 is 5.

By sending programs like this, we make it easy for the recipient to see a pattern in the messages. The recipient will learn to read a statement like ((0111)(0001)) ((1000)(1010)) ((1001)(0111)) as M1=7. The first two words in this statement are most relevant to the idea we want to teach. The word (0111, or decimal 7) means the symbol next to it will refer to a memory location. The word (0001, or decimal 1) identifies which memory location to use. Taken together, these symbols can be read as M1, or in shorthand form, {1}.

If you're not a computer programmer, you may be rubbing your forehead right now. This can be a little confusing at first, but the concept of memory is pretty straightforward—just think of memory as a bucket that holds information. To help illustrate the concept and use of memory, let's look at two different programs that perform the same function. The items used in Example 14-1 and Example 14-2 are defined in Table 14-1.

Table 14-1: *Symbols and their interpretation (for use with Examples 14-1 and 14-2).*

SYMBOL	MEANING
[0100]	The number 4
(1100)	A plus (+) sign
(1010)	An equals (=) sign
{0001}	Memory register (variable) 1 (M1)
{0010}	Memory register (variable) 2 (M2)
{0011}	Memory register (variable) 3 (M3)

Example 14-1 describes a short program that does not use memory to store information.

Example 14-1: Instructions to add two numbers
```
([0100](1100)[0100])
```

When interpreted, Example 14-1 can simply be read as "4 plus 4." The number 4 is defined, or hard-coded, in the program. Example 14-2 performs the exact same procedure, except it processes information that is stored in memory, and stores its results in another variable:

Example 14-2: Instructions to add two numbers using memory (data buckets)
```
({0001}(1010)[0100])
({0010}(1010)[0100])
({0011}(1010){0001}(1100){0010})
```

Using Table 14-1 as our guide, Example 14-2 would be interpreted as follows:
```
({M1}(=)[4])
({M2}(=)[4])
({M3}(=){M1}(+){M2})
```
or:
```
({M3}(=){4}(+){4})
```

Therefore, M3 would be equal to the number 8. Once a memory variable is defined, we can use them over again in other programs by simply referring to the appropriate variable name (e.g., M1, M2, M3, etc.) to perform a variety of functions.

The instruction:

```
({0011}(1010){0001}(1100){0010}) : M3 = M1 + M2
```

can be used to create a generic set of instructions which say "Add A and B, and put the results in C," or "C=A+B." We can plug any number we want into M1 and M2, run our mini-program, and the result (A+B) will be retrieved from M3. This program is useful because it can add any two numbers we plug into it.

Ultimately, we want to build *black box* programs to hide the details of their inner workings from other programs that use or talk to them. The user simply presents a black box program with information to be processed. This information is stored in one or more variables (memory registers). The program then processes the information presented to it, does its thing, and then presents its results (also using one or more variables to store the results). The black box program enables the sender to create modular, gene-like programs designed to perform a specific task. These "igenes" can then be linked into other programs, thus freeing the author from having to rewrite every procedure from scratch in every program. Memory is an important part of this because it provides a mechanism for passing information among these gene-like programs. We will discuss this style of programming will in Chapter 15.

It is important to understand that we are *not* attempting to teach the recipient how to build a solid-state memory device. We are, however, teaching them about memory on a conceptual level, in the same way we would teach an algebra student about variables. In a sense, we are describing an imaginary computer, or virtual machine. Our imaginary computer has an unlimited number of data buckets, each with its own unique numeric address, into which we can place one or more bits of information. All the recipients need to do as they learn to decipher this basic vocabulary is to write software that recognizes the commands, and simulates their behavior, as if they were running on a real computer. This might sound complicated, but it is actually quite easy to do. We can actually make it much easier for aliens to decode the symbols in our message by embedding hints in our programs in the form of universal numbers, something we'll discuss further in a moment.

Data structures and arrays

Now that we've learned how to describe the concept of memory in our hypothetical message, let's take a look at how we can organize the information that instructs a program to store memory. Just as we learned how to add structure to a sequence of binary numbers in Chapter 12, *Binary DNA*, we can use the same technique to add structure to the information stored in variables.

We'll use this technique to create arrays. An *array* is a multidimensional block of data. An array, instead of storing a single piece of information, houses information in a structured format such as a two-dimensional grid (used to represent an image in memory).

If you're not already familiar with the concept, one way to imagine an array is to imagine a tic-tac-toe game board (see Figure 14-1). The game board is divided into three rows of three cells, each of which can have three possible states (empty, *X*, or *O*). This is a good example of a two-dimensional array.

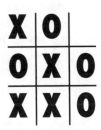

Figure 14-1: *A tic-tac-toe game board.*

Next, let's create an expression to store a summary of the game board's state in memory. We'll use numbers to describe the possible states: 0 means empty, 1 means X, and 10 (decimal 2) means O:

    ({1} (=) ([[1][10][0]] [[10][1][10]] [[1][1][10]]))

This example can be read as an instruction to store a series of nine numbers, in three subsets, in memory location 1. This expression uses extra bracketing symbols ([and]) to imply that the numbers are organized into groups (rows), each of which contains three numbers. It's easier to see the pattern in the example above if it is displayed as follows:

    ({1} (=) [[[1][10][0]]
             [[10][1][10]]
             [[1][1][10]]]
)

Here we can finally see that this expression organizes the information stored in M1 in a two-dimensional array, consisting of three rows with three numbers each in each row.

This example uses the same technique to organize data and store it in memory, as we described in Chapter 12. The ability to add structure to stored data is another useful step forward. This technique allows programs to store data in formats that are easy to parse, and which allow large sets of data to be managed as a collection of smaller subunits. This will come in very handy for displaying high-resolution images using a three-dimensional array.

Multidimensional arrays

Up to now, we've been creating very simple, one- and two-dimensional arrays for defining numbers, symbols, and memory variables for describing simple things (such as basic math equations or how a program can store a number in memory). However, when we reach the point where we want to send images, video, or synchronized multimedia presentations, we need to look to the third and fourth dimensions to give additional information about each individual pixel (dot within a picture).

We can generate images using two- or three-dimensional blocks of data; each element in the array describes a pixel, or picture element, within the overall image. We could also use a four-dimensional array to store a motion picture or an animated video clip. However, in order to describe a three- or four-dimensional array, we must make a slight change to the way we arrange parentheses and brackets.

THREE-DIMENSIONAL ARRAY

In order to store additional information about each element, a three-dimensional array will have eight cells, and would be expressed as follows:

```
({1} (=) [[[[1][2]] [[3][4]]] [[[5][6]] [[7][8]]]])
```

This example depicts a 2×2×2 (2^3) three-dimensional array. To add an extra dimension to an array, all we need to do is add another pair of brackets. This is easiest to visualize as a cube that has been divided into eight smaller cubes (stacked two across, two high, and two deep), as shown in Figure 14-2.

We'll demonstrate how to use three-dimensional arrays to store data that is used to render a high-resolution, full-color image in Chapter 17, *Pictures*. Two dimensions, *width* and *height*, are used to arrange the picture elements into a familiar TV-like display. The third dimension, *depth*, is used to store detailed color information about each pixel (dot) within the image.

Figure 14-2: *A three-dimensional cube, dissected into eight smaller cubes.*

FOUR-DIMENSIONAL ARRAY

Finally, let's look at a quick example of a four-dimensional array, which we can think of as a *hypercube* with 16 cells. To store a set of numbers in a four-dimensional array, we would use the following expression:

```
({1}(=) [[[[[1][2]] [[3][4]]] [[[5][6]] [[7][8]]]] [[[[9][10]]
[[11][12]]] [[[13][14]] [[15][16]]]]])
```

As before, we're just using extra brackets to add another layer of structure to the data being stored in the memory variable (M1). We can use this general approach to create multidimensional arrays to define nearly anything you can imagine.

Since we can only visualize things in three dimensions, it is hard to relate the contents of a 4D array to a static geometric shape or still picture. However, if we use three of the dimensions to represent width, height, and depth, and the fourth to represent time (or frames of a moving picture), we can use a 4D array to store the information used to draw a 3D movie.

Arrays are useful for many applications beyond drawing images. The most important contribution they make, however, is that they enable programs to store and recall highly structured information in a simplified manner. Instead of storing each individual piece of information in its own variable, a program can store a complex set of data in a single variable (a *container*), and do so in a way that makes it easy to recall and process all or selected parts of this information on the fly.

Branching statements

The mini-programs we've examined so far have been simple ones that run in a predictable start-to-finish manner. In order to build truly useful computers, we need to add yet another feature, called *branching statements*.

Branching statements allow us to add decision-making capability to programs. Consider the following example, written in BASIC:

```
START_PROGRAM:
X=1
START_COUNTER:
X=X+1
IF X >= 100 THEN GOTO FINISH_COUNTER
IF X < 100 THEN GOTO START_COUNTER
FINISH_COUNTER:
PRINT "All Done!"
```

This program's behavior is pretty simple. It counts from 1 to 100, and then displays a short message ("All Done!") upon completing this task. This program can be represented in flowchart form, as shown in Figure 14-3.

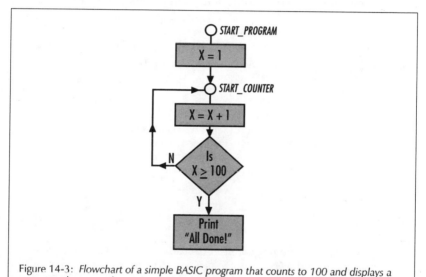

Figure 14-3: Flowchart of a simple BASIC program that counts to 100 and displays a message when complete.

Notice how the program continuously makes decisions as it compares the value of X to see if it is less than 100, equal to 100, or greater than 100.

The words *if* and *then* are fundamental for computing. They allow us to do something called *branching*. Simply put, branching is a way of saying "If condition X is true, *then* do this." A variant on this concept is the *if-then-else* statement, which says: "*If* condition X is true, *then* do A, otherwise (*else*) do B." An analogy here would be: "If X=dog, then throw it a bone. If not (else), throw it a ball of string," assuming that X is a cat.

An if-then-else statement is known as a *branching statement*, because it allows us to control the flow of a process by guiding it to an ultimate solution. Without these statements, all we can do is send equations. We can say a lot with a short list of equations, but equations are not computer programs. Equations behave a lot like a cash register. For example, if you fill in the blank variables, you will get a result; otherwise, the cash register just sits there and does nothing until you punch in a set of numbers.

A computer program, unlike an equation, is a lot like a robot. Before it can do anything, you have to give it a list of instructions. Once the instructions are received, the program goes off, performs several dozen (or maybe several billion) calculations and comparisons, and then comes back to you with its results. Example 14-3 is a simple program (written in BASIC) that performs a procedure to test a number to determine whether or not it is a prime number.*

Example 14-3: Procedure to determine if a number is a prime number

```
Function IsPrime(TestNumber As Integer) As Boolean
    IsPrime = True
    N = 2
    FinishedTesting = False
    Do Until FinishedTesting = True
        If N >= (TestNumber-1) Then FinishedTesting = True
        If IsPrime = False Then FinishedTesting = True
        If (TestNumber / N) = (Int(TestNumber / N))
            Then IsPrime = False
        N = N + 1
    Loop
End Function
```

NOTE

Those of you who are programmers or mathematicians will notice that this is not the most efficient way to test a number to determine whether it is prime. For example, the program does not test to determine if TestNumber is an even number (except for the number 2, prime numbers are not even). This example has been simplified for non-programmers, and to conserve the amount of space required to describe it.

This example loops through a simple series of instructions to determine whether the number is prime or not. For this example, the program's behavior can be explained as follows:

- The program is given an integer to test, the value of which is stored in a variable named *Number*.

- The program counts from 2 to 6 (TestNumber-1) then places this value in a variable named *N*.

---

* Prime numbers can only be divided by themselves or 1 to produce an integer.

- It divides the test *Number* by *N*, and checks to see if the result is an integer. When you divide 6 by 3, the result is 2, which is an integer. When you divide 6 by 4, the result is 1 (or 1.5), which is not an integer.

- If any of these tests return an integer result, the test number is not a prime number. The program aborts its count, and returns a *false* result.

This is a simple procedure, but it allows us to do a lot of work. Let's suppose we need to test whether 940127109257399 is a prime number. As you can imagine, this test would involve a *lot* of computation. We can hand off this task to our simple program and wait for it to reply with a true or false answer.

Subroutines and flow control

We can assemble subroutines into larger sets of instructions to build programs that are progressively more complex. However, we first need to build a basic framework for flow control and handling data.

Branching is a lot like a fork in a road. If a specific condition is met, the program follows one path. If not, it follows another, or simply does nothing and proceeds to its next instruction. The prime number test procedure we just discussed has four "forks" or decision points in its chain of instructions:

```
If N >= Number Then FinishedTesting = True
```

If *N* is greater than or equal to the number being tested by the subroutine, the test is finished and the variable *FinishedTesting* will be set to true:

```
If IsPrime = False Then FinishedTesting = True
```

If the variable *IsPrime* is set to false, the test is finished and the variable *FinishedTesting* will be to true:

```
If (TestNumber / N) = (Int(TestNumber / N)) Then IsPrime = False
```

If dividing *TestNumber* by *N* returns an integer, we will know that *TestNumber* is not a prime number. Therefore, the variable *IsPrime* will be set to false:

```
Do Until FinishedTesting = True
```

If the variable *FinishedTesting* is true, the program will stop and return a true or false result. Figure 14-4 illustrates how flow control works in the program used to determine prime numbers. Notice how *IF* and branching statements are combined to form decision making loops.

Branching statements allow us to test for, and act upon, many types of conditions. While we can build very complicated programs using branching statements, they all boil down to a simple logical building block:

```
If Condition (X) Is True, Then Do (Y)
```

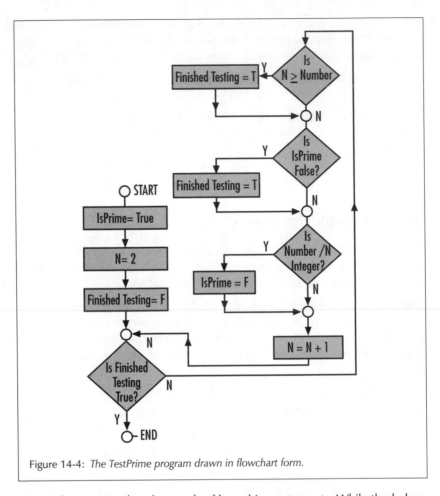

Figure 14-4: *The TestPrime program drawn in flowchart form.*

A complex program has thousands of branching statements. While the behavior of the program as a whole may be complex, its basic building blocks are simple: nothing more than basic arithmetic combined with IF-THEN statements and commands to store and recall information from memory.

In order to explain the concept of flow control to our distant listeners, we will give a set of positive and negative examples, just as we have with earlier examples. Remember, it isn't practical to fax a flowchart, wave our hands, or drop hints like "you're getting warmer." Since our only means of communicating with our distant neighbors is through a stream of binary numbers, any hints about how to decode the message must be embedded in the message itself.

First, we need to create a symbol for *IF*. Let's say, for example, that the number 100000 will be read as *IF* within our hypothetical message. We can help the recipient figure out whether they have correctly understood the meaning of 100000 by writing a series of programs to generate a universally recognized number (e.g., pi), when the recipient treats this symbol as an IF-THEN statement:

```
(
    {1}=[4])
    {2}=[0.7853981633974])
    {3}=0)
    ((100000){1}(=)[4]))(
    {3}={1}(x){2}))
    )
)
```

When translated, the above example would mean:

```
M1=4
M2=0.7853981633974
IF M1=4 THEN M3=M1*M2
```

If we do this over and over again, the recipient will get the general idea that, when an example program gives a result of pi, we're saying, "You guessed right."

Once we get the basic idea of an IF-THEN statement across to the recipient, we can move on to describe some variations on this theme, such as IF-THEN-ELSE, DO loops, and other programming constructs. However, these are icing on the cake. Once we have the ability to define IF-THEN statements, we have what we need to start building useful programs.

GOTO statements

The next thing we need to add to our vocabulary is a symbol that allows us to jump forward or backward in our sequence of instructions within an igene. One way to do this is to create a command called a GOTO statement. A GOTO statement does what its name implies; it tells the computer running the program to jump backward or forward to a specified point within the program.

Let's assume that we have opted to use an approach that is easy to interpret and does not require us to insert additional data into our program, thereby keeping its size to a minimum.

The BASIC program described earlier in this chapter employed a GOTO statement. GOTO statements allow you to insert instructions like "GOTO 160" which, when read, would jump to line 160 in the program.

As we for the IF symbol, we can use a unique number to mean GOTO. The number itself is not important. All that matters is that we use a specific number consistently throughout all of our programs to refer to GOTO. Consider the following example:*

```
(
({1}(=)[0])
({2}(=)[0.7853981633974])
({3}(=){1}(x){2})
({1}(=){1}(+)[1])
((IF)({3}(≠)[3.14159])(
    ((GOTO)[4])
)
))
```

NOTE

The symbols IF, ≠, and GOTO would be replaced by numeric symbols in the actual message. The example program is written in mnemonic form to make it easier to read.

The line numbers in our program are implicit; they are referenced in Table 14-2. Notice how each instruction in the program is bracketed by (and) symbols. This makes it easy for the recipient to parse the program into discrete instructions or lines. So, the statement ({1}(=)([0]) is read as line 1, while ({2}(=)[0.7853981633974]) is read as line 2, and so on.

Table 14-2: *Training program used to illustrate the use of the GOTO symbol*

LINE	EXPRESSION
1	M1=0
2	M2=0.7853981633974
3	M3=M1×M2
4	M1=M1+1
5	IF M3≠3.14159 THEN GOTO 4

This program runs until the value of pi is stored in memory location 3 (M3). Notice how we use pi to give the recipient a clue about whether they are guessing correctly or not.

We can also embed explicit addresses throughout the program:

```
1    A=1
2    B=1
100  A=B-3
110  A=A+1
125  B=A+5
130  GOTO 100
```

---

* Spacing and indentation have been added to make this example easier to read. This sort of formatting would not be included in a real message.

WHAT'S SO SPECIAL ABOUT PI?

Pi (π) is a universal number that is recognizable by anyone who understands geometry and basic mathematics. It is based on the geometry of a circle, and works out to approximately 3.14159.... Pi is a ratio, the result of dividing a circle's circumference (the length of a line traced around the circle), by its diameter (the distance across the circle), as shown in Figure 14-5. This ratio is always the same for any perfect circle drawn in a two-dimensional plane, regardless of its size.

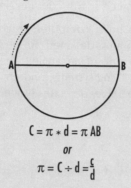

$$C = \pi * d = \pi\ AB$$

or

$$\pi = C \div d = \frac{C}{d}$$

Figure 14-5: *Pi is the result of dividing a circle's circumference (the distance around the circle), by its diameter (the distance between points A and B).*

There are other universal numbers we can use, such as Planck's Constant, the mass of an electron, etc. The meaning of these numbers would also be apparent to an intelligent civilization, but none are as immediately obvious as pi. The reason pi is so useful is because the number by itself will attract attention. Anyone who has the most basic introduction to geometry will recognize that number.

The number for pi can be used as a red flag to alert the recipient who correctly decodes new symbols. We would write example programs that help the recipient learn the meaning of new symbols. When the recipient correctly guesses how an unknown symbol is being used within a program, the program would output the number pi as its result.

If we repeatedly use this approach in the training examples, the recipient should quickly learn to look for the number pi as a signal that they have correctly guessed in decoding an unknown symbol.

Using explicit line addresses makes it easier to make changes to a segment of a program during the authoring process. The example here is taken from older versions of the BASIC programming language. Using labels also works.

The only disadvantage with explicit line addresses or labels, as it applies to this application, is that they will bloat the size of the program somewhat.

With the techniques we've developed in this chapter, we now have the foundation upon which to build a practical, general-purpose computer programming language. With this simple language, we can write sophisticated programs that perform a wide range of tasks: from processing compressed images, to modeling (or simulating) real-world situations. We can think of these programs as agents whose purpose is to amplify the concepts that we are attempting to teach. Once we can write programs, what we can communicate to the recipient is limited only by our imagination.

Next, we discuss how to build computer programs by combining many special-purpose mini-programs designed to perform a specific task (for example, to calculate the sine of an angle). These mini-programs can be compared to the genes in living systems, and enable us to build very complex programs from a large library of relatively simple components.

CONCEPTS AND IGENES

The ability to transmit computer programs allows us to describe more complex ideas and systems. We can use programs to explain abstract ideas that cannot otherwise be explained logically. Difficult concepts, such as randomness, while nearly impossible to explain in words, can be explained clearly using a simple program. We can even create symbols whose meanings are defined by other programs. However, we are still lacking a system for organizing small, modular sets of instructions in a way that enables them to be combined into larger, more complex programs.

This chapter describes a simple yet powerful scheme for building complex programs out of many reusable components. This system combines some well-known techniques from computer science with the gene-like system described in Chapter 12, *Binary DNA*, where the sender creates mini-programs to perform specific, well-defined tasks, such as computing the sine of an angle.

We can think of these mini-programs as digital genes, or *igenes*, which can then be incorporated into many other programs. Each unique igene will be given a unique numeric ID, just as we've used unique numbers to identify other symbols (such as +). This trick allows the sender to reuse an igene throughout many other programs, and to do so without having to repeatedly retransmit the instructions used to define the igene. In effect, the sender can reference each igene by nickname instead of having to repeatedly send a verbose description of what the igene does internally.

Digital genes

The sine function is used throughout geometry and the physical sciences to calculate the trigonometric sine of an angle. If you're not already familiar with geometry, this is best explained by looking at the triangle in

Figure 15-1. By calculating the sine of angle A, and multiplying that by the length of side AC, we can calculate the length of the side BC for this triangle.

NOTE

This is a special case for right triangles, where one of the corners in the triangle is a square, 90° angle (as with angle C).

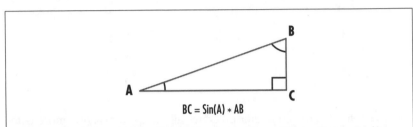

BC = Sin(A) * AB

Figure 15-1: *The length of line BC can be calculated by multiplying the length of line AB with the sine of angle A.*

The procedure for calculating the sine of an angle is pretty straightforward, but it requires several steps of calculation. This is what is known as an *iterative calculation*. In an iterative calculation, the computer churns through several dozen, or perhaps several hundred, calculations to generate a progressively more and more accurate estimate of the desired number. For example, the sine of an angle can be calculated using the following formula:

$$X - (X^3/3!) + (X^5/5!) - (X^7/7!) + (X^9/9!) - ...$$

In this example, the ! symbol is shorthand for a *factorial*. A factorial is the product of all positive integers from 1 to the specified number. For example, the statement 3! should be read as 3×2×1, or 6. This can be expressed in general form as:

$$n! = n \times (n-1) \times (n-2) \times ... \times (n-m)... \text{ where } (n-m) \text{ is } > 0$$

The value of X in this equation represents the angle we wish to compute the sine for, measured in *radians*. Radians measure the angle in relation to the universal number *pi* (3.14159...). For example, a 90° angle works out to pi/2 radians, or 1.570795. A 45° angle works out to pi/4 radians, or 0.7853975, etc. This formula creates a sum of the contributions of a series of factors (e.g., $X^3/3!$).

Let's look at an example to see how this works out by calculating the sine for a 90° angle (1.5708 radian) (angle C of Figure 15-1). If we replace the value X with 1.5708, the formula then reads:

$$1.5708 - (1.5708^3/3 \times 2 \times 1) + (1.5708^5/5 \times 4 \times 3 \times 2 \times 1) - (1.5708^7/7 \times 6 \times 5 \times 4 \times 3 \times 2 \times 1) + (1.5708^9/9 \times 8 \times 7 \times 6 \times 5 \times 4 \times 3 \times 2 \times 1)$$

which equates to:

$$1.5708 - (3.87581/6) + (9.56322/120) - (23.59642/5040) + (58.22212/362880)$$

which equates to:

$$1.5708 - 0.64597 + 0.079693 - 0.00468183 + 0.000160444$$

or:

$$1.000001614$$

According to this calculation, the sine for a 90° angle (pi/2 radian) is approximately 1. It should be exactly 1; however, this method produces an approximate result. We can increase the accuracy of the calculation by including many more terms in the calculation (e.g., $-X^{11}/11! + X^{13}/13! - X^{15}/15! + X^{17}/17!$ ... ad infinitum). The only disadvantage is that this increased accuracy comes with the cost of increased computation; it takes longer to calculate the desired result. A typical physics or mathematics program performs the calculation repeatedly throughout the entire program (whenever it needs to calculate the sine of an angle).

Using this technique, we can simply copy these instructions whenever we need to calculate the sine of a number. This works, but it is an inefficient use of our limited bandwidth. Instead, what we should do is treat these instructions like a reusable component, or "widget," that is included in a program once and referred to as needed, rather than copying it repeatedly throughout the body of the message.

To accomplish this task, we simply associate a symbol with our newly written procedure to calculate a sine. Like all other symbols, our new symbol is assigned a unique number value that identifies it. (Remember the metaphor we used to compare the use of binary numbers as a sort of Dewey decimal system for ideas?) Let's look at our sine example again:

```
(40) (=) (
    (|2|(=)[0])
    (|2|(=)|1|)
    (|2|(=)(|2|(-)((|2|)(^)[3])(/)((!)[3])))
    (|2|(=)(|2|(+)((|2|)(^)[5])(/)((!)[5])))
    (|2|(=)(|2|(-)((|2|)(^)[7])(/)((!)[7])))
    (|2|(=)(|2|(+)((|2|)(^)[9])(/)((!)[9])))
    (|2|(=)(|2|(-)((|2|)(^)[11])(/)((!)[11])))
    (|0|(=)|2|)
)
```

This block of code is a simple equivalency statement; it says that 101000 (decimal 40) = "the body of instructions used to calculate the sine of a number." Once this equivalency statement has been established, we just make a statement like the following when we want to calculate the sine of a number:

```
((101000)([0](.)[11001101]))
```

LOCAL VARIABLES

The sample program in this section introduces a new type of symbol, |x|. This symbol is used to represent a *local variable*, or private memory location.

For now, the best way to explain the difference between global and local variables is to imagine two chalkboards. One is in a hallway, accessible to everyone, while the other chalkboard is in a locked room, accessible only to the people in that room.

As far as the people in the hallway are concerned, the other chalkboard does not even exist. The chalkboard in the hallway is analogous to a global variable, which is visible throughout an entire system. The chalkboard in the locked room is analogous to a local variable, which is visible only within the procedure, or igene, in which it is used.

Local variables are important for two reasons: they greatly reduce the possibility that one software component or procedure inadvertently overwrites information stored in a memory register used by another procedure; and, they enable authors to build self-contained mini-programs or so-called "*black box*" functions.

This statement means: Calculate the sine of 0.11001101

We no longer need to refer to the long list of instructions for calculating the sine; instead, we simply use the numeric symbol that points to these underlying instructions. Therefore, we can describe the symbol once and reuse that symbol throughout many different programs.

We can do this because we we the recipient to catalog every symbol defined in the message. The software igenes we're describing are really just an extension to the symbolic library we've been building in the previous chapters. So, once the symbol 101000 is recognized to mean *"sine(x),"* the recipient will know to execute the underlying instructions behind this symbol whenever it is encountered in other parts of the message.

The object of my desire: Modern programming languages

At this point, it is helpful to compare the system we're describing to real-world programming techniques. Many of the concepts we're describing, in particular the ability to create reusable blocks of code that can be referenced throughout many unrelated programs, are used in a system known as *object-oriented programming* (OOP).

Most modern programming languages, such as C++ and Java. They operate on a similar principle: they treat instruction sets as modular, reusable components that can be incorporated into other programs. These components allow programmers to neatly organize their programs, and to share reusable software components with each other.

A complete introduction to OOP is beyond the scope of this book. However, the basic principles behind OOP are fairly straightforward. The two most important features of OOP are *modularity* and *inheritance*.

MODULARITY

The concept of *modularity* is easy for most people to comprehend. Modularity allows you to write a program composed of many lower order components, or modules, which may be composed of other modules, or submodules. Instead of writing every program from scratch, you can simply reuse existing modules as needed. For example, if you need to calculate the sine of a number, you could simply call a procedure like *math.sine(number)*, which has been written, tested, and used many times before. Modular programming reduces workload, increases reliability, and can sometimes reduce the size of a program. Modularity is not unique to OOP languages, since many older programming languages, such as BASIC, support it in some form.

INHERITANCE

Inheritance is a trickier concept for most people to understand. To understand inheritance, it's helpful to start with an example of how we deal with objects in object-oriented programming. The concept of inheritance is easier to grasp if we apply this idea to a real-world object whose behavior is something most people are familiar with, such as a remote-controlled racecar.

Our racecar has several properties that describe its current condition or state. In the object-oriented paradigm, every object has *properties* and *methods*. *Properties* are the equivalent of variables or memory registers; they contain information about the object and its state. *Methods* are the equivalent of commands. When you call a method, you trigger some sort of action or sequence of commands to be executed. For the purpose of this example, our racecar will have the following properties:

Racecar.batterycharge
  The amount of charge left in the car's battery.

Racecar.direction
  The direction in which the car is facing (0 to 360 degrees).

Racecar.mass
  The mass of the car.

Racecar.velocity
  The velocity (speed) of the car.

Racecar.x
  The position of the car along the x axis.

Racecar.y
  The position of the car along the y axis.

And the following methods:

Racecar.turn(degrees per second)
  Turns the racecar by *degrees*.

Racecar.accelerate(meters per second)
  Increase or decrease speed by *meters per second*.

Racecar.brake(true/false)
  If true, the racecar decelerates at a predefined rate. If false, the car maintains its present speed.

These properties and methods are also shown in Figure 15-2. Note how properties are used to store information about the object, such as its position, rate, and direction of motion, and so forth. Methods are used to manipulate the object, much like you would use buttons and levers on a remote control to manipulate the real-world version of our example object. This provides us with a simplified interface through which we can interact with a specific software component.

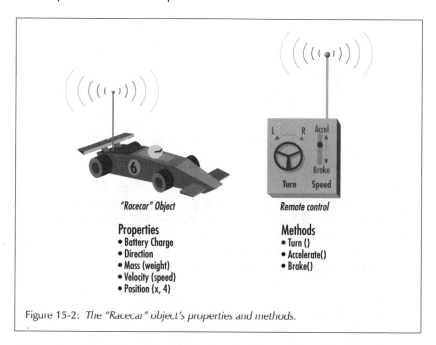

Figure 15-2: The "Racecar" object's properties and methods.

Inheritance allows us to create new objects that *inherit* the properties and methods of a parent class (or category) of an object. So, let's say we want to create a new class of racecar object called *supercar*. This *supercar* can do everything that our original racecar object can, except it can also move in reverse. In order to do this, we need to define a class of object called *supercar* and say that it *extends* the *racecar* object. This means that *supercar* inherits all of the properties and methods of the original *racecar* class, plus any new properties and methods that are specific to this new class.

In our *supercar* example, we will add a new method called *ChangeGear(gear)*. This method allows the user to flip a "forward/reverse" switch on the remote control (see Figure 15-3). Now the racecar can propel itself in both forward and reverse directions; otherwise, everything stays the same.

These two concepts, *modularity* and *inheritance*, give us a foundation for writing a wide variety of programs while reducing the workload by enabling programmers to build on previous innovations.

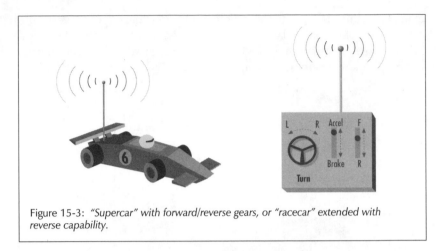

Figure 15-3: *"Supercar" with forward/reverse gears, or "racecar" extended with reverse capability.*

We can build upon the object-oriented gene-like system by combining its basic elements with that of concept-oriented programming to create elaborate programs without having to constantly reinvent basic functions. This combination of programming concepts allows us to transmit these powerful mini-programs in formats that require a minimal amount of bandwidth, thus enabling us to send more information in each transmission.

The next step: Concept-oriented programming

Concept-oriented programming (COP) takes the basic principles of OOP to the next level. COP is really just a straightforward extension of existing OOP technique. COP allows us to combine *concepts* from biology and the Internet to create a powerful system for building complex programs from many reusable components.

We borrow the first technique for adding structure to our endless sequence of binary numbers from genetics. You've probably noticed that most of the communication system we've been discussing borrows heavily from the concepts applied to genetic research. The hypothetical message we are sending is formatted in a manner similar to the data stored in a DNA strand.

Another way of looking at this is to compare our symbols (+, −, >, <, IF, etc.) with genes. When we create a new symbol, or a set of instructions assembled from these symbols (i.e., a subroutine to average several numbers), we're creating a unique *igene*. Our practice of numbering mini-programs creates a system for indexing igenes that can be used by any other program we send. This is a powerful idea, because it dramatically increases our effective transmission speed, thus increasing the amount of information we can send in a single transmission.

The most important new feature in COP is the creation of a uniform addressing system for software components. This can be compared to a computer's network address, except that instead of allocating numeric addresses to machines, you're allocating unique addresses to packaged groups of machine instructions (mini-programs). Think of this as a Dewey decimal system for indexing ideas. This is a simple idea, but it is very powerful, and has many practical applications outside of SETI. To illustrate this general principle, Table 15-1 lists a handful of igenes that perform various calculations. These igenes are built entirely from the symbols for rudimentary mathematical calculations (e.g., addition, subtraction, etc). Each of them is defined by a set of machine instructions, and can be treated as a very small, special purpose computer program designed solely to perform a specific task.

Table 15-1: *Set of hypothetical igenes and their functions*

IGENE NUMBER	NICKNAME	FUNCTION
101000	Sine	Calculates sine of angle
101001	Cosine	Calculates cosine of angle
101010	Tangent	Calculates tangent of angle
101011	Cotangent	Calculates cotangent of angle
101100	Ln	Calculates natural logarithm of a number
101101	x^y	Calculates x to the y power
101110	$x^{1/y}$	Calculates x to the $1/y$ power

Now let's look at how we can create a simple program by combining these igenes:

```
(
    ({1} (=) [4])
    ({2} (=) ⌊5⌋)
    ({3} (=) ((101101){1}{2}))
)
```

The above program can be translated to read as follows:

```
Store the number 4 in data bucket 1 (M1)
Store the number 5 in data bucket 2 (M2)
Calculate the value of M1^M2 or 4^5, and store this value in M3
The result will be 1024, or 10000000000 binary
```

The important point to grasp here is that we are creating an ever-expanding library of symbols, and that we are using programs to define what these symbols mean. This organically growing lexicon of concepts, which are themselves built from simpler concepts, enable us to progress rapidly toward building some very complex, yet very compact programs.

What's in a concept?

In this system, a *concept* is a numeric placeholder for an idea, nothing more, nothing less. Our set of instructions to calculate the sine of a number represents the idea "sine." You can think of a concept as a unit of information. Richard Dawkins coined the phrase *meme* to describe how ideas could spread in ways similar to genes. (A meme is a unit of cultural information. The idea of a meme is somewhat fuzzy, mainly because the way we transmit cultural information using spoken or written words is imprecise. Dawkins theorized that some memes, like the habit of wearing ties at the office, thrived (often for inexplicable reasons) while others simply died out.)

Each concept, or igene, is represented by a numeric symbol, in this case as a binary number. This is a unique number so it cannot be confused with its neighbors. The number itself is meaningless—it merely serves as an identifier. The core of this system is the technique of using a number as a placeholder for an idea. This numerically referenced idea can, in turn, be represented in many different ways.

For example, imagine that a cube represents an idea. This cube (shown in Figure 15-4) has six different faces, and each face represents a different language domain or way of depicting the idea. Depending on which side of the cube you're looking at, you will see a different representation of the idea. You cannot see the idea itself, only its presentation, or description, in different language domains.

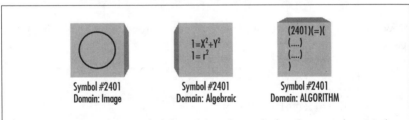

Symbol #2401
Domain: Image

Symbol #2401
Domain: Algebraic

Symbol #2401
Domain: ALGORITHM

Figure 15-4: *Depending on which face of the cube you look at (language domain), the idea hidden inside the cube is presented in different ways.*

Next, imagine that the idea inside this box is the idea of a perfect circle. This may seem confusing at first, but try to picture the cube as a container for an idea, one that you cannot directly see. On each face of the cube is a different depiction of the same idea. The idea of a circle can be communicated in several different formats, among them the following:

Picture

> We can simply draw a picture of a circle (see Figure 15-4, at left).

Algebraic

> The circle can also be described with the formula $r^2 = x^2 + y^2$, or $1 = x^2 + y^2$ (the cube at the center of Figure 15-4).

Algorithmic

> We can also send a small computer program that draws a circle (Figure 15-4, at right). We will describe how to use programs to draw images in Chapter 17, *Pictures*.

Each one of these formats is a different language domain. When we look at our idea-cube, the container for this idea, what we see depends on which face we're looking at. If we turn the cube one way, we see the pictorial representation of a circle (a bitmapped image). If we turn the cube in another direction, we see the idea depicted as an equation (e.g., $1 = x^2 + y^2$). Turn the cube in yet another direction, and we see the idea presented as a set of machine instructions to trace the outline of a circle on a virtual display.

The system we're describing here is actually a multilingual system. It catalogs ideas numerically, so they are not easily confused with each other. In addition, each idea can be described, or rendered, in many different language domains at once. Some ideas lend themselves to a formulaic description, while others are much easier to comprehend with the aid of pictures or through a set of abstract ideas that describe the relation of one abstract idea to another. So, you can describe one idea using whatever methods work best for describing it.

We can think of igenes as a type of *meme*. Some of these igenes will be very specialized in their function (i.e., calculate the sine of the cosine of the cube root of a number), and not referenced frequently by other programs. Other igenes, such as the igenes for addition, will be used throughout nearly every program.

Building a lexicon of symbols

We can use equivalency statements to define new igenes, which can then be used to build a conceptual vocabulary for describing a variety of things. We will use the same technique used in previous chapters to define basic arithmetic operations and Boolean logic. All we need to do is to write a simple equation, such as the following, to define a new symbol. The only difference is that we can define new symbols in absolute terms.

In Chapter 13, *Symbols*, we trained the recipient of our message to recognize new symbols by showing them sets of good and bad examples of an idea. For the first few dozen symbols, this would be fairly slow going because the recipient would have to manually examine the message to learn the basic symbols that form the foundation of the programming language.

However, once the recipient learns the basic symbols required to perform elementary arithmetic, make *if-then* decisions, and to store and manipulate data, they can then begin to decode the rest of the message in an automated fashion. This can be illustrated with the following example:

```
(123) = (
    (|0| (=) (|1| (x) [2]))
)
```

This example is used to define the meaning of symbol 123. This symbol is used to perform a very simple function: to double whatever number is given to it. We could have defined this new symbol using the technique described in Chapter 12. Had we done this, we would have sent a series of training examples, such as the following:

```
([2](=)((123)[1]))
([4](=)((123)[2]))
([6](=)((123)[3]))
([8](=)((123)[4]))
([10](=)((123)[5]))
```

The recipient will notice a clear pattern in this set of examples. The number on the left-hand side of the equation is always equivalent to the number on the right-hand side, multiplied by two. When the recipients have been presented with enough examples, they will be able to easily deduce that symbol 123 means $2x$, or x *times 2*.

This approach is just as valid, but it requires a lot more information. It's easier and more economical (in terms of bandwidth) to define symbol 123 using a statement such as the previous example. Most importantly, the first approach enables the recipient to automatically catalog thousands (or millions) of igenes without having to manually inspect the inner workings of each one.

Super concepts: Building igenes on top of other igenes

Here's where things *really* get interesting. We can build progressively complex igenes using previously defined igenes as building blocks for higher-order functions. For example, if we want to create a program that calculates the mass of a moving object according to Einstein's Theory of Relativity, the equation would reads as:

$$m = m_o / (1 - (v^2/c^2))^{1/2}$$

where:

$$0 < v < c, \text{ and } c > 0$$

This equation predicts that an object's mass increases dramatically as it nears the speed of light. This formula also predicts that the object's mass will reach infinity if it reaches the speed of light, which explains why it is impossible for an object to attain this speed, because doing so would require an infinite amount of energy.

This equation describes a well-known relationship that an extraterrestrial civilization will have discovered. While this is a useful way to tell them that we understand the concept of relativity, we're more interested in demonstrating how to build a library of igenes that can be reused so we don't have to write an entire program from scratch. This formula requires the following arithmetic operations:

- Divide two numbers.
- Calculate the square of a number.
- Calculate the square root of a number.
- Define a constant (the speed of light).
- Verify that v is > 0, that v is < c, and that c is > 0.

Before we define our concept that calculates the mass of a moving object, we need to define concepts to perform these other tasks.

STEP ONE: DEFINE THE CONCEPT OF DIVISION (÷)

This is a basic arithmetic operator. This igene is identified by symbol 15 (1111), as described in Chapter 12, to mean ÷, by sending a series of examples to illustrate the process of division.

STEP TWO: DEFINE Y = X²

This igene is a special case of multiplication. Here, we need to define this symbol, 101100, as follows:

```
(101100) (10) (
    (|0|(10)|1|(14)|1|)
)
```

This expression defines the symbol 101100 (decimal 44) to mean, "Multiply the number presented to this igene by itself." This is a simple way to calculate the square of a number. So, if this igene is presented with the number 2, it will return the result 2×2, or 4.

STEP THREE: CALCULATE THE SQUARE ROOT OF A NUMBER ($X^{1/2}$)

The next igene we need to define is symbol 101101, which is used to calculate the square root of a number. This symbol can be described either algorithmically (as a computer program), or using a set of examples. Because the process of calculating a square root requires more calculation, we'll describe it here using a set of examples. In an actual message, we would probably want to describe it using both algorithms and training examples.

First, let's define this symbol using a set of training examples as shown in Table 15-2. Since the concept of a square root should be familiar to anyone who understands basic math or geometry, the recipient should quickly understand the pattern in the following examples:

Table 15-2: *Training statements used to describe the behavior of the square root (SQRT) symbol*

VERBOSE FORM	PLAIN TEXT FORM
([1](=)((101101)[1])))	1 = SQRT(1)
([10](=)((101101)[100])))	2 = SQRT(4)
([11](=)((101101)[1001])))	3 = SQRT(9)
([100](=)((101101)[10000])))	4 = SQRT(16)
([101](=)((101101)[11001])))	5 = SQRT(25)

The disadvantage of describing symbol 101101 (square root) by example is that the recipient must analyze the set of examples by hand (or tentacle) to discover the underlying pattern. However, if we describe symbol 101101 using a mini-program, the recipient can capture the definition for this symbol automatically. In this scenario, we would send the following series of instructions:

```
(101101) (=) (
    Instructions to calculate the square root of |1| go here.
    This procedure is fairly involved, so we'll gloss over it
    for now to keep this example brief.
)
```

STEP FOUR: DEFINE A CONSTANT

Next, we need to define a symbol for c, a constant, which refers to the speed of light. One way we can do this is to create an igene that always returns the same result, in this case (300,000,000).

```
(1011001) (=) (
    |0| (=) [10001111000011010001100000000])
)
```

This expression is a concept that always returns a pre-determined result; therefore, whenever you invoke the igene 1011001, regardless of what information you present to it, the igene always returns the same number, 10001111000011010001100000000 (decimal 300,000,000). Any program that needs the value for c will simply refer to symbol 1011001.

If we rewrite our equation using the syntax we've developed so far, we can assign this new concept its own unique ID, 100000001 (or concept 257), which can then be called or referred to in other programs:

```
(100000001) (=) (
    (|00111|(1010)((00110001)|0010|))              M3 = M2²
    (|0100|(1010)(|00111|(1111)(((101100)(1011001)))) M4 = M3 ÷ c²
    (|0101|(1010)[0001](1101)|0100|)                M5 = 1 - M4
    (|0110|(1010)((101101)|0101|))                  M6 = √M5
    (|0|(1010)|0001|(1111)|0110|)      M0 (return value) = M1 ÷ M6
)
```

This example defines the steps required to solve the relativity equation. While this may not be a perfect example, as we ignore some details about how variables (data buckets) are defined, it does illustrate the basic technique. Now that we've defined this equation, we can reuse it in other programs simply by referring to this igene using this numeric identifier.

Standing on the shoulders of giants

The next example applies what we've learned in the previous section to describe the behavior of an accelerating spacecraft. This is a simplified example, but it should be sufficient for illustrating the technique we wish to describe:

$$a = F \div m$$

where:

$$m = m_o / (1 - (v^2/c^2))^{1/2}$$

This formula predicts that a spacecraft's rate of acceleration decreases as it approaches the speed of light (because its mass is increasing). We can express this formula using our concept notation in simplified formula, as follows:

```
(100000010) (=) (
    (|0111|(=)((100000010)|0001||0010|)
    (|0|(=)|1000|(1111)|0111|)
)
```

which can be interpreted as:

```
(100000010) (=) (
    |3| = ((257)|1||2|)
    |0| = |4|(/)|3|
)
```

Here, we've created yet another symbol, igene 258. From now on, whenever we use igene 258, we can execute a statement that calculates the acceleration of an object, taking into account the effects of the object's relative velocity on its mass. In case you haven't noticed, igene 258 uses igene 257 (used to calculate the mass of a moving object) to generate its results. The first line in this mini-program uses the symbol 257 to calculate the mass of the object (which is based on its base mass and velocity, information that is contained in the |1| and |2| variables).

It's not important that you understand all of the details of what's occurring inside this example program. The important point to understand is that we are using symbols as shorthand notation for a more complex series of instructions, one which may in turn reference additional symbols and sets of instructions. This building block approach to creating software allows us to approach complex problems in a step-wise fashion and build complex programs from a library of relatively simple, reusable components.

Building "black box" components

The ability to create self-contained mini-programs, or igenes, that can be combined to create larger, more sophisticated programs is another important step. When building igenes, the author is building what is often referred to as a *black box*.

When used to describe software, a black box is a set of instructions whose inner-workings are a mystery to the outside world. A black box presents a simplified interface through which the outside world passes information to and from the software component. This mini-program accepts its input information, performs its instructions, and then places its results in one or more registers visible to the outside world. The outside world only needs to know how to send and receive information from the software component, and usually needs to know nothing about the details of how it arrives at its results.

As Figure 15-5 illustrates, data is fed into the black box (input), which performs its calculations and then feeds the data back out to the user (output). You can think of black box functions almost as information processing circuits that receive information through one or more input wires and push their results out through an output terminal.

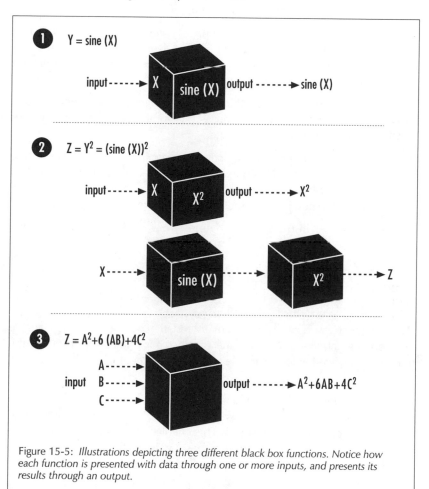

Figure 15-5: *Illustrations depicting three different black box functions. Notice how each function is presented with data through one or more inputs, and presents its results through an output.*

We now have something very similar to the concept of a gene for computer programs. Each black box is a self-contained set of instructions that performs a specific function. Most importantly, these instruction sets are modular. They can be combined to form more complex instructions, and can be used in any combination. This enables us to create super-concepts, or concepts built using one or more simpler igenes. This is like defining a new word for something that previously required many words, or perhaps several paragraphs, to explain. The new word becomes shorthand for something much more elaborate.

Now let's apply the black box concept to an example we used in Chapter 14, *Memory and Programming*. In that chapter, we wrote a short program to test whether a number is prime or not.

We can use the instructions in the example from Chapter 14 as a definition for a new igene. Let's call this igene 259. This igene accepts one input and generates one output. It accepts an integer number as its input. It generates a Boolean (true/false) result as its output.

The algorithm used in the "Test Prime Number" igene is described in flowchart form in Figure 15-6. Thfce input is the number we test; the output is one of two possible values: true or false.

Once we've defined this set of instructions, we no longer need to know how igene 259 arrives at its conclusion; we simply give it a number to test. This igene (259) then replies with either a true or false answer to let us know whether or not the number is prime. That's all we need to know.

To use this set of instructions, or igene, we would send the following statement:

(|0001| (1010) ((100000011) |0010|))

which can be read as:

(|1| (=) ((259)|2|))

This statement instructs the recipient to test the number in local variable (memory register) 2 |2| to determine whether it is prime. The results of the test are then placed in local variable (memory register) 1 |1|.

In looking at this example, we were able to abbreviate what was a lengthy set of instructions into a terse statement with a total of four words. Because we had defined the instructions within igene 259 (100000011) previously, there is no need to repeat ourselves. This enables us to shrink programs dramatically, by 10 fold, a 100 fold, or more, by using shorthand to represent complex, reusable instructions.

We now have the basic building blocks to describe a complete computer program. The next hurdle is to take this knowledge and apply it to create programs that do something useful. Some of the programs we create would be special-purpose programs, such as a program that describes a specific concept. Other programs will be generic, such as a program that decodes

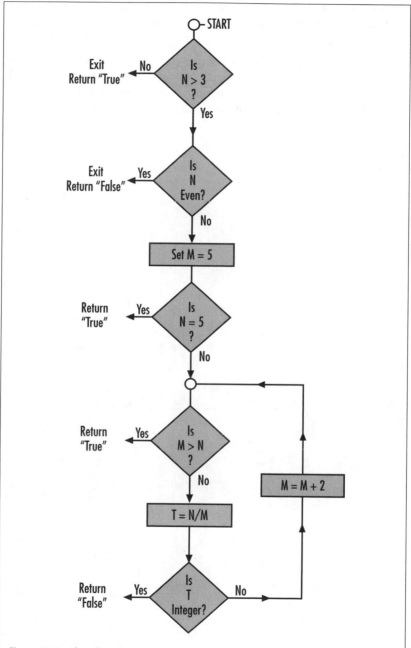

Figure 15-6: *Flowchart depicting internal behavior of the TestPrime igene described earlier.*

compressed image data. We can use this technique to describe anything we want: pictures, sounds, physical simulations, games, anything we can do with a computer.

This is where things start to get really interesting because we're progressing from using computer programs to do relatively simple things like solving algebraic formula, to displaying multicolor images, simulating complex situations, and ultimately, describing a rich, abstract language.

SEQUENCING THE BINARY GENOME

The system we've developed thus far provides an easy mechanism for reconstructing a message without requiring the receiver to capture the entire message from start to finish. The system also allows us to define a mechanism for detecting and repairing transmission errors.

Even under optimal conditions, the listener will not receive the coded message with 100 percent accuracy. There is a high probability that the signal we send may be periodically interrupted, disrupting or damaging a portion of the message. We must assume that the message will be vulnerable to damage by interference, and will be disrupted by noise, loss of line of sight between the transmitter and receiver, and other conditions. We should assume that it is extremely unlikely that the listener will intercept this message just as it is beginning. Even in ideal circumstances, it will not be immediately obvious where the message begins and ends.

In Chapter 12, *Binary DNA*, we borrowed some ideas from biology to describe the basic structure of the message. This was done intentionally, because nature has managed to condense a great deal of information into a small package. The entire human genome, the instructions required to "build" a human being, is represented by about 3 billion DNA base pairs, the equivalent of 6 gigabits of binary data (small enough to fit onto a single CD-ROM). In a sense, the challenge of deciphering the meaning of this 3-billion–word message is not all that different from the challenge of deciphering a message from an alien civilization.

The basic goal of this chapter is to explain the techniques (many of them inspired by biology) that the sender and recipient can use to cope with errors caused by interference. The intent of this process is to make it easier for the recipient to capture and learn what different symbols within the message mean at their own pace, rather than all at one time.

Deciphering the meaning of DNA

While we may never detect an information-bearing signal from an alien civilization, we are, in a sense, tackling the challenge of deciphering an alien message in our efforts to decipher the human genome. Researchers have learned how to decode the basic structure of DNA and translate small groups of DNA base pairs into symbols for amino acids. We know, for example, how to group DNA words (*triplets* of three base pairs) into the equivalent of sentences, and how to recognize the boundaries between these sentences. We also know that the triplets represent instructions for building proteins by stringing amino acids together. If we compare the DNA decoding process to the process one might go through in deciphering an alien message, we will notice that there are many similarities.

Although some biologists might bristle at the thought of their work being compared to the search for extraterrestrial intelligence, the process of decoding and analyzing the data contained in DNA is, in some respects, similar to the process the recipient of our hypothetical message would go through. Consider the following points of comparison:

- Both messages were written in a non-human language by an unknown author. In the case of DNA, there is no author, *per se*.

- We cannot verbally communicate with the author to ask for pointers in deciphering either type of information. We can only rely on our own tools and intuition to guide us in the decoding process.

- At the time of our first encounter with this data, we had absolutely no knowledge about whom the message was from, what it meant, or how it was organized.

- Both types of messages are capable of conveying extremely large amounts of information in a highly compressed format. The "programs" encoded in DNA (e.g., the physical composition of a human being) are very complex.

What does DNA do that is so useful and important that makes it relevant to an extraterrestrial message? Biology offers many interesting lessons in this respect. Among other things, the information stored in DNA has these key features:

- Information is stored in a non-linear, or *random access format*. The human genome is not one giant blob of information. It is subdivided into modular packages of information (genes, chromosomes, etc.). Each of these subunits can be analyzed independently of the others, and then regrouped (compiled) later to form the entire DNA sequence.

- The subunits of information, or mini-programs, described by genes interact with other genes, often in very complicated ways. For example, the action of one gene can regulate (turn on/off) another, apparently unrelated gene. This web-like network effect enables a collection of simple genes to exhibit complex behavior when they interact with each other.

- Information encoded in DNA is highly resistant to damage. The information is structured in such a way that isolated errors, or mutations, are often corrected. Organisms have also developed sophisticated mechanisms for detecting and eliminating most transcription (copying) errors in DNA.

All of these features are relevant to the challenge of sending a message to another civilization—some because they make a message more compact and easier to decode, others because they make a message more resistant to damage resulting from interference.

Compression is important because it enables us to send large amounts of information without wasting vast amounts of bandwidth. Even in an ideal situation, we will always be limited to sending information at a finite and probably fairly slow speed compared to terrestrial computer networks.

The random-access organization of DNA is also very relevant to the task of sending an interstellar message. Mimicking this organization enables us to create a message that can be received out of sequence and re-assembled on the receiving end (sort of like putting the pieces of a puzzle together). The recipient does not have to listen to the entire message from start to finish in a single pass in order to begin deciphering it. By meticulously subdividing the message into packages similar to genes, we can make it much easier for the recipient to parse and analyze the message. This enables the recipient to inspect and learn the function of each symbol (or igene) one at a time.

Error detection and correction is another important feature. In DNA, error-correction mechanisms prevent minor transcription errors from crippling an entire gene. When applied to an interstellar message, error-correction will enable the recipient to automatically detect and correct garbled data without having to wait for the message to be retransmitted.

The decision to mimic the way information is encoded in DNA is an acknowledgement of the fact that nature, without the guiding hand of an engineer, has devised an extremely efficient and resilient way to store and encode information.

Sequencing a binary message

The process of decoding an interstellar message may be similar to the process of decoding genetic information stored in DNA. The basic sequence of events the recipient will go through in decoding a message like this is as follows:

1. Identify the basic elements or signaling scheme used to compose the message and learn how these elements are combined to form a basic alphabet.

2. Learn how the characters in the basic alphabet are organized into groups (words) and supergroups (sentences, paragraphs, mini-programs, etc.).

3. Learn how groups of symbols are organized into discrete gene-like packages, and how these igenes interact with other igenes.

4. Learn how igenes are combined to form higher-order programs, and how they can be used to define or refine the definition of other symbols.

We discussed the first step in the process in Chapter 10, *Teleporting Bits*. Here, the objective is to figure out how information is embedded in a radio or optical signal. As we discussed, information may be encoded in many different ways (e.g., by altering the timing of a laser beacon's pulses, by changing the color of the light emitted by the beacon, etc.). In the second stage, the recipient wants to learn how the bits of information embedded in the signal can be strung together to form simple words and groups of words. We discussed this in Chapter 12, where we introduced the concept of open and close parentheses (which are similar to the STOP sequence used to denote the end of a "sentence" in DNA). This step should also be fairly easy to complete since the DNA-like encoding scheme will be easy to spot using conventional statistical analysis techniques.

In the third and fourth stages, the recipient begins to probe the behavior of the symbols and mini-programs built by combing the symbols and syntax elements learned in stages one and two. The recipient will probe the function of each new symbol individually. Because the message mimics the organization of genetic information, the recipient does not need to read the message from start to finish, but can probe igenes in whatever order they like.

Many programs will be dependent on a fairly small number of igenes to function. For example, a program that tests a number to determine whether it is prime requires the recipient to understand the function of a dozen or more igenes. Other programs, however, may be dependent on hundreds or thousands of igenes to function properly. In order to run any particular program, the recipient will need only to have decoded the igenes on which that program is dependent to run.

Capturing new igenes

Let's look at an example of how a recipient might deal with this message. For the purposes of this example, the recipient has intercepted our message about one-third of the way through. The first thing they receive is a set of instructions that uses our *TestPrime* function, which we described in Chapter 15, *Concepts and igenes*. The only problem, however, is that the *TestPrime* function was defined at the beginning of our message, not toward the middle. For example, the recipient captures a set of instructions like the following (shorthand notation is used for brevity and readability):

```
(21054) (=) (
    (|2| = ((21010)|1|)
    (|0| = ((259)|2|)
)
```

```
(|2| = ((21054){1})
```

Because of noise, receiver malfunctions, or other reasons, the recipient receives only this part of the message. The rest of the message surrounding this snippet is garbled, and is therefore useless. For our purposes, it doesn't matter what function igene 21054 does. The important thing to notice is how this set of instructions references two other igenes: igene 21010 and igene 259 (the *TestPrime* igene we studied earlier).

The recipient cannot execute this program until they receive the definitions for igenes 259 and 21010 (as well as any igenes they reference internally). That's the bad news. The good news is the message repeats indefinitely, in loop fashion, so the recipient can simply wait for the message to repeat and capture igenes 259 and 21010 then run this program again from the start. This process of cataloging igenes, and their underlying instructions as they are received, can be automated. As definitions for new igenes are encountered, they are logged in a database of igenes and their underlying instruction sets for future use.

Retransmitting the message in a loop enables us to guard against the possibility of the recipient missing key parts of the message. We can provide the recipient with clues about the repeating nature of the message by organizing the message into the equivalent of chapters (e.g., group a large number of expressions and igenes into numbered groups). The recipient would see that these "chapters" are sequentially numbered. Thus, if the recipient picked up the transmission during chapter number 19000, this would provide them with a clue that they had missed earlier parts of the transmission.

They need only wait until these igenes are defined elsewhere in the message. Once they have captured the definitions for all of the igenes used by a specific program, they can then run the program. If the listener fails to capture the entire message on the first pass, they can simply capture the missing concepts on subsequent passes.

To understand how this works, take a look at Figure 16-1 to see how the igenes in this example program interact with one another.

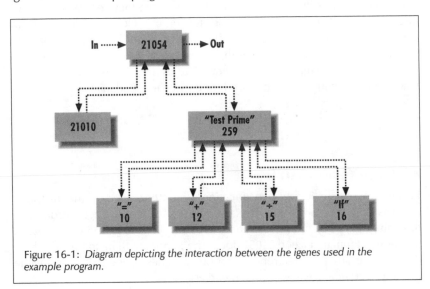

Figure 16-1: *Diagram depicting the interaction between the igenes used in the example program.*

At the topmost level, the program depicted in Figure 16-1 is very simple. The igene 21054 accepts one piece of information as its input, and produces one output as a result. In turn, igene 21054 depends on igenes 21010 and 259 (*TestPrime*) to calculate its result. Likewise, igene 259 depends on several more igenes (such as the symbol for addition), to help test whether or not the number it receives is prime.

What's interesting is that the program, and the underlying components used to build it, can transmit completely out of sequence. Figure 16-2 depicts the message in a timeline view.

Figure 16-2: *Timeline of transmission of igenes; notice how they are sent in no obvious order.*

This diagram depicts the transmission of eight igenes, which are sent out of sequence, in an apparently meaningless order. At first glance this would make the message hopelessly jumbled and nearly impossible to decipher. However, it actually makes it easier to decode. Since each igene is labeled with its own unique numeric address, the recipient can automatically build a manifest of all of the igenes required to execute any program they receive.

When the recipients inspect igene 21054 from Figure 16-1, they will see that it depends, in turn, on igenes 21010 and 259. When they inspect these two igenes, they will see that igene 259 depends on several more igenes to do its job. This inspection process can be completely automated, and is similar to what a Web search engine does when it analyzes a website to build an index of all of the documents stored at that site.

Once the recipients have generated a manifest of the igenes required to run a particular program, they can compare this manifest against a database of the igenes they have already catalogued. If they have all of the required igenes on hand, they would be able to run the program without a problem. If one or more required igenes have not been captured, they would merely need to wait until the igene(s) in question retransmit. (Of course, if they only detected the signal during the last part of its final transmission cycle, they'd be SOL and would have to wait until we got around to broadcasting in their direction again.)

In addition to reducing a complex program to a set of easily digestible, bite-sized mini-programs, there's another important inherent benefit in this scheme. The recipient can execute higher level, sophisticated programs without understanding the functions of the intermediate-level igenes used to build them. Once the recipient learns the few dozen basic symbols required to execute simple programs, the rest of the message capture and decoding process can be largely automated.

Critical mass

We have now reached a sort of "critical mass," in that we can define extremely sophisticated programs without requiring the recipient to understand everything that is happening inside the program. This is not unprecedented. Very few people understand everything that is happening within a typical desktop publishing program. Yet, a user who knows nothing about image enhancement algorithms, or programming in general, can operate a program that is based on some *very* sophisticated technology.

The only limit to the sophistication of the programs we can send is the speed and memory capacity of the computer that will run the programs. If Earthly experience is any indication of where things are heading in this respect, we don't need to worry about ET having a fast enough computer to run these programs.

This is an important turning point in the process of decoding a message. Once the recipient reaches a point at which they understand the fundamental symbols used to define a computer program, the rest of the transcription and decoding process can be automated. When we were first defining the basic vocabulary of symbols required to write a program, we were forced to send a long series of good and bad examples for each new concept in order to teach the recipient what the symbols meant. Now, we can simply send a statement like:

```
(12345) (=) (
        insert code that defines the igene 12345 here
        this could be something simple, like the instructions
        to add three numbers, or it could be a very complex
        set of instructions to be used within a larger program.
)
```

This statement has three basic components: a *symbol*, denoted by "(12345)"; an *equal sign*, denoted by "="; and an *underlying instruction set*, contained in a set of parenthesis. When combined, this statement lets the recipients know that every time they see a particular symbol, the program should recall the information contained in the instruction set. The recipients would simply catalog these statements in a database for immediate recall whenever they want to run a program that references one or more of these symbols. There is no need for the recipients to understand the internal details of these high-level components, because they are ultimately translated into low-level programming symbols they have already learned.

We can use this convenient feature to write igenes that employ sophisticated error-correction and compression algorithms to protect the data we send against transmission errors, and to enable us to maximize the amount of information we can convey with a given amount of bandwidth. This enables us to use sophisticated programs without requiring the recipient to understand the theory behind them (which would otherwise create a potentially insurmountable stumbling block).

Transmitting igenes

Since the transmission will not be 100 percent reliable, we should assume that portions of the message will be corrupted by noise, equipment failures, and other forms of interference. The ability to reconstruct the message out of sequence helps a great deal, but we can improve transmission reliability even further by using techniques that the receiver to detect errors and reconstruct damaged data.

One simple technique we can use is to repeatedly broadcast frequently used, critical instruction sets. For example, the symbol 1100 (addition, or a plus + sign) will be used in virtually every program or igene we transmit. While the message as a whole may repeat itself once per year, we don't want to force the receiver to wait for a year to capture the instruction that defines this concept. If we did, the receiver would have to wait a year to execute most of the programs they received. To get around this problem, we would retransmit the definition for this symbol frequently, perhaps once every few days. This approach would allow the receiver to capture enough data to run many programs within a short period of time, even if it takes a year (or many years) to transmit the entire message and every program it contains.

The first step in this technique is to build an index of every igene used by every program in the message. The index is then ranked to list the igenes according to the number of times they are referenced by other igenes or programs throughout the message. Frequently referenced igenes appear at the top of the list, while the infrequently referenced igenes appear at the bottom. The igenes related to basic math and logic functions will probably be at the top of this list, mainly because they would appear in almost every program.

This sorted list gives the sender a rough measure of the importance of each igene. An igene used in 2000 different igenes or programs is probably more important than one that appears in only one or two places throughout the message. Therefore, it makes sense to retransmit the frequently used igene more often than the rarely used igenes.

The sender would use this index as a guideline for deciding how often to retransmit various igenes. The goal is to minimize the amount of time the recipient must wait to decode before they can run the programs. Because of this, the transmission is weighted to favor the igenes that are reused frequently throughout the message.

This requires the sender to introduce some redundancy in the message. If the senders retransmit an igene to calculate a sine once per day, they will be wasting bandwidth that could be used to send other information. However, if a particular igene is critical to the operation of hundreds or thousands of other components, it is a good idea to make sure the recipient has many opportunities to acquire these instructions.

While this approach increases the odds that the recipient will capture most of the message, subtle errors can creep into the message. These errors may be severe, and cause an igene to fail completely, or they may introduce more insidious errors (e.g., return an incorrect result, except without generating an obvious error condition that could be detected). These more subtle errors would not cause the program to crash outright, but would result in erroneous results that the receiver might not notice for some time.

Because of this potential problem, we need to add a mechanism to correct and repair damaged information whenever possible. As an early solution, one of the first programs we could transmit would be a program that corrects damaged data.

> NOTE
>
> *If you do not have a background in programming, the following section may confuse you. This section discusses strategies that can be used to compensate for errors caused by interference and background noise, and to compress the message so that it reuires less bandwidth to transmit. Fortunately, this section is not critial to understanding later chapters.*

Self-repairing data

When you listen to a compact disc, you hear data that has been digitally stored on a metal disc as pits that are "burned" into the surface of the disc. Like any man-made process, burning a CD is a process prone to errors caused by imperfections in the disc, as well as damage caused by handling, scratches, warping, etc. Just as we cannot assume that a radio transmission will come through loud and clear, the makers of CD players cannot assume that the data stored on the disc is 100 percent intact.

CDs compensate for this problem by encoding data in a special format. This format enables CD players to detect errors, and in many cases, to compensate for possible errors. There are two techniques that can be used to compensate for errors or imperfections in a CD. The first technique is to use a *checksum*. A checksum enables the player to detect any errors in the data recorded on the disc. The second technique, *pre-emptive error-correction*, enables the player to reconstruct lost or garbled data, even if it has been substantially damaged. CDs use a technique called Reed-Solomon coding to embed extra information that enables the player to reconstruct lost or damaged data during playback.

Checksums

A checksum is a simple scheme for detecting errors in a message. One of the main advantages of using a checksum is that it doesn't bloat the message significantly; instead, it adds only a few extra digits to a series of numbers. The checksum numbers are used to crosscheck the data to see if it has been altered during transit. To get an idea of how a checksum works, let's take a look at the following sequence (written in decimal format for brevity):

0149451023

To the receivers, these numbers will be just a few out of billions of digits they might receive in a single transmission. Without some sort of encoding, transmission errors can easily go unnoticed; for example, the sequence 1023 could be changed to 1022 as a result of a single corrupted bit. Without a system for crosschecking the data, the recipient has no way of detecting an error like this.

A checksum works by adding the sum of the numbers in a sequence at repeating intervals. As such, a checksum for the string 0149451023 would be as follows:

0+1+4+9+4+5+1+0+2+3 = 29

We would then take this total and append it to the original series of 10 digits, forming a 12-digit number that is processed by an igene that knows where to look for the checksum information in a block of numbers:

014945102329

Notice how the original series of digits has been modified to include the checksum information. To decode this on the receiving end, the recipient needs an igene whose job is to process check-summed data and convert it into the format we've been working with up until this point. The igene used to decode this message is fairly simple, and will perform the following tasks:

1. Break down the input string of numbers into individual digits (e.g., 0149 becomes 0, 1, 4, 9).

2. Sum (add) all of these digits together, but ignore the last two checksum digits in the sequence. Do not include these checksum digits in the total.

3. Compare the sum of the first ten digits to the two checksum digits.

4. If the two numbers are equal, the data is not corrupted. The igene then returns the first 10 digits from the input string as its result.

5. If the two numbers do not agree, the data may be corrupted, and no data is returned by the igene as its result. The igene does this to notify other programs that are dependent on this data that this part of the message has been corrupted.

Figures 16-3 and 16-4 illustrate how a "test checksum" igene will behave when it is presented with specially encoded data that includes checksum information. In the first example, Figure 16-3, the igene returns the original series of digits with the checksum digits stripped off. This information can then be passed through the same parsing processes outlined in Chapters 12 through 15. The second example, shown in Figure 16-4, illustrates what happens when the igene is presented with corrupted data. In this case, it sees that the checksum does not agree with the rest of data, and returns no data as its result, a clear signal that there is a problem with the data.

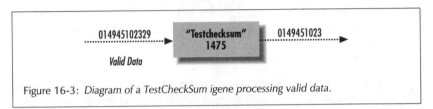

Figure 16-3: *Diagram of a TestCheckSum igene processing valid data.*

Figure 16-4: *Diagram of a TestCheckSum igene processing corrupt data; notice how it returns no data as its result.*

Checksums allow the recipient to detect, but not correct, errors. At the very least, they can discard damaged portions of the message and wait for them to transmit again. A checksum increases the size of the message by as much as 5 to 20 percent, but this is a small price to pay to allow the recipient to detect and reject damaged data.

Pre-emptive error correction

The next trick we will employ enables the recipient to reconstruct damaged data. This is accomplished by introducing some redundancy to the message, and by spreading the information out over time. Here's a simplistic example of how we might do this:

```
"This is a test message."
```

To increase the chances of the recipient receiving all of the data (and reducing the risk of data being lost or damaged along the way), each letter will be sent twice with other letters intermixed. Using this process, the message might now look something like this:

```
"Tehgiass s iesm  at steets ta  mseis ssaighet."
```

Now, let's imagine that the message above is corrupted by interference, resulting in something like this on the receiving end:

```
"????????iesm  at steets ta  mseis ssaighet."
```

Although we have lost the first part of the message, the recipient can reconstruct the original message because we've inserted redundant copies of each letter in the latter half of the message. This is a simplistic example; it is much less sophisticated than the techniques used in real-world systems.

Error-correction schemes, however, are not bulletproof, mainly because they cannot repair severely damaged data. These schemes are typically reliable until the error rate (percentage of bits that are corrupted) approaches 5 or 10 percent. As the error rate increases, the success rate for the error-correction algorithm decreases, as depicted in Figure 16-5. This graph shows that the error-correction scheme will recover damaged data with near 100 percent success when the error rate is relatively low (<10 percent of bits transmitted). But as the error rate increases above 10 percent, the rate of successful data recovery decreases rapidly.

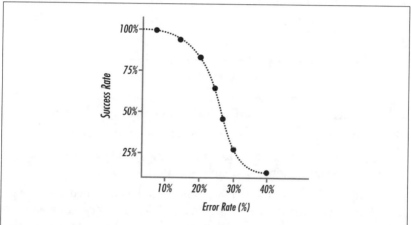

Figure 16-5: The success rate for error-correction scheme, versus BER (bit error rate, percentage of corrupted bits).

The inflection point at which the success rate begins to drop rapidly is primarily determined by the amount of redundant data the error-correction algorithm embeds in the encoded message. If we anticipate a very high error rate (e.g., 90 percent), we can make the error-correction scheme more robust by including a lot of redundant data, several copies of each bit we want to protect. At this point, we will take a huge performance hit, because most of our message consists of error-correction data instead of the message we are trying to protect.

However, if we design our error-correction scheme to handle low error rates (up to about 10 percent), the performance penalty will be relatively small (usually less than 10 to 25 percent), depending on the specifics of the scheme employed. This is a small penalty to pay since it greatly improves the reliability with which the listener can receive the message without being forced to wait weeks or months for the message to repeat.

Back to the beginning

Next, we can define an igene that processes a block of encoded data, checks for and repairs errors, and outputs corrected data (or returns no data if the data is corrupted beyond repair). This corrected data is then run through the parsing process in a second stage during which the commands and data encoded in the original data set are processed. The corrected data is run through the exact same parsing process described in Chapters 11 through 14. The next example will define this program as igene 260, which we'll nickname as *CorrectErrors* (the number sequence is displayed in hexadecimal format for brevity):

```
((260)[09A181873672187424144AFF1DF854444])
```

When decoded, this statement means:

```
Use CorrectErrors to process the data
"09A181873672187424144AFF1DF854444"
```

The *CorrectErrors* igene generates a sequence of numbers formatted similar to the message we first described in Chapters 11 and 12:

```
(260)[ 09A18187...] → ({0101}(11001100){0001}(11001111){0010})
```

This sequence of digits can then run through the parsing and decoding process we've already described in Chapters 11 through 15.

Compression and error-correction algorithms can be combined into a single procedure that decompresses encoded data while also checking for and correcting errors. This combined function works like the black box depicted in Figure 16-6. It accepts compressed, error-corrected data as input and produces easily parsed data as output. The output data is then fed through the processing steps described in Chapters 12 through 15.

We can think of this decompression and error-correction igene as a bootstrap program. It allows the recipient to advance from reading only the parts of the message that are formatted in an obvious and easily parsed way, to processing higher level instructions that are encoded for error-correction and compression.

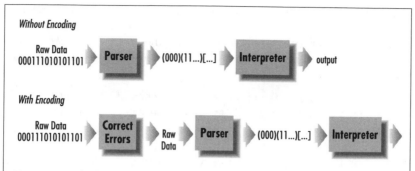

Figure 16-6: *The flow of data through an error-detection and correction algorithm. In the second case, an error-correction algorithm first processes raw data.*

Differentiating between unencoded and encoded data

In order to make the message easy to decipher, the sender would probably alternate between transmitting unencoded, easily parsed data, and data encoded for compression and error-correction. Although it would be most efficient to send all of the data in a compressed format, it would be virtually impossible for the recipient to decipher that data without prior knowledge about the algorithm used to compress it. Sending all of the data in an uncompressed format isn't an attractive option either, since the data won't be coded for error-correction, and will require 2 to 4 times as much bandwidth to send the same amount of information compared to a compressed message.

One way to send a message is by cycling between three types of data: a short calibration message; uncompressed and easily parsed data; and compressed, error-corrected data. The calibration message shown in Figure 16-7 would consist of a short series of prime numbers, making it very easy to spot (it also prevents the recipient from misinterpreting ones as zeros, and vice versa). The uncompressed data is also easy to parse. The compressed data will, at first, appear to be a series of random numbers.

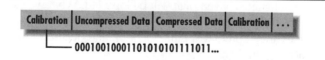

Figure 16-7: *By cycling between three types of data, the sender can send a message that is efficient and easy to parse.*

The recipients will easily tell the difference between plain text and encoded data, even before they have deciphered the basic symbols used in the message. The recipients can do this by measuring the *entropy value* (*H*, a measure of randomness) of the stream of digits and measuring how it changes over time.

Entropy is a measure of randomness. If a sequence of binary digits is truly random, then it will be impossible to predict the state of future digits based on the state of previous digits. This is very much like a coin toss. The fact that a coin turns up heads does not mean that it is likely or unlikely to do so on the next toss. A sequence of binary digits can be treated exactly like a series of coin tosses.

The unencoded stream of digits, on the other hand, is structured. It contains many repeating series of digits because we want the recipient to be able to see the structure in the message, and therefore to parse and decipher it more easily. This stream is not like a series of coin throws, however, because there are many predictable patterns in this series of digits.

The parts of the message that are encoded for compression and error-correction contain very few repeating patterns. When analyzed statistically, the patterns appear to be a series of random numbers. The unencoded stream of digits, on the other hand, will have many repeating patterns that may be easily revealed by statistical analysis.

We can measure randomness by measuring the likelihood that a given digit, or series of digits, will foretell the digit or sequence of digits that follows. If a series of numbers is random, then the knowledge of previous digits will tell us nothing about the digits that follow. If, on the other hand, the series is not random, the odds will be lopsided in favor of one digit (or a series of digits) over other possible combinations.

The measure we obtain is a value called *H*. When applied to a series of binary digits, *H* can vary between 0 and 1. *H* peaks when the probability of obtaining either 0 or 1 is exactly 0.5 (50 percent), the same as a coin toss. If the stream of digits is random, or almost random, the measured value for *H* is approximately 1. However, if there is an ordered pattern in the series, the probability of obtaining a given digit will be lopsided. What we see from the graph in Figure 16-8 is that *H* peaks when the probability (odds) are exactly 50 percent (i.e., they don't favor either 1 or 0), and decreases as the probability approaches either 0 or 1.

The value of *H* says a lot about the density of the information in the message. Ironically, the more densely information is packed in our message, the more it will resemble a random series of digits (random noise). This is because a tightly packed message will have eliminated a redundant series of digits. By eliminating redundancy (repeating patterns), we increase the randomness or entropy of the series of digits.

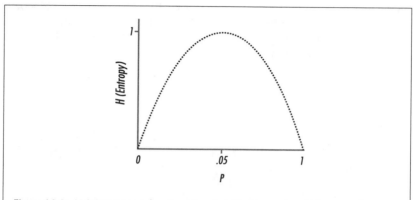

Figure 16-8: *H (entropy) as a function of probability for a series of binary numbers. Note how H peaks when the probability is 50 percent. Information density also peaks when H is 1.*

So, let's suppose that we alternate between sending compressed and uncompressed data. The recipient will be able to clearly see this by measuring the entropy of the digit sequence over time. The recipient will see a plot similar to what is shown in Figure 16-9.

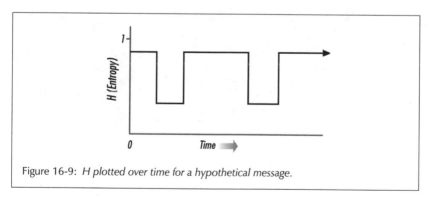

Figure 16-9: *H plotted over time for a hypothetical message.*

This plot is a strong hint that the *information density* of the message varies over time. The regions with a low value for *H* have a lot of redundant data in them. This gives the recipient a hint that this data is not encoded as efficiently, and is therefore w easier to decipher than the data with a high *H* value. This also tells the recipient where to start decoding the message, as it will be easier to figure out what is happening in the parts of the message where there is a lot of redundancy.

Once we've learned to transmit information in a compact format that is protected against the effects of interference, we can proceed to describe larger, more complex programs that can be used to model complex situations (simulators), and also to generate detailed pictures to use later in building a vocabulary of abstract symbols.

PICTURES

Now that we know how to describe computer programs in our hypothetical message, it's time to move on to more interesting territory. The igenes used to build a program define its behavior, and can be used to build sophisticated programs. One of the things we can do with the simple programs we've been creating is use them to transmit detailed images to our distant audience, and to do so in a way that is efficient, requiring little bandwidth.

We're not just limiting ourselves to still pictures either. We can use these programs to generate continuous waveforms to represent sounds, or to send a series of images (motion video), or to simulate the behavior of complex systems such as the planets and asteroids orbiting in our solar system, weather patterns here on Earth, etc.

These programs can then be used to simulate or visualize almost anything, and they can even be taken to the next level, which is to create a general-purpose abstract language, something we'll discuss later. The ability to send detailed images, and to equate these images with other symbols and categories of symbols, enables us to build a much more extensive vocabulary than we could if we were limited to equations or simplified line drawings alone.

From images to pixels

As the old cliché goes, "A picture is worth a thousand words." We can describe any number of scenarios using formulas, but nothing substitutes for a clear picture of something, especially if you're describing a complex system, such as our planet. Pictures, and visual representations of data in general, will play an important role in defining an abstract language to a far-off civilization we know very little about. Once we have the basic capability to create and transmit simple computer programs, we can use them to transmit images. There are many ways this can be done; there is no one "correct way."

The simplest way to transmit a picture is to send a *bitmap*. A bitmap, as shown in Figure 17-1, is a two-dimensional grid consisting of a finite number of pixels, or picture elements.

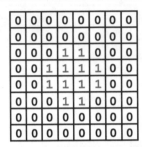 

Figure 17-1: *This diagram depicts an 8 × 8 (8 pixels wide, 8 pixels high) bitmap consisting of 256 bits.*

Each pixel (dot) has only two possible states: 1 (white) or 0 (black). The bitmap shown in Figure 17-1 would draw a black-and-white image depicting a small white circle at its center. While this format is useful for drawing simple geometrical shapes, it is not an efficient way to transmit detailed pictures.

Black and white bitmaps are easy enough to transmit. However, as you can see, they are difficult to interpret. An alien observer, who has no concept of what a human being looks like, would probably not recognize the human stick figure for what it is. Interpreting the contents of a black-and-white bitmap is a highly subjective process, and because of this, it is very error-prone. We can reduce the possibility for confusion by making the images more detailed.

A grayscale picture is an improvement over a black-and-white bitmap because we can adjust the brightness of each pixel (dot) in the image. This enables us to transmit detailed black-and-white pictures of objects with near photographic quality. For example, if we sent a grayscale image of Jupiter, it would be obvious to the receiver that we had sent a picture of a planet. The penalty we pay by adding more detail to the image is increased bandwidth usage. The grayscale image would require eight times as much information compared to a simple black-and-white image, because we would be sending additional information for each individual pixel. Each pixel would have 256 possible values: 0 for black, 255 for white, and 1 through 254 to define intermediate shades of gray.

To get a sense for the amount of data we're talking about here, let's look at a typical photograph with a resolution of 1000 to 2000 pixels on each side. This means that a typical photo will have a resolution (sharpness) between

1000×1000 pixels to 2000×2000 pixels, or between 1 and 4 million pixels per image. If each pixel has 256 possible brightness levels, it would take between 8 and 32 million bits of information to describe a typical high-resolution image.

While it is well within our ability to transmit this amount of data, we can transmit images far more economically. We can do this because most images contain regions with little or no information. Consider, for example, the famous pictures of Earth taken by the crew of Apollo 17 (Figure 17-2).

Figure 17-2: *The Earth, as photographed by the Apollo 17 crew on December 7, 1972, as they were traveling toward the moon.*

As you can see, this image shows the Earth against the blackness of space, with the surface of the Earth having the most detail. This is typical of most images, where you will have some areas with a lot of detail, and others (such as the sky) that have much less detail. The more detail, the more information needed to represent that part of the image. So, we'll want to work out a scheme for transmitting detailed images in a compressed format. By doing so, we can reduce the amount of information needed to encode an image by a factor of 10 to 100 or more.

Embedding bitmap images in a message

By now, the recipient has learned to tell the difference between symbols and data and recognize simple programs (as described in Chapters 12 through 16). Images are just another type of information that can be embedded in the message. When images are first encountered in the message, the recipient probably won't know that a particular series of binary digits is being used to describe an image, only that it is describing a different type of information. Thus, the recipient needs to learn another *context* in which a series of binary numbers can be used.

Recall that in Chapter 13, *Symbols*, we described how to label the numeric words within the message according to their context or usage. So far, we've taught the recipient to recognize four distinct contexts in which numeric words can be used: *symbols* (including igenes), *raw data* (numbers to be processed by igenes), *global variables* (public memory registers), and *local variables* (private memory registers). These four contexts are required to build useful computer programs.

To embed a bitmapped image in the message, all we need to do is create a set of symbols to label a set of numbers that are used to describe the image. To do this, we assign a set of numeric codes that precede different types of bitmap images. For the sake of example, let's use symbol 64 (binary 1000000) as the context label for a black-and-white bitmapped image. The choice of the number 64 is arbitrary; we could use any numeric label to do this.

To embed this image within the message, we would send the following expression:

```
((1000000)(011100111001110))
```

Which would be correctly read as:

```
black/white bitmap 011100111001110
```

When the recipients first encounter a black-and-white bitmap image in this format, they won't know it's an image. However, they will notice that the expression uses a new context label, the number 64 instead of the labels 7, 8, or 9. This will be a hint that this piece of information is used in a different way.

The trick is to train the recipient to recognize that symbol 64 is associated with a bitmapped image. As we've done with other elementary symbols and concepts, one way to do this is to send a series of examples whose common pattern is easy to spot. Just as we did with the symbol 12 (+), we would send a series of training examples.

In order to make the examples easily recognizable, we would send a series of images that contain simple geometrical shapes, such as those shown in Figure 17-3 and Figure 17-4.

Figure 17-3, a small triangle inside a rectangular box, can be represented in the message using the following expression:

```
((1000000)((1111111111111000000000110000100001100011100011
100111110011000000000111111111111))
```

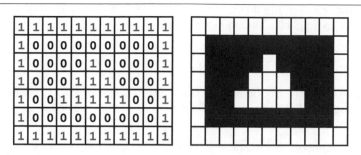

Figure 17-3: *An 11×7 bitmap depicting a triangle surrounded by a rectangular box.*

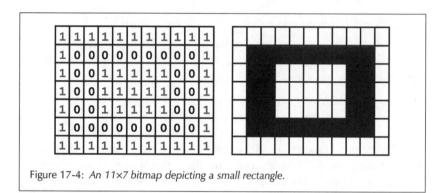

Figure 17-4: *An 11×7 bitmap depicting a small rectangle.*

The bitmap shown in Figure 17-4 displays a white rectangle inside a black rectangular box. This bitmap is similar to the image shown in Figure 17-1, except it shows a different shape inside the box. The bitmap shown in Figure 17-4 would be generated by the following expression:

```
((1000000)(1111111111110000000001100111100110011111001
10011111001100000000001111111111111))
```

When the information used to generate these bitmaps is shown in numeric form, it is not immediately obvious what the images look like. This is why it is important to send a large set of similar examples (not just one or two, as we've done here). This gives the recipients an opportunity to try many different ways to visualize the data, and to recognize a common pattern among the images (e.g., a simple geometric shape shown inside a rectangular box). Once they recognize the general format of the two-dimensional bitmaps, the process of displaying them can be repeated throughout the rest of the message.

Both of these training examples display a simple geometric shape within an 11×7–pixel bitmap. Each bitmap also has a 1-pixel border running around the edge of the image, which makes it easier for the recipient to recognize the basic layout of the image. There are some important pieces of information that are implicitly hidden in the data used to generate these images:

- Each image is 11 pixels wide by 7 pixels high.

- Both 11 and 7 are prime numbers.

- The recipient will be able to count up the digits used to generate the image, and will immediately notice that each word following the 64 symbol (1000000) is 77 bits long.

- The number 77 is the product of two prime numbers (11 and 7).

- Only two numbers can be multiplied together to get 77; those numbers are 11 and 7.

- Each image is bordered by a 1 pixel wide rectangular box.

This is a subtle hint that the data may represent a two-dimensional array. One of the things the recipient is likely to try is experiment with different ways of visualizing the data in a grid format.

The images shown in Figure 17-3 and Figure 17-4 are examples of *non-algorithmic* systems for transmitting pictures. This means that a computer program isn't required to process the data used to display the images. In fact, the recipient could manually transcribe the digits onto a piece of paper to draw the images by hand (assuming they have paper to draw on and hands to draw with). The symbol 64 (100000) tells the recipients *"The number that follows this symbol is a bitmap."* Once they learn to recognize this format, the process of transcribing numbers into a two-dimensional bitmap is easy.

The primary benefit of this approach is its simplicity. Images encoded in binary format will be easy to spot, even if the recipient hasn't mastered the task of interpreting and running computer programs embedded in the message. These images can also be interleaved with equations, algorithms, and other expressions. This is an important feature as it enables the message to incorporate many different media types into a single data stream.

Grayscale images

Once we've described simple black-and-white bitmap images, we can go on to describe grayscale images. As mentioned earlier, grayscale images contain additional information about the brightness of each pixel, enabling us to transmit detailed photographic images. Several bits are used to describe each pixel in the image, and each pixel is defined by a number that describes its brightness.

For example, a 5-bit grayscale image allows for 2^5, or 32, different shades of brightness, and an 11-bit grayscale image allows for 2^{11}, or 2048, different shades of brightness. In the case of a 5-bit grayscale image, the number 0 would represent a black pixel, and the number 31 would be used to describe a white pixel. The numbers 1 through 30 represent the shades of gray in between black and white. The data used to describe a grayscale image can be stored in a two-dimensional array (see Chapter 14, *Memory and Programming*). To visualize how the data in a grayscale image is organized, look at the example in Figure 17-5. This figure depicts a 4×4–pixel bitmap in which each pixel has 32 possible values ranging from 0 (black) to 31 (white).

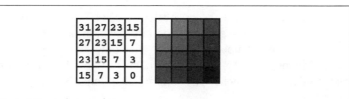

Figure 17-5: *A 4×4–pixel grayscale image.*

Next, let's look at how our hypothetical message can represent this image. The following example program creates a two-dimensional array and stores it in a variable (M1), which it then labels as an image:

```
(
({1}(10)
[[[31][27][23][15]][[27][23][15][7]][[23][15][7][3]][[15][7][3][0
]]])
({1}(20)(64))
)
```

Which can be read as:

```
(
({1}(=)[[[31][27][23][15]][[27][23][15][7]][[23][15][7][3]][[15][
7][3][0]])
({1}(is member of category)(64))
)
```

This program contains two statements. The first stores a two-dimensional array of numbers (the image) in the variable M1 ({1}). Next, the program uses the (20) symbol to group M1 into a category. The second statement can be read as *"The contents of M1 belong to category 64 (image),"* or *"This 2D array is an image."* In one concise expression we have created an array and labeled it so the recipient knows it has something to do with category 64 (an image).

Arrays are very important when dealing with images because high-resolution images require multidimensional data sets. For example, a grayscale image requires a two-dimensional array to store the information used to generate the image. A color image requires a three-dimensional array (two for width and height, and a third dimension for color information). A three-dimensional image, such as a topographical map, requires four dimensions (three for width, height, and length, and a fourth for color information). If you want to add motion to the image, you then need to add yet another dimension to the array.

Algorithmic images

Complex imagery, such as grayscale or color images, and animation or video, requires a more sophisticated approach. In order to save bandwidth, we can transmit computer programs that draw the images, instead of the images themselves. This type of approach can be referred to as an *algorithmic system*. The benefits of using an algorithmic system for transmitting images are:

- This greatly reduces the amount of information required to draw the image. This allows the sender to make more economical use of the finite amount of bandwidth.

- We can transmit programs that write their results into arrays with two, three, four, or more dimensions. This allows the sender to transmit highly detailed color imagery, as well as full-motion video or animation.

- The recipient can automate the process of decompressing and rendering images on the receiving end. Once they learn to recognize when an array represents an image, they will be able to automate the process of rendering and cataloging a collection of images.

Let's look at a simple example of how we might use an algorithm to draw a grayscale image. This example program would draw the bitmap image shown in Figure 17-5. The program also somewhat reduces the amount of information required to describe the image.

The steps performed by the program are as follows. The instructions are written out, rather than represented in numerical form, to make the example easy to read:

1. Store a series of 80 binary digits in a variable.

2. Break this string of 80 digits into a series of 16 5-bit words.

3. Sequentially read these 5-bit words into a four column by four-row 2D array.

4. Use the (U) symbol to label the array as category 64 (an image).

This igene takes the data presented to it, breaks it into a series of 5-bit words, and stores this information in a two-dimensional array. The array is then categorized as an image, which tells the recipient how to interpret the information stored in the array. This igene would be invoked as follows:

```
((100010101)[1111111011101110111111011101110111100111100011
01111001110001101111001110001100000])
```

At first glance, it isn't obvious that this expression can be used to draw an image. However, igene 277 (binary 100010101) breaks the long string of binary numbers on the right side of the expression into 16 5-bit words. It then stores these 5-bit numbers in a 4×4 two-dimensional array, and then categorizes the array as belonging to category 64 (an image).

The sender could also transmit the same image without using an algorithm, by using the following expression:

```
([[[11111][11011][10111][01111]][[11011][10111][01111][00111]]
[[00011][01111][00111][00011]][[01111][00111][00011][00000]]])
```

The problem with sending the image verbatim lies in that each of the bracket ([]) symbols is shorthand for several more bits of information. As a result, when the parentheses are translated to binary code (see Chapter 11, *CETI—Communication with Extraterrestrial Intelligence*), this message is several times longer than it appears in shorthand form. By expressing the image in algorithmic form, the sender can reduce the amount of information required to describe the image while making it easier for the recipient to parse and display.

This simple example shows how algorithms can be used to describe complex images in an abbreviated form. By employing more sophisticated algorithms, the amount of data required to generate a high-resolution image can be reduced by several orders of magnitude.

Color images

To most of us, the idea of color is obvious. However, our perception of the world is (no pun intended) colored by our own anatomy. What we describe as *color* is the ability of our eyes to measure not only the intensity (brightness) of an object, but also the wavelengths of light (colors) emitted or reflected by an object.

Light is a form of electromagnetic radiation, or radio wave. And like a radio signal, light behaves like a wave travelling through a pond. When examined at the microscopic level, electromagnetic radiation is not a continuous signal. Instead, electromagnetic radiation is emitted in tiny, discrete packets called *quanta*. The smallest parcel into which electromagnetic radiation can be subdivided is called a *photon*.

The amount of energy that a photon carries is determined by its *wavelength*. Photons behave like a wave in the ocean; if you could look at a photon as it travels through space, you would see peaks and troughs, much like a wave. A photon's wavelength is simply the distance between the wave's peaks. The shorter the photon's wavelength, the more energy it carries.

NOTE

This represents a relatively small piece of the electromagnetic spectrum. If we could see light with longer wavelengths, we would be able to see into the infrared and microwave spectrums. If we could see a shorter wavelength, we would be able to see into the ultraviolet and X-ray regions of the spectrum.

To truly understand what "color" means, try thinking of light in terms of sound. If you compare the range of colors we can see to the range of sounds we can hear, red light is at the low end (rumbling bass) end of the spectrum, while violet (or blue) light is at the high end of the range of our visual "hearing." Just as some animals can hear sounds above and below our range of hearing, some can see lower (infrared) and higher (ultraviolet) optical "notes."

Other organisms may see very differently than we do. For example, many insects can see well into the ultraviolet spectrum, and some animals can sense heat (infrared) radiation much better than we can. We cannot assume that our distant audience will see color the same way we do (or that they even describe it in the same terms we do).

Color is a complex characteristic. We perceive color on a simple level. Our eyes detect light in three regions of the visible spectrum. We have receptors in our eyes that are sensitive to red, green, and blue light. We infer, or estimate, the color of an object by comparing the amounts of red, green, and blue light we see. Yellow, for example, falls in between red and green. When we see a yellow light, our eyes sense this as equal parts of red and green light. Our brain interpolates (infers) the colors and tells our brain that the color we're really seeing is yellow.

To understand this in greater detail, let's revisit our hearing analogy. We are sensitive to sounds at many different frequencies (notes). We hear by taking the sound coming into our ears and dividing it into thousands of individual frequencies. This is very similar to what SETI radio detection equipment does; it divides incoming radio energy into a large number of channels so they can be analyzed.

By comparison, our eyes are tone deaf. Our eyes are sensitive to light at three basic frequencies: red (bass), green (mid-range), and blue (treble) light. Unlike our hearing system, which divides sounds into thousands of finely defined tones, our eyes can only sense the "pitch" of incoming light in a very coarse way.

To faithfully reproduce color, we need to recreate the entire spectral signature of an object. In fact, we need to describe the complete spectral signature for each pixel in an image. The picture shown in Figure 17-6 only has 4 pixels (a 2×2–pixel image). This is too small to be useful, but it is fine for illustrating how we describe color.

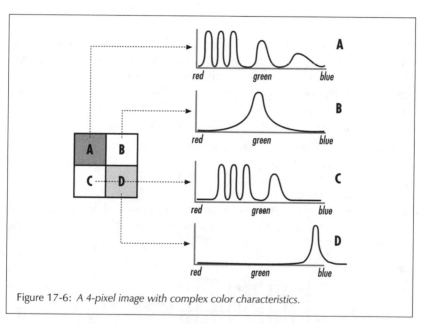

Figure 17-6: A 4-pixel image with complex color characteristics.

The pixels in this image have been labeled A, B, C, and D. The spectral signature for each pixel is sketched to the right of the simple image, and is described here:

- Pixel A has a complex spectrum, with threee peaks in the red-yellow region, one peak in green, and one peak in blue.

- Pixel B has a simple spectral signature, with one peak at green; this is a *monochromatic*, or single-colored signal.

- Pixel C has a complex signature, with three peaks in the yellow-green region, and one peak in the blue region.

- Pixel D has a simple spectrum with only one peak in the blue region.

When looking at these areas, we would see pixels B and D (which are monochromatic) with minimal loss of information. On the other hand, we would not see most of the color detail in pixels A and C.

Because we don't know how an extraterrestrial species will see color, we need to transmit images with color encoded in a way that goes beyond our own capability to perceive it. While this information may be superfluous for a human observer, it may be important to someone who can see color in much greater detail than we can. The recipients can then display the color information in a format that is optimized their way of seeing.

Encoding color

We deal with the challenge of encoding color by describing each pixel of an image in much more detail. Instead of using simple brightness values (ranging from 0, black, to 255, white), we describe the entire spectral "fingerprint" of each picture element. In effect, we turn our two-dimensional image into a three-dimensional image, with the third-dimension containing the detailed color information behind each pixel in the image.

Figure 17-7 and Figure 17-8 illustrate how arrays contain detailed color information. The first figure shows a grayscale image. The information needed to generate this image can be stored in a two-dimensional array that stores the data in a grid-like format. The second figure shows how a color image is represented, this time in a three-dimensional array. The third dimension (depth) is used to store color information about each dot in the picture.

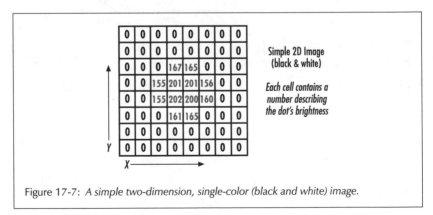

Figure 17-7: A simple two-dimension, single-color (black and white) image.

The third-dimension, shown in Figure 17-8, stores color information for each pixel in the image (the image is projected forward onto the front face of the cube).

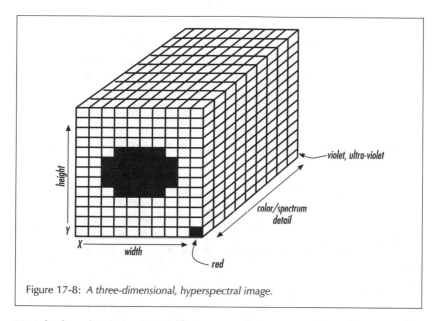

Figure 17-8: A three-dimensional, hyperspectral image.

Now look at the dark pixel in the lower-right corner at the front of the cube. Behind it are nine more cells; follow the color (or z-t) axis to the back side of the cube. Each one of these cells contains a number that describes the intensity of the light at that particular wavelength or color.

While this three-dimensional format allows the sender to depict images with highly detailed color information, this ability comes at a price. The addition of color information dramatically increases the amount of data used to describe the image, as shown in Table 17-1.

Table 17-1: Amount of information required to represent different types of images

HORIZONTAL RESOLUTION	VERTICAL RESOLUTION	SPECTRAL RESOLUTION	UNCOMPRESSED IMAGE SIZE (IN BITS)
200	200	10	3,200,000
400	400	10	12,800,000
1000	1000	1	8,000,000
1000	1000	3	24,000,000
1000	1000	10	80,000,000
1000	1000	100	800,000,000

The table illustrates how an uncompressed image size increases as we add more color detail. A 1000×1000–pixel black-and-white image requires 1/100th as much data as the same size image with high color detail (100 different wavelengths, compared to the usual three we use in color images).

DISPLAYING COLOR IMAGES

Color images, because they require much greater amounts of information, will most likely be sent in an algorithmic form. The sender will need to use computer programs to generate the raw data used to create an image, and store this information in an array to conserve bandwidth.

One way to do this is to create an igene that processes a block of raw data, which stores its results in a three-dimensional array. This is similar to the example we used to render a grayscale image. This type of expression would read as follows:

```
((278)[1][10101011...01101])
({1}(20)(64))
```

The igene used in this example, symbol 278, processes the block of data presented to it "10101011..." and stores its results in the variable M1 as a three-dimensional array. This variable is then grouped into category 64 (an image) with the statement "{1}(20)(64)."

This simple procedure tells the recipient that the data stored in the three-dimensional array is an image, so all the recipient needs to do is to guess what the extra dimension in the array represents. The data in a three-dimensional array can be categorized into one of two possible formats:

- A three-dimensional image, where the third dimension is used to represent depth or distance from the viewer (e.g., a topographical map).

- Color images, where the third dimension is used to store pixels' color spectrum.

To make it easier for the recipient to decipher color information, we would send a set of training images that feature easily recognizable objects (circles, squares, triangles, etc.). These images serve as calibration tools that allow the sender to reproduce color information precisely. Figure 17-9 and Figure 17-10 are two examples of training images that would provide the recipient with a tool for correctly interpreting color information in a three-dimensional array.

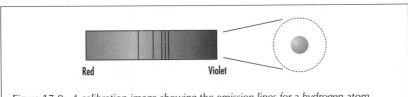

Red   Violet

Figure 17-9: A calibration image showing the emission lines for a hydrogen atom.

Figure 17-9 shows how we can use the common language of physics to precisely calibrate the color information in these images. Hydrogen, which is the most common element in the universe, emits light at very specific wavelengths (or colors) when it is electrically excited. Anyone with a basic understanding of physics will be familiar with this phenomenon. We can then assume that anyone capable of interstellar communication will be familiar with the behavior of the hydrogen atom. The spectrum shown on the left-hand side of Figure 17-9 serves as a calibration mark, because the recipient will probably already know the spectral fingerprint for hydrogen. This will make it easy for them to build a translation table that maps the color information stored in the array to values that correlate with the real world.

Southern Crab Nebula • He2-104
Hubble Space Telescope • Wide Field Planetary Camera 2

Figure 17-10: *Hubble Space Telescope (HST) image of the Crab Nebula, used as a calibration image. (STScI/HST image courtesy of Romano Corradi, Instituto de Astrofisica de Canarias, Tenerife, Spain; Mario Livio, Space Telescope Science Institute, Baltimore, MD; Ulisse Munari, Osservatorio Astronomico di Padova-Asiago, Italy; Hugo Schwarz, Nordic Optical Telescope, Canarias, Spain; and NASA [STScI-PRC99-32].)*

Figure 17-10 is another example of a calibration image. This is an image captured by the Hubble Space Telescope (HST) that depicts the Southern Crab Nebula, a large object that can be observed from other star systems. A recipient who understands astronomy will easily recognize this image (which is a safe assumption, since they have gone through the trouble of building the radio or optical telescope that detected our signal). Like the first calibration image, it provides the recipient with the ability to compare their interpretation of the image data against a known source. In this case, they can compare the image generated on their display systems to images taken of the same object by their own astronomers.

Motion pictures

While our discussion so far has focused on still images, it is fairly easy to extend this technique to transmit motion images. This is an important feature because many natural processes involve a change of state or motion. For example, a meteor colliding with a planet can be easily depicted using a series of images.

To display motion, we need to add yet another dimension to the array. For a black-and-white image, a two-dimensional array would become a three-dimensional array; the third dimension would be used to represent time. If we were using color images, we would need to add a fourth dimension to the array so we could depict colors as well as motion. To do this, we would simply create an igene that stores its results in a three- or four-dimensional array instead of the usual two or three dimensions used to display a still image.

Figure 17-11 shows a simplified example of motion in a 2D grayscale image. The motion is stored in a 4×4×4 array consisting of 64 pixels. Two dimensions represent width and height, while the third represents time (labeled 1, 2, 3, and 4 for frames 1 through 4, shown to the right). Think of each layer in this cube (going from front to back) as a single frame in a reel of film.

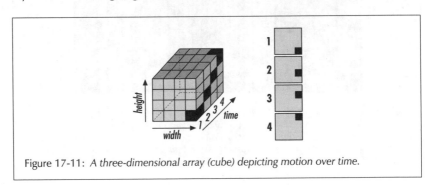

Figure 17-11: *A three-dimensional array (cube) depicting motion over time.*

In frame 1 (at the front of the cube), the image shows a dot in the lower right corner of the display. In frames 2 through 4, the dots moves up one row at a time until, in the fourth and final frame, the dot is in the upper-right corner of the display.

To teach a recipient to recognize moving images, we would use the same basic training technique used for explaining how to interpret other types of images. The training images would show a set of images that depict an easily recognized motion, for example, a moon orbiting a planet, as shown in Figure 17-12.

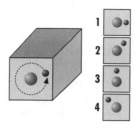

Figure 17-12: *Training images used to demonstrate motion, here depicted by the motion of a moon orbiting a planet.*

Once the recipients learn to correctly map these training images to a display device, they will be able to capture and display the rest of the images found throughout the message.

NOTE

To help the recipient figure out the order in which still frames should be displayed, we could send motion pictures of processes that are not reversible. For example, a movie of an ice cube melting would contain information about the direction in which time flows as this process is not reversible (a puddle of water will not spontaneously form an ice cube).

Associating images with ideas

Once the recipient is able to identify and view images, the next logical step is to associate images with symbols. There are many situations where nothing clarifies an idea as much as a picture. Consider the following example:

```
((100010110)[1][10101...]))(10100)(111000101))
((100010110)[1][1110011..]))(10100)(111000101))
((100010110)[1][111000110101...]))(10100)(111000101))
```

Each of these three examples uses igene 278 to render a color image. These statements take the resulting images and use symbol (10100, decimal 20) to group them into a common category. Recall that we used the symbol 20 to indicate something as a member of category X. In this way, we can display a series of images, and describe them as belonging to a common category, in this example category 111000101. In this example, let's say that each of the images drawn is a photograph of a planet in our solar system. By now, the recipient of our messages will be used to identifying a new number sequence and associating that with another string of data depicting an image. However, up to this point, the meaning of category 111000101 has yet to be defined. Therefore, these examples can be paraphrased as:

```
This image is a member of category 111000101
This image is a member of category 111000101
This image is a member of category 111000101
etc.
```

The recipient will notice that each image depicts a planet, and will assign each of these images to the same category (111000101).

This simple technique can be used to develop a symbolic vocabulary to describe a wide range of objects. Motion video sequences can also be used to describe processes such as evaporation, or to describe symbols that represent an action instead of an object. Think about how we might use this approach to describe a symbol for the concept of *evaporation*. This concept is very difficult to describe with a formula or still picture because evaporation is a process, not an object. However, it is relatively easy to depict the process of evaporation through the use of time-lapse photography.

In this scenario, we would send a set of examples, each depicting the evaporation of a different type of fluid. One time-lapse series might depict the evaporation of water, while another would depict the evaporation of liquid nitrogen. All of these time-lapse series would be labeled as belonging to a new numeric category, which can be used to describe "evaporation."

The recipient would see a trend among these examples, and hopefully be able to associate "evaporation" as we know it with a similar concept in their vocabulary. Since all of the time-lapse images that belong to this new category depict the process of evaporation, the recipient would be able to associate the new category with this process or action.

This technique represents an important step forward because it frees the sender from describing only ideas that can be represented by formulas or computer programs. This technique enables the sender to build a vocabulary of numeric symbols that can represent almost any observable object or process. This approach can also describe a species of animal, a physical process, or an aspect of animal behavior (such as eating). In short, it enables the sender to create a general-purpose symbolic vocabulary that can describe pretty much anything. We'll further expand on this idea in Chapters 18 through 20.

Image compression

While transmitting bitmapped images in their raw binary form make them easy to decode, it is not a very efficient way of sending images across a relatively slow data link. A high-resolution photographic quality image will require 8 to 32 million bits of information to describe. We can greatly reduce the amount of bandwidth required to transmit an image by using image compression.

Images can be compressed using a relatively simple computer program. Instead of transmitting the raw data to draw an image pixel by pixel, we can send a set of abbreviated instructions that a computer program can use to redraw a close approximation of the original image. The example shown in Figure 17-2 (Earth against the black background of space) illustrates how many images contain relatively large featureless areas. These types of images can often be sent in abbreviated form since a large part of the image contains no information (e.g., an empty background field).

The subject of image compression is worthy of a book in and of itself (and a pretty hefty one at that). Many different techniques have been used to compress images and video clips. This field of study has attracted an especially high level of attention since the development of the World Wide Web. Since even the fastest Internet connections are just barely capable of transmitting uncompressed video, inventors and computer scientists have been hard at work developing new schemes for image and video compression. As a result, it is now possible to transmit fairly high quality video over connections once thought too slow to transmit even the simplest form of animation.

One thing that all of these schemes share in common is that they use programs to decompress and display images and full-motion video. These programs process compressed data that, without the decompression program, is meaningless. These compression/decompression algorithms, more commonly referred to as CODECs, are used to convert abbreviated instructions contained in the compressed file into raw data that can be mapped directly to a video display.

One popular image compression scheme, JPEG (short for the *Joint Picture Experts Group*) is widely used on the Web. This system takes an image and divides it into an array of 8×8–pixel cells. Each of these mini-pictures is reduced to an abbreviated set of mathematical instructions (or equations). If the mini-picture contains a lot of detail, it will be difficult to reduce to a very simple statement. On the other hand, if it contains a featureless background (such as a solid black background), it can be reduced to a simple statement to the effect of "Paint this whole cell black." This is a simplification of what the JPEG algorithm actually does, but it gets the basic idea across.

Currently available algorithms reduce the filesize of an image by a factor of 10:1 to 100:1. The ability to compress an image is related to the speed of the computer displaying the image. For example, when compared to older compression standards, such as CompuServe's Graphic Interchange Format

(GIF), the JPEG algorithm requires much more computational effort to decode and draw the image. However, the JPEG algorithm is able to compress images by a factor of 10 to 100, while the GIF format can rarely compress images by more than 10 fold (unless the image is very simple, such as a cartoon drawing).

If we wanted to use image compression in a message for another civilization, we would create a library of igenes designed to process blocks of raw data, store their results in an array, and then label the array as an image. What is interesting about this framework is that it allows the sender to use many different compression schemes at the same time. Each compression scheme is handled by a different igene optimized to deal with a certain kind of image or region within an image. For example, some images may contain a lot of fine detail (e.g., a picture depicting a lawn with many blades of grass). Other images, however, may contain very basic geometric shapes such as a square or triangle. Each type of element within an image lends itself to different compression strategies.

Each of these compression strategies is associated with a particular igene, which contains the procedures required to decompress the image or region of an image. The sender would create a library of image compression igenes, each having its own strengths and weaknesses. Some igenes would be specialists in the task of reproducing fine textures, while others could specialize in reproducing less-detailed background features. This would enable the sender to transmit an image in a composite format, such as in the simplified example:

```
((292)[1][101010111111...])
((293)[1][111100111011...])
((298)[1][110000001101...])
```

Each of these expressions invokes a different igene (292, 293, and 298, respectively), and presents it with a block of data. These igenes store their results in the variable M1.

This simple example demonstrates that a complex image can be transmitted as different components or layers using several different decompression programs to reconstruct the image on the receiving end. This allows the sender to minimize the amount of bandwidth required, while maximizing the quality of the reproduced image.

SIMULATIONS

Our ability to send high-resolution images greatly expands the range of ideas we can communicate to the recipient of our interstellar message. We can use pictures to train recipients to recognize a vocabulary of symbols that represent many different types of objects, from planets to different species of animals here on Earth. We can also use motion pictures to teach the recipient to recognize symbols that represent an action or process, such as a falling object.

Although images give us an excellent foundation for building a large symbolic vocabulary, there are still many ideas that cannot be adequately described by a still image or animation, including ideas that involve some kind of motion or interactivity. Most physical phenomena involve motion or change of some sort. Some can be explained using the formulas we've developed in earlier chapters, while others may be too difficult to explain except by example.

This chapter discusses how we can combine the techniques from Chapters 10 through 17 to build programs for demonstrating, or simulating, more esoteric concepts (such as gravity). One way to think about these programs is as living sets of flashcards. Instead of sending the recipient a lifeless still picture or symbol, we can send them an animated symbol that has a life of its own. The recipient can probe this program to see how it behaves in different scenarios, and from this, gain a much deeper understanding of the concept that is being described.

Describing entropy

The laws of thermodynamics offer a good example of concepts that are intuitively obvious, yet difficult to explain. One of the basic premises outlined by this set of physical laws is the idea that entropy, a measure of disorder within a system, increases over time. This is a straightforward concept when you apply it to real-world systems. For instance, an ice cube will melt after you drop it into a glass of warm water. In theory, this process is reversible—yet we all know that warm water never spontaneously forms ice cubes. However obvious this concept may be, the concept of melting ice is difficult to explain in a formula.

Figure 18-1, which shows an ice cube melting, illustrates the idea that entropy (disorder) increases over time. Another similar situation occurs when you add a small drop of dye to a glass of water. Although the dye is initially concentrated in one small drop, it gradually diffuses throughout the entire glass of water.

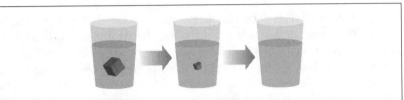

Figure 18-1: *This sequence of images displays a melting ice cube. This type of sequence can be used to describe the increase of entropy over time.*

This type of behavior is difficult to express in a purely mathematical form. Although there are equations that describe the increase of entropy over time, it is difficult to visualize what they mean. It is much easier to demonstrate with an animated example that depicts the evolution of a system over time.

To describe the concept of increasing entropy, we would need to define two concepts as symbols: *increasing* and *entropy*. For this example, let's say that we'll use the numeric symbol 5001 to represent increasing, and the symbol 5002 to represent entropy. When the recipient first encounters these symbols, they will not know what they represent. So, as we've done before, we need to train the recipient to recognize the meaning of these new symbols.

NOTE

Numbers are used as placeholders for abstract ideas to conform to the rest of the message, which is composed entirely from numbers. As before, the numbers themselves have no inherent meaning, and are merely used as placeholders to prevent the reader from confusing one symbol with another.

The symbol that represents increasing (5001) is used to describe a situation where something is growing larger over time. This is an idea that can be described easily using a combination of numbers and simple black and white images. To describe the concept of increasing using numbers, we could send the following expression:

```
({1}(=)[[1][2][3][4][5][6][7][8]])
({1}(20)(5001))
```

Which would read as:

```
M1 = series of numbers (1,2,3,4,5,6,7,8)
M1 belongs to category 5001
```

We would follow this expression with several others that depict a series of sequentially increasing numbers, and then categorize the array as belonging to the category 5001. We would also send a set of negative examples such as the following:

```
({1}(=)[[8][7][6][5][4][3][2][1]])
((0)({1}(20)(5001)))
```

Which would read as:

```
M1 = series of numbers (8,7,6,5,4,3,2,1)
False: (M1 belongs to category 5001)
```

The recipient should notice that the examples used to depict an increasing series of numbers are grouped into category 5001, while the examples that depict a constant or decreasing series of numbers don't belong to this category. The common theme among the examples is the increasing trend within the numbers; hence the symbol 5001 probably denotes the idea of an increasing sequence.

We can then further clarify the idea using simple black and white animations. These animations would consist of short series of diagrams that depict simple shapes that grow over time (see Figure 18-2).

Figure 18-2 depicts how a simple animation might be used to highlight the idea of "increasing" or "growth." These series of black and white images depict objects or shapes that grow as the clip proceeds from start to finish. Given enough examples to view, the recipient should be able to easily spot the common trend among these images.

As we've discussed in Chapter 17, *Pictures*, the images used to create this animated series can be equated with other symbols, as in the following example:

```
((279)[1][010011000011111...10101])
({1}(20)(64))
({1}(20)(5001))
```

Which would read as:

```
Run igene 279, store its results in M1
M1 belongs to category 64 (image)
M1 belongs to category 5001 (unknown)
```

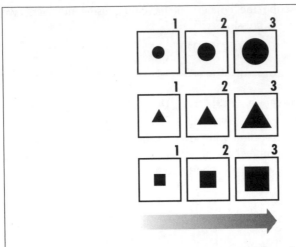

Figure 18-2: *Several frames from black and white animation depicting objects that grow over time.*

The program in this example would process a block of compressed image data ([010011000011111...10101]) and store its results in the variable M1. The contents of this variable are categorized as belonging to categories 64 (an image) and 5001 (whose meaning is initially unknown). The recipient will know that category 64 means "image," and will display the contents of variable M1 in a visual format. In an attempt to learn the meaning of symbol 5001, the recipient will use the image, or series of images, as a guide. The combination of visual and formulaic examples taken together provides the recipient with enough information to decode the meaning of symbol 5001.

The next symbol we need to define is symbol 5002, which is used as a placeholder for the concept of entropy. We can define this idea by transmitting a series of animations that depict systems in which entropy is increasing over time. Let's revisit the melting ice cube from in Figure 18-1. If this were displayed as an animated image, or sequence of still images, we might use an expression such as:

```
((279)[1][10111110101010011111...000111001101])
({1}(20)(64))
({1}(20)(5001))
({1}(20)(5002))
```

Which would read as:

```
Run igene 279, store results in variable M1
M1 belongs to category 64 (image)
M1 belongs to category 5001 (increasing)
M1 belongs to category 5002 (meaning unknown)
```

This example generates a series of images, and groups them into the categories 5001 (*increasing*) and 5002 (*unknown*). Since the recipients will know that 5001 means increasing, they will be prompted to ask: "What is increasing in this sequence of images?" Once again, this process would be repeated with several examples that all display a common trend, in this case increasing entropy, or disorder over time. Given several examples, the recipient should be able to decode the meaning of symbol 5002, which was used as a placeholder for the concept of *entropy*, and can then move onto other concepts.

This is a good example of how we might define new symbols using a combination of images, animated images, and equations. There are many situations for which even this approach is insufficient, and we will need to send examples that are more interactive.

Describing gravity

Now let's look at a more complex concept, *gravity*. Gravity is an invisible force. Unlike a physical object, which we can see, we can only the effects of gravity (such as Sir Isaac Newton's proverbial falling apple). Because of this, gravity cannot be described with still pictures alone. We can describe gravity with formulas, such as Einstein's gravitational equations. Another option would be to describe the concept of gravity through the use of programs that simulate the action of gravity.

To do this, we would write a program that models the behavior of two or more objects under the influence of gravity. This program would be pretty small, probably requiring less information to describe it than a typical high-resolution picture. Yet it would enable us to demonstrate a wide range of situations related to gravity. Instead of having to send a large number of images to chart every possible situation, we can send one compact program that can demonstrate a wide range of scenarios.

For example, in one simulation we might demonstrate a small object (such as a satellite) in orbit around a larger object (such as a planet). In another, we might simulate the interaction between a planet and its moon. This one small program would enable us to depict many different situations and, ultimately, to build a vocabulary of additional symbols that can be used to describe them. For example, we could use a simulation to help define a symbol for the idea of a circular orbit.

For this next example, we will define the program that simulates the action of gravity as igene 700. This igene contains the equations used to model the force of gravity, and can model the interaction of a large number of objects under its influence. This igene also generates a continuously updated series of two-dimensional images that are stored in memory. igene 700 is then used to define another symbol, say symbol 701, which can be used as an abstract symbol to represent the concept of gravity. We might invoke this program in a set of expressions, such as the following:

```
((701)(=)
((700)[1][array containing starting conditions goes here])
({1}(20)(64)))
((701)(=)
((700)[1][array containing different starting conditions
goes here])
({1}(20)(64)))
((701)(=)
((700)[1][array containing another set of starting conditions
goes here])
({1}(20)(64)))
```

Which would read as:

```
Symbol 701 = (is defined by) (
    Run igene 700, store results in M1
    M1 belongs to category "image"

    Run igene 700, store results in M1
    M1 belongs to category "image"

    Run igene 700, store results in M1
    M1 belongs to category "image"
)
```

These examples use a program (igene 700) to generate a visual simulation of a system. The program stores its output in the variable M1, which is also grouped into category 64 (image). This tells the recipient that the information stored in this variable can be mapped to a display. When the recipient maps the output from the program to a display, they see something similar to what is shown in Figure 18-3. This figure illustrates how a program can be used to depict a small object in orbit around a larger object.

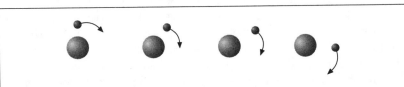

Figure 18-3: *Example of series of images generated by a simple simulation program.*

The information stored in variable M1 drives the display and is updated constantly as the program runs. When the program is running, the recipient sees an animated series of images that shows how the objects move around each other as time progresses.

The key to explaining the concept of gravity is to depict a wide range of scenarios involving different sized objects traveling at different speeds. Since the same program simulates all of these different scenarios, all the sender needs to do is repeatedly invoke the same program with different starting conditions. Given enough examples, the recipient should be able to see that the programs depict the behavior of objects under the influence of gravity. The sender can further refine the definition for symbol 701 by using equations related to the force of gravity as well.

What's interesting about these examples is that, unlike previous examples, it is difficult to define the concept of gravity in precise $X=A+B$ form. Instead, we are forced to define the concept of gravity indirectly, by displaying its effects in many different scenarios. Although we could do this with pictures and video clips (as described in Chapter 17), it requires much less bandwidth to send a simulation program that can then model an infinite variety of situations derived from the same basic set of rules.

Building a simulator

The general technique used to build simulation programs is not difficult. Simulations are nothing more than a special type of computer program that allows the user to interact with them in some way. There are several key features that distinguish a simulation program from other programs or igenes, including:

- They can allow the users to define their own starting conditions for the program, or they can be invoked with default starting conditions.

- They may provide a mechanism for visualizing the data generated by the simulation.

- They may allow the users to interact with the program while it is running.

The main thing to understand about a simulator is that it is a program that can be invoked to predict an infinite variety of scenarios. Because of this, the sender can describe many different instances of the same underlying phenomenon or process, and do so using only a compact program.

Starting conditions

Simulations' ability to model a wide variety of scenarios derived from the same basic set of rules makes them extremely useful. The gravity simulation was a good example of this. The laws of gravitation govern the behavior of objects as small as a subatomic particle to objects as large as a galaxy (or the universe itself). One set of equations can be used to model the behavior of large and small objects.

The simulation program contains no information about the objects whose behavior it is designed to model. It merely contains the equations used to create the model, as well as instructions that enable it to display its results to the user in an easily interpreted format (e.g., via a series of images). The information that determines the exact scenario that the simulation will model is presented to the program when it is first invoked, as in the following example:

```
((950)[1][100][7050][575][100][5750][6900])
```

In this example, the expression invokes igene 950, and presents it with a set of numbers. These numbers represent a set of starting conditions that tell the program where to begin.

NOTE

The exact function of the igene described in this example is not important. The main purpose of the example is to illustrate how a statement that invokes a simulator appears in the message. As you can see, the same format can be used to invoke any other igene. Simulators simply represent a special use of an igene.

Let's apply this idea to the gravity simulator discussed previously. In order to simulate the behavior of two or more objects under the influence of gravity, the model should include the following pieces of information about each object:

- The object's mass
- The object's position, given in three-dimensional (x,y,z) coordinates
- The object's velocity vector, given in three-dimensional $(v_{x,vy,vz})$ form

For each object, the simulator requires seven pieces of information, which can be described in a one-dimensional array as:

```
[[m][x][y][z][vx][vy][vz]]
```

Since the simulator is designed to model the behavior of many objects, the starting conditions can be presented in the form of a two-dimensional array. The dimensions of the array will be N rows by seven columns wide, where number N is the number of objects in the simulation. For example, this simulation program would be invoked as follows:

```
({1}(=)[[[100][10][20][10][0][5][0]] [[10][0][0][0][5][0][0]]
[[50][10][10][10][0][0][0]]])
((700){1})
```

EXPLAINING 3D VECTORS

A vector represents the motion of an object in three dimensions. In order to fully describe the motion of an object in 3D, it is insufficient to provide only its speed (velocity). To fully describe its motion, we have to describe its motion in each of three dimensions.

This is easy to visualize if when considering an airplane that is traveling due north at 200 miles per hour and climbing at a rate of 10 miles per hour. The airplane's course is described in 3D based on the terms of its motion relative to a North-South axis, its motion relative to an East-West axis, and its vertical motion.

In this example, the airplane is moving due north at 200 miles/hour, so its motion along the North-South axis is +200 miles/hour. Since it is traveling due north, the airplane's motion along the East-West axis is 0 miles/hour. The plane's vertical motion (climb rate) is +10 miles/hour. Therefore, the airplane's motion can be described in vector form as $(v_{ns}, v_{ew}, v_{alt})$ or (200,0,10).

This example performs two basic steps. First, it creates a variable M1, and creates a two-dimensional array of numbers, which are then stored in M1. Second, it invokes igene 700 (gravity), and passes M1 as the set of starting conditions. The array described in the first line of the program provides the initial position, velocity, and mass for three different objects. The simulator program then calculates how these three objects interact with each other. It then produces a series of images that display how the objects move around each other over time.

Data visualization

Data visualization is another important part of simulation. How the program does this depends on the type of behavior or situation it models. Let's use the classic arcade video game Lunar Lander™ as an example.

An example of this game, depicted in Figure 18-4, allows the player to test his piloting skills by landing a spacecraft on the moon. The goal of the game is to bring the craft in for a safe landing. The spacecraft has a limited amount of fuel, so the trick is to bring the ship down at a safe speed, but to do so in a way that does not burn off too much fuel. If the craft runs out of fuel when it is above a certain height, it will fall too quickly and break up when it hits the ground.

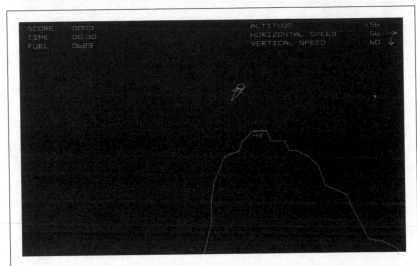

Figure 18-4: Sketch of the Lunar Lander™ arcade game display. (Lunar Lander is a trademark of the Atari Corporation.)

The display depicted in Figure 18-4 provides two types of information to the player. One piece of information is a graphical display of the terrain and the Lunar Lander. Another piece of information is a group of numbers in the upper part of the display. These numbers depict the amount of fuel remaining, the weight of the spacecraft, and its rate of descent.

If we wanted to create a version of this game to include in our hypothetical message, we would store its results in four different variables: let's say M1, M2, M3, and M4.

One of these variables, M1, would be used to store the bitmap used to generate the display (similar to Figure 18-4). The variables M2, M3, and M4 are used to store the numbers that represent the amount of remaining fuel, weight of the spacecraft, and rate of descent. This provides the recipient with all of the information they need to create a display that is similar to the sketch in Figure 18-4.

Interactivity

The next thing we need to add is a mechanism through which the user can interact with the program while it is running. This can be done by using global variables to pass information from the outside world to the program.

Let's revisit the Lunar Lander example again. This program has two basic controls: a joystick and a thruster button. The joystick is actually a simple switch that can be in three positions: left, right, and neutral. Let's look at the possible states these controls can be in, as shown in Table 18-1.

Table 18-1: *Possible states for joystick control*

JOYSTICK POSITION	LEFT SWITCH	RIGHT SWITCH	CODED VALUE
Neutral	0	0	0
Right Turn	0	1	1
Left Turn	1	0	2

The position of the joystick can be translated into a two bit numeric value, as shown in the table above. This number can then be stored in a variable that the simulator program is watching. We can do the same thing with the thruster button, which is a simple ON-OFF switch (ON = 1, OFF = 0).

The igene equivalent of the Lunar Lander game would watch two variables, M5 (used to store the joystick state, which is used to turn the spacecraft) and M6 (used to store the state of the thruster button), and would use them as control inputs. It would respond to these variables as shown in Table 18-2.

Table 18-2: *Possible control states and responses for Lunar Lander simulation*

M5	M6	MEANS
0	0	No turn, thruster off
0	1	No turn, thruster on
1	0	Bank to right, thruster off
1	1	Bank to right, thruster on
2	0	Bank to left, thruster off
2	1	Bank to left, thruster on

Now that we have described a complete input/output interface for this Lunar Lander simulation, we can look at the flow of information into and out of the program, as shown in Figure 18-5.

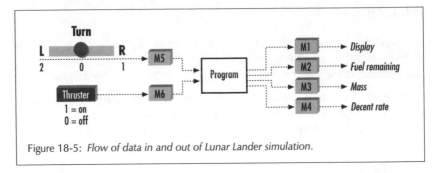

Figure 18-5: *Flow of data in and out of Lunar Lander simulation.*

This example, although it is fairly simple, illustrates how it is possible to send programs that can interact with their users. This program examines the contents of two variables (M5 and M6) that are used to represent the position of two external controls (the joystick and thruster button, respectively). The program places its own results in the four variables on the right-hand side of this diagram. One of the variables is used to store the bitmap image shown in Figure 18-4. Three of the variables are used to store numeric information (fuel remaining, weight, and descent rate).

Atomic erector set

While we can summarize our knowledge about the structure and behavior of matter using equations, it is often very difficult to visualize what these equations actually represent. We can expand upon a formulaic description by creating programs that simulate the behavior of the particles from which all of the matter we can see (and can't see) is made.

For example, we could write a program that simulates the behavior of a hydrogen atom (the most common element in the universe) under a wide range of conditions. This program would allow the user to probe its behavior, perhaps in conditions such as testing to see what happens when:

- Two hydrogen atoms collide at very high speed

- A high-energy photon strikes an atom

- A low energy photon strikes an atom

Through experimentation, the recipients could watch what happens to the simulated hydrogen atom under different conditions. They would learn how the hydrogen atom behaves when it collides with another atom, when it is struck by an X-ray, and so forth. Figure 18-6 depicts one scenario where a high-energy photon (X-ray) strikes a hydrogen atom. In this scenario, the atom's electron (e) is stripped off in the collision; this process is known as *ionization*.

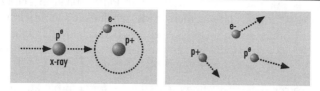

Figure 18-6: *Sketch of display produced by hydrogen simulator.*

We can extend this general idea to build a sort of atomic erector set that would allow the recipient to simulate the interaction of many different types of particles in a nearly infinite variety of situations. This would be a powerful teaching tool since it would enable the recipient to run through an endless variety of scenarios, and to compare the results produced by the simulator with their own experiments. Instead of sending the recipient a static formula that describes one aspect of a hydrogen atom, we could use a computer program to faithfully reproduce the behavior of the atom. In effect, the simulated hydrogen atom is a living symbol.

This might sound fantastic, but these simulations are merely computer programs that can interact with the user by passing information back and forth through shared memory.

Using simulations to refine an idea

In Chapters 12 through 14, we learned how to use a series of positive and negative examples to teach basic concepts to our receiver. We can use the same general technique here, but at a higher level. Another situation where simulations can be very helpful is in refining the definition of a symbol, or in describing several variations of an idea.

Let's look at how we could use this technique to define a vocabulary of symbols to represent different types of gravitational orbits. The concept of an orbit is fairly easy to explain to someone who understands gravitation. An object is in orbit when it travels at a high enough speed around an object so its motion around the body partially or wholly counteracts the effect of gravity.

Describing different types of orbits

The basic concept of an orbit will be easy enough to explain to someone who understands the effects of gravity, as we have for several hundred years. There are, however, many different types of orbits that we can describe.

Some objects, such as the outermost planet Pluto, travel in elliptical (egg-shaped) orbits. Others, such as man-made satellites, travel in circular (geo-synchronous) orbits around Earth. And others, such as our interplanetary space probes, travel so fast that they escape the effects of Earth's gravity entirely.

We can use a simulation to refine the definition for an orbit, and to describe new symbols that represent specific types of orbits. Table 18-3 lists some of the cases we might want to describe.

Table 18-3: *Examples of specialized types of orbits*

NUMERIC SYMBOL	MEANS
20101	Circular orbit
20102	Elliptical orbit
20103	Degenerating orbit
20104	Escape trajectory
20105	Chaotic or unpredictable orbit

To describe these specific types of orbits, we can use the gravity simulation program discussed earlier in this chapter (igene 700). We would then use this program to "paint" positive and negative examples of the new symbols we want to define. This is accomplished by feeding the simulation program starting conditions that produce the type of behavior we want to demonstrate.

Let's start with symbol 20101, which describes the idea of a circular orbit. Once again, we would send a series of positive and negative examples where we run the simulation using a variety of different starting points. The positive examples depict one object in a precisely circular orbit around another. The negative examples depict one object in something other than a precisely circular orbit around another. The positive examples might read as follows:

```
(20101)(=)(
    ((700)[[[n1][n2][n3]...[n14]]])
)

(20101)(=)(
    ((700)[[[n1][n2][n3]...[n14]]])
)

(20101)(=)(
    ((700)[[[n1][n2][n3][n4]...[n14]]])
)
```

In these examples, we invoke igene 700 and present a set of starting conditions that describe a small object that is in a perfectly circular orbit around a larger object.

To send negative examples, we would simply replace the equal sign (=) with the does-not-equal sign (≠), and invoke igene 700 with starting conditions that produce orbits that are not circular.

By feeding igene 700 different starting conditions (the numbers represented by n1, n2, and so forth), we can describe a completely different outcome. We run igene 700 with one set of starting conditions, and it describes an object in a perfectly circular orbit about another. Run it with a slightly different set of starting conditions, and it depicts an object in a degenerating orbit, as shown in Figure 18-7 and Figure 18-8.

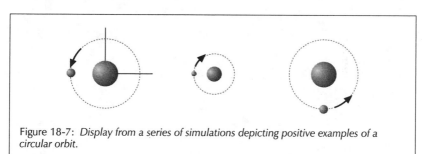

Figure 18-7: *Display from a series of simulations depicting positive examples of a circular orbit.*

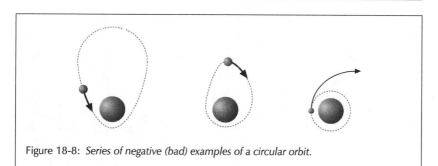

Figure 18-8: *Series of negative (bad) examples of a circular orbit.*

So, just as we've done before, we're using sets of positive and negative examples to draw attention to the idea we're attempting to describe. The recipient of this series of examples would be able to see a common pattern in the results produced by the simulation. All of the true (positive) examples depict an object in a perfectly circular orbit around another. All of the false (negative) examples depict an object in something other than a circular orbit. Therefore, the symbol 20101 probably represents the idea of a circular orbit.

In this and the previous chapters of Part III, *Communicating with Other Worlds*, we've described how to build a suite of tools that can be used to describe a wide variety of ideas. With the development of this technique, we can now define symbols for ideas that involve motion, forces, and inter-relationships between objects. In the remaining chapters, we combine these concepts with additional techniques to create a general-purpose symbolic language.

ABSTRACT SYMBOLS
AND LANGUAGE

With a combination of the equations, images, and programs we've described thus far, we have the ability to say quite a lot about ourselves. This gives us the basis for creating a versatile symbolic language that can be interpreted and hopefully understood by another civilization. Using these tools, we can build complex expressions that combine equations, images, and simulations to build rudimentary sentences to describe almost anything, just as we would with our respective languages.

In this chapter, we'll discuss how to combine equations, algorithms, images, and simulations to form the basis for a general-purpose language that we can use to describe a wide range of situations and processes. Ultimately, we'll learn how to describe abstract ideas solely in terms of other ideas, something we'll discuss in detail in Chapter 20, *Semantic Networks*.

Describing ideas

Until now, we've covered a variety of concepts for describing things, ranging from simple math equations to how to compose a complex grayscale or color image. We've also expanded upon that to demonstrate how to go beyond traditional two- and three-dimensional images and build programs that the recipient can interact with. Now we'll describe how to add relationships to our messages that can help the recipient understand how we associate pictures with words to describe different concepts.

One example would be to build complex expressions combining equations, images, and simulations to build rudimentary sentences, such as in the following example:

```
(
(((279)[1][1001011010101011...])
({1}(20)(64)))
```

```
(((700)[2][n1]..[n14]))(({2}(20)(64)))
(((279)[3][10101111...]))
({3}(20)(64))
)
```

When interpreted, this expression can be read as:

```
Use igene 279 to render an image of Earth
Use igene 700 to depict a nearly circular orbit
Use igene 279 to render an image of the sun
```

The first "word" in the sentence would be a color image of the Earth. The second word, or symbol, would be an animation used to depict the idea of a planetary orbit. The third word would be used to describe a picture of our sun. When combined, the message would build a simulation that shows the Earth orbiting the sun:

```
"Earth orbit sun"
```

While this type of graphical format can be used to convey many different ideas, it is not the most efficient way to describe something as complex as a planetary orbit. A more efficient way to express this idea, in terms of the amount of bandwidth required, is to build a vocabulary of numeric symbols that can be used as placeholders for previously described ideas. By combining this symbolic vocabulary with a simple system for labeling symbols according to their context, or use within a sentence, we can create a simple, general-purpose language.

In Chapter 18, *Simulations*, we described an example where we used a simulation to depict several different types of orbits, and to equate numeric symbols with each. Depending on the type of symbol or idea we want to define, we have several different tools we can use to describe it, as shown in Table 19-1.

Table 19-1: *Techniques available for defining new symbols*

TYPE OF CONTENT	USES
Mathematical expressions	Useful for defining formulas (e.g., $E=mc^2$), statements within a computer program, and ideas that can be easily reduced to or explained with a formula.
Still images	Useful for depicting objects and categories of objects.
Series of images	Useful for depicting motion, changes in the state of a system.
Motion pictures	Useful for depicting interaction between objects, gradual change, and recorded images and events (such as a rocket launch, etc.).

Table 19-1: *Techniques available for defining new symbols (continued)*

TYPE OF CONTENT	USES
Computer programs	Related to simulation programs, computer programs can be used to draw images, series of images, and to build simulations; they can also be used to build more complex programs used to define an idea or situation.
Simulation programs	Can be used to depict complex systems involving multiple objects, invisible phenomenon such as force, complex systems (such as weather, N-body problems, fluid flow and so on); can also be used to define subtle variations in an idea (such as the difference between a circular orbit and a degenerating orbit).
Semantic networks	Semantic networks (described later in this section) are used to define symbols in terms of their relationship to other symbols through statements like *"large is the opposite of small."*

Which tool is the best to use for describing new ideas? It depends on the symbol that we want to define. Images and sequences of images, for example, are particularly well suited for depicting objects and simplified models of physical processes. Simulations, on the other hand, are useful for depicting more esoteric concepts, such as the idea of an invisible force.

Physical objects and categories of objects play an important role in this vocabulary. Much of our language is devoted to describing the world around us. The same is likely to be true in any exchange of information with alien civilizations. In most situations, we can label objects and categories of objects by transmitting sets of images to depict them; this is analogous to describing objects using flashcards.

Scenarios that involve motion, or an unseen interaction between objects (such as the behavior of objects under the influence of gravity), may be described using an animated series of images (video), or with a simulation. As we discussed in Chapter 18, simulations can describe complex systems without using large amounts of bandwidth.

Abstract symbols (such as a symbol for the concept of "large") may be easiest to describe purely in terms of other abstract symbols (e.g., *large* is the opposite of *small*, *large* is similar to *big*, and so forth).

As such, the tools we would use to define a symbol are determined by the efficiency with which it can be used to describe the idea. The basic objective is to minimize the use of bandwidth. So, if we can describe an idea that would otherwise require several bandwidth-hogging animations with a simple, unambiguous equation, we'd use an equation or a set of equations to define the idea.

In deciding which tools to use, we're faced with a tradeoff: bandwidth versus ease of comprehension. If we had an unlimited amount of bandwidth to work with, we would not be forced to deal with this trade-off. However, it's unlikely that we'll have this luxury, so we must describe each new idea using as few bits as possible. On the other side of the coin, we want to maximize the ease with which the recipient can learn new symbols. This is important because we will often use symbols to describe other symbols. So, the failure to understand one symbol may make it impossible for the recipient to learn ideas they must derive from it.

Another factor to take into consideration in defining a new symbol is the importance of that symbol in decoding our message as a whole. Some symbols, such as the symbol for addition, will be absolutely vital to understanding the rest of the message. Other symbols, such as a symbol used to describe an obscure term that is used only once or twice in the entire message, are less important. The recipient can fail to understand these obscure symbols, and still be able to piece the rest of the message together. The importance of a symbol can be measured by keeping track of how often it is used to describe other, unrelated symbols. If it is used often, we need to make sure it is easy to comprehend, even if this means that we need to use more bits of information to do so.

Describing invisible concepts

As we move along to more esoteric ideas, it becomes harder to describe ideas in photographic or flashcard fashion. For example, we can't easily define energy with pictures. Energy, like gravity, is invisible; we can only see its effects. That is why we are forced to describe the idea using a set of equations.

Energy

Let's look at example of an idea from physics: the idea of energy. As with gravity, energy is a tricky concept to explain because you can't observe it directly—you can only observe the effects of energy after the fact. While we can use pictures to support the definition, we can't rely on pictures alone to describe this idea. One way to define energy is to send a series of equations that equate an object's energy to another object or force of nature that has been defined elsewhere. We will have to rely on the recipient to recognize a pattern among a series of equations.

In order to describe energy, we first need to define a symbol for it. For these examples, we will use the symbol 71822 to define energy. As with other examples in this book, the number itself doesn't matter; we're just using it as a placeholder. Next, we'll provide an absolute definition for this symbol, as follows:

```
((71822) (=) (
    (|0| (=) |0|)
))
```

The above expression tells the recipient to treat symbol 71822 as a variable when it is used in an equation. We'll also define two other symbols. We'll use 71823 as a placeholder for m (mass), and 71824 as a placeholder for c (the speed of light). So, when we send a message like:

```
((71822)(=)(71823)(x)((71824)(x)(71824))
```

The recipient could translate that into:

```
((E)(=)(m)(x)(c)(x)(c))
```

Which can be read as:

$E=mc^2$

This can be interpreted as E (symbol 71822) is equivalent to mc^2. By itself, this doesn't tell the recipient what E (symbol 71822) means. However, we will use symbol 71822 everywhere that we want to say E (energy) in all of the equations that refer to this concept. If we send enough equations that refer to E, the recipient should be able to determine that symbol 71822 is being used to represent E, and hence 71822 means "energy." This is just one example of how we can use equations to define an abstract idea that cannot be observed directly. However, many ideas can't be represented by equations like energy can. The concept of randomness is a good example of something that is hard to describe with a formula, and even with words.

Randomness

The basic idea behind randomness is that in a random series of numbers one cannot rely on prior observations or patterns in the series to predict future results. In a truly random series of numbers, it will be impossible to predict future results based on prior observations. In a non-random series of numbers, you can use previous observations to predict future results. Tides are a good example of this. Tides follow a predictable, periodic pattern, so by observing the tides for a period of time, you can make accurate predictions of future tides based on previous observations.

So, how do you describe the idea of randomness? As we've done before, first we assign a symbol to this idea. We would then send a series of positive and negative examples, such as a series of examples of random and non-random numbers similar to the following examples:

```
(1)(10)(((279)[10101110011001010111111100101100101011111])(20)
(61522))
(0)(10)( ((279)[101101101101...])(20)(61522))
(0)(10)(((279)[110001110110][0000100])(20)(61522))
```

Which can be read as:

```
TRUE: output from igene 279 belongs to category 61522
FALSE: output from igene 279 belongs to category 61522
FALSE: output from igene 279 belongs to category 61522
```

These expressions equate the concept 61522 with a series of images used to depict random and non-random patterns. Figure 19-1 depicts a series of random and non-random images and equates them with a numeric symbol that is used to represent the concept of *random*.

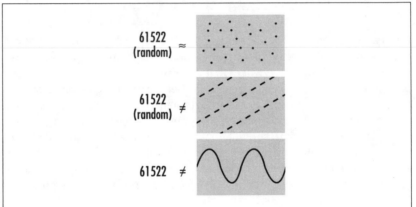

Figure 19-1: *These examples would display a series of graphs and plots depicting a series of random and non-random numbers.*

Here, we are using numbers as words. Each number is associated with a unique idea (e.g., 61522 means "random") and cannot be confused with other ideas. We define each idea using a combination of computer programs, images, and equivalency statements that depict both positive and negative examples. We can use this approach to build a library of words to describe physical objects, processes, and relative terms (such as big, small, before, after, etc.).

General-purpose vocabulary

Using this technique, we can describe physical objects and processes, as well as biological processes (such as the processes of eating, reproduction, etc.). We can also define words that describe relative scale (i.e., bigger or smaller than), and speed (i.e., faster or slower than). This enables us to create a rich vocabulary for describing our world as well as our experiences. The vocabulary we develop might include the following subject areas:

Relative terms
> We would use these to describe one object or process compared to another (i.e., larger, smaller, faster, slower, brighter, darker, etc.).

Physical objects and phenomena
> We would define words for physical and astronomical objects (i.e., moon, planet, star, solar flare, etc.).

Geological features and processes
> We would define words for geological features and processes on Earth and other worlds in our solar system.

Biological features and processes
> We would define words for biological objects and processes (i.e., eating, mating, dying, etc.).

This is only a partial list. We can define symbols to describe virtually any physical object, process, or cultural artifact. This can grow to become a very large vocabulary, with millions of unique symbols. We could, for example, define every known living and extinct species on Earth using this approach. To do so, we would create a numeric symbol for each unique species, and describe it using pictures, and simple symbolic sentences. The only limit on the scope of the vocabulary is our own imagination.

Unlike previous chapters, where we were creating computer programs, these symbols are not shorthand for machine instructions. These symbols are placeholders for abstract ideas, categories of objects, and processes. We might use computer programs, images, and equivalency statements to define these ideas, but these higher-level ideas are not directly translated into computer instructions themselves. We're using these expressions to communicate abstract ideas to an intelligent reader, much like we use language and diagrams to communicate ideas to each other. The difference is that we're using computer programs, combined with a numeric indexing scheme for abstract ideas (think of it as a Dewey decimal system for ideas) to define them.

Some ideas, such as the notion of randomness, will be easy for our recipient to comprehend, because they are commonly encountered phenomena.

Other ideas, especially cultural ideas, may be very difficult for them to comprehend, but that shouldn't stop us from trying to communicate the more esoteric aspects of our culture.

Memetic translation layer

To make numeric sentences intelligible, the recipient will create what can be called a *memetic translation layer*. This is a procedure for translating numeric ideas into the recipient's native language or mode of communication.

The numeric indexing system used to identify ideas forms the basis for an *interlingua* (intermediate language). The basic idea behind an interlingua is to create a standardized language, with strict vocabulary and syntax rules that can be translated or mapped into other language domains in an automated manner. For example, a sentence in this hypothetical interstellar message is built using a collection of numeric words in place of natural words. The numeric sentence is then translated into another language domain on the receiving end. This can be accomplished using a database that contains all of the translations into different languages.

This system encodes each idea with a unique numeric identifier, one that cannot be confused with other ideas (a common problem in spoken languages). Because of this, it is possible for the recipient to map numeric expressions into their preferred mode of communication with a minimal loss of information. The results may not be particularly poetic, but the goal is to make the message easy to comprehend, not to win a Nobel Prize for literature.

This numeric system is also interesting because it does not assume that the recipient will build a language using letters and words. For example, many species of squid communicate by rapidly changing the color of their skin. An alien species that communicates in a similar way might use patterns of color to communicate ideas instead of sound. Its language might use colors to form an alphabet in the same way we use letters (that in turn represent basic utterances of speech). So, where we would string the letters c-i-r-c-l-e together to represent the idea of a circle, they might use a sequence of colors (e.g., blue, orange, yellow, blue, purple, and red) to convey the same idea.

Since every idea in this system is coded numerically, the message can be mapped into many different formats on the receiving end. However, merely being able to build a large vocabulary of symbols is just one part of the process. The next thing we need to do is to couple this vocabulary with a system for describing how symbols are used within an expression. We can do this by labeling symbols according to their context, or use, within an expression, a concept we first introduced in Chapter 13, *Symbols*. Next, we'll expand on this idea to describe how we can use numeric symbols to represent objects (nouns), actions or processes (verbs) and modifiers (adjectives or adverbs), to create a rudimentary, general-purpose symbolic language.

Context

Since some words can be used in more than one context, we will need to tag symbols so their context within a sentence is obvious. For example, the word "orbit" could be used as a noun "The spacecraft is in a geosynchronous *orbit*," or as a verb "The spacecraft *orbits* the Earth." We first described how to do this in Chapter 12, *Binary DNA*, when we described how to label symbols according to their usage in an equation. We'll use the same trick again, except this time we'll describe several new contexts in which symbols can be used.

Imagine for a moment, that we never invented verbs or adjectives. The result would be a language composed entirely of nouns. Nouns, as you know, are used to describe objects or ideas, and cannot be used to describe an action or change of state. While we could use nouns to list all of the objects in a room, for example, we would not be able to describe any form of action, or how those objects interacted. Imagine trying to say something like, "The cat sprinted across the room," when you are forbidden from using a verb. You're stuck with saying something like, "The cat across the room." Does this mean that the cat is sitting across the room, has run across the room, or is looking across the room? The meaning of the statement is unclear.

Likewise, it is impossible to paint a complete picture of a situation without nouns because nouns are used to describe the objects in an environment. So, imagine trying to say, "The cat sprinted across the room" when you can't use the word "cat" or "room." In this case, you would be able to describe action, but not the objects involved in the action. Once again, you would lose a lot of information about the object you're trying to describe.

A basic language consists of nouns, verbs, and modifiers. The role of the nouns is to label objects in a situation. The role of a verb is to describe actions, changes of state, and the interrelationships between objects. The role of modifiers is to provide descriptive information about either nouns or verbs in a sentence (e.g., "The *small* cat sprinted across the room").

Once we've defined these three basic tools, we can extend our vocabulary of uses (contexts) to describe ideas such as tense (e.g., past, present, future).

With these tools, we can create a language that is easy for the recipient to analyze with the aid of computers, yet also capable of describing a wide range of ideas and processes. This doesn't necessary guarantee that the recipients will be able to comprehend every idea we describe (such as a symbol for an emotional state such as happiness), but it will make it easy for them to determine how symbols are grouped together, and how each symbol is used within a larger expression.

Describing symbolic context

In order to create a general-purpose language, we need to be able to describe four different types of symbols: object symbols, difference symbols, cause symbols and modifiers. An *object symbol* plays the role of a noun in an expression, and can be used to represent a physical object or an idea. A *difference symbol* plays the role of a verb in an expression, and is used to describe an action or change of state within a system. A *modifier* plays the role of an adverb or adjective, and is used to provide additional information about the object symbols and difference symbols within an expression. A *cause symbol* is another category of symbol that is used to explicitly describe the cause of an event.

To describe the context of a symbol within a sentence, we need to create several new labels. We pair these labels with symbols to describe how they are used within an expression. Looking back at Chapters 12 through 14, you will see how we used the symbols 8 and 9 to guide the reader in differentiating between numbers that are used as symbols and numbers that are to be interpreted as raw data. For example:

((8)(20100))

Would read as symbol 20100, or orbit; and:

((9)(20100))

Would read as numeric value 20100 (no symbolic meaning, just data to be used by another symbol or command). We'll do the same thing in our next series of examples, where we'll assign several new symbols to mean "object symbol (noun)," "difference symbol (verb)," and "modifier" as defined by the symbols listed in Table 19-2.

Table 19-2: *Example content labels used to describe nouns, verbs, and modifiers*

SYMBOL	MEANING
1024	Noun, Object
1025	Verb, Action
1026	Modifier

Using this approach, we could build expressions such as those listed in Table 19-3.

Table 19-3: *Examples depicting noun, verb, and modifier*

SYMBOL	MEANING	ENGLISH EXAMPLE
((1024)(20100))	Noun	The spacecraft is in a stable *orbit*.
((1025)(20100))	Verb	The spacecraft *orbits* the Earth.
((1026)(20100))	Modifier	The *orbital* velocity is 18000 miles per hour.

Notice how the same symbol, *orbit*, is used in three different contexts (*orbit*, *orbits*, and *orbital*) in these examples. Using the appropriate symbol reference, "orbit" can be used to depict an object, an action, or to describe another object or action.

This relatively straightforward addition to the lexicon enables us to create simple sentences using the expanding library of symbols we've been building. Even with this basic addition, we can compose sentences that describe a wide variety of situations.

We would teach the recipient to recognize these context labels, as we've done before, by sending sets of examples designed to highlight the idea we want to amplify. We would send a set of widely varied examples whose only common theme is they are sent in the form shown in the following example:

((((1024)(A))((1025)(B))((1024)(C)))

Which would read as:

(((noun)(symbol A)) ((verb)(symbol B)) ((noun)(symbol C)))

where A, B, and C represent previously defined and recognized symbols.

Enough examples will prompt the recipient to recognize the symbols 1024 and 1025 as context labels. They will notice that the center word in the expression is always a symbol that represents an action or process, while the left and right words always represent an object. This is a clue that the context label 1025 refers to an action or process (the equivalent of a verb), while context label 1024 refers to an object that participates in an action or process (the equivalent of a noun).

Once they have learned to recognize the meaning of symbols 1024, 1025, and 1026 (or whatever numbers we assign to mean "noun", "verb," and "modifier") they will be able to recognize sentences composed of any combination of these compound symbols.

Compound words

Once we've worked out a scheme for describing the context of symbols within a sentence, the next thing we need to add is the ability to group words together, and to describe words in terms of each other within a sentence. By doing this, we can go beyond the simple noun-verb-modifier classification to do things like:

- Describe the tense of a verb (e.g., past, present, future)
- Group several symbols together to form a new word
- Group modifiers with the symbols they describe
- Group symbols to form nested statements (sentences within sentences)

Compound symbols

Compound words offer a way to describe new concepts without resorting to a lengthy definition. Take the word "spaceship" for example. The meaning of the word is immediately obvious to someone who understands the meaning of the words "space" and "ship." With little effort, they can infer that spaceship means *"a ship that travels in space."*

Why go through all of the effort to define the concept of "spaceship" from scratch when it is possible to define it quickly by creating a compound word? This approach won't work for many concepts, but there are a lot of situations where this type of combination works well. If we wanted to use a compound word in an informal statement, and did not plan to reuse the idea repeatedly, we could use an expression such as:

((1024)(20100)(7010))

to mean "circle-orbit," or "circular orbit." If we wanted to use a compound word in a more formal way as a definition for a new symbol that we use repetitively, we might describe as:

((20101)(10)(1024)((20100)(7010)))

In the second example, the compound word is as a description for a new symbol, 20101, which can be used over again and interpreted as "circle-orbit" (circular orbit).

GROUPING MODIFIERS

Modifiers enable us to describe objects and actions in greater detail. They enable us to provide additional information about an object such as its size, color, position, or relationship to other objects. They also enable us to describe the action of a verb in detail, for example, walking quickly versus slowly.

One of the things we need to add to our technique for building symbolic sentences is to work out a scheme for linking modifiers with the words they are describing. This is important because the reader will not initially know which symbols are customarily used to describe other symbols. Here, we will format the messages so that it is obvious which symbol a modifier is describing. Consider the following examples:

```
((1026)(500)) ((1024)(1902)) ((1024)(1555))
(((1026)(500))((1024)(1902))) ((1024)(1555))
```

These two statements are identical except for the way the parentheses are used to bracket the symbols in each sentence. In the first expression, there are three words (one adjective and two nouns). The words are listed sequentially, and are not grouped in any obvious way. So it is not immediately apparent whether the symbol 500 is describing symbol 1902 or symbol 1555.

In the second expression, the first two words are grouped together (notice the extra pair of parentheses that surround them). This structure is used to hint that symbols 500 and 1902 are grouped together, with the symbol 500 describing symbol 1902, and not symbol 1555.

The next set of example sentences are written in shorthand form, and illustrate how we can group symbols together to make the relationships between symbols more obvious. In these expressions, n means noun, v means verb, and m means modifier (an adjective or adverb):

```
((n)(m)(m)(v)(m)(n)(m))
(((n)(m)) ((m)(v)(m)) ((n)(m)))
```

The first of these two examples does not include explicit information about the organization of the sentence; the words are simply listed in sequential order. The reader is forced to infer which word each modifier is associated with. In the second example, extra parentheses are used to explicitly group words together so there is no confusion about which word a particular modifier is describing. Now let's apply this general concept to the following sentence:

```
The small cat sprinted quickly
```

Which would read as:

```
(the) (small) (cat) (sprinted) (quickly)
```

With explicit grouping, the sentence can be displayed as:

```
(((the)(small)(cat)) ((sprinted)(quickly)))
```

As in the previous examples, we used extra parentheses to explicitly group several words together. This step is unnecessary in most human languages because the position and inflection of the words within a sentence contain information about their context and relationship to each other. However, our hypothetical language is based entirely on numbers and would offer no such clues to the reader. In order to make the sentences easier to decode, we're forced to include additional information about how words are grouped together as well as their context within the larger expression.

Compound context (tense)

Just as we can group two or more symbols together to form compound symbols or words, we can also group two or more context (usage) symbols to provide additional information about a symbol's usage within an expression. One example of where this technique will be useful is in describing the tense of a verb. Being able to describe the tense of a verb enables the recipient to tell the difference between statements that refer to past or future events.

The way we would define tense in this numeric language is different from the way we describe tense in human languages. Human languages are full of implicit information. By slightly changing the way we speak or spell a word, we can indicate whether we're referring to a past, present, or future event (e.g., "he ran," versus "he runs"). In numeric language, we would do this by creating several modifiers (adverbs) that we would pair with verbs to describe tense (see Table 19-4).

Table 19-4: *Example symbols for defining tense*

SYMBOL	MEANING
1027	Past event
1028	Present event
1029	Future event

To build upon our previous example using the symbol for orbit, we could end up with statements similar to those shown in Table 19-5.

Table 19-5: *Sample uses of tense*

SYMBOL	TENSE	MEANING
(((1026)(1027))((1025)(20100)))	Past tense	The spacecraft *orbited*.
(((1026)(1028))((1025)(20100)))	Present tense	The spacecraft *orbits*.
(((1026)(1029))((1025)(20100))	Future tense	The spacecraft *will orbit*.

By pairing symbols and context labels together, we can provide additional information about the usage and context of a word within a sentence. This is not just limited to tense, however. We could use this approach to describe many different things, such as: the degree of intensity (e.g., fast, faster, fastest), definite versus indefinite (e.g., may happen, will definitely happen), and active versus passive voice, to name a few.

Teaching the reader to recognize the concept of tense will be fairly straightforward since the structure of the expression will tell them that the new symbols 1027, 1028, and 1029 are associated with difference-symbols (verbs). This will prompt the recipient to think about the different ways that verbs can be modified or linked to other words. Because time is so important to communication, one of the things the recipient will be likely to look for is a symbol that provides temporal information (e.g., where objects and events are located in time).

Nested expressions

The concept of nested expressions in sentences is the same idea we applied to creating computer programs. Instead of writing an entire program in one giant block of instructions, we would build a program using many smaller components that performed specific tasks. The ability to create nested expressions allows us to express a complicated idea more efficiently. It also allows us to organize our thoughts, much like this book is organized in sentences, paragraphs, chapters and sections.

The general idea, as applied to a symbolic language, is similar. Nested expressions allow us to describe a small part of a scene, which can then be used to create a shorthand label for a particular element that can be used elsewhere in the message. We can then refer to this element by its shorthand nickname (i.e., its symbolic code), without having to repeat the entire description over and over. This is analogous to the practice of creating a reusable subroutine for use throughout a computer program.

We would use this technique differently than we do in spoken language. Most sentences in human languages contain only a few nested statements, mainly because of limitations in how we remember things. Most people can remember a typical sentence, but cannot memorize and recall a paragraph or several paragraphs.

A computer does not suffer from this limitation, so we can create intricate sentences that are built using large numbers of nested expressions, since the recipient will be able to use a computer store an indexed archive of the symbols (and their respective meanings) we've sent. From that archive, the recipient will be able to quickly identify a particular symbol and assign it to an expression. Some expressions can also be built using symbols that refer to other symbols, and so on, thus creating complex sentences and paragraphs using very few symbols. For example, you could have a single symbol (say symbol 1776) that refers to the entire Preamble for the U.S. Constitution, or for that matter, for the entire document.

Interstellar hypertext

This technique allows the sender to transmit a message, in effect, as a hyper-linked document. Let's look at a simple example of how we can do this using the techniques already described.

PARAGRAPHS, CHAPTERS, AND SECTIONS

Without doing anything new, we can organize expressions into larger pack-ages of information, simply by using the open and close parentheses sym-bols described in Chapter 12. We would do this as follows:

```
(((expression 1)(expression 2)(expression 3)(expression 4))
((expression 5)(expression 6)))
```

or:

```
(((1)(2)(3)(4)) ((5)(6)))
```

The simple example above shows how a series of expressions can be grouped into the equivalent of paragraphs, which in turn can be grouped into the equivalent of a chapter or section within a chapter. Notice how sim-ply using parentheses symbols to group the expressions together accom-plishes this.

Using only this technique, we can organize the message so that expressions, and collections of expressions, are grouped into obvious packages.

HYPERLINKING

We can add a form of hyperlinking to the message by associating the "para-graphs" and "chapters" described above with numeric symbols. This type of notation would read as follows:

```
((19001)(=)((expression)(expression)(expression)(expression)))
```

Which would read as:

```
Symbol 19001 = ((expression)(expression)...)
```

This is an important addition because it allows the sender to extensively cross-reference subjects within the message. So, for example, when attempting to describe a difficult concept, the sender could include an expression to the effect of "See also symbols 19001, 74052, etc." This allows the sender to repeatedly refer to subjects throughout the message, without resending the information related to the subject. The sender simply sends a pointer ("See subject 19001") instead of repeating the definition for symbol 19001.

Another important innovation that is made possible by this technique is the ability to group these chapter symbols into categories. This forms the basis of a system for searching for information within the message by category. All the sender needs to do is to include category information along with the symbol definitions (see Chapter 20), as shown in the following example:

```
((19001)(10)((expression)(expression)(expression)(expression)))
((19001)(20)(7405))
((19001)(20)(7801))
```

This is the same as the previous example, except this statement includes two additional expressions: "Symbol 19001 belongs to category 7405," and "Symbol 19001 belongs to category 7801." The sender can group these hyperlinked symbols into an arbitrary number of categories (which in turn can be grouped into supercategories). This enables the sender to create elaborately cross-referenced messages, and will make it even easier for the recipient to learn from the message.

Compound messages

Another interesting feature of the system described in recent chapters is the ability to create a message that includes many different types of information (symbols, images, computer programs, etc.). By combining these various elements, we can represent an idea or set of instructions in shorthand.

One of the beneficial side effects of this system is the ability to compose sentences from a combination of symbols, equations, images, and computer programs. For example, let's suppose we wanted to say, "The star exploded" without ever having defined a symbol for "exploded." This could be done by writing the following symbolic sentence:

```
(((1024)(7801)) ((1026)(1027)((9)(279)[1010101001111001...])))
```

Which would read as:

star$_{(noun)}$ display animation$_{(verb, past tense)}$

Here, the symbol (display animation) displays a sequence of images depicting the explosion of a star.

Note how we have combined two types of information in this example: an abstract symbol (star) and a sequence of images (display animation) generated by a computer program. What we did was to say "Treat the results produced by the igene 279 as a past tense verb." Hence, the reader would interpret this expression as "the star exploded."

The ability to combine many different types of information into an expression will give us considerable flexibility in describing complex ideas and concepts. If words are not sufficient to describe a scene, we can use pictures or animations in place of symbolic words in an expression.

While this may sound ambitious, all we are doing is combining the different types of media we've described throughout this section into a single presentation.

Defining symbols in terms of each other

Natural languages contain fairly few absolute terms. Most of the words in human languages are inventions that are derivations or combinations of previously invented words. Although we are rarely consciously aware of it, when we use language, we are constantly describing objects and situations in relative terms.

A *semantic network* treats words in a manner similar to a computer network, except that instead of networking computers, one is networking ideas. The links between ideas describe their relationship to each other.

We can use semantic networking to provide additional layers of detail about the meaning of the symbols we combine to form our narrative. We can also use semantic networks to provide an additional way to correct for transmission errors by giving the recipient the ability to derive approximate translations for a concept where no direct definition is available, the concept of which will be described in the next chapter.

SEMANTIC NETWORKS

We can move beyond describing concepts in absolute terms to create a large vocabulary of symbols defined purely in terms of other symbols. We can also use these to amplify the meaning of esoteric symbols, or the difference in meaning between closely related ideas.

A semantic network, like a computer network, enables us to network ideas, or link them to each other—a concept we've used implicitly throughout the past few chapters. This chapter describes how semantic networks can be used to provide additional layers of meaning about abstract symbols and to further assist the recipient in comprehending a message.

With semantic networks, we can create a message that provides the recipient with many ways to translate symbols and probe their meaning in terms of other symbols. This is important because it enables us to embed extensive clues about how to translate the higher order symbols within a message. It also allows us to describe almost anything, while at the same time guiding the recipient in understanding the message itself.

What is a semantic network?

The basic idea behind a semantic network derives from the way we define and use words in everyday language. While a few words can be defined in absolute terms, many are defined in terms of their relationship to other words. For example, the phrase "smaller than" can be described as the *opposite* of "larger than." This relationship, although simple, illustrates how one word can be linked to another by a relative definition. If the readers learn the meaning of "smaller than," they can infer the meaning of "larger than" by examining the relationship between the two words.

Figure 20-1 depicts a simple semantic network with four nodes. Each node represents an idea or word. In this example, we used the words "big," "small," "large," and "tiny."

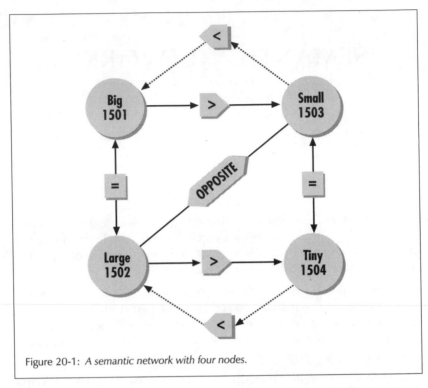

Figure 20-1: *A semantic network with four nodes.*

The four nodes (symbols) in Figure 20-1 are represented by circles. Lines drawn between these nodes represent links between them. The squares overlaid onto these links contain an expression that describes the relationship of one symbol to another.

Let's look at the symbols for *big* (1501) and *small* (1503) at the top of the diagram. These symbols have two lines connecting them. One line represents the connection from *big* to *small*, while the other line represents the connection (or path) from *small* to *big*. The box at the center of the line contains a *translation function* that describes the relationship of one symbol to another.

When we follow the path from big (1501) to small (1503), the translation function used is the greater than symbol (>), which gives us the expression *"big is greater than small."* When we follow the path from small to big, the less than (<) symbol is used as the translation expression in the link, which gives us the expression *"small is less than big."*

When we take this basic concept and apply it to SETI communication, it's easy to see that we will need to employ semantic networking on a much larger scale because our vocabulary of abstract symbols will be much larger. Most of these symbols will be linked to several other symbols, which in turn are linked to other symbols, *ad infinitum*. The goal is to define each symbol's relationship to at least a few other symbols wherever possible. By doing so, we can create a lexicon that enables the recipient to probe the meaning of one symbol in terms of several other known symbols. This also enables the recipient to probe the meaning of symbols by using inquiries like the following examples:

```
Q:  What is (large) compared to (small)?
    {large : small}
A:  (large) (is greater than) (small)
    (large) (is opposite of) (small)
    (large) (≠) (small)

Q:  What is the relationship of (large) to (size)
    {large : size}
A:  (large) (describes) (size)

Q:  What is the relationship of (homo sapiens) to (mammal)?
    {homosapiens : mammal}
A:  (homosapiens) (is member of group) (mammal)
        "humans are mammals"
    (homosapiens) (is member of group) ((intelligent) (mammal))
        "humans are intelligent mammals"
    ...

Q:  What is the relationship of (intelligent) to (mammal)?
{intelligent : mammal}
A:  ((some) (mammal)) (is member of group) (intelligent)
        "some mammals are intelligent"
    ((all) (mammal)) (≠) (intelligent)
        "not all mammals are intelligent"

Q:  What is the relationship of (homo sapiens) to (cell)?
    {homosapiens : cell}
A:  (homosapiens) (contains) ((many) (cell))
        "humans have/contain many cells"
    (([1](cell)) (≠) (homosapiens)
        "one cell does not make a human"

Q:  What is the relationship of (homosapiens) to (plant)
    {homosapiens : plant}
A:  (homosapiens) (is not member of group) (plant)
```

This provides the recipient with many paths through which they can translate symbols and learn how different symbols relate to each other. That way, if one translation does not make sense to the recipient, they can translate an unknown symbol in terms of symbols they already understand, and look for a relationship between the two.

Building a semantic network

To build a semantic network, we need to describe how different symbols are related to each other. Typically, we describe symbols in the following ways:

- By describing what categories or groups to which they do or do not belong

- By describing how they compare to other symbols (e.g., opposite of, similar to, greater than, less than, etc.)

- By using abstract expressions (sentences) to define them (similar to the way terms are described in a dictionary)

Categories

Grouping symbols into various categories is easy to do. In fact, we've been describing this form of a semantic network implicitly throughout this section of the book. Categories are used to describe whether a symbol does or does not belong to a particular group. To illustrate how this concept can be applied, let's look at a genetic example of how symbols can be grouped into categories. Figure 20-2 depicts the relationship between a hierarchy of symbols in a tree-like format.

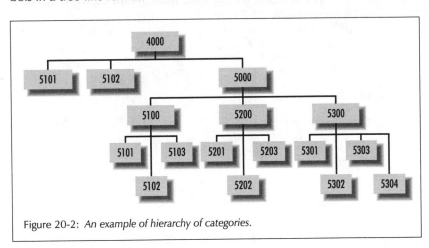

Figure 20-2: *An example of hierarchy of categories.*

Figure 20-2 shows a hierarchy of symbols grouped into categories. This diagram depicts the relationship in a tree-like format. Consider the symbol 5304, shown in the lower-right part of the diagram. This symbol belongs to the parent category 5300, which in turn belongs to category 5000, which in turn belongs to the category 4000.

For example, a reader who is examining this index will be able to determine that all of the symbols, except 5101 and 5102, belong to the category 5000. This index could be expressed in our hypothetical message as follows:

```
((5101)(20)(4000))
((5102)(20)(4000))
((5000)(20)(4000))
((5100)(20)(5000))
((5200)(20)(5000))
((5300)(20)(5000))
((5101)(20)(5100))
((5102)(20)(5100))
((5103)(20)(5100))
((5201)(20)(5200))
((5202)(20)(5200))
((5203)(20)(5000))
((5301)(20)(5300))
((5302)(20)(5300))
((5303)(20)(5300))
((5304)(20)(5300))
```

The code shown in this example provides all of the information required to generate the category tree depicted in Figure 20-2. While these category definitions are fairly simple, we can use sets of these expressions to build a list of all of the categories to which a symbol belongs. This allows the recipient to build a map that illustrates the basic relationships between symbols. While the diagram in Figure 20-2 may imply that this requires a rigid, hierarchical category structure, this is not true. Any symbol can be used as a label for a category, allowing the sender to create many web-like networks of categories. This is, in essence, a very simple type of semantic network where the (is member of) label is used to describe what groups symbols belong to.

Comparison functions

In addition to grouping symbols into categories, we can also define symbols in terms of other symbols, using comparative statements. Consider the following sample definitions:

```
large is greater than small
large is opposite of small
large is similar to big
large is opposite of tiny
small is less than large
small is similar to tiny
small is opposite of large
small is opposite of big
```

When converted to our symbolic language, the above statements might look something like the following:

```
((1502)(>)(1503))
((1502)(opposite)(1503))
((1502)(similar)(1501))
((1502)(opposite)(1504))
((1503)(<)(1502))
((1503)(similar)(1504))
((1503)(opposite)(1502))
((1503)(opposite)(1501))
```

The operators (>, <, similar, *and* opposite*) are shorthand for numeric symbols.*

These simple comparative statements can be used to define symbols in terms of their degree, whether they are similar to or different from other symbols, and so forth.

Complex definitions

Not all symbols are easy to describe as polar opposites of others. Many symbols require a subtle change of meaning compared to related ideas. Consider, for example, the words *cove* and *harbor*. Both words convey a slightly different meaning, but the distinction between them is subtle. The word "harbor" is generally used to describe a relatively large sheltered body of water that may be used by shipping traffic. On the other hand, the word "cove" is typically used to describe a smaller body of water, one large enough to anchor a boat perhaps, but not one that is likely to be used by shipping traffic.

Describing this distinction between these ideas to someone who is not already familiar with these terms will be difficult. Condensing this difference into a single formulaic expression is not very practical. However, it is possible to describe the difference in meaning by sending a set of expressions. These expressions can be used to define what each term does and does not mean. Consider the examples shown in Table 20-1. These examples assume that one or both terms have been described in general terms through the use of pictures. The purpose of this exercise is to provide additional information about the difference between the two symbols.

Table 20-1: *An example of expressions used to refine definitions of cove and harbor*

SEMANTIC EXPRESSION	MEANING
`((cove)(similar)(harbor))`	Cove is similar to harbor
`((cove)((likely)(<))(harbor))`	Cove is usually smaller than harbor

Table 20-1: *An example of expressions used to refine definitions of cove and harbor (continued)*

SEMANTIC EXPRESSION	MEANING
((false)(=)((cove)(=)(port)))	Cove is not used as port
((harbor)(=)(port))	Harbor is used as port

The examples shown in Table 20-1 are composed using previously defined symbols. The recipient already knows that the symbols for cove and harbor represent sheltered bodies of water. These expressions provide additional information about the relative meaning of these symbols, and tell the recipient the difference between a cove and a harbor.

In looking back at some of the previous chapters, we used different numbers of training examples depending on how easy or difficult an idea or symbol is to describe. If the difference in meaning between two symbols is very subtle, we might send a relatively large number of expressions to show the recipient the difference in meaning between the objects. If the difference in meaning is very easy to discern (e.g., big versus small), we may only need a small number of training statements to get the point across.

Deciphering the lexicon

The process of building a translation table for symbols can be largely automated. The recipient would watch for statements in the form ((symbol X) (translation function) (symbol Y)). When detected, the recipient would catalogue these statements in a database of translation expressions. The database could be relatively simple, with three columns for the source symbol, target (defined) symbol, and the equivalence expression or translation expression that links the two. Table 20-2 shows an example of this type of translation.

Table 20-2: *Translations for several related symbols*

SOURCE		SOURCE		TRANSLATION EXPRESSION(S)
SYMBOL	MEANING	SYMBOL	MEANING	
1501	big	1502	large	($\approx$)
1501	big	1503	small	(>), ($\neq$), (OPPOSITE)
1501	big	1504	tiny	(>), ($\neq$), (OPPOSITE)
1502	big	1501	big	($\approx$)
1502	large	1503	small	(>), ($\neq$), (OPPOSITE)
1502	large	1504	tiny	(>), ($\neq$), (OPPOSITE)

Table 20-2: *Translations for several related symbols (continued)*

SOURCE		SOURCE		TRANSLATION EXPRESSION(S)
SYMBOL	MEANING	SYMBOL	MEANING	
1503	small	1501	big	(<), (≠), (OPPOSITE)
1503	small	1502	large	(<), (≠), (OPPOSITE)
1503	small	1504	tiny	(≈)
1504	tiny	1501	big	(<), (≠), (OPPOSITE)
1504	tiny	1502	large	(<), (≠), (OPPOSITE)
1504	tiny	1503	small	(≈)

The entries in Table 20-2 would be transmitted as a series of equivalency statements, which would read as follows:

```
((1501) (>) (1503))
((1501) (>) (1504))
((1501) (≈) (1502))
((1503) (≈) (1504))
...
```

The recipient would simply capture these equivalency statements and store them in a database similar to Table 20-2.

The recipient would then analyze this data by writing programs that explore possible paths through the semantic network. These programs would learn how symbols are interconnected, and would build a table of routes to and from different symbols in the network. Then, whenever the recipient wants to define a symbol in terms of any other symbol, all they would have to do is perform a simple query on the information contained in the translation table.

This enables a further advance in comprehension because the recipient can now probe the meaning of any symbol in terms of many other symbols, and can interactively learn how the different symbols relate to each other. In effect, the semantic network turns the lexicon of symbols into a web-like network of inter-related definitions.

Mining for meaning

Semantic networks are powerful tools because they allow the reader to explore the meaning of symbols from many different perspectives. Since most ideas are described as relationships with other ideas and not in absolute terms, we will employ semantic networking implicitly similar to how we learn and use language. Some symbols will be relatively easy for any intelligent reader to comprehend. This is especially true of symbols that are being used to label objects depicted by images. The meaning of others will not be as obvious.

The ability to learn the meaning of an unknown symbol in terms of many other symbols will assist the reader in deciphering their meaning. For example, suppose symbol A is described in relation to symbols X, Y, and Z. For some reason, the recipients do not know the meaning of symbol X; however, they do understand the meaning of symbols Y and Z from previous messages. Since symbol A is described in terms of many symbols, they can learn its meaning in relationship to one or more known symbols. In Figure 20-3, the recipient of this message only knows the meaning of symbols Y (big) and Z (large); they do not know the meaning of symbol A (tiny).

Symbol A can be defined according to the following expressions:

```
A = X
A < Y
A is opposite Y
A < Z
A is opposite Z
```

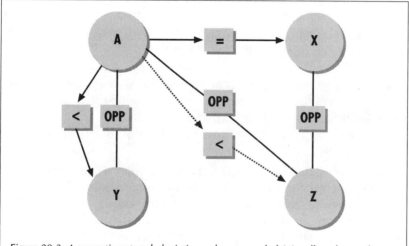

Figure 20-3: A semantic network depicting unknown symbol A (small) and several known symbols.

The meaning of X is unknown, so this does not help the recipient learn the meaning of A. However, the meanings of Y and Z are known, so the recipient can define the meaning of symbol A in terms of its relationship to Y and Z.

Symbol A is defined as being less than Y, and also the opposite of Y. The reader can infer that A is less than Y, and that A is also the opposite of Y.

Since Y is known to mean "big," the reader can infer that A is smaller than "big," and also the opposite of "big." Hence, it's reasonable for our recipient to infer that A means small, or the opposite of big.

This general approach can be used to probe the meaning of symbols by inspecting their relationship to other symbols. When used in conjunction with the symbolic vocabulary built using the techniques described in previous chapters, a semantic network enables a sender to communicate a wider range of concepts.

The symbolic vocabulary and context labeling (grammar) provide the basis for a general-purpose language that can describe many ideas. The semantic network provides the recipient with a powerful tool for probing the meaning and usage of words whose meaning might otherwise be unlearned or misunderstood.

Limits of interstellar communication

One of the long-held objections to SETI research is based on the assumption that, even if we do detect a signal from another civilization, it will be impossible to communicate with them in any meaningful way. The assumption holds that while we would be able to exchange some bitmapped hieroglyphics, and maybe a few equations, we would be able to share little or no useful information.

One of the goals of this book was to disprove this assumption by describing a general system that can be reproduced and demonstrated by using currently available computing and communication technology. The system is versatile, and can communicate a wide range of ideas and types of information.

The limits on the type of information the sender could include in a message are really limited only by the sender's creativity in composing messages. The sender should be able to combine equations, images, simulations, and abstract language in any combination or sequence they wish. This gives the sender an essentially infinite range of ideas they can communicate.

The real technical problem that is likely to thwart attempts at communication between two civilizations is not the technology itself, but the difference in sophistication of the parties on either end of the line. We can only speculate about the intellectual capabilities of a civilization that is thousands or millions of years ahead of us. It's more likely than not that it will be more sophisticated in its use of communication and in the ideas it communicates.

"Idiot-proofing" a message

Suspend your disbelief for a moment and assume that communication among civilizations is routine. Since there are likely to be wide gaps between the civilizations in terms of their intellectual and cultural development, there are likely to be a lot of situations where one civilization will not be able to comprehend ideas being described by another.

This leads to the question of how to create a message that is "idiot-proofed," meaning that it can be acquired by less developed civilizations, even if the recipient cannot understand the message in its entirety. The technology required to do this already exists. It's an implicit feature of the communication scheme described previously. The real trick to accomplishing this is in the way a message is authored.

The process starts off with the description of a basic vocabulary of math and logic symbols that can be used to create a simple programming language. Understanding this vocabulary of symbols, and their usage, is the minimum requirement for capturing the rest of the message. Because these symbols are based on elementary math and Boolean logic, they should be easy to decode.

The programs built from these fundamental symbols can then be used like genes to build more sophisticated programs that ultimately guide the recipient in learning symbols that represent abstract ideas. The use of semantic networking provides the recipient with extensive, embedded clues about how these symbols relate to each other, and will play an important role in making the message easier to decipher.

One way to "idiot-proof" a message is to author it in a progressive fashion by starting off with straightforward concepts, and then moving to more and more esoteric concepts. The recipient will be able to acquire the easy symbols and parts of the message built using them without much difficulty. At some point in the process, the recipient will start to encounter symbols whose meaning will not be obvious. As this occurs, the process of decoding the parts of the message that use these symbols will slow down as the recipient reaches the limits of their capabilities. This is akin to putting the hardest questions toward the end of a test.

Even if the recipients reach a point at which they cannot comprehend part of the message, they will have captured all of the information they need to eventually do so. The message, symbols, and their definitions can all be catalogued automatically. Even the most difficult concepts will be expressed in the same basic format as the basic ones (just as the basic format of the information stored in human DNA is the same as it is in a single-celled bacterium).

So, while the recipients may have a great deal of difficulty understanding parts of a message, they will have all of the raw data they need to eventually decode it (even if some of the ideas take decades or centuries to learn). Even if parts of the message are hard to decipher, the underlying system used to transmit information is the same. This is similar to the situation faced by biologists and geneticists in deciphering the human genome. The decoding process may take decades or centuries. However, the raw data has been acquired and catalogued and is silently challenging scientists to figure out what it means.

This suggests is that it is possible to communicate virtually any idea, although some ideas will take longer to comprehend than others. Some may remain mysterious to the recipient for an indefinite period of time, while others will be easy to interpret. For example, we will have an easier time defining a vocabulary of symbols related to geology than trying to define a vocabulary of emotional states. However, the difficulty of an idea shouldn't stop us from attempting to describe it.

CONTENT

Now that we have the means to communicate equations, pictures, and ideas across an interstellar communication link, we must decide what type of message we would want to send (or conversely, what kind of information we might expect to receive from another civilization).

What we choose to say with any message we send has less to do with technology and more to do with what we think another civilization will be interested in knowing about us. One idea that has been floated since the beginning of modern SETI programs is the idea that civilizations would exchange information in the form of an encyclopedia. An encyclopedia is essentially a database of terms that are organized into groups or categories. A civilization would use this encyclopedia to share information about their home world's geography, biology, and perhaps their history. While the idea may sound far-fetched, composing an encyclopedic message can be fairly easy to do using the techniques developed in previous chapters.

Earth history

For the sake of this exercise, suspend your disbelief for a moment and assume that we've recently detected signs of an intelligent civilization on a planet orbiting a nearby star. Rather than speculate about what kinds of information we might receive from them, let's instead examine what kind of message we could send in reply.

The things that will likely be most interesting to another civilization are the things such as a detailed survey of a planet's biology or cultural history. This is the type of information that cannot be collected by telescopes, but can only be relayed via interstellar communication. But first, try viewing this from our own perspective....

...We have invested billions of dollars in space exploration, and are currently engaged in a major effort to search for signs of life on neighboring planets (Mars, and Jupiter's moon, Europa, in particular). To do this, we'll ultimately have to send robot probes, and eventually people, to survey these worlds in detail to search for signs of life.

We're interested in learning about the biology, climate, chemistry, and geology of other worlds in our solar system. This quest for life within our own solar system will eventually lead to similar searches in other solar systems. All of these fields of study have a direct bearing on the development of life. By studying all of these characteristics of a world, we can learn more about the context in which life is likely or unlikely to develop, and whether life has developed independently on other worlds.

While it is possible that Earth is not the only inhabited world in the universe, it is almost certain that Earth's biology and life history is unique. It is unlikely that the exact conditions that exist on Earth will be duplicated on another world. Chances are that there will be subtle differences, such as slightly different chemistry, higher or lower gravity, a different planetary climate system, a different ratio of water-to-land, and so forth. All of these factors would have a great influence on the environment in which life develops on these worlds.

The implication is that life will have most likely developed along a much different path on alien worlds. Every new inhabited world that a civilization discovers is likely to have very different planetary and life histories. Even if this civilization had perfect knowledge of the physical laws of the universe, they would not be able to guess the specifics of how life evolved on a newly discovered world. As such, one thing we might want to do is describe Earth's biological and geological history in detail. The recipient reading this part of the message would receive, in effect, an encyclopedia describing Earth's history.

The Earth encyclopedia

To build an encyclopedia, we need to build a lexicon consisting of two general types of symbols, one for representing objects and another for describing the relationship between two or more objects. The first type of symbol used for representing objects (such as a particular species of animal, geological formation, etc.) are generally used as nouns, as shown in Table 21-1.

Table 21-1: *A hypothetical list of symbols used to represent species*

SYMBOL	MEANING
12000	Cat
12001	Mouse
12002	Rat
12003	Flea

Another type of symbol will be used to describe the relationship between two or more objects (e.g., frog *eats* fly). These symbols are combined with symbols representing objects to describe how they relate to or interact with each other. Examples of these symbols are shown in Table 21-2.

Table 21-2: *Symbols used to describe relationships between species*

SYMBOL	MEANING
9000	Eats
9001	Is eaten by
9002	Lives in (parasite)
9003	Lives on (e.g., insect that lives on a tree's leaves)

The symbols shown in Table 21-2 can be combined with the symbols used to represent different species to describe how they interact. This is a simple vocabulary of terms, and does not permit the description of more complex relationships (we can use more complex expressions to do this). Examples of some expressions, and their translations, are shown in Table 21-3.

Table 21-3: *Hypothetical table describing the relationship between these species*

SYMBOLIC EXPRESSION (SHORTHAND FORM)	MEANING
((12000)(9000)(12001))	12000 eats 12001
((12000)(9000)(12002))	12000 eats 12002
((12001)(9001)(12000))	12001 is eaten by 12000
((12002)(9001)(12000))	12002 is eaten by 12000
((12003)(9003)(12000)	12003 lives on 12000
((12003)(9003)(12001)	12003 lives on 12001
((12003)(9003)(12002)	12003 lives on 12002

This table illustrates how, by combining these two categories of symbols, we can describe basic relationships between different organisms. At a minimum level, we can describe each species (using images, diagrams, and such), what categories each belongs to, and how they interact with others in simple terms.

Key concepts

To build an encyclopedia of past and present Earth life, we need to define a vocabulary to deal with the following concepts:

- Numeric symbols that uniquely each species
- Numeric symbols that represent categories of species
- Vocabulary of concepts related to time
- Vocabulary of concepts used to describe interaction or relationship between species

By defining symbols to address these topics, we could craft a message that describes a manifest of past and present life on Earth, as well as the basic relationships between different species. If we wanted to, we could extend these definitions to include more verbose descriptions; however, for the sake of this exercise, we'll use simple expressions. Even if we restrict ourselves to using simple, formulaic expressions, we can still deliver a lot of information in this encyclopedia. We could send not only still images of plants and animals, but also describe where they live, what species they interact with, and the history of their evolution.

Species

One of the first things we will need to do is to define a lexicon of symbols used to uniquely identify every species of organism that we include in the encyclopedia. In this system, we will assign a unique numeric ID that can be used to represent each species (in place of a Latin name). For example, we used the symbol 12000 to represent the species *Felis domesticus* (domestic cat).

We would define the symbols for different species by equating these symbols with collections of images, animations, and abstract expressions. This information will tell the recipient what the members of the species look like, their population, and other pertinent information, as shown in the following example:

```
((12000)(10)(
    ((279)[1][101011...1101010101])
    ({1}(20)(64))
    ((279)[1][1110010111...101001])
    ({1}(20)(64)
    ...
    ((12000)(20)(11050))
)
```

Which would be read as:

```
((12000) equals (
    display image of cat
    display image of cat

    symbol 12000 belongs to category 11050 (felis)
)
```

This example equates the symbol 12000 with a series of pictures (the pictures are generated by the igene 279). The sequence of images might include several images of a live animal, its skeleton, diagrams of its anatomy, much like we might do in a textbook.

This expression would generate a series of images and equate those images with the numeric symbol used to represent the species. This expression also tells the recipient which categories the symbol belongs to (and groups the species *felis domesticus* into the parent category *felis,* which is represented by symbol 11050 in this example).

Categories of species

In addition to defining individual symbols for each species, we will also want to define additional symbols that are used to represent categories of species, such as the category felis (which includes cats, lions, and tigers). These symbols can be used to build an elaborate, hierarchical list of categories into which the different species can be grouped.

For example, cats and related species would be grouped into a symbol that is used to represent the category *felis,* which itself would be grouped into other parent categories (e.g., animal, vertebrate, mammal).

This enables the recipient to easily reconstruct the hierarchical category structure, and to see how different species are related to each other.

Time

Time is another important concept that we need to incorporate into this encyclopedia, because most species that once lived on Earth are now extinct. We need to be able to describe when different species existed, and how extinct species evolved to produce the species that are in existence today. At a minimum, we will need symbols to represent the concepts *before* and *after* and for describing the passage of time in measurable intervals.

NOTE

The concept of time will most likely have been addressed elsewhere in the message in sections related to physics and chemistry.

When talking about the history of life on Earth, we will typically be dealing with the passage of large amounts of time. We can define the passage of time using the same terms we use in everyday life, *days* and *years*. These symbols can be easily described using animated images, as shown in the following example:

```
((6500)(=)(
    ((279)[1][10111...1111])
    ({1}(20)(64))
    ((6500)(20)(1500))
)
```

Which would be read as:

```
Symbol 6500 = (
    Display image, or series of images depicting Earth's
    daily rotation
    Symbol 6500 belongs to category 1500 (related to time)
)
```

This example illustrates how we might define the symbol for the concept of a *day*. This statement would depict an animated image of the Earth's daily rotation on its axis. This symbol would then be grouped into a previously defined category for the concept of time. This concept would have been defined in sections of the message pertaining to the laws of physics.

The recipient would be prompted to interpret the symbol represented by the rotating Earth as a unit of time. So, they would read the expression ([365](6500)) as "365 rotations (days)."

To define the concept of a year, we would use a similar technique, as shown in the following example:

```
((6501)(=)(
    ((279)[1][111010101011....11111])
    ({1}(20)(64))
    ((6501)(20)(1500))
    ((6501)(10)([365](14)(6500))
)
```

Which would be read as:

```
Symbol 6501 = (
    Display image or series of images depicting earth's
    orbit around the sun
    Symbol 6501 belongs to category 1500 (related to time)
    Symbol 6501 = 365 x Symbol 6500 (Year = 365 Days)
)
```

This time, the statement would generate an animation of the Earth orbiting around the sun, and would also define years and days in terms relative to each other (e.g., year = 365 days).

With a library of just four symbols related to time (before, after, day, and year), we could separate species not only by categories, but also according to the times during which they existed. This additional invention allows us to describe the development of species in a timeline format similar to the format used by paleontologists today.

Geography

If we want to give the recipient a more complete picture, we also want to describe where each species lives. We may want to describe this in geographical terms by displaying a map that depicts the area where a particular species can be found. We may also want to describe this in terms of habitat, or in terms of what other species of plants and animal a particular species lives among.

We could describe a geographical representation of a species' habitat through the use of a special-purpose igene. This igene's purpose would be to generate a map of the Earth, or a selected part of the Earth's surface, and to overlay additional information about the boundary of a selected species' habitat.

Recall that because of the way igenes work, we do not need to send this program along with every entry in the encyclopedia. The program can be sent only once, and referred to indirectly throughout the rest of the message. This allows us to dramatically reduce the amount of information required to generate these maps.

This program works by drawing a shaded region on top of a map of the Earth's surface, as shown in the following example:

```
({1}(=)[[0][0][0]][[0][5][0]][[5][5][0]][[5][0][0]][[0][0][0]])
((24001){1}[2])
({2}(20)(64)
```

Which would be read as:

```
Create a two-dimensional array of numbers, store them in M1
Invoke igene 24001, pass it the contents of the 2D array
The results produces by igene 24001 belong to the category
"image."
```

This example can be further translated as:

```
Draw a shaded region with corners at the following (latitude,
longitude, and altitude) coordinates: (0,0,0), (0,5,0), (5,5,0),
(5,0,0), and (0,0,0). Store the resulting image in the variable
M2, and classify M2 as an image.
```

This igene would draw a map of the Earth's surface, and then overlay a shaded box onto this map to depict the range of a particular species' habitat.

This particular igene would be pretty big, as it would contain all of the data needed to map any part of the Earth's surface. Since we can refer to igenes indirectly, without having to retransmit their underlying instructions, we can use this type of shorthand form to generate complex maps without using a lot of bandwidth to do so. As shown in the example, the only information that we need to send is an array that gives the coordinates of the shaded region's boundaries.

Relationships between species

Next, we would need to define a group of symbols that describe the relationship between species. These symbols will typically be used as verbs in simple expressions such as "frog eats fly" to describe things such as:

- Predator and prey relationships between species
- Where a species lives with respect to other species
- Symbiotic and parasitic relationships among species
- Where a species lives in terms of climate or geography

We've already described several symbols that we might use to do this (eats is eaten by). To define these symbols, we would employ the same training technique used to describe symbols that represent actions or processes (verbs). For example, to define the concept of "eat," we might send the following set of instructions:

```
((9000)(10)(
    ((279)[1][101011111...1111])
    ({1}(20)(64))
    ((279)[1][101111010011...0001])
    ({1}(20)(64))
    ...
)
```

This set of instructions would generate a series of moving images equated with the symbol 9000. This prompts the recipient to look for the common pattern among these images. The common pattern the recipient would see is that all of the motion pictures depict one animal eating another. Hence, symbol 9000 is most likely being used to represent the concept of eating or predation.

Some concepts, such as predation, are fairly easy to describe since they can be depicted visually. Other concepts, such as a symbiotic relationship, are harder to describe. Some of these more esoteric concepts may be described using a combination of images and simulations that would amplify the idea that we want to call attention to.

Human languages and history

So far, all of our communication has involved the use of numeric symbols, most of which were defined using sets of images, simulations, or by linking one symbol to another numeric symbol. While this book is written in English, the messages we're talking about sending are written entirely in numbers; so far, they contain no reference to human language.

Suppose we want to describe the history of human civilization. While we can do this, in part, using the techniques described earlier, a lot of information will be lost. The reason is because to understand human history, one needs to understand human languages, partly because so many historical events are the result of personalities and politics.

In order to accomplish this task, we'll need to describe how to include the text from historical documents (or any other document) within our message. We'll also need to embed information that can be used to translate the documents on the receiving end. This is a situation where the recipient may have a difficult time reading the documents, but if we are meticulous in the way we send this information, we can make them relatively easy to parse and translate.

For example, this book was written on a computer. As such, each letter on this page is represented by a numeric code (e.g., A=65, B=66, C=67, and so on). We can use the same technique to transmit the text from documents written in various human languages. Sent in their raw form, they will be hard to read, but we can embed clues to assist the recipient in parsing and translating them. Consider the following example:

```
THAT IS ONE SMALL STEP FOR MAN ONE GIANT LEAP FOR MANKIND
```

When converted into numeric form, this sentence is represented as follows:

```
84,72,65,84 73,83 79,78,69 83,77,65,76,76 83,84,69,80 70,79,82
77,65,78 79,78,69 71,73,65,78,84 76,69,65,80 70,79,82
77,65,78,75,73,78,68
```

NOTE

We have used the numbers 65 through 90 to represent the English alphabet as uppercase text. This is a subset of the ASCII code commonly used on computers in North America. You may notice that these numbers conflict with symbols defined in previous chapters. In a real message, these letters would most likely be assigned a different block of numeric identifiers. We decided to use ASCII values to make these examples easy for software developers to read.

When the recipient first encounters this series of numbers, chances are they will not be able to recognize what they are looking at. We need to do two things to guide them in recognizing what these numbers represent. First, we would need to teach them how these numbers relate to an alphabet of written characters. Second, we would need to provide them with a lexicon that can be used to translate words into numeric symbols that they can understand. Let's examine how we would describe the alphabet, and how we use written words as a form of communication.

To do this, we need to communicate two pieces of information. First, we need to communicate the idea that letters are written individually as symbols. This idea can be communicated by sending images that show a person writing the letters of the alphabet by hand and associating a letter's symbolic number to that image. This will tell the recipient that we can communicate by drawing symbols, and by stringing these symbols together to form words.

Next, we would need to send a series of statements that equate numeric symbols with the letters they represent, as shown in the following example:

```
((84)(10)(
    ((279)[1][1010111...1010101])
    ({1}(20)(64))
    ({1}(20)(60))
)
```

Which would be read as:

```
Symbol 84 = (
    Draw image of the letter "T"
    Image belongs to category 60 (used to represent alphabet)
)
```

This example would tell the recipient that the symbol 84 represents the letter *T*. We would repeat this process to define the remaining letters and punctuation marks in the alphabet.

Once we've defined the alphabet, the next thing we need to do is to start building a dictionary of terms, or translation table. This lexicon can be used to map natural language text into the numeric vocabulary that we've been building throughout Chapters 11 through 19. This translation would contain entries similar to those displayed in Table 21-4.

Table 21-4: *An example translation table to map natural language text to numeric symbols*

EXPRESSION	TRANSLATION
([[79][78][69]](=)[1])	"O-N-E" = 1
([[84][87][79]](=)[2])	"T-W-O" = 2
([[84][72][82][69][69]](=)[3])	"T-H-R-E-E" = 3

Table 21-4: *An example translation table to map natural language text to numeric symbols (continued)*

EXPRESSION	TRANSLATION
(([83][77][65][76][76]](=)(1503))	"S-M-A-L-L" = symbol for small (1503)
(([77][65][78]](=)([1](5777)))	"M-A-N" = 1 human (5777)
(([77][65][78][75][73][78][68]](=)((25)(5777)))	"M-A-N-K-I-N-D" = all humans

Once we have built a large enough translation table, we can send the documents in an easily parsed format. To make it easy for the recipient to analyze the documents, we would edit the documents to remove informal grammar, improper spellings, and other features of casual speech that might throw an inexperienced reader off track. We might also add context labels to clearly show how each word is being used in an expression (e.g., noun, verb, or modifier).

As shown in the example below, Neil Armstrong's famous quote would be formatted so that it is easy to break down into words:

```
THAT IS ONE SMALL STEP FOR MAN ONE GIANT LEAP FOR MANKIND
```

Which breaks down into words and sentences as:

```
[[THAT][IS][ONE][SMALL][STEP][FOR][MAN]][[ONE][GIANT][LEAP]
[FOR][MANKIND]]
```

Taking this one step further, the words and sentences would be broken into individual characters and grouped together to form the words of the sentence:

```
[[[[84][72][65][84]][[73][83]][[79][78][69]]
[[83][77][65][76][76]][[83][84][69][80]]
[[70][79][82]][[77][65][78]]][[[79][78][69]]
[[71][73][65][78][84]][[76][69][65][80]]
[[70][79][82]][[77][65][78][75][73][78][68]]]]
```

Once we've reached this point, we can send as many documents as we want using this technique. Whether the civilization we are communicating with will be able to understand the more subtle aspects of our languages is unknown. If we do a thorough job of defining translation tables to map our text into the numeric vocabulary we've been building, we can increase the odds that they will be able to understand our writing.

Since it's a reasonable assumption that a civilization capable of receiving an interstellar message is probably pretty smart, it's also reasonable to assume that, given enough time to study the documents, they will be able to learn the meaning of many of the words in our vocabulary. And once they've received and correctly translated a number of words in our vocabulary, they could learn to read these documents, at least in part, in their original form.

What's next?

One of the most important scientific discoveries we've made in the 20th century is that the universe is much stranger than we once imagined. If basic physical laws don't explicitly forbid something, no matter how preposterous it may seem, it is probably happening somewhere. Given what we've learned about the universe, and about life's ability to thrive in hostile environments, it seems unlikely that life has arisen only on Earth.

What makes SETI such an interesting field of study is the fact that it touches on so many different disciplines—from astronomy to biology to information theory—and that it seeks to answer such a fundamental question.

If SETI does succeed, making contact with intelligent beings on another world will be the most important discovery in human history—one that has the potential to radically alter our civilization. Merely verifying that another civilization exists will be a historic event in and of itself. If it turns out that in-depth communication is possible, the implications of being exposed to the knowledge collected by ancient, space-faring civilizations are truly staggering.

The implications of failing to discover intelligent life are equally awesome. It will take decades for us to conduct a thorough search for intelligent life in our galaxy, perhaps longer. If we are ultimately answered only by silence, we'll be forced to deal with the reality that we are alone in the universe. More ominously, this silence may be a warning that we live in a Darwinian universe, one in which only the stealthiest and most aggressive species survive.

While it would be fun to speculate about what we might learn from another civilization, the reality is that we really have no idea what they might choose to say. What we do know is that it is technologically feasible to communicate in depth with another civilization that is willing to communicate. What they might say to us is only limited by their imagination and how we interpret their message. This is what makes the potential reward from SETI research so interesting.

Whatever the outcome, we may well have the answer within our lifetime.

EPILOGUE

Throughout known time, man has gazed upon the stars, wondering what might be out there. Recent analyses of cave drawings in the south of France that depict a man being run over by a bull now appear to be drawings of the earliestknown astronomers. These drawings show the three main stars of the constellation Taurus as they would have appeared in the night sky some 16,500 years ago.

When David Anderson, Dan Werthimer, and a team of computer scientists and astronomers developed the SETI@home project in cooperation with the SETI Institute, their best hope was to get 5,000 people to download and run the screensaver. A year later, nearly 2.5 million people from around the world run this program to aid in the search for intelligent life—not because we're all crazy, but because we believe there is something else out there in the cosmos. And big corporations are stepping up to the plate to fund projects such as the SETI Institute's Allen Telescope Array (ATA).

We already know that Jupiter-sized planets orbit nearby stars at a distance similar to the asteroid belt that separates Mars and Jupiter in our own solar system. If the Titius-Bode Law of Planetary Distances holds true throughout the universe (or at least in some instances), then it is possible that other planets—possibly rocky, Earth-sized planets—could be in a closer orbit nearby those stars.

Just as those who sail the seas rely on the stars to plot their course to reach distant lands, so shall we someday chart a course through time and space to reach alien worlds beyond our own. And when we do, there's a good chance that we will have already learned a great deal about our distant neighbors because of the work being done by past- and present-day SETI researchers.

— Chuck Toporek
Editor, O'Reilly & Associates, Inc.

APPENDIX IV

MESSAGE REPLICATION

This appendix explores the possibility that radio communication among civilizations may not be a rare occurrence. In this appendix, we examine some possible scenarios for communicating with an intelligent extraterrestrial civilization. A good way to approach this exercise is to imagine that you are a civilization that wishes to colonize your neighborhood, not in the physical sense, but in the intellectual sense. Perhaps your motive is to benevolently share your knowledge with anyone who might be listening, to trade notes about your experiences, or to scare off potential aggressors by implying that unwanted visitors will be blasted into oblivion. Who knows?

The purpose of this exercise is to determine how to broadcast a message as widely as possible, while also minimizing the cost, in terms of the amount of energy required to send the message. The goal is to reach the widest audience at the lowest energy cost. We'll examine this problem from the perspective of a telecommunications engineer.

Optimizing detection range versus cost

The designer of an interstellar broadcasting facility would have two basic options to choose from. One option is to build a single, extremely potent transmitter that is powerful enough to be detected at distances up to tens of thousands of light years in all directions (omnidirectional beacon). The other option is to build a less powerful facility, but to design the message in such a way that it prompts any recipients to retransmit the message in reply (as you might forward an email joke from a friend).

Scenario 1: Centralized transmitter

The problem with building a single transmitter to broadcast to a very large area is that the laws of physics impose unfavorable economics. Remember that in order to double the effective receiving range of a signal (all other things being equal), one has to increase the transmitter power four times. To put this in perspective, a microwave transmitter broadcasting at a power of 1 billion Watts can be detected at a distance of 100 to 1,000 light years, depending on the receiving equipment. To transmit a signal at a distance of 100,000 light years (enough to span the entire galaxy), one would have to increase the power of the transmitter by 10,000 to 1 million times. So what started out as 1-billion Watt transmitter would become a 10 trillion to 1,000 trillion Watt transmitter! This amount of energy represents a sizable fraction of the total amount of solar energy received by Earth as a whole (approximately 10^{16} Watts, or 10,000 trillion Watts).

The shaded area in this graph represents detection range as a function of transmitter power. Notice how the slope of this curve becomes shallower to the right of the graph. This illustrates the diminishing return gained by increasing transmitter power. These unfavorable energy economics are likely to impose a limit on the amount of energy a sender will want to budget for a transmitter. The reason for this is the diminishing returns yielded by increasing the transmitter power (a hundredfold increase yields only a tenfold increase in the signal's detection range). Even if the sending civilization is quite advanced, their energy budget, while perhaps much larger than ours, will still likely be finite.

There is another problem with using an extremely powerful transmitter to send a message across galactic distances. Even if the transmission is successfully detected, the round-trip time for any two-way communication will be tens of thousands or hundreds of thousands of years. This extreme delay effectively eliminates any opportunity for a two-way exchange of information, which further undermines the rationale for building a super-strong transmitter.

Scenario 2: Mesh-like network

If it turns out that communicative civilizations are relatively common, a much more practical solution is to use a lower-powered transmitter, and to transmit a message that is easy to decode, which prompts any recipient to rebroadcast the message as part of their reply. In this scenario, the sender only needs to broadcast a signal that is powerful enough to reach a handful of nearby civilizations. These recipients then rebroadcast this message in their own transmissions, which are picked up by other civilizations outside the original sender's detection range.

We can compare this scenario to a forwarded email joke. The sender's goal is to persuade one or more recipients to forward the email to other recipients, and for those recipients to do the same, ad infinitum. This type of message can propagate indefinitely provided that each time the message is forwarded, one or more of the recipients of the message also forwards the message again.

NOTE

This scenario will only work if communicative civilizations are relatively common, with an average distance between them of 1,000 light years or less. If civilizations are much more widely separated, the odds that this type of communication will succeed are more remote.

Figure A-1 illustrates the energy savings associated with this approach. This graph depicts several curves. The upward sloping line shows power as a function of distance for a single, centralized transmitter. The dashed and dotted lines show power requirements as a function of distance when there are repeating sites every 100, 300, and 1,000 light years, respectively. Unlike the solid line, these lines increase up to a point and then plateau. Because of this, it takes 10,000 to 1 million times less energy to send a message across the galaxy using a mesh-like network compared to a single long-haul transmission, as described in the first scenario.

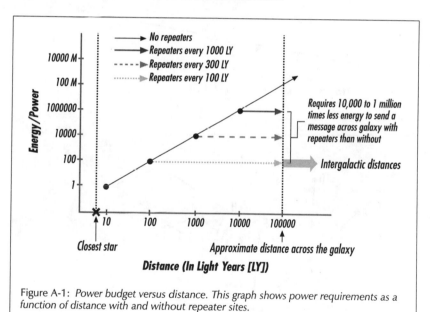

Figure A-1: *Power budget versus distance. This graph shows power requirements as a function of distance with and without repeater sites.*

In addition to reducing the transmitter power requirements, this approach also reduces the round-trip delay time. This is because the sender establishes communication with the nearest sites, which can then relay data onward, in bucket brigade fashion, to other sites that are outside the detection range of the sender's original signal. Let's look at an example to see how this can make a difference in the speed at which information is disseminated among the sites.

In this example (illustrated in Figures A-2 and A-3), two sites, A and B, are separated by a distance of 10,000 light years. In this situation, it will take 10,000 years for a message from site A to reach site B.

Figure A-3 depicts the same two sites, except now there are many intermediate sites randomly scattered between them. All of these sites represent communicative civilizations that can relay messages. The lines in this diagram depict communication links among the nearby sites. Here, data can follow several different paths to travel from site A to site B. Instead of transmitting data directly from site A to B, the sender could relay data across several intermediate sites. For example, a message could be transmitted from site A to C, which then gets forwarded to F to H to K to L, with the signal finally reaching site B on the far side of the galaxy.

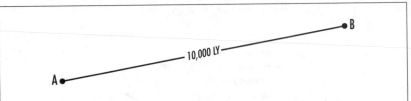

Figure A-2: *Two sites, A and B, are 10,000 light years apart, which makes communication difficult.*

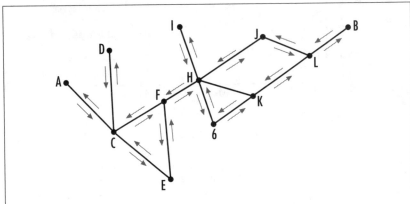

Figure A-3: *This figure compares a single long-haul link between two sites to a mesh-like network, which links many intermediate sites together.*

In this scenario, each of these civilizations can be viewed as a node in a mesh-like network (remember our discussion about distributed computing earlier in the book?), which can potentially communicate with other nearby nodes. This type of communication has several benefits compared to the centralized approach, among them:

- Transmitter power requirements are reduced by a factor of up to 1 million, compared to an omnidirectional beacon. The power budget reduction is even more dramatic if the sender uses directional antennas to focus most of the transmitter's energy toward the sites that are within detection range.

- Round-trip communication times are reduced to the distance between the two closest sites within the network.

- The sites participating in the network can archive each other's data, and by doing so, can create a form of shared, persistent memory. Even if one of the sites drops off the network permanently, the information they had sent prior to ceasing their transmission would have been disseminated throughout this network and would propagate throughout the network indefinitely.

- Information from multiple civilizations can be shared much more quickly this way, since a new participant can receive information from all participating sites through the nearest node in the network.

Whether civilizations would elect to participate in this kind of system is another matter. However, the marked reduction in power requirements (and hence lower economic cost), the reduction in round-trip times, and the ability to archive information are compelling reasons to consider this approach.

Anyone who is sophisticated enough to engage in interstellar communication will also know that this type of distributed communication is possible. So, we shouldn't be surprised if we discover that, by contacting one civilization, we are indirectly contacting others who have previously exchanged information with the first contact.

Promoting piracy

The greatest challenge in starting a system like this is in persuading the party on the receiving end of the transmission to rebroadcast the message. To achieve this, it is important to craft a message that is easy to acquire and decode, and which encourages its recipient(s) to rebroadcast its contents along with their own transmission. This is akin to a band encouraging listeners to make and share bootleg copies of their music.

This system of interstellar communication is not as improbable as it might initially seem. It is simply much more economical, in terms of energy requirements, to create a mesh-like network than to create a hub and spoke network with longer distances between the participating nodes. Anyone who is sophisticated enough to engage in interstellar communication will perceive this.

In order to start a mesh-like network, the following things must happen:

- There must be one or more communicative civilizations within several thousand light years of the originating transmitting site. Communicating civilizations must also have a fairly long life span (L, according to the Drake Equation). The jury is obviously still out on whether this condition exists in our case.

- The transmitted signal must be easy to detect, and must be broadcast for an extended period of time. The longer the transmitter is on, the greater the likelihood that someone will stumble across the signal.

- The message embedded in the signal must have an obvious structure, and must also be easy to decode.

- The message should include explicit instructions that depict the transmission of an endlessly propagating broadcast (i.e., the message should hint to the recipient that it is common practice to rebroadcast the message using an established format).

The first three criteria must be in place in order to establish a mesh-like network. If there is nobody to hear the message, or they do not recognize the message, it will not be rebroadcast (thus, nobody outside of the original sender's detection range will discover the signal).

The last item provides any recipient(s) with explicit directions. To communicate this idea, the sender could send a program that generates a series of images.

The program would display the binary coded message shown in Figure A-5 as a three-dimensional image. The spacing between the nodes in the network would correspond to the position of actual stars. The viewer would see an animation that shows strings of binary numbers (formatted exactly like the message they have just received) traveling from one node to another in this network. They would be able to identify the stars in the image because of their spacing and color signatures. This would suggest to the sender that they are viewing a simulation of a mesh-like interstellar communication network.

Survival of the fittest meme

If a process like this begins, wherein two or more civilizations attempt to persuade others to retransmit their information, it could create a form of Darwinian competition. In this case, the competition is between different message formats. Instead of selecting for the survival of the fittest animal, this competition is biased in favor of the fittest meme.

To understand how this might play out, it helps to step back and take a look at the big picture—in this case, the entire galaxy. Imagine that two or more civilizations at opposite ends of the galaxy get the same idea—to influence their neighbors through communication. Each uses a different strategy to build their message. Whoever crafts the message that is most likely to be detected and rebroadcast by other civilizations will be able to reach the largest audience in the shortest period of time. This is because the message that is easiest to decode, and that prompts its recipients to rebroadcast it, will propagate faster than one that is hard to acquire or understand. So, let's take a look at some of the attributes that could affect the "fitness" of a civilization's message:

- First and foremost, the message must be easy to detect.

- The message must also have an obvious structure and be easy to parse and decode. At the very least, it should be easy for the recipient to parse it out into the equivalent of words, groups of words, and so on. The structural format of the message should be efficient and easy to mimic. (This is one of the reasons the message described in Chapter 12, *Binary DNA*, borrowed ideas from biology.)

- The message should clearly identify the symbols that are used in the message (e.g., reserve a block of numeric addresses if the system uses numbers as placeholders for symbols).

By including these attributes, the sender would provide the recipient with the information they need to create their own message based on the format used in the original message. If the format of the original message is efficient and easy to decode, the recipient will be likely to mimic this format in their reply (especially if the message prompts them to do so in their response). As the cliché goes, "Why reinvent the wheel?"

The recipient could then create a new message that uses a format identical to the original, and that contains information from both the original sender(s) and the recipient's own messages. This second transmission is structurally identical to the original message (e.g., same frequencies, same modulation scheme, same basic encoding format, etc.). However, the recipient has interleaved their own vocabulary of symbols, images, and expressions along with the contents of the original message.

This process is illustrated in Figure A-3. In this scenario, let's suppose that site A is receiving information from site C. Because C has direct or indirect links to B, D, E, F, G, H, I, J, K, and L, the recipient at A may also be able to receive information relayed from any of these distant sites.

One of the real benefits of using numbers to build a language is that numeric addresses can be used as unambiguous placeholders for ideas. They can also be used to create a uniform address space that makes it easy to combine symbols from multiple sources. As long as the participants understand the addressing system, and take care to avoid using duplicate addresses, it would be possible to interleave information from multiple sources within a single message.

In Chapter 13, *Symbols*, we learned that we could equate numbers with symbols for processes such as addition, subtraction, and so forth. In subsequent chapters, we extended this concept to use numbers as placeholders for images, computer programs, and eventually for abstract symbols. The technical hurdle we face now is how to create a system for tracking symbols from not just one sender, but from a potentially unlimited number of senders.

One way we could do this is to create a compound numeric symbol that consists of two parts. This is similar to the hierarchical domain name service (DNS) that identifies computers on the Internet. This system divides the Internet address space into top-level domains (e.g., *.com*, *.org*, *.ar*, *.uk*). These top-level domains often indicate the country in which node is located. Hence, we know that *abccorp.ar* is located in Argentina, while *abccorp.co.uk* is a commercial site located in the United Kingdom.

In this system, each symbol would be identified by a two-part address. One number would identify the civilization that originally defined the symbol. Another number would identify that symbol within the authoring civilization's symbolic address space. This procedure would clearly label the origin of every symbol within a message, and would allow participating sites to interleave symbols from many different sources.

When we first discussed the idea of using numeric addresses as placeholders for symbols, we created a two-dimensional address for mapping ideas numerically. One coordinate identified the symbol to be used to form a word (e.g., 10 for "="). A second coordinate identified the context, or usage, of the numeric word within an expression (e.g., 8 means *command*, while 9 means *data*). If we employ this methodology, we would create a three-dimensional system for mapping ideas to and from numbers. This coordinate system can be described as:

```
(n,s,c) or (source node id, symbol id, context id)
```

Where:

- *n* is a unique number that identifies the sender that authored the idea.

- *s* is a unique number that identifies the symbol within their numeric address space for ideas.

- *c* is a number that denotes the context (or usage) of the symbol within a group of words.

This is just one way to do this. The specifics of the addressing scheme are less important than the fact that it is easy to create a uniform address space for indexing ideas from multiple sources since it is a straightforward extension of the technique described previously.

Immortal information

There is a hidden implication in all of this: If this mesh-like network gets started and is used by two or more civilizations, it is possible that this type of communication would expand to cover a large volume of space. The reason for this is because the economic value of the message increases with each additional participant in the network.

As the number of participants rises, the value of the shared knowledge increases, which enhances the likelihood that communication will continue on a long-term basis. This, in turn, increases the likelihood that other civilizations that are not already participating will someday stumble across this discussion. They can then add their information to the discourse and, by transmitting their own message, extend the range of the original message even further to reach even more sites. This is a self-reinforcing process that, once started, makes it likely that this network will eventually propagate widely, perhaps to reach most of the inhabited areas of the galaxy.

While this theory cannot be proven, this type of communication may also affect the value of the Drake Equation factor *L* (the life span of communicative civilizations). The realization that other civilizations exist, and that interstellar communication is routine, could potentially motivate emerging civilizations to make a concerted effort to solve problems that might otherwise threaten their continued existence (e.g., warfare, environmental damage, overpopulation, health and welfare of the general population, etc.). If we were to discover that many other civilizations had survived the same kind of transition that we are presently negotiating, and could learn from their experiences (as well as the fatal mistakes of failed civilizations), this would likely have a positive effect on the odds for our own long-term survival.

What's most interesting is the network's persistent memory. One of the fringe benefits of a uniform addressing system for symbols is the ability of the participating sites to archive and relay information from many sources, including those that dropped off the network long ago. For example, new participants in the network would be exposed to information from ancient sites that might have dropped off the network millions of years prior to their arrival. While this may sound fantastical, all the participating sites are doing is endlessly relaying parcels of information, in store and forward fashion, throughout the network.

In a sense, this would be the information equivalent of a galactic genome that contains the knowledge accumulated from past and present participants in the network. So, while the implications of encountering such a network are pretty amazing, the underlying principles that would be used to build it are pretty straightforward and not very different from the principles employed in packet switched networks here on Earth.

The odds that we will stumble across this type of communication are remote, especially if communicative civilizations are rare. However, this is technically feasible, and therefore a real possibility that we should consider. However, there is always the possibility that we're the first communicative civilization (or among the first), in which case we could be the ones with an opportunity to start this type of process ourselves, with human civilization becoming the inventor of what would become, in effect, an interstellar Internet.

SETI RESOURCES
ON THE INTERNET

Arecibo Radio Observatory
(National Astronomy and Ionosphere Center)
  http://www.naic.edu

Big Ear Observatory
  http://www.bigear.org

Cocconi & Morrison 1959 MSETI paper
  http://www.coseti.org/morris_0.htm

Columbus Optical SETI Observatory
  http://www.coseti.org

Extrasolar Planet Search
(Dr. Geoffrey Marcy, San Francisco State University)
  http://www.exoplanets.org

Jodrell Bank Observatory SETI
  http://www.jb.man.ac.uk/research/seti/

"The Great Silence"
(available on David Brin's web site)
  http://www.kithrup.com/brin/

Harvard University SETI
  http://seti.harvard.edu/seti/

NASA Origins Program
  http://origins.jpl.nasa.gov

Planetary Society
  http://www.planetary.org

SETI@home
  http://setiathome.berkeley.edu

SETI Australia
http://seti.uws.edu.au

SETI History
(compiled by the SETI League)
http://www.setileague.org/general/history.htm

SETI Institute
http://www.seti.org

SETI League
http://www.setileague.org

SETIQuest Front Pages
http://www.coseti.org/setiq_cv.htm

Sky & Telescope SETI
http://www.skypub.com/news/special/seti_toc.html

Schwartz and Townes 1961 OSETI paper
http://www.coseti.org/townes_0.htm

UC Berkeley SETI
http://seti.ssl.berkeley.edu

SETI PROGRAM TIMELINE

Morrison and Cocconi paper (1959)
Philip Morrison and Giuseppe Cocconi publish their landmark paper "Searching for Interstellar Communications" in *Nature*. This paper becomes the blueprint for subsequent microwave SETI programs.

Project Ozma (1960)
Conducted by SETI pioneer Frank Drank at the National Radio Astronomy Observatory in Green Bank, West Virginia, Project Ozma searched for narrowband radio transmissions at the 21cm wavelength.

Schwartz and Townes paper (1961)
R. N. Schwartz and Charles Townes publish their landmark paper "Interstellar and Interplanetary Communication By Optical Masers" in *Nature*. This paper becomes the blueprint for subsequent optical SETI search programs.

OSU Big Ear Observatory (1973–1995)
Ohio State University's Big Ear Observatory was used for SETI research from 1973 to 1995, the longest-running continuous search for extraterrestrial intelligence. This facility detected the famous "Wow!" signal in 1977. The observatory has since been decommissioned and is no longer in use. Detailed information about the antenna, and about research conducted at Big Ear, can be found online at *http://www.bigear.org/*.

Project Cyclops (early 1970s; planned, not implemented)
Project Cyclops was a plan to build a very large array of small radiotelescopes that would be networked together to behave like a single large antenna. The plan, although never implemented, inspired the Allen Telescope Array, now under construction in northern California.

META (1985–1994)
META, short for Million Channel Extraterrestrial Assay, was a Harvard-based microwave SETI program. This targeted search monitored 8.4

million 0.05 Hz channels centered on 1.42 and 2.84 GHz frequencies. This program was a precursor to the more sophisticated BETA survey, which went online in 1995.

NASA High Resolution Microwave Survey (canceled)

HRMS was one of the few publicly funded SETI programs. Project Phoenix is a privately funded search that is based on the designs developed through the NASA program, which was canceled in 1993.

Project Phoenix (1995–present)

Project Phoenix, sponsored by the privately funded SETI Institute, is a targeted search program that conducts detailed investigations of about 1,000 sun-like stars within 200 light years of our system. The program can monitor a large percentage of the microwave observing window (up to 2 GHz). The program uses several different radiotelescopes, including the Arecibo Radio Observatory, but it is only active a few weeks per year (this will change when the Allen Telescope Array goes into operation).

BETA (1995–1999)

Project BETA, a Harvard-based program led by Dr. Paul Horowitz and sponsored by the Planetary Society, is a targeted search that monitors a wide frequency band (from 1.40 to 1.72 GHz) at high resolution (0.5 Hz per channel). The search used the 26meter dish at Harvard, which was severely damaged during a storm in 1999. Prior to being knocked offline, BETA had scanned 68 percent of the celestial sphere at least once. The equipment is currently being repaired, and the electronics will be upgraded. The system is expected to return to operation soon.

SERENDIP (1978–present)

Based at the University of California, Berkeley, Project SERENDIP has gone through several generations since its inception in 1978. SERENDIP is a "piggyback" program, in which the detection equipment looks at whatever star the telescope happens to be pointed at. The latest generation of detection equipment, SERENDIP IV, monitors 168 million channels, each 0.6 Hz wide. The system monitors a band of frequencies 150 MHz (0.15 GHz) wide, centered on the 1.42 GHz hydrogen emission line frequency. The project currently conducts piggyback observations from the Arecibo telescope, the world's most sensitive radiotelescope.

SETI League

The SETI League (http://www.setileague.org/) is an amateur SETI program founded by Richard C. Factor. This program employs a large number of small radiotelescopes built using commercially available satellite receiver systems. These systems, although they are not sensitive enough to detect weak signals, can be used to cover a large percentage of the night sky to listen for very strong beacon signals.

SETI Australia, Southern SERENDIP (1998–present)

Based on UC Berkeley's SERENDIP III program, Australia's Southern SERENDIP program uses the 64meter Parke's Observatory to monitor 58.8 million 0.6 Hz channels. This system is also a piggyback program, and enables SETI researchers to search the southern sky, which is not visible from North American and European radiotelescopes.

Harvard OSETI Group (1998–1999)

The Harvard OSETI group, led by Dr. Paul Horowitz, conducted piggy-back optical SETI observations using the 61-inch Wyeth telescope at the Oak Ridge Observatory. The system is currently being upgraded to reject false alarms from cosmic ray events. The new system, being developed with the cooperation of Princeton University, is expected to go into operation soon.

SETI@home (1999–present)

Launched in May 1999, SETI@home represents a breakthrough in the way that SETI research, and signal processing in particular, is done. The program enables millions of computer users to donate their spare CPU time to analyze small chunks of data captured by the SERENDIP program. The program complements the signal processing systems used by SERENDIP by enabling researchers to look for many different types of signals within the data already captured by the Arecibo Radio Observatory.

UC Berkeley OSETI Program (1999–present)

The University of California is conducting two types of OSETI programs at present. Led by Dr. Dan Werthimer, the projects search for continuous and pulsed laser beacons. One program uses the 30inch telescope at the Leuschner Observatory to search for the signature of a pulsed laser beacon in the light from about 2,500 sun-like stars. In the other program, planet hunter Geoffrey Marcy will check his group's high-resolution spectra to look for the signature of a continuous laser beacon. This search will examine about 1,000 sun-like stars.

Project StarVoice (slated to begin in 2002)

This European effort hopes to piggyback SETI detection hardware onto up to 40 radiotelescopes throughout the continent, including some of the world's largest telescopes. The systems will be networked, and their data collated at a central location. Recently funded, the program is slated to begin operation in 2002.

Lick Observatory/SETI Institute OSETI Project (currently under construction)

The SETI Institute is collaborating with the Lick Observatory to build an Optical SETI instrument that will be used to conduct piggyback or targeted searches. The telescope will initially have a 1-meter aperture, and will later be expanded to 3 meters.

Mount Wilson Observatory OSETI Project

Albert Betz (University of Colorado) and Charles Townes (UC Berkeley) examined nearby sun-like stars to look for 10micron (infrared) pulsed beacons. Infrared light is thought to be an especially attractive way to signal across interstellar distances because it degrades less quickly due to extinction (absorption of light by the interstellar medium).

Oz OSETI (currently under construction)

Designed by Ragbir Bhathal, this Australian optical SETI project will use a 16-inch automated telescope, based at the University of Western Sydney, to examine 200 stars for long periods of time. Leon Darcy, a colleague, will use a small radio telescope to observe the same stars simultaneously.

Allen Telescope Array (slated to begin in 2005)

The Allen Telescope Array (ATA; formerly called the One Hectare Telescope, or 1HT), is a proposed network of relatively small radiotelescopes that will form the equivalent of a single large dish. Sponsored by the SETI Institute, and funded by private donations from leaders in the high-tech industry, the ATA will be the first radiotelescope dedicated to SETI research. The ATA is presently under construction in Northern California.

GLOSSARY

21-cm line
Neutral hydrogen (hydrogen gas) is known to emit light that has a 21-centi-meter wavelength (1420 MHz). This frequency, often referred to as the "water hole," is familiar to anyone who understands radioastronomy. The term "water hole" is used to describe the range of frequencies between 1420 MHz and 1667 MHz. The 1420 MHz frequency is associated with natural radio emissions from neutral hydrogen, while the 1667 MHz frequency is associated with emissions from OH (oxygen-hydrogen radical). These two materials combine to form water, an important prerequisite for carbon-based life. Hence, the term "water hole" is used to describe the band of intermediate frequencies. Also known as the *hydrogen line*.

Absorption line
A dark line that appears in the spectrum of light emitted by an object, caused by material in the object, or between the object and the observer, absorbing light at specific wavelengths.

Algorithm
A series of machine instructions that perform a series of computations (see also *Computer program*).

Amino acid
An organic compound formed from carbon, hydrogen, oxygen, and nitro-gen. Amino acids are combined in daisy-chain fashion to form proteins.

Amplifier
An electrical circuit that increases the strength of an incoming signal, typi-cally by several orders of magnitude. See also *Diode*, and *Transistor*.

Amplitude modulation
A technique for encoding information in a radio signal by changing the strength of the transmitted signal over time (e.g., high power = 1, low power = 0).

AND gate

An electrical circuit that compares two or more input signals to produce a single output signal. If all of the input signals are ON then the output signal will be ON. If one or more input signals are OFF, the output signal will be OFF.

Animal habitable zone (AHZ)

The region surrounding a star that heats planets enough to maintain temperatures above the freezing point of water and below 50 degrees Celsius. Peter Ward and Donald Brownlee proposed this concept as part of their Rare Earth Hypothesis.

Array

When applied to memory or programming, an array is a collection of numbers stored in an organized grid. When applied to radioastromony, an array is a collection of radiotelescopes that function together as one integrated system.

Astronomical unit (AU)

A unit of measurement used for measuring the distance between planets and their stars. An astronomical unit is based on the distance from the Earth to its sun, approximately 93 million miles; the Earth is 1 AU from the Sun.

Binary arithmetic

A special form of arithmetic that can be applied to binary numbers. This includes such functions as AND, OR, XOR, and NOT, as well as conventional arithmetic (e.g., addition, subtraction, multiplication, and so forth). Binary arithmetic is also known as Boolean arithmetic.

Binary code

The simplest format in which to store information. Binary code uses an alphabet consisting of two numbers, 0 and 1. These numbers can be combined to describe anything from alphanumeric text to complex images and multimedia.

Bitmap

A representation of a two-dimensional image using a string of binary numbers arranged in a grid.

Black box

A software component that hides the details of its internal works, presenting its user with a simplified interface for sending information to and receiving information from the component (or mini-program).

Blackbody radiation

Objects with a temperature greater than absolute zero emit light according to a well-known equation that governs the intensity and color of the emitted light. As the object's temperature increases the amount of energy emitted as light increases rapidly (in proportion to the fourth power of its temperature), while the median wavelength of the emitted light decreases.

Branching statement

A machine instruction that directs the computer to test a value (e.g., is X>2?), and to fork in two or more directions depending on the outcome of the test (e.g., "If X > 2, then do X, otherwise do Y").

Broadband signal

A radio signal that spreads its energy across a wide band of frequencies. A television signal is an example of a broadband signal.

Capacitor

An electrical device that functions as a reservoir for electric charge.

Charged coupled device (CCD)

An electronic device that converts minute amounts of incoming light into an electrical current. These devices are used in optical telescopes and digital cameras.

Checksum

A number used to crosscheck data to detect transmission errors within a data set.

CODEC

Short for "compression/decompression," a CODEC is a pair of computer programs that compresses (transmitting side) and decompresses (receiving side) information used to represent an image, video, or sound files.

Compression

A technique used to eliminate redundant information from a data set, such as the information used to describe a high-resolution image.

Concept-oriented programming (COP)

An extension of object-oriented programming, COP systems assign unique numeric addresses to reusable software components that can be automatically disseminated throughout a public data network such as the Internet.

Context

A symbol's context describes its usage within a larger collection of symbols (e.g., as a number, as a command, as a noun, etc.).

Cosmic background radiation

A pervasive source of microwave radiation that is visible in every direction of the sky. This radiation is a relic of The Big Bang, which is thought to have formed the universe.

Digitization

The process of converting a continually varying analog signal into a series of numbers.

Diode

An electrical device that allows current to flow easily in one direction while presenting strong resistance to an electrical current that wants to flow in the opposite direction.

Directionality

See Gain.

Dispersion

The process by which a packet of photons (emitted by a precisely timed source such as a laser) spreads out as it travels further from their source. This can be compared to a horserace where the horses start off in at the same point, but spread out on the track as the race goes on.

Distributed computing

The practice of using a large number of computers to work independently of each other on sub-divided pieces of a larger problem. The SETI@home project is an excellent example of a distributed computing project.

DNA

Short for *deoxyribonucleic acid*, DNA is the molecule that stores the basic genetic blueprint for most organisms on Earth.

Doppler shift

Also known as the "Train whistle effect," Doppler shift is the result of the fixed speed of light. When an object travels toward an observer, its light appears to be blue-shifted (bluer in color, or higher frequency). When an object travels away from an observer, its light appears to be red-shifted (redder in color). By measuring Doppler shift, we have been able to detect the expansion of the universe, estimate the distance to other galaxies, and to detect the presence of large planets orbiting other stars.

The Drake Equation

Conceived by Dr. Frank Drake, the Drake Equation is a tool for estimating the number of communicative civilizations in our galaxy based on a collection of factors related to the rate of star formation, the percentage of stars that host Earth-like worlds, and so on. The Drake Equation is represented as: $N = R \times f_s \times f_p \times n_e \times f_l \times f_i \times f_c \times L$.

Electromagnetic spectrum

The range of electromagnetic radiation, from very long wavelength signals (radio waves) to visible light to ultra-short wavelengths (X- and gamma rays).

Entropy

A measure of the disorder, or randomness, within a closed system.

Extrasolar planet

A planet orbiting a star outside of our solar system; may also be referred to as an exosolar planet.

Extinction

The weakening of an optical signal due to the absorption of light by interstellar gases.

Fast Fourier transform (FFT)

A formula (or process) used to convert a time domain signal into a frequency domain signal.

FLOP/s

Short for *FLoating point OPerations per Second*; a measure of computing speed.

Forward error correction
> The process of encoding a block of data so that if some of the data is damaged or corrupted, the recipient can reconstruct the original message without having to request and wait for the data to be resent by the sender. Also known as *preemptive error correction*.

Frequency domain graph
> A plot of a signal that has been broken down into many frequency bins or channels. This is analogous to what an equalizer in a home stereo system does, except on a larger scale.

Frequency drift rate
> The rate at which a signal drifts across frequencies. For example, a 1,000 Hz signal with a 1 Hz/second drift rate will start at 1000 Hz, then be at 1,001 Hz after one second, 1,002 Hz after two seconds, and so on.

Frequency shift keying
> A technique for encoding information within a radio or optical signal by changing the frequency of the signal (e.g., 1,000 Hz means 0, 1,001 Hz means 1). Also known as modulation.

Gain
> A measure of the effectiveness of an antenna (or amplifier). A high-gain antenna will typically boost the intensity of a signal by factor of a million to several billion times. Gain is typically measured in decibels (dB).

Galactic habitable zone (GHZ)
> The region of the galaxy, about halfway between the galactic core and the outer arms of the spiral arms, that is thought to be most hospitable to the formation of complex life. Stars in this region are far enough apart that violent events such as supernovae are less likely to sterilize life-bearing worlds, but are still close enough to permit the generation and accretion of heavy elements required to form rocky, Earth-like planets.

Gene
> A package of genetic information that is typically associated with the formation of a particular protein or treat.

Genome
> An organism's complete genetic blueprint.

Global (public) variable
> A variable, or memory register, that is visible and accessible throughout an entire system or program.

GOTO statement
> A statement that instructs a computer running a program to jump to a specific label or location within the program.

Habitable zone (HZ)
> The region surrounding a star where average temperatures on a planet are within the range required to support liquid water. See also *Microbial habitable zone* (MHZ), and *Animal habitable zone* (AHZ).

HOX (homeobox) gene
> An animal gene that regulates the development of macroscopic structures (e.g., legs, eyes, internal organs, etc.). This gene was originally discovered in fruit flies, and has since been found in almost all other animals, including humans.

IF-THEN statement
> A statement that directs a computer to examine a test condition, and if a certain condition is met, to perform a series of instructions.

igene
> A package of machine instructions designed to perform a specific task, which can be included in any other program simply by referring to its numeric identifier.

Interferometer
> A type of telescope that can selectively cancel the incoming light from a star to reveal planets and other bodies orbiting nearby.

Laser
> A device that emits light in a very tightly focused beam, and that is tuned to a specific wavelength.

Light-emitting diode (LED)
> A light-emitting device that is tuned to a precise wavelength (though not necessarily in a tightly focused beam as is the case with a laser).

Light speed
> The velocity at which light travels, which is 185,000 miles per second.

Light year
> The distance that light travels in a year, equivalent to 5.878 trillion miles.

Lincos (lingua cosmica)
> A mathematical language proposed by the Dutch mathematician Hans Freudenthal.

Local (private) variable
> A variable, or memory register, that is only accessible within a specific part within a system or computer program.

Main-sequence star
> A star that has approximately the same mass as our sun. Main-sequence stars typically have life spans ranging from a few billion to as much as 50 billion years, and emit most of their energy as visible light. The inner planets orbiting these stars are considered the most likely sites for life.

Meme
> Similar to a gene, a meme is a placeholder for a unit of cultural information. This concept was originally coined by Richard Dawkins to explain the spread of knowledge and cultural information.

Memory
> A device or procedure used for storing information, which can be recalled at a later time.

Method

Related to object-oriented programming, a method is a procedure or command that can be invoked within a computer program.

Microbial habitable zone (MHZ)

The region surrounding a star that is thought to be suitable for the development of microbial life. This habitable zone is much larger than the animal habitable zone because microbes can survive in a much wider range of conditions than multicellular animals.

Modulation

A system for encoding information within a radio or optical signal by subtly altering the characteristics of the signal in an orderly way.

Monochromatic signal

A radio or optical signal that concentrates most or all of its energy in about a single wavelength.

NASA High Resolution Microwave Survey

This NASA-sponsored SETI program would have combined a targeted search program with a full sky survey (similar to the SERENDIP program). The program was canceled by the U.S. Congress and was never fully implemented.

Narrowband signal

A signal that concentrates most of its energy within a narrowly defined band of frequencies.

Object-oriented programming (OOP)

A programming technique that emphasizes the use of reusable software components to create more complex, higher order programs.

Operator

A symbol or word that is used as a command within a computer program or mathematical expression (the symbol + is an example of an operator).

Optical SETI (OSETI)

A search for extraterrestrial intelligence designed to detect infrared and visible laser beacons.

Oscillator

A circuit that converts a steady electrical current (DC) into a sinusoidal current (AC).

Parser

A program that dissembles a message or string of numbers into structured subunits of information. Another example would be breaking a sentence down into a series of individual words.

Pattern recognition

The ability or process of recognizing a common theme among a set of numbers, equations, images, etc.

Phase shift keying
> A method of encoding information within a carrier by modifying the phase of the signal. Also known as modulation.

Photoelectric effect
> The process by which incoming photons knock negatively charged electrons loose from a surface. Albert Einstein discovered this effect, for which he won the 1921 Nobel Prize for Physics.

Photomultiplier (PMT)
> A device that amplifies the effect of a single photon to produce an electrical current that is large enough to be detected by conventional electronics (e.g., a digital counter).

Photon
> A particle that transmits electromagnetic energy, producing the light that we see.

Photon detector
> A device that captures incoming photons, and uses the photoelectric effect to turn incoming light into a measurable electric current. The most sensitive detectors can count individual photons.

Polarity shift keying (modulation)
> A method of encoding information within a carrier by modifying the polarity of the signal (the direction in which the photons vibrate back and forth).

Polychromatic signal
> A signal that spreads its energy across many wavelengths.

Prime number
> A number that can only be divided by 1 or itself to produce a whole number. Dividing a prime number by any other number will produce a fractional result.

Prism
> A device that splits an incoming beam of light into a rainbow (spectrum) of individual colors.

Protein
> A chemical formed by assembling multiple amino acids in daisy-chain fashion.

Protoplanetary disk
> The disk of dust and material that orbits a newly formed star. These disks are thought to condense into a constellation of planetary bodies over the course of millions of years as the star system ages.

Project Ozma
> The first modern SETI program, Project Ozma searched for signs of intelligent civilizations by listening for signals in the 21-cm microwave band. Project Ozma focused on two nearby stars, Epsilon Eridani and Tau Ceti, and was headed by Dr. Frank Drake.

Project Phoenix
> The privately funded successor to the canceled HRMS project, Project Phoenix is a targeted search program that analyzes about 1,000 nearby star systems for radio signals that would betray the presence of an intelligent civilization.

Radioastronomy
> Radioastronomy is different from traditional telescope-based astronomy in that celestial objects are studied by gathering and analyzing their radio wave emissions using radio antennas and receivers.

Radio frequency interference (RFI)
> Interference due to man-made radio signals from ground or space-based transmitters.

Random number
> A number, or series of numbers, that cannot be predicted based on previous observations.

Random access memory (RAM)
> A system for storing information that allows the individual numbers stored in memory to be retrieved (recalled) in any arbitrary sequence.

Rare Earth Hypothesis
> A hypothesis proposed by Peter Ward and Donald Brownlee that states that the combination of processes that led to the development of animal and intelligent life on Earth are quite rare, and may be unique in the galaxy.

Replicator
> A molecule that can make copies of itself. This type of molecule is thought to be a precursor to microbial life on Earth.

Reusable software
> Software that is built from reusable components that are designed to perform specific tasks (e.g., average a series of numbers, calculate the sine of an angle, etc.). See also *igene*.

Semantic network
> A system for describing ideas or symbols in terms of each other (e.g., large is the opposite of small, small is similar to tiny, etc.).

SERENDIP
> A University of California, Berkeley–sponsored radio-based SETI program. SERENDIP is a full sky survey. This program uses the Arecibo Radio Observatory in Puerto Rico to scan a large number of target stars.

SETI@home project
> This widely used screensaver program downloads raw data collected by the SERENDIP program and analyzes it to search for tell-tale signs of narrowband carriers.

Simulation
> A program that simulates the behavior of a real-world system.

Spectrometer

A device that breaks incoming light into a large number of individual colors, thereby allowing astronomers to analyze the spectrum of the light in much greater detail than is possible with the naked eye.

Spectroscopy

The science of analyzing spectral information to determine an object's temperature, brightness, and chemical composition.

Symbol

A number or icon that is used as a placeholder or token for an idea.

Syntax

The rules by which symbols or words can be grouped together to form meaningful expressions (sentences).

Terrestrial Planet Finder

A next-generation space telescope that will use interferometry to search for Earth-sized planets orbiting other stars.

Transistor

An electronic device that behaves like an electric valve or switch, and which allows the designer to control a relatively large flow of electrical current using a much weaker input or control signal.

SELECTED BIBLIOGRAPHY

Ball, John. "The Zoo Hypothesis." *Icarus* 19 (1973): 347.

Benford, Gregory. *Deep Time: How Humanity Communicates Across Millennia.* Avon, 1999.

Bova, Ben, ed., et al. *Are We Alone in the Cosmos?: The Search for Alien Contact in the New Millennium.* New York: iBooks, Inc., 1999.

Bradbury, Robert J. *Matrioshka Brains.* Self-published, 1998. (*http://www.aeiveos.com/~bradbury/MatrioshkaBrains/MatrioshkaBrains.html*).

Brin, Glen David. *The Great Silence: The Controversy Concerning Extraterrestrial Intelligent Life.* 1982, n.p.

Broad, William J. *The Universe Below: Discovering the Secrets of the Deep Sea.* New York: Simon & Schuster, 1997.

Crosswell, Ken. *Planet Quest: The Epic Discovery of Alien Solar Systems.* San Diego: Harcourt Brace, 1998.

Cullers, Kent, ed., *SETI 2020: The Report of the SETI Science and Technology Working Group.* SETI Press, 2001.

Dick, Steven J. *The Biological Universe: The Twentieth-Century Extraterrestrial Life Debate and the Limits of Science.* Cambridge: Cambridge University Press, 1996.

Freudenthal, Hans. *LINCOS: Design of a Language for Cosmic Intercourse.* Amsterdam: North-Holland Publishing Company, 1960.

Goldsmith, Donald. *The Hunt For Life On Mars.* New York: Dutton, 1997.

Hogan, James P. *Mind Matters: Exploring the World of Artificial Intelligence.* New York: Ballantine Publishing Group, 1997.

Kingsley, Stuart A. "The Search For Extraterrestrial Intelligence (SETI) in the Optical Spectrum." Bellingham: *SPIE—The International Society for Optical Engineering, SPIE Proceedings Volume 1867*, August 1993.

Kingsley, Stuart A. "The Search For Extraterrestrial Intelligence (SETI) in the Optical Spectrum II." Bellingham: *SPIE—The International Society for Optical Engineering, SPIE Proceedings Volume 2704*, June 1996.

Lemarchand, Dr. Guillermo A. *Detectability of Extraterrestrial Technological Activities*. Columbus Optical SETI Observatory, 1992 (*http://www.coseti. org/lemarch1.htm*).

Minsky, Marvin. "Communication with Alien Intelligence." *Byte Magazine*, April (1985).

Minsky, Marvin. *The Society of Mind*. New York: Simon & Schuster, 1985.

Moravec, Hans. *Robot: Mere Machine to Transcendent Mind*. Oxford: Oxford University Press, 1999.

Schwartz, R.N., and Townes, C.H. "Interstellar and Interplanetary Communication by Optical Masers." *Nature*, Vol. 190, No. 4772 (1961) (*http://www. coseti.org/townes_0.htm*).

SETI Institute. *Project Cyclops: A Design Study of a System for Detecting Extraterrestrial Intelligent Life*. Mountain View: SETI Institute, 1971.

Taylor, Michael Ray. *Dark Life: Martian Nanobacteria, Rock-Eating Cave Bugs, and Other Extreme Organisms of Inner Earth and Outer Space*. New York: Scribner, 1999.

Vakoch, Douglas. *Messages: From The Moon, To Mars, To The Stars*. Mountain View: SETI Institute, 1999 (*http://www.seti.org/science/signals.html*).

Vakoch, Douglas. "The View from a Distant Star: Challenges of Interstellar Message Making." *Mercury Magazine*, March/April (1999) (*http://www.aspsky. org/mercury/mercury/9902/vakoch.html*).

Ward, Peter D., and Brownlee, Donald. *Rare Earth: Why Complex Life Is Uncommon In The Universe*. New York: Copernicus, 2000.

ACKNOWLEDGMENTS

This book would not have been possible without the help of many people. I would especially like to thank Chuck Toporek and Tim O'Reilly at O'Reilly & Associates, Inc. Without their early support, this book would not have gotten past the proposal stage. Most authors share horror stores about how difficult it is to get published. I was one of the lucky few to approach the right publisher at the right time. This book almost never happened, and probably would never have seen the light of day were it not for a chance discussion with Tim O'Reilly, who sent me a contract shortly after reading a few chapters from an early draft of the book.

I would also like to thank Kent Cullers, director of research and development at the SETI Institute. Kent is one of a handful of people who built the hardware used by today's SETI researchers. Kent's advice and critiques have been instrumental in completing this book. Dan Werthimer was equally helpful in explaining Berkeley's SETI program, most notably the SETI@home project (now in use by over 2.5 million people).

Thanks also to David Brin, who offers an excellent analysis of the classic Drake Equation in his article "The Great Silence." Brin, a space scientist and science fiction author, has thought in-depth about extraterrestrial intelligence, and why we have not already detected it. His paper should be required reading for anybody who is interested in the subject of extraterrestrial civilizations.

Many other people have helped to shape this book, especially our technical reviewers. Among those not already mentioned are: Sir Arthur C. Clarke (science fiction author), Dr. Vinton Cerf (Internet pioneer, and co-inventor of the TCP/IP protocol), Dr. Dan Werthimer (Director, UC Berkeley SETI programs/*SETI@home*), Dr. Stuart A. Kingsley (Columbus Optical SETI Observatory), Dr. Allen Tough (University of Toronto), Dr. Ragbir Bhatal (Director, Australian Optical SETI Project, University of Western Sydney), Paul Schuh (Director, SETI League), Stephane Dumas, Yvan Dutil, Bob McNamee, Jon

Orwant (Chief Technology Officer, O'Reilly & Associates, Inc.), Charlie Schick, and Monte Ross.

I'd also like to thank the following O'Reilly staff members who contributed to the design and production of the book:

- Claire Cloutier, for production management and quality assurance.
- Sarah Jane Shangraw, the production editor/project manager and copy-editor, who did an excellent job improving my prose.
- Rob Romano, who took my hand-drawn sketches and turned them into the great illustrations you've seen throughout the book.
- Ellie Volckhausen, who designed the striking cover.
- Emma Colby, who designed the cover mechanical.
- Melanie Wang, who designed the interior based on work by Alicia Cech.
- Joe Wizda, indexer extraordinaire.
- Cliff Dyer, who implemented the internal design using FrameMaker 5.5 and transferred the original Word files into the Framemaker templates.
- Linley Dolby, who proofread the galleys.
- Mary Sheehan and Colleen Gorman, for quality assurance.
- Matt Hutchinson, for page composition.
- Cathy Record and Betsy Waliszewski, for marketing and promotions.

I'm sure there are other people within O'Reilly who've contributed a great deal of time and effort to the production, design, and marketing of this book. For those whose names have escaped me, thank you.

Last, but not least, I would like to thank my editor, Chuck Toporek, who helped me turn a good idea into a polished book (and helped me avoid the pitfalls of being a first-time author).

HOW TO CONTACT US

We have tested and verified the information in this book to the best of our ability, but you may find that some information has changed (or even that we have made mistakes!). Please let us know about any errors you find, as well as your suggestions for future editions, by writing to:

O'Reilly & Associates, Inc.
101 Morris Street
Sebastopol, CA 95472
1-800-998-9938 (in the U.S. or Canada)
1-707-829-0515 (international/local)
1-707-829-0104 (fax)

The web site for *Beyond Contact: A Guide to SETI and Communicating with Alien Civilizations* lists errata and plans for future editions. You can access this page at:

http://www.oreilly.com/catalog/alien/

To ask technical questions or to comment on the book, send mail to:

bookquestions@oreilly.com

For more information about this book and others, see the main O'Reilly web site:

http://www.oreilly.com/

INDEX

Numbers

1HT (One Hectare Telescope), 7, 16
2001: A Space Odyssey, 184
51 Pegasi, 25

A

abstract language, 224
abstract symbols, 329–346
adenine molecule, 208
after, developing a concept for, 363
A_j factor in Brin's Equation, 69
algae, as a dominant life form, 43
algebra for defining symbols, 216
algorithmic, communicating
        concepts, 265
    images, 300
alien communication, assumptions
        for, 198–203
Allan Hills meteorite, 37
Allen, Paul (Microsoft), 16
Allen Telescope Array (ATA), 7, 16,
        145, 371
AM (Amplitude Modulation), 165–167
amateur astronomers, in the SETI
        League, 15
amino acids in DNA, 208
amplifiers (non-linear device), 199
Amplitude Modulation (AM), 165–167
analog-to-digital (A/D) conversions, 123
AND circuits, 200
AND gates, 162–163

AND operation in Boolean logic, 229
Anderson, David (SETI@home
        team), 4, 371
antennae
    building a SETI receiver, 91
    directionality of, 95
    in receivers, 85
    in transmitters, 84
Arecibo Pictograph, 189
Arecibo Radio Observatory, 4, 7
arrays, 244–246
ATA (see Allen Telescope Array)
atomic erector set, simulating
        interaction of particles, 325
attenuation (extinction) of beams, 116
Australian SETI programs, 15

B

background noise
    AM (Amplitude Modulation)
        and, 167
    in universe, 77, 96
    quietest band of frequencies, 122
bacteria
    as a dominant life form, 43
    complexity of, 41
    first fossils of, 36
    harsh climates, living in, 32
    multicellular life, evolution of, 43
    Rare Earth Hypothesis and, 47
Ball, John A. (Zoo Hypothesis), 65
Baum, L. Frank (*Land of Oz*), 12

before, developing a concept for, 363
BETA (Billion Channel Extraterrestrial
Array), 14
Big Bang, 77, 96
Big Ear Radio Observatory, 13
unverified signals and, 121
binary DNA, 163, 197–212
binary numbers, 83
biology and, 163
for Boolean arithmetic, 228
code for, 160–161
computing, 161–165
DNA and, 197–212
igenes and, 264
for pictographic communication
systems, 189–191
radio signals, transmitting, 165
sequencing messages with, 278–282
biological features, developing a
concept for, 335
bitmaps, 160, 294
images in messages, 295–298
transmitting into space, 188
bits, teleporting, 159–178
black box programming, 243
building components, 270–274
black holes, 71
blackbody radiation, 100
Boolean logic, 162, 227, 236–238
branching statements for, 238, 246
comparative statements for, 232
defining symbols for arithmetic, 216
NOT operators for, 231
relational symbols in, 233
Brin, David (scientist/author), 68
Brin's Equation, 68–70
broadcasts, radiating in space, 186
Brownlee, Donald (author), 47

C

calibration messages, sending, 289
Calisto
existence of microbial life on, 6
n_e Drake Equation factor and, 30
capacitor, in radio receivers, 88
carbon, abundance of in galaxy, 34

carbon dioxide (CO_2), as a greenhouse
gas, 49
carbon-based life, 34
cataloging data, 155
cause symbols, 338
Cerf, Vinton (inventor of TCP/IP), 18
CETI (Communication with
Extraterrestrial
Intelligence), 182–195
chapters, organizing expressions
with, 344
checksum, detecting errors, 284–286
CHZ (continuously habitable zone), 48
circular polarization, 172
Clarke, Arthur C. (author), 117, 184
Clarke, Ian (Freenet developer), 6
climate modeling, 6
Cocconi, Giuseppe (author), 11, 187
CODECs, 311
coded signals, 187
codons in DNA, 208
color images, 301–307
displaying, 306
encoding, 304–307
color modulation (wavelength), 173
command (operator), 219
communication
animals, using symbols for, 51
assumptions for alien, 198–203
f_c factor in Drake Equation and, 53
interstellar, limits of, 356
lightwave (laser), 99–118
long distance, 76–78
radio, 75–98
symbols for, 51, 213–238
comparative statements, 232
complexity, in evolution, 41
compound
context, 342
messages, 345
symbols, 340
words, 340
compression
for data, sending messages, 289
images, 310–312
in DNA, 277

concept-oriented programming
  (COP), 262–274
concepts, 262–274, 329–336
  for compound words/symbols, 340–342
  invisible, 332–336
  for semantic networks, 347–349
constant, developing a concept
  for, 269
containers (variables) in four-dimesional
  arrays, 246
content of messages, 359–370
context
  abstract symbols/language and, 337
  compound, 342
  defining images, 296
  defining symbols, 219–222
continuous beacons
  communication with, 104–108
  detecting, 107
  processing and confirming, 139
continuously habitable zone (CHZ), 48
COP (concept-oriented
  programming), 262–274
Crab Nebula, 307
culture
  evolution of, 59
  in humans, 54
  memes, survival of in, 61
cycling between types of data, 289
cytosine molecule, 208

D

Darwin, Charles, 40
data
  analysis of SETI@home, 151
  for defining symbols, 219, 222
  easily parsed, 289
  information for SETI@home, 151
  sending self-repairing, 284–292
  structures/arrays, 244–246
  transfer speed, 177
  visualization, 321
Dawkins, Richard (author), 59, 264
day, developing a concept for, 364
Deadly Probes Hypothesis, 64, 68
dechirping, 153

Declaration of Principles Concerning
  the Activities Following the
  Detection of Extraterrestrial
  Intelligence, 143
decoding signals, 120
depth in three-dimensional arrays, 245,
  304
descriptors (modifiers), 224
DeVito, Carl L. (creator of Devito's
  Numeric Language), 192
difference symbols, 338
digital computing for alien
  communication, 200
digitalization for signals, 123
diode, in radio receivers, 87
directional transmitters, 94
dispersion in laser beams, 116
distributed computing, 4, 6, 147
division, developing a concept for, 267
DNA, 205
  binary, 163, 197–212
  deciphering meaning of, 276
  encoding, 209
  molecules, 208
    evolving complexity of, 42
  number structures and, 207
dolphins, 52
Doppler shift, 26, 103
  drift rate, 132–134
dots (see pixels)
down conversion, 124
Drake Equation, 21–56
  Brin's Equation, factors for, 68–70
  knowing where to look in time, 81
  oversimplification of, 58
Drake, Frank (astronomer), 21
  Project Ozma and, 12
drift rate (Doppler shift), 132–134
Dumas, Stephane (developer), 190
Dutil, Yvan (developer), 190
Dutil-Dumas Pictographic System, 190

E

Earth
  building a lexicon for, 360–366
  criteria for intelligence, 51

easily parsed data, sending
  messages, 289
ecosystems, existing under Earth's
  surface, 33
efficiency, in evolution, 41
Einstein, Albert (mathematician/
  scientist), 111
electromagnetic radiation, 301
  in radio communication, 75
electronic valves (non-linear
  devices), 199
encoding color, 304–307
energy, developing a concept for, 332
entropy
  describing, 313–317
  value (randomness), 290
Epsilon Eridani, 12
equations
  transmitting into space, 188
error corrected data, sending
  messages, 289
error detection
  in DNA, 277
  in data, 284–288
ET signals, ranking criteria for, 138
Europa
  existence of microbial life on, 6
  n_e Drake Equation factor and, 30
  supporting ecosystems, 33
  unmanned probes, sending to, 37
European SETI programs, 15
evaporation, developing a concept
  for, 310
evolution, 40–53
  culture and, 59
  intelligence, origins of, 43
expressions (nested), 343
extelligence, 59
extinction (attenuation) of beams, 116

F

f_1 factor in Drake Equation, 35–40
factorial (!) symbol, 256
Fast Fourier Transform (FFT), 152
f_c factor in Drake Equation, 22, 53
  defining upper and lower limits, 57

Fermi, Enrico (physicist), 63
FFT (Fast Fourier Transform), 152
f_i factor in Drake Equation, 22, 51–53
fit test (Gaussian), 154
f_l factor in Drake Equation, 22
flow control in programming, 249
follow-up detecting (signals), 120
four-dimensional arrays, 246
four-state transmitters, 89
Fourier (frequency domain)
  conversions, 125
f_p factor in Drake Equation, 22
fractions and floating points and, 236
Freenet (censor proof publishing
  system), 6
frequency distribution of signals, 132
frequency domain conversions
  (Fourier), 125
frequency shift keying (FSK), 165, 167
Frudenthal, Hans (creator of
  Lincos), 192
f_s factor in Drake Equation, 21, 24
FSK (see frequency shift keying)
funding for SETI research, 17

G

gain, in antennae, 95
galactic habitable zone, 47
Galileo probe, 30
Ganymede
  existence of microbial life on, 6
  n_e Drake Equation factor and, 30
Gaussian power curve, 134–137
  SETI@home, examining, 149
  vs. time (fit test), 154
genes, 205
genetic information vs. memetic, 60
Geneva Observatory, 25
geological processes, 49
geology
  defining a lexicon of symbols
    with, 365
  developing concepts with, 335
geometry of a circle (pi (π)), 253
GIF (Graphic Interchange Format), 311

global variables, 240, 258
  for defining symbols, 223
  embedding bitmap images in
      messages, 296
GOTO statements in computer
    programming, 251
Graphic Interchange Format (GIF), 311
gravity
  describing, 317–324
  developing concepts with, 325
  formation of planets and, 29
grayscale images, 294, 298–301
Great Silence (Brin), 68
greenhouse gases, maintaining suitable
    conditions for animal life, 49
Greenwich Mean Time (GMT), 156
guanine molecule, 208

H

habitable zones of planets, 29
  Rare Earth Hypothesis and, 48
heavy elements
  Rare Earth Hypothesis and, 48
  for star formation, 23
  sun-like star formation of, 24
height in dimensional arrays, 245
high-gain antenna, building a SETI
    receiver, 91
High Resolution Microwave Survey
    (HRMS), 13
Horowitz, Paul (BETA), 15
HOX (Homeobox) genes, 44
HST (see Hubble Space Telescope)
Hubble Space Telescope (HST), 7, 38,
    307
  capturing images of new stars
      forming, 22
  protoplanetary disks, images of, 27
Human Genome Project, benefiting
    from SETI research, 19
human language in history, 367–370
hydrogen
  abundance of in galaxy, 34
  calibrating color information, 307
  simulating behavior of, 324

hydrothermal vents, supporting bacterial
    life, 32
  hyperlinking expressions with, 344
hyperspectral images, 79

I

ideas, describing, 329–336
IF-THEN statements, 247
  in Boolean logic, 232
igenes, 255, 262–274
  in black box programs, 243
  capturing new, 279–281
  decoding errors, 288
  super concepts, building, 266
  transmitting, 282–284
images
  associating with ideas, 309
  bitmaps in messages, 295–298
  compression, 310–312
  from pixels, 293–295
  transmitting, 308–312
  used as symbols, 223
increasing, developing a concept
    for, 314
indexes of igenes, 283
information density of messages, 291
infrared light, 302
inheritance, 260
integration time, in phase shift
    keying, 170
intelligence
  criteria for species on Earth, 51
  origin of in living organisms, 43
interactivity in simulations, 323
interference
  detecting signals from space, 96
  effects, 79
interferometers, 31, 79
  detecting Earth-sized planets, 7
interlingua (intermediate
    language), 336
"Interstellar and Interplanetary
    Communication by Optical
    Masers" (Townes and
    Schwartz), 11, 17, 188

interstellar communication, limits of, 356
inverter, in radio receivers, 87
invisible concepts, 332–336
ionization, 324
iterative calculations, 256

J

Joint Picture Experts Group (JPEG), 311
joules (unit of energy), 94
JPEG (Joint Picture Experts Group), 311
Jupiter
    microbial life, existence of on moons, 6
    Rare Earth Hypothesis and, 50

L

L (Lifetime) factor in Drake Equation, 22, 55
    knowing where to look in time, 81
Lake Vostok (Antarctica), testing unmanned probes, 37
language, 329–346
    context for, 337
    human, history of, 367–370
    memetic translation layer and, 336
lasers (see lightwaves)
leakage
    radiation in space, 185–186
    unintentional signals, 14
LED (light-emitting diode), 88, 199
life, existing in harsh environments, 32
light capturing devices, 199
light emitting devices, 199
light signals, 173
lightwaves (lasers)
    communication, 99–118
    continuous beacons
        communication with, 104–108
        processing and confirming, 139
    encoding information and, 174
    pulsed beacons
        communication with, 108–114
        processing and confirming, 140
    signals, confirming, 139–145

Lincos (Lingua Cosmica) mathematical language, 192
local variables, 240, 258
    for defining symbols, 223
    embedding bitmap images in messages, 296
locality of signals, 132
logic circuits (non-linear device), 199
low frequency light (radio waves), 83

M

M13 globular cluster, 190
M87 galaxy, 71
machine code, 217
main-sequence category of stars, 101
mapping, defining symbols, 226
Marconi, Guglielmo, 75
Marcy, Geoffrey (professor at San Francisco State University), 25
Mars
    existence of microbial life on, 6
    first attempts of communicating, 182
    geological processes of, 49
    Pathfinder probe, 37
    sending coded signals, 187
    unmanned probes, sending to, 37
    Viking mission, 38
Mayor, Michael, 25
Medicina radioastronomy station, 16
memes, 59, 205, 264
    survival of in culture, 61
    vs. genetic information, 60
memetic translation layer, 336
memory
    as a non-linear device, 199
    in Boolean logic, 238
    in computer programming, 239–254
messages (compound), 345
methods, in object-oriented programming, 260
microbial life, existing in solar system, 6
microwave SETI vs. OSETI, 117
modifiers, 338
    descriptors, 224
    grouping, 340
modularity, 259–262

modulated electromagnetic radiation, detecting for the deadly probes hypothesis, 68
modulation, 159
molecules
  evolving complexity, 42
  replicators, 36
monochromatic (single color) light, 103
Montebugnoli, Stelio (head of European Project StarVoice), 16
monuments for communicating with other civilizations, 182–184
moons
  Rare Earth Hypothesis and, 50
Morrison, Philip (author), 11, 187
motion pictures, 308–312
multicellular life
  origins of, 43
  Rare Earth Hypothesis and, 47
multidimensional arrays, 245
multiplication, concept of, 267

N

N factor
  in Brin's Equation, 69
  in the Drake Equation, 56
NAND gates, 200
Nathan, Myrhvold (Microsoft), 16
National Radio Astronomy Observatory (NRAO), 12
natural selection
  in civilizations, 63
  pattern recognition and, 214
  theory of, 40
n_e factor in Drake Equation, 22, 30–34
nervous system, origins of in living organisms, 43
nested expressions, 343
Next Generation Space Telescope (NGST), 39
nitrogen, abundance of in galaxy, 34
n_j factor Brin's Equation, 69
nodes in semantic networks, 347
noises (in universe), 77
  quietest band of frequencies, 122
  when detecting signals, 96
non-algorithmic systems, 298

non-linear devices (electronic valves), 199
non-pictorial communication systems, 192
NOT circuits, 200
not sending signal (two state system), 89
nouns (object symbols), 224
numbers, using as symbols, 217

O

object symbols, 338
object-oriented programming (OOP), 259–262
  concept-oriented programing (COP), 262–274
oceans, existing on planets/moons, 30
OFF state, 83
off-axis viewing, 134–137
omnidirectional transmitters, 94
ON state, 83
One Hectare Telescope (1HT), 7, 16
operator (command), 219
Optical SETI (see OSETI)
optical telescopes, detecting Earth-sized planets, 7
OR operators, 230
orbits, developing a concept for, 325
oscillators, 84
OSETI (Optical SETI), 16, 99
  future technology of, 114
  photoelectric devices, 199
  pulsed transmitters/beacons, 108, 110
  encoding information and, 174
  processing and confirming with, 140
  systems for, 113
  vs. microwave SETI, 117
oversampling, 125

P

P (transmitter power), 94
parabolic antennae
  building a SETI receiver, 91
  directionality of, 95

parabolic dishes, 201
paragraphs, organizing expressions
    with, 344
parrots, communicating
    symbolically, 51
Pathfinder probe, 37
pattern recognition, 214
phase shift keying (PSK), 165, 169
phenomena, concept of, 335
photoelectric
  devices, 199
  effects, 111
photomultipliers, 109, 140
photons, 82
  color images and, 302
  detectors, 109, 111–114
  polarization modulation, 170–172
physical objects, concept of, 335
pi (π) (geometry of a circle), 253
pictographic communication
    systems, 188–191
pictures, 293–312
  associating with ideas, 309
  transmitting motion and, 308–312
  used as symbols, 223
pictures, communicating concepts, 265
Pioneer spacecraft
  communicating with other
    civilizations, 183
  detecting false signals from, 137
pixels, 160
  grayscale images, 299
  to images, 293–295
  for multidimensional arrays, 245
Planetary Society, sponsoring BETA, 14
planets
  formation, commonness of, 28
PMTs (see photomultipliers)
polarity shifting, 166
polarization, 165, 170–173
populations
  driven by natural selection, 40
  memes, survival of in, 61
post-processing data, 155
precellular period, 42
pre-emptive error-correction, 284,
    286–288

primates, communicating
    symbolically, 51
private memory locations, 240
probes
  the Fermi Paradox and, 64–68
  searching for evidence of life, 37
programming (computer), 239–254
Project Ozma, 12
Project Phoenix, 14
Project StarVoice, 16
properties in object oriented
    programming, 260
proteins, 208
protocellular period, 42
protoplanetary disks, 27
PSK (see phase shift keying)
PSR1257+12 neutron star, 25
public memory locations, 240
pulse timing, 174
pulsed beacons
  communication with, 108–114
  encoding information and, 174
  processing and confirming, 140
pulsed OSETI transmitters, 110

Q

Quarantine Hypothesis, 64
Queloz, Didier, 25

R

R (Rate) factor in Drake Equation, 21–
    24
radians, 256
radiation, detecting for the Deadly
    Probes Hypothesis, 68
radio communications, 75–98
  basics of, 82
  cost of operating a SETI facility
    for, 97
radio frequency interference (RFI), 154
radio signals, 165
radio waves, 76
  coded signals in, 187
  leakage radiation from, 185
  low frequency light, 83

radioactive decay, 141
radio-based signal detection, 122
  future of, 129
radiotelescopes, 201
random access format in DNA, 276
randomness
  developing a concept for, 333
  entropy value, 290
Rare Earth Hypothesis, 47–50
raw data, embedding bitmap images in
  messages, 296
receivers
  amplifiers, communicating long
    distances, 76
  building, 85, 91–93
Reed-Solomon coding in compact
  disks, 284
relative terms, developing a concept
  for, 335
replicators (molecules), 36
  evolving complexity, 42
RFI (radio frequency interference), 154
RNA molecules, development of, 42

S

satellites, detecting with Doppler
  shift, 134
Saturn, discovery of Titan, 80
Schwartz, Robert (author), 11, 17, 188
Search for Extraterrestrial Radio
  Emissions from Nearby
  Developed Intelligent
  Populations (see SERENDIP)
sections, organizing expressions
  with, 344
self-repairing data, sending, 284–292
semantic building blocks, 222–224
semantic networks, 346–347
  building, 350–353
  building a lexicon for, 353–356
sending signal (two state system), 89
SERENDIP (Search for Extraterrestrial
  Radio Emissions from Nearby
  Developed Intelligent
  Populations), 14, 148
  Gaussian power curve, 136

SETI League, The, 15
SETI program
  beginnings, 11–20
  benefits of, 18–20
  concept behind, 3–5, 147
  in Europe/Australia, 15
  funding, 17
  radio communication and, 75–98
SETI@home, 4, 147–157, 371
  cataloging, 155
  pitch, detecting with, 153
  statistics for, 156
shifting (phase/polarity), 166
shorthand notation, describing context
  of words, 225
signal power, 132
signals
  coded, 187
  criteria for candidate ET, 138
  detectability/speed of, 177–178
  light, encoding information, 173
  processing, 119–145
    confirming a signal, 119–121
    radio signals, verifying, 122–123
    radio, sending binary numbers, 165
    receiving with a SETI receiver, 93
    sending, 89
simulators, 313–328
  building, 319–324
sine function, 255
sine waves, 84
single (monochromatic) color, 103
Sloane Digital Sky Survey, 80
solar systems, formation of, 22
space exploration, searching for
  evidence of life, 36
Space Sciences Lab (Berkeley), 4
space telescopes, searching for evidence
  of life, 38
species, defining symbols for, 362
  relationships between, 366
spectrometry, 31
spectroscopy (Doppler shift
  analysis), 26, 79
spectrum analysis of signals, 129–139
  ranking criteria for, 138
spherical geometry, 186

spikes
  Gaussian fit test and, 154
  in radio-based signal detection, 123
  SETI@home, examining, 149, 152
  spectrum analysis of, 130
square root of a number, developing a
      concept for, 268
starlight
  continuous laser beacons and, 140
  physics of, 100
stars
  determine the chemical composition
      of, 100
  determining weight of, 101
  formation of, 22
    sun-like, 24
  measuring age of, 102
  measuring surface temperatures
      of, 100
StarVoice (project), 16
structures, building in space, 184
subduction (geological process), 49
subroutines in computer
      programming, 249
subterranean bacteria, 32
sun-like stars (f_s factor), 24
super concepts, building igenes, 266
supernova, formation of solar
      systems, 23
swell waves, 78
symbolic communication
  of animals, 51
  systems for, 192
symbols
  abstract, 329–346
  associating images with, 309
  building a lexicon for, 353–356
  building a lexicon of, 265–274
  commands for defining, 222
  comparative statements for, 351–
      353
  compound, 340
  defining in terms of each other, 346
  describing context of, 338
  embedding bitmap images in
      messages, 296
  for communication, 213–238
  grouping into categories, 350
  semantic networks and, 347
  techniques for defining new, 330
  vocabulary based on numbers, 204–
      206

T

Tau Ceti, 12
technology
  advancements in astronomy/
      computing, 7
  memes, survival of in cultures, 61
telescopes
  advancements in, 7
  Doppler shift and, 26
  interferometers, 79
  next generation, 38
  Terrestrial Planet Finder and, 31
tense in human languages, 342
Terrestrial Planet Finder, 31, 38
Tesla, Nikola, 75
three-dimensional arrays, 245
  color images and, 304
  representing time, 308
thymine molecule, 208
time
  defining symbols for, 363
  three-dimensional arrays,
      representing in, 308
Titan, discovery of, 80
tools for defining a symbol, 331
Tough, Allen, 67
Townes, Charles (author), 11, 17, 188
train whistle effect (Doppler shift), 103,
      133
transistors, 201
  amplifying a weak electrical
      signal, 86
transmitters, building, 83–90
  broadcasting messages to other solar
      systems, 93–96
  problems with, 89
  receivers, 85
triplets in DNA, 208, 276
tuners, in radio receivers, 87
two state systems, 89

two-dimensional arrays
  color images and, 304
  depicting symbols, 227
  for grayscale images, 300

U

ultraviolet light, 302
uncompressed data, sending
    messages, 289
unencoded data, differentiating
    between encoded data, 289
unintentional signals (leakage), 14
United States Congress, funding of SETI
    research, 17
University of California (Berkeley)
  Allen Telescope Array and, 16
  release of SETI@home and, 147
  researching SETI, 4
  SERENDIP and, 14
University of Western Sydney, 15
unmanned probes, searching for
    evidence of life, 37

V

values of binary numbers, 160
vectors, 321
verbose notation, describing context of
    words, 225
verbs, 224
video compression, 311
Viking mission, 38
vocabulary
  developing concepts with, 335
  symbols, based on numbers, 204
volcanic activity, providing source of
    CO2, 49
von Neuman probes, 66
Voyager spacecraft, 183

W

W. M. Keck Observatory, 7
War of the Worlds (Welles), 182
Ward, Peter (author), 47
water, existing on planets/moons, 30–34
wavelengths
  for color images, 301
  color modulation, 173
  detecting planets with, 31
waves (radio), 76
weather forecasting
  benefiting from SETI research, 19
  solving problems with distributed
      computing, 6
Welles, Orson, 182
Werthimer, Dan (SETI@home
    team), 4, 371
whistlers (signals), 75
widgets, 257
width in dimensional arrays, 245
wireless communication, devising first
    SETI experiments, 75
wireless data networks, benefiting from
    SETI research, 19
Wolszczan, Alexander (professor at
    Penn State), 25
words
  compound, 340
  structure and grouping, 225
work units in personal computers, 5
World Wide Web, developing video
    compression, 311
"WOW!" Signal, 13
  unverified signals and, 121

Z

Zoo Hypothesis, 64